D1505391

Untold Stories, Unheard Voices

Truman Capote and *In Cold Blood*

MERCER UNIVERSITY PRESS

Endowed by

TOM WATSON BROWN
and
THE WATSON-BROWN FOUNDATION, INC.

Untold Stories, Unheard Voices

Truman Capote and *In Cold Blood*

Jan Whitt

MERCER UNIVERSITY PRESS

Macon, Georgia

1979–2019

40 Years of Publishing Excellence

MUP/ H974

© 2019 by Mercer University Press
Published by Mercer University Press
1501 Mercer University Drive
Macon, Georgia 31207
All rights reserved

9 8 7 6 5 4 3 2 1

Books published by Mercer University Press are printed on acid-free paper
that meets the requirements of the American National Standard for
Information Sciences—Permanence of Paper for Printed Library Materials.

Printed and bound in Canada.

This book is set in Adobe Caslon.

ISBN   978-0-88146-704-8
Cataloging-in-Publication Data is available from the Library of Congress

Breanna Draxler,
Nicole Lilienfeld,
and
Kathryn J. Miller,

students extraordinaire

Contents

Acknowledgments

This book is a testament to continuing interest in crime novels, the criminal mind, cultural studies, media practices, murder and its aftermath, psychology, sociology, and other areas of inquiry. It also represents an enduring interest in nonfiction, especially literary journalism, and the ethical issues that accompany any study of the borderland between fiction and nonfiction.

The book pays tribute to the interest that students exhibit in historical events, literary criticism, and social issues, such as capital punishment, incarceration, law enforcement, and other topics related to crime. In particular, I want to thank a former graduate student, Breanna Draxler, and two former undergraduate students, Nicole Lilienfeld and Kathryn J. Miller, to whom this book is dedicated.

During a graduate course in literary journalism in 2011, Breanna Draxler, an editor and environmental journalist, took a special interest in the life of Truman Capote and the narrative strategies of his work *In Cold Blood*. While doing research about the nonfiction novel, she discovered references to Michael Nations, the son of a former Kansas editor and publisher. An engaging writer and an inquisitive journalist, Breanna also found an online reference to Starling Mack Nations, who wrote a manuscript titled *High Road to Hell* about the murder of Herbert, Bonnie, Nancy, and Kenyon Clutter. Although she graduated before I began regular correspondence with Michael Nations, Breanna's discovery was the catalyst for a chapter in this book.

Michael Nations, now in his sixties, spent much of his career in law enforcement in Houston. At the time when Breanna and I first sought him out, he was suspicious of our motives, although he eventually began mailing family documents, including original correspondence between his father and Richard Eugene Hickock, one of the men convicted of murdering the Clutter family. After a trial and several years in prison, Hickock and his accomplice Perry Edward Smith were hanged in Kansas. Capote considered Mack Nations a competitor; in fact, as discussed at greater length in chapter five, in a letter to friends Capote called Nations "the newspaper bastard who has caused me so much trouble."[1] In correspondence, Capote even expresses his delight that Nations suffered from financial trouble.

---

[1]Gerald Clarke, ed., *Too Brief a Treat: The Letters of Truman Capote* (New York: Random House, 2004) 343.

Although Breanna identified an important source, two undergraduate students contributed to this study in other ways. In 2012, I had the privilege to teach a course in media ethics. Together, we read *In Cold Blood*, *Into the Wild* (Jon Krakauer), and *Midnight in the Garden of Good and Evil* (John Berendt) in order to explore several ethical issues of particular interest to scholars of literary journalism, including the boundaries between fiction and nonfiction, didacticism, first-person point of view, and immersion.

Fortunately for me, an especially engaged student, Kathryn J. Miller, told me after class one day that she needed to catch up on the reading assignment for *In Cold Blood*. She mentioned casually that her grandmother, Sally Anduss, was a neighbor of the Clutters in the 1950s who had remained a friend of Beverly Clutter English and Eveanna Clutter Mosier, the only immediate family members to escape the carnage. English and Mosier gave interviews to Capote with the promise that he would let them read the family's story before he published it in serialized form in *The New Yorker*. Stunned that he did not keep his word and concerned about his portrayal of their family, the sisters have refused all other interviews with the exception of a 2005 news article in which they explain their desire not to share their story. In that short piece, written by Patrick Smith, the women describe their commitment to collecting material about their parents and brother and sister for the scrapbooks they plan to give their grandchildren. English and Mosier describe "three thick red binders"[2] of family documents that they collected as a tribute to their parents. Although the Clutter sisters remain determined to protect their privacy (and did not respond to requests to participate in this study), Kathryn's interest in the nonfiction novel and her understanding of an event that impacted so many Kansans—including her grandmother—inspired the class and encouraged me to return to this project.

Another student, Nicole Lilienfeld, took an undergraduate seminar in literary journalism with seven other students in 2015. During the class, we met with the authors of two of the nonfiction novels on the reading list, Sara Davidson of Boulder, author of *Loose Change: Three Women of the Sixties*, and Patricia Raybon of Denver, author of *My First White Friend: Confessions on Race, Love, and Forgiveness*. Other books included *Travels with Charley in Search of America* (John Steinbeck), *Blue Nights* and *A Year of Magical Thinking*

---

[2]Patrick Smith, "Sisters, Family: Surviving Clutter Daughters Hope to Preserve their Parents' Legacy," *Lawrence Journal-World*, 4 April 2005, web (accessed 25 July 2018).

(Joan Didion), *Into the Wild* (Jon Krakauer), and *Midnight in the Garden of Good and Evil* (John Berendt).

Nicole selected *In Cold Blood* for her presentation, which was to be an informal twenty-minute discussion about the author and nonfiction novel. Instead, she amassed enough material to write a graduate thesis, and I began to encourage her to consider making the study an honors project. After I had postponed my work on Capote in order to pursue other book projects, Nicole inspired me to return to the Capote masterpiece—in large part because her interest reminded me that *In Cold Blood* remains, even for twenty-somethings, one of the most intriguing examples of crime fiction, literary journalism, and nonfiction studies in American literature.

Three additional contributions are especially important. Michael Nations forwarded information and talked with me by phone about his father, Starling Mack Nations. In the manuscript, I refer to our telephone and e-mail conversations. Diana Selsor Edwards agreed to let me include her article "The Rest of the Story," originally published in *Desert Exposure* in November 2009. In a September 6, 2016, e-mail message, her editor, Elva K. Österreich, called her piece "very touching and human, an excellent addition to any publication." Finally, Donald Cullivan allowed me to include his essay "Truman Capote and Perry Smith." Nations, Edwards, and Cullivan are working on memoirs in which they include the essays featured here in chapters five and eight.

I acknowledge permission by Bridgeman Images to publish a photograph of Truman Capote in Milan on the cover of this book. I also acknowledge the Library of Congress for providing the image for the back cover. The black-and-white photograph is a three-quarter-length portrait of Capote standing in the living room of the Clutter house after the 1959 murders. Titled "Return to the Scene," the editorial copy that accompanies the photograph reads, "Author Truman Capote stands in the living room of the Clutter ranch house where four members of the Kansas family were murdered in 1959. Capote's account of the crime and its solution, 'In Cold Blood,' was a best-seller and is being filmed in the actual locales. Despite critical comment, Capote declares his 'non-fiction novel' was an advance in literature." Chapter one explores both the "critical comment" that made the nonfiction novel even more alluring to readers and the unprecedented history of a novel that began as a study of Holcomb, Kansas, and became an international bestseller and a polemic about capital punishment.

Taken by an Associated Press photographer, the untitled photograph of Capote in the Clutter house is part of the *New York World-Telegram and Sun* collection and is used courtesy of the Prints & Photographs Division, Library of Congress (LC-USZ62-119332). Although not directly relevant to a study of *In Cold Blood*, that collection is a valuable resource made possible by the contributions of several newspapers: *The New York Herald*, *The Evening Telegram*, *The Telegram*, the *New York Sun*, and the *New York World*. In 1950, after a series of acquisitions and sales, the *New York World-Telegram and Sun* was founded. It survived until 1966, and then, after a brief merger with a William Randolph Hearst newspaper, it shut down in 1967. Major newspapers that remain in New York include the *Times*, the *Post*, and the *Daily News*. Chapter two of this book addresses the evolution of literary journalism and its eventual separation from what was in the 1950s and 1960s a traditional and detached "just-the-facts-ma'am" approach to newsgathering and news dissemination. Although not part of this study, New York newspaper history requires more than a nod.

First, I thank Penguin Random House for permission to cite from Truman Capote's *In Cold Blood: A True Account of a Multiple Murder and Its Consequences* (New York: Random House, 1965). I also thank the Truman Capote Literary Trust, established by Capote's literary executor, Alan U. Schwartz, for its support of research about Capote and his work.

I appreciate permission to use an excerpt from the poem "Asphodel, That Greeny Flower" (By William Carlos Williams, from COLLECTED POEMS 1939-1962, VOLUME II. Copyright 1944 by William Carlos Williams. Reprinted by permission of New Directions Publishing Corp.).

I also appreciate permission to cite the poem "Design" from THE POETRY OF ROBERT FROST (Edited by Edward Connery Lathem. Copyright 1947, 1969 by Henry Holt and Company. Copyright 1975 by Lesley Frost Ballantine. Reprinted by permission of Henry Holt and Company, LLC).

Updated chapters from *Dangerous Dreams: Essays on American Film and Television* (New York: Peter Lang, 2013) appear in this study. I appreciate permission to include portions of *"Shutter Island:* Martin Scorsese's Allegory of Despair" (17-24) and "Changing Faces: Dr. Jekyll, Mr. Hyde, and Films of the 1980s" (47-60).

I thank Grey House Publishing for permission to use a portion of a chapter originally published as "'And a Little Child Shall Lead Them': Scout and Jem Finch in Novel and Film" in *Critical Insights: Horton Foote* (Copyright 2016 Grey House Publishing. All rights reserved.).

I acknowledge the *Popular Culture Studies Journal* for permission to include "'I Did Them Things So You Wouldn't Have To': *Secret Window* and the Characters Who Won't Stay Dead," 1.1/2 *Popular Culture Studies Journal* (2013): 84-99.

In addition, I would like to thank Rowman & Littlefield for their permission to include excerpts from *Settling the Borderland: Other Voices in Literary Journalis*m, which I published with University Press of America, a Rowman & Littlefield imprint, in 2008.

Finally, as a former journalist and professor of journalism, I especially thank five editors and their reporters for a commitment to their profession and for permission to quote from several news stories. I thank Jon Alverson, editor and publisher, *Delta* (Mississippi) *Democrat-Times;* M. Olaf Frandsen, editor and publisher, *Salina* (Kansas) *Journal;* Chad Lawhorn, editor, *Lawrence* (Kansas) *Journal-World;* Dena Sattler, editor and publisher of the *Garden City* (Kansas) *Telegram;* and John Vahlenkamp, managing editor of the *Longmont* (Colorado) *Times-Call.*

In particular, I am indebted to David Abrahamson, the Charles Deering McCormick Professor of Teaching Excellence, Northwestern University; Thomas B. Connery, professor and dean emeritus, St. Thomas University; John C. Hartsock, professor, the State University of New York at Cortland; John Pauly, Gretchen and Cyril Colnik Chair in Communication, Marquette University; Nancy Roberts, professor, the State University of New York at Albany; Willard D. (Wick) Rowland, dean emeritus, School of Journalism and Mass Communication, University of Colorado at Boulder; and Norman Sims, professor emeritus, University of Massachusetts at Amherst. These scholars and friends introduced me to the confounding and inspiring universe of literary journalism.

Introduction

On November 15, 1959, Herbert and Bonnie Clutter and two of their children were terrorized and murdered in a farmhouse in the small town of Holcomb, Kansas. Bonnie Clutter and her daughter Nancy were shot in their upstairs bedrooms. Herbert Clutter and his son Kenyon were killed in the basement, Kenyon on a couch and his father on the floor. Both were shot at close range. Herbert Clutter also had his throat cut. Friends found the bodies the next morning before church services.

The murders immobilized, shamed, and shattered a close-knit community that—until the deaths occurred—had lived and worshipped together as friends in their rural neighborhood. Their social interactions were characterized by church gatherings, school functions, and other activities in Holcomb and nearby Garden City. After gunshots forever changed a community in which many residents did not lock their doors, no one knew whom to trust. The world they had known was gone.

Author of *Other Voices, Other Rooms* (1948), *A Tree of Night and Other Stories* (1949), *The Grass Harp* (1951), *The Muses Are Heard* (1956), and *Breakfast at Tiffany's* (1958), Truman Capote read a short newspaper article about the murders in *The New York Times* and became obsessed with their context and aftermath. Eventually, the title *In Cold Blood* would refer broadly to the murders in the Clutter home, the executions of those responsible, and, according to some critics, the techniques Capote employed while writing his magnum opus. In hindsight, it is no surprise that a famous gay author from New York would be captivated by a story about death in a rural locale known for its white, heterosexual, religious population, nor is it strange that the nation itself would be drawn into an allegory about the presumed end of American innocence.

By the time readers engaged Capote's masterpiece, they already were familiar with the news stories about the event and the investigation, arrests, and executions that followed; however, they were interested in learning how Capote would describe a series of events that absorbed more than five years of his life and produced several file cabinets full of research. What could possibly explain the deaths of four family members who kept no money on the premises? How could a strong and healthy farmer—accustomed to physical labor—allow two invaders to bind him and his family? Why would he believe their promises? And why would anyone kill a family for a pair of binoculars, a transistor radio, and about forty dollars in cash? Such a crime might occur in New York City, they told themselves, but how could it happen in the American heartland?

Eventually, two men who had previously served time for other crimes were apprehended, tried and found guilty, and sentenced to death by hanging. First, however, Richard Eugene Hickock and Perry Edward Smith would spend years in prison in Lansing, Kansas, with few visitors except Capote himself. Capote and his childhood friend Nelle Harper Lee, celebrated author of *To Kill a Mockingbird* (1960), would come to Holcomb to investigate the murders and would visit the two men on Death Row. At first, Capote intended to write a book about what he called a "village"[1] and its shattered innocence. *In Cold Blood* became that and much more. Ultimately, the narrative captured the imagination of a nation and highlighted issues including the death penalty, justice, violence, and the very nature of humankind. Having befriended and identified with one of the murderers, Capote shocked and engaged his readers and created a masterpiece that would eclipse his previous work; however, not even the author himself could have known the personal price he would pay for his obsession with the deaths and their aftermath.

This book, *Untold Stories, Unheard Voices: Truman Capote's* In Cold Blood, gives expression to the narratives omitted from the nonfiction novel, which Capote wrote during his whirlwind race to an imaginary finish line. In addition to his lifelong quest to believe in himself and to be the center of every party, Capote was determined to compete with his childhood friend Harper Lee and her unprecedented success after the publication of *To Kill a Mockingbird* and the release of the film by the same title two years later. Her book would win a Pulitzer Prize, and the film starring Gregory Peck as Atticus Finch would garner three Academy Awards and be nominated for eight more.

The title of this study borrows from the idea behind the phrase "voices in the wind-bent wheat"[2] in the final paragraph of *In Cold Blood*. Focusing on some of the untold stories and unheard voices that are linked to the publication of the nonfiction novel, it analyzes the place of *In Cold Blood* in the history of creative nonfiction and literary journalism, placing it into cultural, historical, literary, and regional contexts. More important, it explores the

---

[1]Truman Capote, *In Cold Blood: A True Account of a Multiple Murder and Its Consequences* (New York: Vintage, 1965) 3.

[2]Ibid., 343.

stories of those whose experiences were omitted from the crime novel, including much of Harper Lee's own contribution. Although Capote dedicated *In Cold Blood* to Lee and his partner Jack Dunphy, he did not credit Lee appropriately for the time and access to sources that she provided.

In the final (invented) scene of the much-beloved and disparaged novel, Alvin A. Dewey, who investigated the murder of the Clutter family in Holcomb, meets a friend of the late Nancy Clutter in the cemetery near the four Clutter graves. Dewey considers how the young woman he meets, Susan Kidwell, is the age Nancy Clutter would have been had she lived, and he chats briefly with Kidwell. Capote describes the encounter, although he did not observe it, and says that eventually Dewey turned to go: "Then, starting home, he walked toward the trees, and under them, leaving behind him the big sky, the whisper of wind voices in the wind-bent wheat."[3]

Following the 1967 film *In Cold Blood*, starring Robert Blake as Perry Smith, two other films, *Capote* (2005) and *Infamous* (2006), were drawn from two different biographies about Capote and posthumously fulfilled the author's unrelenting desire to make *In Cold Blood* his most widely celebrated work. The film *In Cold Blood* did not feature Capote himself; instead, Richard Brooks created a reporter to observe and comment upon the events. Seeking fame, Capote attacked those whom he saw as threats to his genius; made up dialogue and scenes; misrepresented facts; manipulated law enforcement officers, FBI investigators, and killers Hickock and Smith; and alienated some of the Kansas residents most wounded by the murders. He also produced a riveting and mysterious tale about the unpredictability of criminals and the tenacity of law enforcement.

Capote's obsession with the murders and his desperation to cement his legacy as the author of the greatest nonfiction novel came at a terrible personal cost. Critics argue that after the nonfiction novel appeared, Capote had a breakdown from which he never recovered; in fact, until his death in 1984, he never published another book. In *Chronicling Trauma: Journalists and Writers on Violence and Loss*, Doug Underwood suggests that *In Cold Blood* was responsible for Capote's "physical and mental decline."[4] Capote died in 1984 at the home of Joanna Carson, ex-wife of talk-show giant Johnny Carson, after years of abusing his body with alcohol and drugs. By

---

[3]Ibid.

[4]Doug Underwood, *Chronicling Trauma: Journalists and Writers on Violence and Loss* (Urbana: University of Illinois Press, 2011) 173.

most accounts, he was alienated from many of his friends and in deep despair.

In Cold Blood *in Context*

Introductory chapters in this study place *In Cold Blood* into a historical context and provide a chronological summary of the events that led to its publication. They also rely on biographical information about Capote, his insecurities, his reputation among the New York literati, and his childhood, including his relationship with Harper Lee.

Part one, titled "Contexts," includes four chapters. Among other topics, the first chapter ("The Enduring Popularity of *In Cold Blood*") addresses well-documented inaccuracies in what Capote purportedly considered the first nonfiction novel and prepares readers for subsequent analyses that locate the book in everything from literary journalism, a subgenre of creative nonfiction, to American crime stories with doppelgängers as protagonists. It helps to answer the question: Why is *In Cold Blood* a landmark work in an interdisciplinary genre?

The second and third chapters ("*In Cold Blood* and American Literary Journalism" and "*In Cold Blood, Handcarved Coffins*, and 'Then It All Came Down'") address Capote's commitment to nonfiction based on newsworthy events. Before introducing some of the missing perspectives in the nonfiction novel in part two ("Voices"), this portion of the study concludes with chapter four, titled "*In Cold Blood*, the Doppelgänger, and Murder." It locates the book in additional genres of American literature, introduces possible reasons for the widespread appeal of certain American crime stories (for example, the murder of JonBenet Ramsey in Boulder, Colorado; the murder of a mother and her daughters in Cheshire, Connecticut; the death of Casey Anthony; the trials of Amanda Knox, etc.), and deals with their allegorical, universal, and popular exposure. From novels by Norman Mailer to films such as *The Shawshank Redemption* to *People* magazine's contemporary coverage of assaults, murders, and robberies, the chapter helps to explain our obsession with crime and its aftermath.

However, chapter four focuses on the books *In Cold Blood* and *True Story* (2005)—and several films and literary texts that appeared between the two. Written by Michael Finkel, *True Story* became a film starring Jonah Hill as Finkel and James Franco as convicted murderer Christian Longo in 2015. The comparative study helps to answer these questions: Why does the murder of a farm family in 1959 hold such a powerful sway? What is the history of sensationalism—both in extended nonfiction and daily journalism—and what role does it play in Capote's novel? Finally, which contemporary texts best illustrate the relationship that can develop between a reporter and his or her source? What happens when Truman Capote and Michael Finkel meet murderers face to face and begin to immerse themselves in those men's realities? Most important, what occurs when they begin to recognize aspects of themselves in the criminals whom they interview? This final question suggests other texts that explore the doppelgänger in literature and film, including the films *The Talented Mr. Ripley* (1999), *Shutter Island* (2003), *Secret Window* (2004), *Mr. Brooks* (2007), and *The Two Faces of January* (2014).

Part two includes four chapters that profile a few of the people and perspectives left out of *In Cold Blood*. Chapter five ("Starling Mack Nations and *High Road to Hell*") introduces Starling Mack Nations, the newspaper owner and publisher who wrote an unpublished book-length account of the murders. Some of his interviews with convicted murderer Richard Hickock appeared in an article in the now-defunct *Male* magazine, included in its entirety in this study. His son Michael Nations provided biographical information about his father, who served in the governor's office in Kansas and at the time of his death was a Walsenburg, Colorado, newspaper publisher. He also provided correspondence between his father and Hickock.

The chapter focuses on Nations and a manuscript that is based on interviews with Hickock instead of Smith. At least thirty researchers have produced studies that deal with the shortcuts Capote took in writing *In Cold Blood*, a book that some of them consider to be more fiction than fact. This study necessarily refers to that body of literature, all secondary sources. However, the assessment of *In Cold Blood* relies equally on ethnographic research and literary criticism and introduces *High Road to Hell*, which, had Random House been more interested, would have predated *In Cold Blood* and might, in fact, have dimmed some of the attention that Capote craved. As we will learn, Capote knew of Nations's work and actively sought to undo him.

The chapter answers the following questions: Why was Capote allowed extensive contact with the murderers, while Nations, other reporters, and even Harper Lee, Capote's "assistant researchist,"[5] were denied access? What do the answers to this question tell us about celebrity authors and their roles

---

[5]Charles J. Shields, *Mockingbird: A Portrait of Harper Lee* (New York: Henry Holt, 2006) 139.

in constructing national narratives? How was Capote able to exclude Kansas journalists, gain the trust of local law enforcement officials, and become friends with one of the convicted killers? Could he achieve the same access today?

Chapter six ("Nelle Harper Lee and *In Cold Blood*") focuses on author Harper Lee. It specifically addresses the role Lee played in producing *In Cold Blood*. Capote advocates have muddied the truth about the time she spent as Capote's assistant, and Lee maintained her privacy and her silence on the matter until her death in 2016. What did Harper Lee actually provide Capote? Did he take some of her advice and dismiss the rest? More important, is Lee's sister Alice Lee correct when she argues that Capote's rejection of his childhood friend was part of his undoing and a possible explanation for his depression and his death at age 59?

Chapter seven ("*In Cold Blood* in Documentary and Film") continues to unveil the role Lee played in the interviews at the heart of *In Cold Blood* by exploring her portrayal in other related films. The chapter deals with the films *In Cold Blood*, *Capote*, and *Infamous* and the impact of the latter two on a new generation of readers of *In Cold Blood*. The two biographies of Capote that inspired the films lie at the center of this section. Why did each creative team select one of the biographies for its film project and exclude the other? Are the films accurate? Should they be? What does scholarship about film adaptation suggest? The chapter also addresses the portrayal of Jean Louise (Scout) Finch, her brother Jeremy Atticus (Jem) Finch, and Charles Baker (Dill) Harris in the novel and film *To Kill a Mockingbird*. Dill is modeled on Truman Capote, and the novel portrays him as an affectionate, animated, compassionate, curious, and deeply wounded child.

Chapter eight ("River Valley Farm and Beyond") introduces the voices of people whose names appear in *In Cold Blood*. Where are Perry Smith's Army buddy Don Cullivan, Nancy Clutter's friends Nancy Ewalt and Susan Kidwell, and others today? What happened to Beverly Clutter English and Eveanna Clutter Mosier, the sisters who were not home when Richard Hickock and Perry Smith murdered their family? The chapter answers other questions, too: Who were the Clutters? Why did Capote all but ignore their lives in telling his extraordinary tale? Why did he portray Bonnie and Herbert Clutter in the way he did, ignoring information from the surviving Clutter sisters and other residents of Holcomb and Garden City? Did his narrative goals determine his characterization of a farm family? Why does the novel begin in medias res—like Nathaniel Hawthorne's novel about

Hester Prynne and other "crime stories"—and what does his emphasis on the forensic study, the trial, and Perry Smith tell us about his objective in documenting the crime?

The chapter also addresses others who remained in Holcomb, Kansas, after the murders and the trial. Much has changed, but the murders still help to define the community, where people drive past the former Clutter home, visit the gravesites, and go to church in Garden City to see the stained-glass window dedicated to the family. Chapter eight describes both Garden City and Holcomb more than fifty years after *In Cold Blood* and the memorials and other tributes that document the lives of Herbert, Bonnie, Nancy, and Kenyon Clutter. With the exception of one short local interview, the sisters have refused to talk to reporters since they believed Capote betrayed them more than a half-century ago. The final chapter takes readers into the former Clutter home that was advertised for sale and then taken off the market. It provides interviews with the homeowners who for many years gave tours of the house and farm. Questions that drive this portion of the study include the following: Why do so many visitors descend upon Holcomb and Garden City? Why are so many residents willing to talk with them? Why did some of the central figures in the novel—including Bobby Rupp, who was Nancy Clutter's boyfriend—remain in their hometown following the murders, the trial, and the executions? What have their lives been like?

Untold Stories, Unheard Voices *in Context*

Studies about creative nonfiction, including *Settling the Borderland: Other Voices in Literary Journalism*, help to place *In Cold Blood* in its historical context. Since a great deal of research falls into the netherworld between journalism and literature, literary and media scholars often address Capote's nonfiction novel and explore ethical dilemmas related to the use of literary techniques (allegory, denouement, description, dialogue, narration, rising and falling action, symbols, tropes, etc.) in creating a nonfiction text. They also consider the ways that marketing, reportorial strategies, timeliness, and other factors are involved in producing and sustaining memorable fact-based narratives.

Literary journalists can be said to be all about themselves, often employing allegory to uncover universal themes and using first-person point of view and established literary techniques to make everyday events appear immediate and deeply personal. Sara Davidson, Joan Didion, Jane Kramer, Norman Mailer, Susan Orlean, Hunter S. Thompson, Tom Wolfe, and others write themselves into existence by listening to and appropriating the stories of others, providing sources with confessional moments while they eavesdrop on their lives, caring about them while seeking deeper truths. In part, this study addresses the ego at play in *In Cold Blood* and other seminal texts.

In Cold Blood remains among the 100 greatest novels of the twentieth century, a study of crime and a polemic against capital punishment that is without equal. Capote purportedly considered it one of the first examples of a nonfiction novel, helping to usher in the era of New Journalism as defined by Tom Wolfe. *In Cold Blood* is also the catalyst for a century of crime reporting in America, which drew upon popular narratives about heightened human conflict in England, France, and Italy. Of course, crime coverage is by definition popular, involving dramatic conflict, human interest, and questions of morality. Certainly, *In Cold Blood* provides nail-biting realism, although it does much more.

This book does not ignore previous investigations into Capote's character and his determination to produce a Pulitzer Prize-winning nonfiction novel to rival his friend Harper Lee's *To Kill a Mockingbird*, which is an example of fiction laced with memoir. However, it begins with an acknowledgment that *In Cold Blood* has outlasted negative criticism and will endure as a fusion of fiction and nonfiction and as a stylistic masterpiece. *Untold Stories, Unheard Voices: Truman Capote and* In Cold Blood seeks to explain the hold of the nonfiction novel on generations of readers by focusing on its allegorical significance, its didacticism, and its description of law enforcement officials and Capote himself. The study addresses multiple layers of the crime and its aftermath; its role in what literary journalist Sara Davidson describes as "The Gray Zone" between fiction and nonfiction; and the centrality of memory in autobiography, memoir, personal essays, and other literary forms.

Untold Stories, Unheard Voices: Truman Capote and In Cold Blood recognizes the ongoing obsession with the Clutter family murders and what they represent. From the desire to link Hickock and Smith to the murder of a family in Florida, to the debate among investigator Harold R. Nye's family with respect to releasing existing records, to authors and filmmakers who mirror relationships between journalist and murderer (especially in *True Story*)—*In Cold Blood* holds sway over our imaginations and contemporary studies of crime and the criminal mind. Although he suffered from alcoholism, drug abuse, and depression and died in 1984, Capote—ever the showman seeking the spotlight—would no doubt be even more proud of what he considered his best work if he had lived to see at least a part of its continuing literary ascendance.

In a foreword to Lawrence Grobel's *Conversations with Capote*, James Michener highlights the popularity of *In Cold Blood* and calls it "exceptional in its mastery."[6] "At the time of the publication of *In Cold Blood*, I was working in widely scattered parts of the world," Michener writes, "and wherever I went *In Cold Blood* was being translated into the local language with all the impact it had had in English. Critics, readers, other writers were all mesmerized by it, and no other book during my productive years enjoyed such popular and critical acclaim."[7] Michener dubbed Capote a "later-day Thomas Chatterton, indubitably brilliant, indubitably incandescent, indubitably doomed."[8]

Chapter one addresses why *In Cold Blood* remains a compelling nonfiction novel, even as it competes with continuous coverage of crime and crime-related stories featured on entertainment and news networks and websites and in magazines, newspapers, and online venues. The first and subsequent chapters pose and seek to answer questions such as these: Where does the novel fall in the history of crime coverage? What trends did it introduce, if any? Why locate *In Cold Blood* in the traditions of American literary journalism and crime stories? Chapters two and four place *In Cold Blood* into particular themes, literary movements, and genres including allegory, doppelgängers, literary journalism, sensationalism, and crime. Chapter three compares the nonfiction novel to other texts in Capote's own canon.

What are the "voices in the wind-bent wheat"[9]—the phrase drawn from the final line of *In Cold Blood*—that were omitted from critical consideration of the novel? For example, as chapter five explores, what might Starling Mack Nations, who interviewed Hickock instead of Smith, say about the veracity of *In Cold Blood*? And what about the role of the late Nelle Harper Lee as a friend to and "assistant researchist" for Capote in Kansas, a topic explored in chapter six? And, as addressed in chapter seven, what should we make of the documentaries and films that transported Capote and *In Cold*

---

[6]James A. Michener, "Foreword," in Lawrence Grobel, *Conversations with Capote* (New York: New American Library, 1985) 11.

[7]Ibid., 8.

[8]Ibid., 9.

[9]Capote, *In Cold Blood*, 343.

Blood into the twenty-first century and appealed to a new generation of readers, film critics, and moviegoers?

Finally, what has happened to the residents of Holcomb and Garden City, Kansas, whose personal lives were affected both by the release of the novel and by the hundreds who annually drive past River Valley Farm to catch a glimpse of the Clutter family's former home? Chapter eight explores what *In Cold Blood* might have been if Capote had adhered to his first inclination, which was to investigate the impact of murder on a close-knit community. The tone for the nonfiction novel is set in his first paragraph:

> The village of Holcomb stands on the high wheat plains of western Kansas, a lonesome area that other Kansans call "out there." Some seventy miles east of the Colorado border, the countryside, with its hard blue skies and desert-clear air, has an atmosphere that is rather more Far West than Middle West. The local accent is barbed with a prairie twang, a ranch-hand nasalness, and the men, many of them, wear narrow frontier trousers, Stetsons, and high-heeled boots with pointed toes. The land is flat, and the views are awesomely extensive; horses, herds of cattle, a white cluster of grain elevators rising as gracefully as Greek temples are visible long before a traveler reaches them.[10]

Holcomb, Kansas—what Capote calls a "haphazard hamlet"[11]—ceased to be what it was for millions of Americans when Truman Capote stepped off the train and created a mythological place that inhabitants would never fully reclaim. What are Holcomb and Garden City, Kansas, today, and what do those who are willing to discuss the nonfiction novel and its legacy say now?

---

[10]Ibid, 3.
[11]Ibid.

PART 1

CONTEXTS

Chapter 1

The Enduring Popularity of *In Cold Blood*

In 1959, World War II had ended, although the Vietnam War loomed. The national economy was stable. More than fifty million homes had television sets, and viewers enjoyed *The Ed Sullivan Show*, *Father Knows Best*, *Gunsmoke*, *Leave It to Beaver*, *The Mickey Mouse Club*, and *Perry Mason*. Civil rights activists demanded an end to segregation, and movements for racial, ethnic, gender, and economic equality proliferated. Dwight D. Eisenhower was president, Richard M. Nixon was vice president, and among white Americans, there existed a general sense of optimism, a desire for safety and continuing prosperity. The homicide rate was approximately 4.9 percent per 100,000 citizens, and concern about crime was not prevalent; in fact, homeowners in rural communities across the Great Plains and elsewhere often did not lock their doors.

On November 15, 1959, Perry Edward Smith and Richard Eugene Hickock slid into Holcomb, Kansas. Recently released from prison, Hickock took a twelve-gauge pump-action shotgun and traveled with Smith 400 miles to Holcomb, Kansas. Without attracting attention, they drove Hickock's 1949 black Chevrolet down a long driveway toward a quiet farmhouse. The two walked through an unlocked door, and after waking Herbert, Bonnie, Nancy, and Kenyon Clutter, discovered there was no safe in the house in spite of what they had heard. They then killed the family, took a transistor radio, binoculars, and about forty dollars, and disappeared into the night. Hickock and Smith were arrested December 30, 1959, and executed April 14, 1965.

On November 16, 1959, Truman Capote read an account of the murders in *The New York Times*. Having sought a news story that he might turn into a piece of extended nonfiction, he believed he had found one. He traveled to Kansas soon after, and six years later, *In Cold Blood: A True Account of a Multiple Murder and Its Consequences* was published. Considered one of the greatest books of the twentieth century, *In Cold Blood* has sold millions of copies and been translated into more than thirty languages. It remained on the bestseller list thirty-seven weeks,[1] and in 2005 alone sold 1.5 million copies after the release of the Academy Award-winning film *Capote*.

Truman Capote and Kansas

As is evident from several biographies, news stories about his life, obituaries that followed his death in 1984, and the films about his life and work, Truman Capote has withstood the test of time. For this study, *In Cold Blood* is central to the discussion of classics in American literature, crime coverage, film studies, and literary journalism. *In Cold Blood* gives us Perry Smith, a cold-blooded murderer and an anti-hero akin to the protagonist in Albert Camus's *The Stranger*. In fact, Capote dedicates almost one-third of the nonfiction novel to Smith. A translation of the poem "Ballade Des Pendus" by Francois Villon at the beginning of the novel suggests the way the reader is supposed to feel about Smith: "My brothers who live after us, / Don't harden your hearts against us too. / If you have mercy now on us, / God may have mercy upon you."[2] Discussion of Capote's sympathy for Smith and the way his feelings for the killer might have distorted the truth of the novel continues.

Most important, four members of the Clutter family were killed on their farm in a town with a population of approximately 270,[3] a town in which people knew and supported one another. Capote's title reflects the headline in the November 1959 issue of *Time* magazine about the murders, "In Cold Blood." Ultimately, the title may refer to the manner in which the murderers were put to death by the state, to the manner in which the family was killed, and/or to the manner in which Capote was thought by many to have exploited his sources and excused one of the killers. In an interview with biographer George Plimpton in *Truman Capote: Conversations*, Capote said he didn't know immediately that the story of the murder was what he had been looking for:

> ...But after reading the story it suddenly struck me that a crime, the study of one such, might provide the broad scope I needed to write the

---

[1]Paul Rudnick, "Midnight Snack at Tiffany's: Answered Prayers," *Los Angeles Times*, 27 September 1987, web (accessed 27 July 2018).

[2]Francois Villon, "Ballade Des Pendus," trans. A. S. Kline (2004), web (accessed 27 July 2018).

[3]Ed Pilkington, "In Cold Blood, Half a Century On," *The Guardian*, 15 November 2009, web (accessed 27 July 2018).

kind of book I wanted to write. Moreover, the human heart being what it is, murder was a theme not likely to darken and yellow with time.

I thought about it all that November day, and part of the next; and then I said to myself: Well, why not *this* crime? The Clutter case. Why not pack up and go to Kansas and see what happens?[4]

What followed Capote's fascination with the news story were 6,000 pages of notes, three years of research, and three more years of writing. Most likely, part of the reason for his fascination with the murders was how unusual such an event was in rural Kansas. The former sheriff of Finney County and special agent of the Kansas Bureau of Investigation, Alvin A. Dewey, conducted the investigation. In a news story titled "The Clutter Case," Dewey said that in his home state murders "were virtually unheard of."[5] By the time the criminal investigation, trial, and execution were over, Capote had built relationships with each of the killers and had become especially fond of Smith. Whether that relationship was sexualized, as some have suggested, is unclear, but it was a powerful connection for both men. In answer to a question about whether or not Hickock and Smith had sex, Capote said, "No. None at all."[6] Capote described his own relationship with the killers by saying that Hickock and Smith "were very very good friends of mine (I mean became very close friends, very very close intimates in every conceivable way)." He said they "would have gladly given me the things they wrote."[7]

The investigation into the murders changed Truman Capote forever. In one of his most provocative and insightful statements about the impact his research in Kansas had on him, Capote said to Lawrence Grobel, "The experience served to heighten my feeling of the tragic view of life, which I've always held and which accounts for the side of me that appears extremely frivolous; that part of me is always standing in a darkened hallway, mocking tragedy and death. That's why I love champagne and stay at the Ritz."[8] Toward the end of his life, Capote would say that if he knew the effect that the research, the trial, and the executions would have on him, he would never

[4]George Plimpton, "The Story Behind a Nonfiction Novel," *Truman Capote: Conversations*, ed. M. Thomas Inge (Jackson: University Press of Mississippi, 1987) 51.

[5]Alvin A. Dewey, "The Clutter Case: 25 Years Later KBI Agent Recounts Holcomb Tragedy," *Garden City Telegram*, 10 November 1984, 2A.

[6]Plimpton, "The Story," 60.

[7]Ibid., 71.

[8]Lawrence Grobel, *Conversations with Capote* (New York: New American Library, 1985) 110.

have begun the project, although, with characteristic hyperbole, Capote said his nonfiction novel was near perfect: "Every time I pick up *In Cold Blood* I read it all the way through, as if I didn't write it," he told Grobel. "It's really quite a perfect book, you know. I wouldn't change anything in it."[9]

The journey to Holcomb and back would deeply affect Capote, and it would change forever the genre of extended nonfiction. "Wealthy Farmer, 3 of Family Slain," reads the November 16, 1959, headline in *The New York Times.* The details that followed engaged the writer from New York City— in part because he already was looking for a subject for a piece of extended nonfiction and in part because whatever he knew about Kansas, which was almost nothing, he understood from his childhood years in Monroeville, Alabama: murders in a small town alter forever the way neighbors relate to one another. The story reads as follows:

> A wealthy wheat farmer, his wife and their two young children were found shot to death today in their home. They had been killed by shotgun blasts at close range after being bound and gagged.
>
> The father, 48-year-old Herbert W. Clutter, was found in the basement with his son, Kenyon, 15. His wife Bonnie, 45, and a daughter, Nancy, 16, were in their beds.
>
> There was no sign of a struggle and nothing had been stolen. The telephone lines had been cut.
>
> "This is apparently the case of a psychopathic killer," Sheriff Earl Robinson said.
>
> Mr. Clutter was founder of The Kansas Wheat Growers Association. In 1954, President Eisenhower appointed him to the Federal Farm Credit Board, but he never lived in Washington.
>
> The board represents the twelve farm credit districts in the country. Mr. Clutter served from December, 1953, until April, 1957. He declined a reappointment.
>
> He was also a local member of the Agriculture Department's Price Stabilization Board and was active with the Great Plains Wheat Growers Association.
>
> The Clutter farm and ranch cover almost 1,000 acres in one of the richest wheat areas.
>
> Mr. Clutter, his wife and daughter were clad in pajamas. The boy was wearing blue jeans and a T-shirt.

---

[9]Ibid., 16.

The bodies were discovered by two of Nancy's classmates, Susan Kidwell and Nancy Ewalt.

Sheriff Robinson said the last reported communication with Mr. Clutter took place last night about 9:30 P.M., when the victim called Gerald Van Vleet, his business partner, who lives near by. Mr. Van Vleet said the conversation had concerned the farm and ranch.

Two daughters were away. They are Beverly, a student at Kansas University, and Mrs. Donald G. Jarchow of Mount Carroll, Ill.[10]

Capote read the staccato facts arranged in characteristically brief paragraphs and made plans to go to Holcomb. Years later he produced the controversial and riveting *In Cold Blood*. Perhaps only a writer known for her or his fiction would emphasize the phrase "true account," and perhaps only Capote would claim that every word in his nonfiction novel was accurate. Whether or not he ultimately understood the import of his magnum opus, the beginning of his pilgrimage was nondescript: "Why not pack up and go to Kansas and see what happens?" he said to Plimpton. He added:

Of course it was a rather frightening thought!—to arrive alone in a small strange town, a town in the grip of an unsolved mass murder. Still, the circumstances of the place being altogether unfamiliar, geographically and atmospherically, made it that much more tempting. Everything would seem freshly minted—the people, their accents and attitudes, the landscape, its contours, the weather. All this, it seemed to me, could only sharpen my eye and quicken my ear.[11]

In Cold Blood is not only a masterpiece of storytelling but also belongs with other classics of American literary journalism and stories of crime and punishment. What began as an exposé about a village became a polemic about capital punishment and a topic of conversation for authors, historians, literary critics, psychologists, readers, and sociologists for decades to come. Perry Edward Smith—who Capote believed killed Herbert, Bonnie, Nancy, and Kenyon Clutter—became an anti-hero, a symbol of a life misspent, and Capote's own doppelgänger. Dan Futterman, screenwriter for the Academy Award-winning film *Capote* (2005), wrote these lines for Philip Seymour

---

[10]"Wealthy Farmer, 3 of Family Slain," *The New York Times*, 16 November 1959, web (accessed 27 July 2018).

[11]Plimpton, "The Story," 51.

Hoffman, who played Capote: "It's as if Perry and I started life in the same house. One day he stood up and walked out the back door while I walked out the front. With some different choices, he's the man I might have become." In fact, Capote told Plimpton, "I think Perry could have been an entirely different person. I really do. His life had been so incredibly abysmal that I don't see what chance he had as a little child except to steal and run wild."[12]

In Cold Blood complemented Capote's existing canon as much as it drove him in another direction. "Truman Capote's stories, much like the author himself, are driven by feelings of isolation, rejection, sadness, and other-ness,"[13] writes Courtney Watson in "Other Rooms: Safe Havens and Sacred Spaces in the Works of Truman Capote." Certainly, the nonfiction novel underscored themes in *Other Voices, Other Rooms* (1948), *A Tree of Night and Other Stories* (1949), *The Grass Harp* (1951), and *A Christmas Memory* (1966) at the same time it rocked Capote personally and professionally in a way he would address often before his death. Leslie A. Fiedler argues that a nonfiction novel set in Kansas farmland also introduced characters that are a part of the literary tradition of the Deep South, a topic addressed more thoroughly in the conclusion of this study. Writing that Capote's early work comprised "an accomplished anthology of all Southern literature," Fiedler believes that several authors haunted him, whether Capote noticed or not: "Poe is there, first of all, in the ambivalent image, half fairytale, half psychopathic revelation; Faulkner does the décor; the young girls are by Carson McCullers, the freaks by Eudora Welty. That contrived world is his inheritance, and, with assurance, Capote takes possession."[14]

It is not an exaggeration to suggest that Perry Smith is akin to characters in startling stories by Flannery O'Connor and novels by Cormac McCarthy. Perry Smith and Richard Hickock were hanged five and one-half years after Capote set foot in Holcomb with his childhood friend and accomplished author Nelle Harper Lee. Capote both celebrates his collaboration with Lee and alludes ominously to the impact the project had on him:

> In the end, I did not go alone. I went with a lifelong friend, Harper Lee. She is a gifted woman, courageous, and with a warmth that in-

---

[12]Ibid., 64.

[13]Courtney Watson, "Other Rooms: Safe Havens and Sacred Spaces in the Works of Truman Capote," *Studies in American Culture* 37/1 (October 2014): 101.

[14]Leslie A. Fiedler, "The Fate of the Novel," *Kenyon Review* 10/31 (1948): 522.

stantly kindles most people, however suspicious or dour. She had recently completed a first novel (*To Kill a Mockingbird*), and, feeling at loose ends, she said she would accompany me in the role of assistant researchist....

If I had realized then what the future held, I never would have stopped in Garden City. I would have driven straight on. Like a bat out of hell....

She kept me company when I was based out there. I suppose she was with me about two months altogether. She went on a number of interviews; she typed her own notes, and I had these and could refer to them. She was extremely helpful in the beginning, when we weren't making much headway with the town's people, by making friends with the wives of the people I wanted to meet. She became friendly with all the churchgoers. A Kansas paper said the other day that everybody was so wonderfully cooperative because I was a famous writer. The fact of the matter is that not one single person in the town had ever heard of me.[15]

Capote describes this period in his life by saying, "I decided to go and do *In Cold Blood*, which meant a fantastic period of my life living in ghastly motels in the windswept plains of western Kansas on and off for six years."[16] Capote went to the execution of Hickock and Smith. Before Smith walked up the stairs to the gallows, he is said to have kissed Capote on the cheek and said, "Adios, amigo."[17] However, Daniel Axelrod suggests in a detailed and scathing assessment of the truthfulness of *In Cold Blood* that Capote "even invented a final apology for Smith on the gallows."[18] Of the nonfiction novel itself, Axelrod writes, "In short, Capote was shamelessly unfaithful to the truth and ethically bankrupt in his information-gathering practices. He turned real people into characters and fit them into his artistic motifs by adding and omitting information and inventing conversations and entire scenes."[19] Smith and Hickock were executed April 14, 1965, between midnight and 2 a.m. after their petition for a rehearing of their case was de-

---

[15]Plimpton, "The Story," 51-52.

[16]Grobel, *Conversations*, 99.

[17]Plimpton, "The Story," 65.

[18]Daniel Axelrod, "In Cold Fact, In Cold Blood: Exposing Errors, Finding Fabrication and Unearthing Capote's Unethical Behavior," *The Newsletter of the International Association of Literary Journalism Studies* (Winter 2014): 18.

[19]Ibid., 18-19.

nied March 1, 1965. One of Plimpton's sources, Joe Fox, writes of Capote's trip back to New York after the execution:

> After the hanging, I sat next to Truman on the plane ride back to New York. He held my hand and cried most of the way. I remember thinking how odd it must have seemed to passengers sitting nearby—these two grown men apparently holding hands and one of them sobbing. It was a long trip. I couldn't read a copy of *Newsweek* or anything like that...not with Truman holding my hand. I stared straight ahead.[20]

In Cold Blood *Under Fire*

Few literary critics would describe themselves as Truman Capote apologists. Even fewer practitioners and scholars of journalism and media studies would seek to explain away the ethical breaches that mar one of the greatest nonfiction novels of all time. English professor emeritus Ralph F. Voss, in particular, explores in detail the errors, exaggerations, and omissions in the international bestseller in *Truman Capote and the Legacy of* In Cold Blood.

Nonetheless, *In Cold Blood* remains one of the most riveting tales of murder and its aftermath in American literary history. Readers mesmerized by convicted killers Richard Eugene Hickock and Perry Edward Smith and by the pages of forensic evidence—interspersed with narratives about the Clutter family, law enforcement officials, and townspeople—often forgive the license Capote took with the truth. Journalistic and literary critics, however, express their disappointment in Capote's claim that he could memorize hours of interviews, and they also lambast his inclusion of events that never occurred and his recreation of others. Although impossible to prove, his negative portrayal of victims such as Bonnie Clutter made it even more unlikely that anyone would ever interview the two daughters who survived the carnage that took place on November 15, 1959. Their story may never be told, except to their children and grandchildren. On the defensive, journalists committed to accurate reporting and dissemination of the news remind readers that Capote was never a journalist—much less one trained in news values.

Phillip K. Tompkins suggests in the essay "In Cold Fact" that *In Cold Blood*—composed of four main parts and eighty-six unnumbered chapters—reads as though it is a series of short stories, arguing that "many of them

---

[20]George Plimpton, "Capote's Long Ride," *The New Yorker*, 13 October 1997, 70.

could stand by themselves with little or no additional context."[21] Tompkins's most dramatic contribution to historical and literary criticism, however, is rooted in his own journey to Kansas in 1966. After spending nine days researching the veracity of the interviews Capote conducted, Tompkins concludes that *In Cold Blood* is hardly a true account. To ground his study, Tompkins cites an interview in the *Saturday Review* in which Capote said, "And then I got this idea of doing a really serious big work—it would be precisely like a novel, with a single difference: every word of it would be true from beginning to end." To this Tompkins added, "One doesn't spend almost six years on a book, the point of which is factual accuracy, and then give way to minor distortions."[22] Unfortunately, Tompkins finds much to fuel his suspicions. Examples include Capote's exaggerations and inaccurate statements about Bobby Rupp, Nancy Clutter's boyfriend; Capote's anecdote about Babe, Nancy Clutter's horse; and conversations with Undersheriff Wendle Meier and his wife Josephine (Josie) Meier. Specifically, Rupp told Tompkins he was not a great athlete and didn't run back and forth to the Clutter house,[23] as Capote claimed. No Mennonite farmer bought Babe for $75, nor was she used as a plow horse; instead, the YMCA used her to train children to ride.[24] "Capote's version of Babe's fate was a cheap bid for pathos,"[25] argues Daniel Axelrod. The Meiers are quoted at length in chapter 65 of *In Cold Blood,* but according to them, much of what Capote describes "had not taken place";[26] furthermore, Mrs. Meier is cited in chapter 77 as saying that she heard Smith crying. She denies that this occurred.[27]

These examples, which a reader might forgive as the result of inaccurate notes, are in a list of more troubling omissions and commissions. For example, Bill Brown, former editor of the *Garden City Telegram,* heard Smith's last words before he was hanged, as did the wire-service reporters. Their reports are identical. Capote, they said, had walked away and out of earshot, so he cannot have known what Smith said before his execution. Nonetheless, Capote claims that Smith told him, "Good-bye. I love you and I always have."[28] Although Capote claims that Smith apologized for the

---

[21]Phillip K. Tompkins, "In Cold Fact," *Esquire* 65/6 (June 1966): 125.
[22]Ibid.
[23]Ibid., 125, 127.
[24]Ibid., 127.
[25]Axelrod, "In Cold Fact, In Cold Blood," 28.
[26]Tompkins, "In Cold Fact," 168.
[27]Ibid.
[28]Grobel, *Conversations,* 117.

murders, the journalists said he did not. They also suggested that Smith probably did not commit all four murders, believing that Hickock probably killed the women.[29] Brown is joined by Kansas Bureau of Investigation detective Alvin A. Dewey and County Attorney Duane West in drawing this conclusion.[30]

Two of Capote's most persuasive critics, David Hayes and Sarah Weinman, understand why Capote made certain artistic decisions with respect to In Cold Blood, but they hold him accountable nonetheless. Hayes and Weinman write in "The Worthy Elephant: On Truman Capote's In Cold Blood" that in the decades since the nonfiction novel was published, "Capote's elastic attitude toward the truth surfaced"; in addition, they say In Cold Blood "really should have carried the disclaimer 'based on a true story,'" with Weinman adding, "It seems another example of Capote's self-absorption, valuing himself above the story. But it worked." They are especially harsh with respect to the ending of In Cold Blood because "nonfiction often doesn't allow you to craft such perfectly symbolic moments."[31]

Indeed, the most egregious violation of fact is probably the final scene of In Cold Blood, where Susan Kidwell meets Dewey in a fictional universe filled with drama and narrative import. As Nick Nuttall notes, it is, in fact, "pure invention": "It clearly suits the demands of a fictional narrative, providing a sense of life carrying on, bringing us full circle, back to the place where the story began, rather than the requirements of a piece of journalism that it stick to the facts."[32] Furthermore, as masterful as the last scene is, even Capote said he "could probably have done without that last part": "I was criticized a lot for it. People thought I should have ended with the hangings, that awful last scene. But I felt I had to return to the town, to bring everything back full circle, to end with peace."[33]

Capote, on the other hand, continued to claim that his motives and the execution of his literary purposes were without reproach. He said he changed the name of the man who picked up Smith and Hickock when they were hitchhiking: "There are only three people in the book whose names I've

---

[29]Tompkins, "In Cold Fact," 168.

[30]Ibid., 170.

[31]David Hayes and Sarah Weinman, "The Worthy Elephant: On Truman Capote's In Cold Blood," Hazlitt, 27 January 2016, web (accessed 29 July 2018).

[32]Nick Nuttall, "Cold-Blooded Journalism: Truman Capote and the Nonfiction Novel," The Journalistic Imagination: Literary Journalists from Defoe to Capote and Carter, ed. Richard Keeble and Sharon Wheeler (New York: Routledge, 2007) 137.

[33]Gerald Clarke, Capote: A Biography (New York: Simon and Schuster, 1988) 359.

changed—his, the convict Perry admired so much (Willie-Jay he's called in the book), and also I changed Perry Smith's sister's name."[34] He also stands by his interview techniques:

> Twelve years ago I began to train myself, for the purpose of this sort of book, to transcribe conversation without using a tape-recorder. I did it by having a friend read passages from a book, and then later I'd write them down to see how close I could come to the original. I had a natural facility for it, but after doing these exercises for a year and a half, for a couple of hours a day, I could get within 95 per cent of absolute accuracy, which is as close as you need. I felt it was essential. Even note-taking artificializes the atmosphere of an interview, or a scene-in-progress; it interferes with the communication between author and subject—the latter is usually self-conscious, or an untrusting wariness is induced.[35]

Furthermore, Capote claims an objectivity that few if any journalists would believe possible, basing his bravado on the third-person point of view in *In Cold Blood*:

> My feeling is that for the nonfiction-novel form to be entirely successful, the author should not appear in the work. Ideally. Once the narrator does appear, he has to appear throughout, all the way down the line, and the I-I-I intrudes when it really shouldn't. I think the single most difficult thing in my book, technically, was to write it without ever appearing myself, and yet, at the same time, create total credibility.[36]

In addition to challenging Capote's interviewing techniques, Tompkins questions Capote's claims that he memorized interviews and attacks Capote for his relationship with Smith, believing that it compromised his ability to be balanced and fair. Capote told *Life* magazine that within three hours of his interviews for *In Cold Blood*, he went to the hotel to record his notes and said he "had it all in his head."[37] With respect to Smith, Tompkins accuses Capote of "transforming an unexciting confession into a theatrical cathar-

---

[34]Plimpton, "The Story," 53.
[35]Ibid., 54.
[36]Ibid., 55.
[37]Tompkins, "In Cold Fact," 170.

sis"[38] and argues that Smith was an "obscene, semiliterate and cold-blooded killer."[39] In one of his most scathing attacks, Tompkins writes, "For premeditated murder performed in cold blood, Capote substituted unpremeditated murder performed in a fit of insanity. Art triumphs over reality, fiction over nonfiction."[40] Tompkins complains that Capote creates a murderer who possesses "conscience and compassion," "inner sensitivity," and a "final posture of contrition" and who becomes Capote's "hero."[41]

It is true that Capote identified strongly with Smith and felt intense compassion for him: "I believe Perry did what he did for the reasons he himself states—that his life was a constant accumulation of disillusionments and reverses and he suddenly found himself (in the Clutter house that night) in a psychological cul-de-sac."[42] Describing the killer, Capote wrote, "His own face enthralled him. Each angle of it induced a different impression. It was a changeling's face."[43] In an interview in *Newsweek*, Capote described himself by saying, "If you looked at my face from both sides you'd see they were completely different. It's sort of a changeling face."[44] The doppelgänger—a literary explanation for the ways in which Capote and Smith identify with one another—is explored in detail in chapter four.

Whether or not Capote was in love with Perry Smith is a subject for biographers. Certainly, screenwriters involved in both *Capote* (2005) and *Infamous* (2006) suggest he was. With characteristic candor, Harper Lee offered a first-person perspective into the relationship between Truman Capote and Perry Smith: "I'm told that the idea is that Truman fell in love with Perry Smith, one of the killers, and had an affair with him. No he didn't. I was there and the film-makers weren't."[45] Just as open for debate is Smith's emotional connection to Hickock. In Thomas Fahy's reading of the nonfiction novel, "Perry's attraction to Dick's masculinity appeared to be sexually

---

[38]Ibid.

[39]Ibid., 171.

[40]Ibid.

[41]Ibid.

[42]Plimpton, "The Story," 55.

[43]Truman Capote, *In Cold Blood: A True Account of a Multiple Murder and Its Consequences* (New York: Random House, 1965) 15.

[44]Tompkins, "In Cold Fact," 171.

[45]Wayne Flynt, *Mockingbird Songs: My Friendship with Harper Lee* (New York: HarperCollins, 2017) 32.

charged."[46] As evidence, Fahy mentions Smith's scrapbook photos of weightlifters, the nude sketches of Hickock, and his considering Hickock his "most intimate companion."[47] For his part, when Hickock and Smith are getting along, Hickock calls Smith "honey," "sugar," and "baby"; when they are not on good terms, Hickock compares Smith to a wife he'd like to leave behind: "Dick was sick of him—his harmonica, his aches and ills, his superstitions, the weepy, womanly eyes, the nagging, whispering voice. Suspicious, self-righteous, spiteful, he was like a wife that must be got rid of."[48] According to Fahy, Hickock's "allusion to marriage" suggests the "extent of their closeness, while feminizing the 'nagging' Perry with 'womanly eyes' hinted at his homosexuality."[49]

Most compellingly, when Jane Howard of *Life* magazine asked Capote whether or not he liked Smith and Hickock, he responded, "That's like saying, 'Do you like yourself?'"[50] According to Tompkins, "Capote's characterization of Smith clearly tells us more about the former than the latter."[51] And, finally, Tompkins challenges Capote's contention in *The New Yorker* installments, which included the following editor's note: "All quotations in this article are taken either from official records or from conversations, transcribed verbatim, between the author and the principals."[52] Even Capote's collaborator on *In Cold Blood*, Harper Lee, told *Newsweek*, "And if it's not the way he likes it, he'll arrange it so it is."[53] It is impossible to know whether she was being humorous or judgmental when she uttered this critique.

One of the most descriptive episodes in the nonfiction novel involves a dog. Critics war over whether or not the dog existed or whether he was simply a convenient tool for Capote to employ in illustrating Hickock's utter lack of compassion and empathy. In an interview, Capote addresses the issue directly and expands his defense of his journalistic integrity by focusing on his portrayal of Nancy Clutter:

---

[46]Thomas Fahy, *Understanding Truman Capote* (Columbia: University of South Carolina Press, 2014) 142.
[47]Ibid.
[48]Capote, *In Cold Blood*, 214-15.
[49]Fahy, *Understanding*, 142.
[50]Tompkins, "In Cold Fact," 171.
[51]Ibid.
[52]Ibid., 125.
[53]Ibid., 171.

No. There was a dog, and it was precisely as described. One doesn't spend almost six years on a book, the point of which is factual accuracy, and then give way to minor distortions. People are so suspicious. They ask, "How can you reconstruct the conversation of a dead girl, Nancy Clutter, without fictionalizing?" If they read the book carefully, they can see readily enough how it's done. It's a silly question. Each time Nancy appears in the narrative, there are witnesses to what she is saying and doing—phone calls, conversations, being overheard. When she walks the horse up from the river in the twilight, the hired man is a witness and talked to her then. The last time we see her, in her bedroom, Perry and Dick themselves were the witnesses, and told me what she had said. What is reported of her, even in the narrative form, is as accurate as many hours of questioning, over and over again, can make it. All of it is reconstructed from the evidence of witnesses—which is implicit in the title of the first section of the book—"The Last to See Them Alive."[54]

Of course, nothing in Capote's lengthy explanation addresses why his descriptions of the dog and Nancy Clutter are factual when the conversation between Nancy Clutter and Alvin Dewey that concludes *In Cold Blood* is not.

Truman Capote as Author and Celebrity

In spite of the flaws that exist in *In Cold Blood*, one of the first generally acknowledged and celebrated literary journalists who penned an American classic is Truman Capote. *In Cold Blood* is rarely omitted from anyone's list of historically significant works of literary journalism, partly because Capote seemed to believe *In Cold Blood* was one of the first novels in a new genre of nonfiction and marketed it as such. Perhaps the reasons for his popular appeal are as much a result of who he was as what he produced. In an obituary published in *Newsweek* in 1984, Jack Kroll writes of Capote:

> Most people who knew his name probably thought of him as some odd little gadfly among the glitterati, flitting from party to party, from talk show to talk show, telling faintly outrageous tales in that Little Lord Fauntleroy voice and forever feuding with Norman Mailer and Gore Vidal. It's doubtful that Capote ever prayed to be thought of in that

---

[54]Plimpton, "The Story," 62-63.

way. If he prayed at all, it was certainly to be a true artist, a man who could move others with his vision of the world. And at his best that's what he was. In "Other Voices, Other Rooms," the book that made him famous at 23, in "Breakfast at Tiffany's" and in his best stories and journalism, he produced a unique verbal music, a blend of shrewdness and sentimentality that revealed human beings as hybrids both baroque and banal.[55]

James Wolcott writes similarly of the young Capote in "The Truman Show," his *Vanity Fair* article published in 1997:

Being the center of attention at least gave him a fixed position. When Capote was in the second grade, he learned that he would be leaving Alabama to live up North with his mother. "He said he wanted to throw a party so grand that everybody would remember him," Jennings Faulk Carter, a cousin, recalls. He decided to host a Halloween costume party, and created elaborate games for the other children to play. The party was nearly stampeded by a visit from the Ku Klux Klan, who had heard tell that there might be Negroes present and set upon one scared (white) boy dressed as a robot, whose cardboard legs prevented him from fleeing. After Harper Lee's father and other powerful townsfolk gave the sheeted rednecks the big stare, the Klansmen slunk off to their cars. With its giddy buildup and unexpected drama, this going-away party was the forerunner to the masked Black and White Ball Capote would host for Kay Graham [the late owner and publisher of the *Washington Post*] in 1966, a night of operatic intrigue which was the Woodstock of the tuxedo brigade.[56]

Truman Streckfus Persons was born in New Orleans on September 30, 1924, to Lillie Mae Faulk and Archulus (Arch) Persons, who divorced when he was six years old. His mother tried but was unable to get an abortion in the 1920s in the Deep South.[57] When he was a child, she sent him to Monroeville, Alabama, to live with relatives. In 1933, young Truman Persons went to New York to live with his mother and Joseph Capote, who renamed

[55]Jack Kroll, "Truman Capote: 1924–1984," *Newsweek*, 3 September 1984, 69.
[56]James Wolcott, "The Truman Show," *Vanity Fair* (December 1997): 126.
[57]Fahy, *Understanding*, 1.

him "Truman Garcia Capote." According to Fahy, Capote "was a neglected child" who "developed a profound fear of abandonment":[58]

> Not only was she in love with her husband, but she was also ashamed of and repelled by Truman's effeminacy. In fact she would terminate two pregnancies with Joe in large part because she refused to have another child like Truman. Mostly Nina feared that her son was becoming a homosexual, and she tried desperately to prevent this. She took him to numerous psychiatrists and then sent him to a military academy in the fall of 1936 (just before his twelfth birthday)...She ridiculed him publically and privately, calling him a "fairy," a "pansy," and a "monster"...It is no wonder that Capote later described her as "the single worst person in my life."[59]

However, Capote was tougher than his small frame suggested. He left school at seventeen and worked as a copyboy for *The New Yorker*. In 1942, he published "Miriam" in *Mademoiselle* and won an "O'Henry Award" for "Best First-Published Story." In 1948, Capote published *Other Voices, Other Rooms*, followed by *The Grass Harp* (1951) and *Breakfast at Tiffany's* (1958).

Capote himself knew that as an adult he sought the attention that had been denied to him when he was a child. In "Literature's Lost Boy," David Gates cites Capote, who said of himself, "It's as if two different people were inside of me. One is highly intelligent, imaginative and mature, and the other is a fourteen-year-old."[60] Nothing in Capote's life better illustrated how different he was from others than his time in the Midwest. When Capote traveled to Holcomb to conduct interviews for *In Cold Blood*, residents were taken aback by his demeanor and his accent: "If Kansas was strange to Capote," writes Kenneth T. Reed, "Capote was just as strange to Kansas...A Holcomb resident's recollection is typical: 'We did feel pretty put off by Truman at first, with that funny little voice of his and the way he dressed and all, but after we'd talked to him only for an hour, we just got so we thoroughly enjoyed him.'"[61]

Because of his extravagant nature, his genuine affection for others, his need for attention, and his talent, what has become increasingly apparent is

---

[58]Ibid., 2.

[59]Ibid., 3.

[60]David Gates, "Literature's Lost Boy: The Self-Destruction of an American Writer," *Newsweek*, 30 May 1988, 62.

[61]Kenneth T. Reed, *Truman Capote* (Boston: Twayne, 1981) 164.

that Capote has never lost his appeal. Accolades were heaped upon the head of the late actor Philip Seymour Hoffman, who played the author in *Capote*, a film based on Gerald Clarke's *Truman Capote: A Biography*. In a film review titled "Hoffman Gives Soul to the Role of Capote," John DeFore of the *Austin American–Statesman* writes:

> In an early scene in small-town Kansas, we see the friction between the man and his image. Interviewing a friend of one of the murder victims who is reluctant to confide in this strange creature from New York, Capote unexpectedly makes what feels like a confession, indirectly giving the girl permission to find him odd while offering her something to identify with. Within moments, the interviewee has decided to share a piece of evidence she has previously kept hidden.
>
> Is this interview a rare miracle of empathy, or an example of a journalist's genius for working his subject? That issue is the heart of the movie, as Capote meets and conducts marathon interviews with the killers, particularly the strangely magnetic Perry Smith.[62]

In the film, Capote's relationship with Harper Lee, played by Catherine Keener, disintegrates as her book *To Kill a Mockingbird* becomes popular. Capote grows increasingly jealous of her success and wants his book to be published in order to gain the recognition he craves. According to DeFore, Capote is a "mess by the picture's end, praying for the killers' execution while pretending to be on their side." DeFore also notes, "[Director Bennett] Miller and screenwriter Dan Futterman, though, refuse to condemn the author, preferring to dig as deep as they can into the contradictory justifications for what he did and to portray him as a tragic figure whose masterpiece, *In Cold Blood*, came at the price of his soul."[63]

As chapter seven discusses in depth, *Capote* and *Infamous*, another film about Capote's life, were in production simultaneously. The latter film stars Sandra Bullock, Gwyneth Paltrow, Sigourney Weaver, Jeff Daniels, Isabella Rossellini, Hope Davis, and Peter Bogdanovich. Toby Jones plays Capote. This film is based on George Plimpton's *Truman Capote: In Which Various Friends, Enemies, Acquaintances and Detractors Recall His Turbulent Career*. In "Capote's Long Ride," an essay published in 1997 in *The New Yorker*, Plimp-

---

[62]John DeFore, "Hoffman Gives Soul to the Role of Capote," *Austin American-Statesman*, 28 October 2005, 1E/10E.

[63]Ibid., 10E.

ton refers to the literary form Capote introduced as "oral narrative" or "oral biography,"[64] which, in addition to Capote's use of description and dialogue, makes the nonfiction novel especially appropriate for adaptation into film.

Capote excelled not only because he wrote a bestselling nonfiction novel but also because of his admiration for journalists. He called journalism the "last great unexplored literary frontier"[65] and "the most underestimated, the least explored of literary mediums."[66] In fact, Reed writes in his biography *Truman Capote* that the author of *In Cold Blood* was an "inveterate devourer of newspapers."[67] Certainly, the newspaper story that inspired his greatest work suggests the power that real life held over Capote. Of the day in 1959 when he read *The New York Times* story, Capote writes:

> I found this very small headline that read "Eisenhower Appointee Murdered." The victim was a rancher in western Kansas, a wheat grower who had been an Eisenhower appointee to the Farm Credit Bureau. He, his wife, and two of their children had been murdered, and it was a complete mystery. They had no idea of who had done it or why, but the story struck me with tremendous force. I suddenly realized that perhaps a crime, after all, would be the ideal subject matter for the massive job of reportage I wanted to do. I would have a wide range of characters, and, most importantly, it would be timeless. I knew it would take me five years, perhaps eight or ten years, to do this, and I couldn't work on some ephemeral, momentary thing. It had to be an event related to permanent emotions in people.[68]

Criticism of *In Cold Blood* continues, partly because of techniques Capote employed, such as stream of consciousness, and partly because of Capote's questionable reportorial strategies. John Hellman believes that, like conventional journalism, *In Cold Blood* employed the "illusion of objectivity."[69] For example, the reader is privy to the thoughts of the characters but is not told how the reporter knows these thoughts. For a journalist, however,

---

[64]Plimpton, "Capote's Long Ride," 62.

[65]Eric Norden, "*Playboy* Interview: Truman Capote," in *Truman Capote: Conversations*, ed. M. Thomas Inge (Jackson: University Press of Mississippi, 1987) 122.

[66]Plimpton, "The Story," 47.

[67]Reed, *Truman Capote*, 102.

[68]Ibid.

[69]John Hellman, *Fables of Fact: The New Journalism as New Fiction* (Champaign: Illinois University Press, 1981) 20.

this fact is more than troublesome. As we have seen, Capote's interview techniques—treated with suspicion by both journalists and literary scholars—are often attacked. Reed, one of Capote's defenders, writes:

> In earlier years, Capote had trained himself not to write or use a tape recorder during interviews, but instead to make notes from memory afterwards, a technique that provoked criticism from various reviewers when *In Cold Blood* was published. Some were never satisfied about the authenticity of the information and took the time to retrace all of Capote's steps to check the facts. There were, however, many more defenders than detractors, and the subject provided a long and lively debate amongst the critics.[70]

Capote would win praise for other works—especially *Other Voices, Other Rooms*; *Tree of Night*; *The Grass Harp*; *Breakfast at Tiffany's*; and *Music for Chameleons*—but it would be *In Cold Blood* that would guarantee him a place in American literary history. Much has been made of Capote's inability to produce more writing after *In Cold Blood*, but in all he wrote a memoir, novellas, novels, personal sketches, plays, poetry, screenplays, short stories, and travel articles. Surely his literary legacy speaks for itself.

In Cold Blood *as Allegory, Literary Journalism, and Naturalism*

In Cold Blood was serialized in four installments in *The New Yorker* before its publication. The allegorical nature of the novel was central to its popularity. In "The Truman Show," Wolcott writes, "The Clutters—mom, pop, son, daughter—are ready-made symbols: the model American family, America in microcosm, their murders a blow to the heartland and a desecration of the American dream."[71] What also interested readers were the parallel narratives that allowed them to immerse themselves in the lives of the Clutters, the police and other investigators pursuing the fugitives, and the murderers themselves. What interested literary scholars was Capote's use of stream of consciousness and other techniques and the book's place in the canon of naturalism. For example, Capote treats Smith as a victim, somehow destined to kill because of the trauma he endured. Capote also refers to the "annihilating sky,"[72] suggesting that—in addition to Smith's being fated to

---

[70]Reed, *Truman Capote*, 142.
[71]Wolcott, "The Truman Show," 130.
[72]Capote, *In Cold Blood*, 95.

pursue crime—the natural world itself is not a hospitable place. Studies about criminal behavior were especially compelling during the 1960s, when many previously entrenched attitudes and values were in flux. When Capote's project became less about the feelings, interactions, and thoughts of Kansas residents and more of a polemic on the death penalty, it sparked even greater interest.

Southern author Flannery O'Connor is well known for her creation of allegorical figures that are larger than life. Asked why she created such unusual characters, she explained that readers have become so desensitized to evil and to their inhumanity toward one another that she had to draw "large and startling figures"[73] in order to remind them that what is familiar might not be normal and might not deserve to be tolerated. Certainly, Perry Smith, a large and startling figure, dominates Capote's nonfiction novel. *In Cold Blood* captivated America because of Smith, but it also became a bestseller for at least three other reasons: First, on one level the nonfiction novel is dreadfully realistic, but on another level it is an allegory, a tale of lost innocence for residents of rural Holcomb, for readers of the nonfiction novel, and for Capote himself. Second, *In Cold Blood* is an example of phenomenology—or the science of knowledge and making meaning—as Capote tries to make sense of four senseless murders. Finally, it is an example of naturalism—the concept that human events are random and that decisions such as those made by the tortured Perry Smith often seem inevitable.

Like Robert Frost's poem "Design"—in which Frost speculates about the cruelty that seems to "govern" even small events among insects—*In Cold Blood* raises questions about coincidence; about the actuality and motivation for evil unleashed in the world; about the existence of a benevolent, omniscient God; about goodness as accidental; and about the rationality of natural processes. The nonfiction novel raises important questions about the effects of seemingly random events such as car accidents, the genetics involved in mental illness, and the violent home lives into which some people are born. Frost's darkly beautiful and disturbing poem reads as follows:

> I found a dimpled spider, fat and white,
> On a white heal-all, holding up a moth
> Like a white piece of rigid satin cloth—
> Assorted characters of death and blight

---

[73]Flannery O'Connor, "The Fiction Writer and His Country," *Mystery and Manners* (New York: Farrar, 1969) 34.

Mixed ready to begin the morning right,
Like the ingredients of a witches' broth—
A snow-drop spider, a flower like a froth,
And dead wings carried like a paper kite.

What had that flower to do with being white,
The wayside blue and innocent heal-all?
What brought the kindred spider to that height,
Then steered the white moth thither in the night?
What but design of darkness to appall?—
If design govern in a thing so small.[74]

Capote ties the concepts of fate and chance to another aspect of *In Cold Blood*—its tribute to bravery in the face of catastrophe—and links it to his compassion for Smith. He also alludes to the powerful sway of a narrative set in the bucolic heartland, writing about the "collision between the desperate, ruthless, wandering, savage part of American life, and the other, which is insular and safe, more or less."[75] Of readers of *In Cold Blood,* Capote said:

It has struck them because there is something so awfully inevitable about what is going to happen: the people in the book are completely beyond their own control. For example, Perry wasn't an evil person. If he'd had any chance in life, things would have been different. But every illusion he'd ever had, well, they all evaporated, so that on that night he was so full of self-hatred and self-pity that I think he would have killed somebody—perhaps not that night, or the next, or the next. You can't go through life without ever getting anything you want, ever.[76]

Human beings need explanations for daily events, reasons for another's behavior, clear causes and effects, and the opportunity to pursue "the blessed rage for order"[77] suggested in Wallace Stevens's poem "The Idea of Order at Key West." As Wes Chapman writes in "Human and Divine Design,"

---

[74]Robert Frost, "Design," in *The Poetry of Robert Frost: The Collected Poems*, ed. Edward Connery Lathem (New York: Henry Holt, 1969) 302.

[75]Plimpton, "The Story," 67.

[76]Ibid.

[77]Wallace Stevens, "The Idea of Order at Key West," in *The Norton Anthology of Modern Poetry,* ed. Richard Ellmann and Robert O'Clair, 2nd ed. (New York: W.W. Norton, 1988) 292.

Frost's poem is "a meditation on human attempts to see order in the universe—and human failures at perceiving the order that is actually present in nature."[78] *In Cold Blood* is Capote's rationale—an inevitable ordering system—as he seeks answers to why he was obsessed by *The New York Times* story about the Clutter murders. It's as if Capote set out to complete himself by immersing himself in the lives of two killers, and he certainly learned more about his interests, his compassion, his philosophy about evil, and his role as interviewer.

One of the perils of literature is an author's desire to create an invincible, unassailable conclusion, to have narrative threads come together and affirm a reader's sense of order. *In Cold Blood* suffers from this tendency—in part because Capote pursued stylistic and thematic perfection when he wrote the nonfiction novel and because readers who survived a tale of betrayal and murder longed for resolution. *In Cold Blood* contains rising action, a climax, a denouement, and a near-perfect conclusion. Did Capote ask the questions he asked in order to draw the conclusion he wanted to draw? Perhaps. As he constructed the conclusion, did Capote want to remain true to facts and verifiable information? If not, why not? Operating with a certain false authority, Capote invents the conclusion and offers us a questionable—albeit affirming and optimistic—ending. Not a journalist, Capote allowed his expertise as a writer of fiction to overtake his limited understanding of the role of journalism and its higher purposes in a civilized society.

What is most important, though, is to remember that Capote's phenomenological quest leads to more than an explanation of how people who have bad childhoods can hurt Christian, law-abiding families who live in idyllic communities. If that were all *In Cold Blood* were, readers would simply ask, "So what?" The nonfiction novel gained the readership and accolades it received because—like stories about the murder of JonBenet Ramsey in Boulder, Colorado, and Matthew Shepard in Laramie, Wyoming—it captured the human imagination and suggested larger themes and larger questions.

Even the setting is significant to Capote's construction of allegory and naturalism: "Mr. Clutter seldom encountered trespassers on his property; a mile and a half from the highway, and arrived at by obscure roads, it was not a place that strangers came upon by chance."[79] The innocent, quiet, safe life

---

[78]Wes Chapman, "Human and Divine Design: An Annotation of Robert Frost's 'Design,'" *American Poetry*, 8 March 2006, web (accessed 1 August 2018).

[79]Capote, *In Cold Blood*, 23.

possible for residents of Holcomb was part of the American consciousness, extending even to popular culture where television ruralcoms such as *The Andy Griffith Show* (1960–1968), *The Beverly Hillbillies* (1962–1971), *Green Acres* (1965–1971), and *Petticoat Junction* (1963–1970) would thrive. *In Cold Blood* reminded mainstream, white America that unknown dangers lurked both at home and abroad. In fact, in "American Gothic: What Rushes into the Newsless Void?" Jeffrey Toobin writes, "This kind of dialectic—the worthy clashing with the sinful, high-minded with the debased—is a classic part of the Gothic tradition. We identify with its pulls and pushes because, of course, they're going on inside us all the time."[80]

The naturalism that pervades *In Cold Blood* links the novel to *An American Tragedy* and *Sister Carrie* (Theodore Dreiser), *Maggie: A Girl of the Streets* (Stephen Crane), and other nineteenth- and twentieth-century novels based on news events of the day. As noted throughout this study, the existence of fate is reflected in Capote's perspective on everything from landscape to human development. "How was it possible that such effort, such plain virtue, could overnight be reduced to this—smoke, thinning as it rose and was received by the big, annihilating sky?"[81] he asks. The sky is not, of course, "annihilating," but such a personification suggests there is no escape from the possibility of malevolence. Later in the nonfiction novel, Capote quotes a local teacher who tells him:

> Feeling wouldn't run half so high if this had happened to anyone *except* the Clutters. Anyone *less* admired. Prosperous. Secure. But that family represented everything people hereabouts really value and respect, and that such a thing could happen to them—well, it's like being told there is no God. It makes life seem pointless. I don't think people are so much frightened as they are deeply depressed.[82]

Another startling example of naturalism occurs after the investigators interview one of Smith's siblings. In an example of stream of consciousness, perhaps drawn from notes Harold R. Nye or one of his colleagues took, Capote writes about Perry Smith's sister Barbara Johnson and the sadness that settles over her after the detectives leave. Waiting until the house is quiet

---

[80]Jeffrey Toobin, "American Gothic: What Rushes into the Newsless Void?" *The New Yorker* 73/21 (28 July 1997): 5.

[81]Capote, *In Cold Blood*, 79.

[82]Ibid., 88.

and the children are fed and ready for bed, she thinks about whether she is afraid of her brother Perry or simply everything he represents, including her mother Florence Buckskin and father Tex John Smith. One brother had shot himself; another sibling died after falling out of a window, accidentally or intentionally; and Perry Smith would end his life on Death Row. In Capote's appropriation of her thoughts, which may or may not be accurate, she fears that she might face a terrible fate—insanity, a natural disaster, or a terminal illness. Capote describes not only the reality he experiences when he is with Perry Smith's sister but also the fears that lurk in his own subconscious. Some people escape their fates; some meet a desperate end. Understanding that part of him feels as though he is "standing in a darkened hallway," Capote compensates—as he says—by loving champagne and staying at the Ritz.[83]

Alvin A. Dewey also focuses on the illogical series of events that contributes to the sense of dread in *In Cold Blood*. Capote writes of Dewey, "For it appeared to him 'ludicrously inconsistent' with the magnitude of the crime and the manifest cunning of the criminals, and 'inconceivable' that these men had entered a house expecting to find a money-filled safe, and then, not finding it, had thought it expedient to slaughter the family for perhaps a few dollars and a small portable radio."[84] Later in the novel, Dewey observes that the murders were so odd as to appear almost accidental. Like Capote, he considers how Smith became who he is:

> The crime was a psychological accident, virtually an impersonal act; the victims might as well have been killed by lightning. Except for one thing: they had experienced prolonged terror, they had suffered. And Dewey could not forget their sufferings. Nonetheless, he found it possible to look at the man beside him without much anger—with, rather, a measure of sympathy—for Perry Smith's life had been no bed of roses but pitiful, an ugly and lonely progress toward one mirage and then another.[85]

Certainly, Capote's portrayal of Smith suggests that he believed his anti-hero was almost preordained to commit crimes. At one point, Smith says he sees himself and Hickock as "'running a race without a finish line'—that

---

[83]Grobel, *Conversations*, 110.
[84]Capote, *In Cold Blood*, 190.
[85]Ibid., 245-46.

was how it struck him."[86] Smith later tells Capote that during the murders he wasn't aware of hatred, rage, or other motivations for killing the family. His description of killing Herbert Clutter is the most startling: "I didn't want to harm the man. I thought he was a very nice gentleman. Soft-spoken. I thought so right up to the moment I cut his throat."[87] Capote also quotes Smith as saying, "They [the Clutters] never hurt me. Like other people. Like people have all my life. Maybe it's just that the Clutters were the ones who had to pay for it."[88] Smith's capacity for random violence seems to surprise even himself.

Throughout the nonfiction novel, Hickock appears far more diabolical than Smith, and although he may not be the one who killed the family, Capote's personal perception of the killers dominates the narrative. Hickock's paralyzing cruelty is best illustrated not by the murder of the Clutter family but by the dogs he slaughters when he drives. In one incident, Hickock's cruelty is horrifically documented:

> A hundred feet ahead, a dog trotted along the side of the road. Dick swerved toward it. It was an old half-dead mongrel, brittle-boned and mangy, and the impact, as it met the car, was little more than what a bird might make. But Dick was satisfied. "Boy!" he said—and it was what he always said after running down a dog, which is something he did whenever the opportunity arose. "Boy! We sure splattered him!"[89]

In spite of the description of Hickock's premeditated cruelty and the delight he experiences when animals and people suffer, Capote is unfaltering in his belief that criminals such as Hickock and Smith are the result of a lifetime of neglect and brutality and that society itself must accept some responsibility. The heart of *In Cold Blood* is a compressed allegory similar to Joseph K's visit to the cathedral in Franz Kafka's *The Trial*. In each literary classic, a symbolic interlude represents the full plot. The pages that describe the crowd watching Smith and Hickock arrive at the courthouse are laden with symbolism, as Capote associates the killers with two starving stray cats. It is perhaps the most significant allegorical moment in Capote's canon. He writes, "Among Garden City's animals are two gray tomcats who are always

---

[86]Ibid., 202.
[87]Ibid., 244.
[88]Ibid., 290.
[89]Ibid., 112-13.

together—thin, dirty strays with strange and clever habits."[90] What follows is a compassionate and intricate description of the starving cats that stay alive by eating the remains of birds in the grills of automobiles parked near the Windsor and Warren hotels and at the Courthouse Square. At the end of the scene—whether it is real or imagined—the first snow of the season begins to fall.

Although Capote may believe that Smith might have been redeemed had he been born into a loving family and extended community, Capote's ability to understand the harrowing murder story is disturbingly limited. It lies with Dewey to represent the contributions and promise of the four members of the Clutter family who lost their lives for no particular reason. It is his grief—not Capote's—that reminds readers of the horror of the murder scene. *In Cold Blood* would no doubt be a less effective psychological analysis of the criminal mind if it contained crime photos from the basement and the bedrooms of River Valley Farm. "But even if I hadn't known the family, and liked them so well, I wouldn't feel any different," Dewey says. "Because I've seen some bad things, I sure as hell have. But nothing so vicious as this. However long it takes, it may be the rest of my life, I'm going to know what happened in that house: the why and the who."[91] Of course, neither Capote nor Dewey nor the reader will ever know entirely "the why and the who."

A Legacy of Masterful Storytelling

At the time *In Cold Blood* appeared, Truman Capote already had secured his place in literary history. The nonfiction novel was the exclamation point. Capote (and those who compiled and edited his work after his death) published *Other Voices, Other Rooms* (1948); *A Tree of Night and Other Stories* (1949); *Local Color* (1950); *The Grass Harp* (1951); *The Muses Are Heard* (1956); *Breakfast at Tiffany's* (1958); *Selected Writings* (1963); *In Cold Blood* (1965); *A Christmas Memory* (1966); *The Dogs Bark: Public People and Private Places* (1973); *Music for Chameleons* (1980); *One Christmas* (1983); *Three by Truman Capote* (1985); *Answered Prayers: The Unfinished Novel* (1986); and *Truman Capote: A Capote Reader* (1987).

Capote was driven to tell stories—at parties, in his living room, and on paper. Writers, psychologists, sociologists, and others argue that storytelling, like breathing, is not a choice and occurs in multiple forms—oral expression,

---

[90]Ibid., 246.
[91]Ibid., 80.

poetry, prose. In *Waterland,* Graham Swift argues that human beings inevitably tell stories:

> But man—let me offer you a definition—is the story-telling animal. Wherever he goes he wants to leave behind not a chaotic wake, not an empty space, but the comforting marker-buoys and trail-signs of stories. He has to go on telling stories, he has to keep on making them up. As long as there's a story, it's all right. Even in his last moments, it's said, in the split second of a fatal fall—or when he's about to drown—he sees, passing rapidly before him, the story of his whole life.[92]

Roger Rosenblatt, too, argues in "Once Upon a Time" that we tell stories "because it is in us to do so—like a biological fact—because story-telling is what the human being does, to progress, to learn to live with one another."[93] In "Dreaming the News: Stories Are the Way We Tell Ourselves to Ourselves," Rosenblatt provides context for a perspective that grounds his work:

> Yet the effect of fiction preceding fact was just that: I began to dream my way into the news. Ordinarily, I would skitter over the papers quickly, the way an animal might take note of possible dangerous places on a journey; it is the stuff I need to know. But now I bored into language; I invented; I expected revelation. What was real became surreal, or perhaps it was that already. I read the news not as the first draft of history but as the first draft of a work of art.
>
> Writers like Truman Capote and Norman Mailer discovered this opportunity a long time ago. But they were approaching the matter from the creative end: How do I dream my way into the wanton murder of a Kansas family, or into Gary Gilmore's frightened, deadly little mind?...
>
> So much of living is made up of storytelling that one might conclude that it is what we were meant to do—to tell one another stories, fact or fiction, as a way of keeping afloat. Job's messenger, Coleridge's mariner, the reporter in California all grab us by the lapels to tell us their tale. We do the same; we cannot help ourselves. We have the story of others to tell, or of ourselves, or of the species—some monumentally elusive tale we are always trying to get right. Sometimes it seems

---

[92]Graham Swift, *Waterland* (New York: Vintage, 1983) 62-63.

[93]Roger Rosenblatt, "Once Upon a Time," *Online NewsHour with Jim Lehrer,* 24 December 1999, web (accessed 1 August 2018).

that we are telling one another parts of the same immense story. Fiction and the news are joined in an endless chain. Everything is news, everything imagined.[94]

Rosenblatt, who has told many stories during his rich career, published "Dreaming the News" in 1977, and the central theme of that essay remains at the heart of his work—and at the heart of much of this study about Capote and *In Cold Blood*. In "Once Upon a Time," Rosenblatt describes the diary entries, poems, letters, and news stories that Jews wrote in the final days of the Warsaw ghetto, even when they knew they would soon die:

> Why did they do it? Why bother to tell a story that no one would hear? And why make the telling of that story their last act on earth? Because it is in us to do so, like a biological fact—because story-telling is what the human animal does, to progress, to live with one another.
>
> Horses run, beavers build dams; people tell stories. Chaucer's pilgrims go back and forth from Canterbury and feel compelled to pass the time by telling tales. The Ancient Mariner, crazy as a loon, grabs the wedding guest and forces him to listen to an incredible yarn.[95]

Literary journalists, like other tellers of stories, have devoted themselves to a craft that alienates some readers and scholars because it relies upon personal point of view and because it employs techniques that many of them consider to be the particular province of literature. However, their belief in the higher truths of nonfiction—and in the power of reality when it is conveyed with description, dialogue, and stream of consciousness—has gained a growing number of adherents. The importance of allegory and phenomenology in the best works of literary journalism is undeniable, and whether the "lessons" are stated directly or subtly, human beings will continue to hunger for the stories told to children before bedtime, for the local news, for the commentary that follows national and international disasters, for gossip—for all the once-upon-a-times of our lives.

Although Capote was not a journalist, he was a storyteller with an interest in creative nonfiction and a burgeoning curiosity about social issues. When Plimpton interviewed Capote January 16, 1966, Capote said he want-

---

[94]Roger Rosenblatt, "Dreaming the News," *Time*, 14 April 1997, 102.
[95]Roger Rosenblatt, "Once Upon a Time."

ed to study "homicidal mentality" and chose to write a "true account of an actual murder case":[96]

> It seemed to me that journalism, reportage, could be forced to yield a serious new art form: the "nonfiction novel," as I thought of it. Several admirable reporters—Rebecca West for one, and Joseph Mitchell and Lillian Ross—have shown the possibilities of narrative reportage; and Miss Ross, in her brilliant *Picture*, achieved at least a nonfiction novella. Still, on the whole, journalism is the most underestimated, the least explored of literary mediums.[97]

During the interview, Capote argued that the more truthful the critique, the more the people who are profiled will retaliate—"the more accurate the strokes, the greater the resentment."[98] However, this was not the only negative Capote anticipated with the publication of *In Cold Blood*:

> When I first formed my theories concerning the nonfiction novel, many people with whom I discussed the matter were unsympathetic. They felt that what I proposed, a narrative form that employed all the techniques of fictional art but was nevertheless immaculately factual, was little more than a literary solution for fatigued novelists suffering from "failure of imagination." Personally, I felt that this attitude represented a "failure of the imagination" on their part.[99]

Significantly, Capote commits himself to interviews with real people engaged in real time and addresses the shelf life of traditional journalism: "But, above all, the reporter must be able to empathize with personalities outside his usual imaginative range, mentalities unlike his own, kinds of people he would never have written about had he not been forced to by encountering them inside the journalistic situation. This last is what first attracted me to the notion of narrative reportage."[100] Capote makes it clear that he selected his topic because the murder of a Kansas family and its aftermath would remain important to American readers, although he acknowledged that murders are common: "There was nothing really excep-

---

[96]Plimpton, "The Story," 47.
[97]Ibid.
[98]Ibid., 48.
[99]Ibid.
[100]Ibid.

tional about it; one reads items concerning multiple murders many times in the course of a year."[101] In the same interview, Capote appears to contradict himself, suggesting that with "the human heart being what it is, murder was a theme not likely to darken and yellow with time"[102] and stating, "If you intend to spend three or four years with a book, as I planned to do, then you want to be reasonably certain that the material will not soon 'date.'" He adds, "The content of much journalism so swiftly does, which is another of the medium's deterrents."[103] Capote seems to suggest that although murder is itself common, particular murders—when heightened with allegory and phenomenology—have the potential to become art.

Chapter two, "*In Cold Blood* and American Literary Journalism," addresses journalism practices and principles and places *In Cold Blood* into the literary journalism genre. In *The Journalistic Imagination: Literary Journalists from Defoe to Capote and Carter*, co-editor Richard Keeble states in his introduction ("On Journalism, Creativity, and the Imagination") that he joins journalists in helping to "identify some of the elements that make up the journalistic imagination and explore the reasons why it has so long been devalued and misunderstood."[104] Keeble writes:

> Journalism and literature are too often seen as two separate spheres (one "low," the other "high")…Journalistic genres constantly avoid neat categorizations and theorizing, thriving on their dynamism, contradictions, paradoxes and complexities. And journalism's functions are diverse and ambiguous—being variously associated with democratic debate, education and entertainment as well as myth, fabrication, disinformation, polemic and propaganda.[105]

In a section of the introduction about journalism's "low status," Keeble tips his hat to the history of journalism, stating that "complex factors (historical, cultural, ideological, political) lie behind journalism's low literary and academic status—and the marginalization of the journalistic imagination. Since their emergence in the early seventeenth century in Europe's cities,

---

[101]Ibid., 51.

[102]Ibid.

[103]Ibid., 50.

[104]Richard Keeble, "Introduction: On Journalism, Creativity, and the Imagination," *The Journalistic Imagination: Literary Journalists from Defoe to Capote and Carter*, ed. Richard Keeble and Sharon Wheeler (New York: Routledge, 2007) 2.

[105]Ibid.

particularly London, the 'news media'…have been associated with scandal, gossip, and 'low' culture."[106] In a section that examines journalism and the literary marketplace, Keeble writes:

> On a basic level, journalism has provided writers with an income. Yet this very fact has reinforced journalism's position as a sub-literary genre. For while literature is often seen as the fruit of "scholarship"—hence pure and disinterested and above market considerations, including those of being readable and accessible—journalistic writing is viewed as distorted by the constraints of the market, tight deadlines or word limits. Moreover, journalism tends to be identified in Anglo-American mainstream debates with a mass audience (uncultivated) as opposed to an elite (cultivated). Accordingly, mass audiences are characterized as being easy to manipulate, emotional and irrational.[107]

Although chapter two explores these issues in more depth, this chapter summarizes the popularity and controversy associated with *In Cold Blood*. Although far more harsh in his assessment than is reflected in this book, Daniel Axelrod is correct when he argues that Capote's own words have come back to haunt him: "When it comes to judging the work, Capote himself set the terms," Axelrod writes. "He deemed it a historical narrative, written like a novel, commensurate with great literature—and forged with a journalist's devotion to accuracy, independence and objective methods for gathering and interpreting evidence."[108] The latter claim, Axelrod argues, is entirely untrue. Capote writes, "All art is composed of selected detail, either imaginary or, as in *In Cold Blood*, a distillation of reality."[109] Is "distillation of reality" a not-so-elaborate dodge, or does it suggest what Capote understood the nonfiction novel to be? In other words, does the word "novel" in the phrase suggest something to Capote that it does not suggest to Joan Didion, Jon Krakauer, and other practitioners of extended nonfiction? We shall see.

---

[106]Ibid., 3.

[107]Ibid., 5.

[108]Axelrod, "In Cold Fact, In Cold Blood," 19.

[109]Truman Capote, "Ghosts in Sunlight: The Filming of *In Cold Blood*," in *Truman Capote: A Capote Reader* (New York: Penguin, 2002) 623.

Chapter 2

In Cold Blood and American Literary Journalism

In Cold Blood does not stand alone, although critics often are inclined to see it as a singular achievement. Understanding allegory, crime stories, film, literary journalism, naturalism, sensationalism, and various historical and literary images, movements, and themes enhances the nonfiction novel, giving it texture and elevating it beyond cliché. It is not—no matter what Capote actually believed, claimed publically, or stated when talking with editors and friends—a masterpiece unto itself, nor is it entirely a study of the criminal mind, the death penalty, forensics, or a glimpse into what motivated Truman Capote. One of the intellectual spaces in which to locate *In Cold Blood* is literary journalism, itself a controversial, engaging, and multifaceted field of inquiry.

Chapter one, "The Enduring Popularity of *In Cold Blood*," introduces allegory, fate, naturalism, sensationalism, and the place of the nonfiction novel among post-1970 texts in American literary journalism. This chapter defines literary journalism and how it informs *In Cold Blood* and other nonfiction essays and novels. Chapter three, closely connected to chapter two and the history and impact of literary journalism, is titled *"In Cold Blood, Handcarved Coffins*, and 'Then It All Came Down,'" three examples of Capote's focus on crime and its aftermath. Chapter four (*"In Cold Blood*, the Doppelgänger, and Murder") links previous chapters with a study of the films *The Talented Mr. Ripley* (1999), *Shutter Island* (2003), *Secret Window* (2004), *Mr. Brooks* (2007), *The Two Faces of January* (2014), and *True Story* (2015). The chapter addresses the doppelgänger, the gothic, murder, mystery, and the symbols that enrich *In Cold Blood*. Other films—*In Cold Blood* (1967), *Capote* (2005), and *Infamous* (2006), which are based on Capote's novel—are excluded from this particular study of film but are dealt with in detail in chapter seven (*"In Cold Blood* in Documentary and Film").

Capote was both a writer and a critic, carefully considering the place of creative nonfiction in the continuum of American life and letters. In "Preface to *The Dogs Bark*," Capote writes, "Everything herein is factual, which doesn't mean that it is the truth, but it is as nearly so as I can make it. Journalism, however, can never be altogether pure—nor can the camera, for after all, art is not distilled water: personal perceptions, prejudices, one's sense of selectivity pollute the purity of germless truth."[1] Capote is adamant in expressing his admiration for and commitment to literary nonfiction: "It was my contention that reportage could be as groomed and elevated an art form as any other prose form—the essay, short story, novel."[2]

In art, even the techniques of literary journalism—description, dialogue, first-person point of view, immersion, narration, universal themes, etc.—should not be intrusive or call attention to themselves. Capote went so far as to say that taking notes in an interview "creates artifice and distorts or even destroys any naturalness that might exist between the observer and the observed."[3] Although most journalists would argue that this is not an accurate description of the interviewing and note-taking process, it makes clear Capote's desire to challenge journalistic practice. Capote writes:

> For several years I had been increasingly drawn toward journalism as an art form in itself. I had two reasons. First, it didn't seem to me that anything truly innovative had occurred in prose writing, or in writing generally, since the 1920s; second, journalism as art was almost virgin terrain, for the simple reason that very few literary artists ever wrote narrative journalism, and when they did, it took the form of travel essays or autobiography...I wanted to produce a journalistic novel, something on a large scale that would have the credibility of fact, the immediacy of film, the depth and freedom of prose, and the precision of poetry.[4]

In this quotation, Capote is alluding, of course, to *In Cold Blood*, and after its publication he doubled down on the accuracy of the text: "Many people thought I was crazy to spend six years wandering around the plains of Kansas; others rejected my whole concept of the 'nonfiction novel' and pronounced it unworthy of a 'serious' writer; Norman Mailer described it as a 'failure of imagination'—meaning, I assume, that a novelist should be writing about something imaginary rather than about something real."[5] Of

---

[1]Truman Capote, "Preface to *The Dogs Bark*," in *Truman Capote: A Capote Reader* (New York: Penguin, 2002) 643.

[2]Ibid.

[3]Ibid., 644.

[4]Truman Capote, "Preface to *Music for Chameleons*," in *Truman Capote: A Capote Reader* (New York Penguin, 2002) 719.

[5]Ibid., 719-20.

course, Mailer wrote *The Armies of the Night*, *Of a Fire on the Moon*, and *The Executioner's Song*, suggesting that he, too, understood the significance of biography, history, and other nonfiction texts.

This chapter addresses at some length first-person point of view and immersion—arguing that readers are more likely to trust writers who acknowledge their personal biases and predilections. Because Capote was not trained as a journalist and did not see himself in the company of Joan Didion, Norman Mailer, and Tom Wolfe, he anguished over the author's vantage point in his nonfiction novel:

> From a technical point, the greatest difficulty I'd had in writing *In Cold Blood* was leaving myself completely out of it. Ordinarily the reporter has to use himself as a character, an eyewitness observer, in order to retain credibility. But I felt that it was essential to the seemingly detached tone of that book that the author should be absent. Actually, in all my reportage, I had tried to keep myself as invisible as possible.[6]

In "The Story Behind a Nonfiction Novel," George Plimpton sweepingly claims that *In Cold Blood* is "remarkable for its objectivity—nowhere, despite his involvement, does the author intrude."[7] Capote often underscores Plimpton's opinion, nowhere more strikingly than when he tells Lawrence Grobel that the "great accomplishment" of *In Cold Blood* is that he "never" appears: "There's never an *I* in it at all,"[8] he says. Although there is no reason to doubt Capote's intention, his fingerprints appear throughout *In Cold Blood*; in other words, avoiding first-person point of view does not muzzle a writer. It, too, is an artifice. In short, an autobiographical story may appear to represent multiple voices and reveal universal themes, while a more objective essay might be deeply self-revelatory. Capote's impressions of Garden City, Holcomb, the murderers, and the townspeople are obvious and are quintessentially his. Nothing about *In Cold Blood* is coy or detached or dispassionate. From the description of the village on page one to the fictional conversation in the cemetery on the final page, Capote transforms both characters and

---

[6]Ibid., 722.

[7]George Plimpton, "The Story Behind a Nonfiction Novel," *Truman Capote: Conversations*, ed. M. Thomas Inge (Jackson: University Press of Mississippi, 1987) 47.

[8]Lawrence Grobel, *Conversations with Capote* (New York: New American Library, 1985) 116.

places imaginatively, providing not only a story based on fact but a glimpse into his own personal connections, priorities, and values.

Rupert Thomson's "Rereading: Truman Capote's *In Cold Blood*" is one of the most articulate critical essays about the nonfiction novel as an American classic and the reasons for its inclusion in the celebrated texts of literary journalism. "For many critics, the 'non-fiction novel,' as Capote was calling it, belonged to a tradition dating back to Daniel Defoe's *The Storm* (1704), in which Defoe used the voices of real people to tell his story,"[9] writes Thomson. Thomson lists James Agee, Charles Dickens, Lillian Ross, John Steinbeck, and Mark Twain as a few of the literary journalists who influenced other writers. He challenges Capote's sense that he was doing something new with *In Cold Blood*, quoting Harold Bloom's critique of Capote and his "quest to be self-generated"[10] and his determination not to be influenced by William Faulkner, Carson McCullers, Eudora Welty, or other writers (and not being *perceived* as being influenced by these or other established authors).

Thomson praises Capote for being an "exquisite stylist" and quotes Norman Mailer, who called Capote "the most perfect writer of my generation."[11] He locates Capote's work in the "swamp gothic" and in the literature of the American South: "*Other Voices, Other Rooms* (1948) and *The Grass Harp* (1951) were carefully wrought examples of swamp gothic— unashamedly ornate, lush and impressionistic, and for all its metropolitan sass, *Breakfast at Tiffany's* (1958), Capote's third novel, in which he gave us the kooky, amoral Holly Golightly, also had its roots in the deep south."[12] Thomson has respect for the artist himself, celebrating Capote's ambitious efforts in packing his bags and boarding a train for a region as foreign to Capote as Bangladesh might be. "*In Cold Blood* gave him the opportunity, allowing him to ditch his attachment to childhood and nostalgia, the literature of the backward glance, and to immerse himself in something that was both current and universal,"[13] Thomson writes.

Literary journalism relies on description, dialogue, and narration— techniques that fiction makes a claim to but does not own. In fact, literary

---

[9]Rupert Thomson, "Rereading: Truman Capote's *In Cold Blood*," *The Guardian*, 5 August 2011, web (accessed 3 August 2018).
[10]Ibid.
[11]Ibid.
[12]Ibid.
[13]Ibid.

journalists from Willa Cather to Stephen Crane to Ernest Hemingway would be surprised if told that nonfiction cannot explore the depths of human experience. Most important, Thomson understands Capote's desire to create reportage and acknowledges what appears to be a superficial understanding of news gathering and reporting.

> Capote saw journalism as a horizontal form, skimming over the surface of things, topical but ultimately throwaway, while fiction could move horizontally and vertically at the same time, the narrative momentum constantly enhanced and enriched by an incisive, in-depth plumbing of context and character. In treating a real-life situation as a novelist might, Capote aimed to combine the best of both literary worlds to devastating effect.[14]

Capote himself said in an interview with Grobel that a conversation about fiction and nonfiction is not rooted in something as simplistic as truth or untruth: "It is really a question of narrative writing, that's what it's really about," he said. "It's a question of learning to control the narrative so that it moves faster and deeper at the same time."[15] Although Capote is correct about the ability of literature to go both "faster and deeper," he fails to appreciate what the creative nonfiction and literary journalism of his day already had accomplished. "His intention was to produce a tightly controlled forensic piece that examined the effects of a savage, senseless killing on an obscure community, and what interested him at the outset was the climate of wariness and suspicion, the insomnia, the loss of faith, the dread,"[16] Thomson writes. As late as 1962, Capote said *In Cold Blood* would be the "story of a town."[17] A psychological study of a rural community took second place to an exploration of the criminal mind and the horrors of state-sanctioned execution, but both themes represent Capote's ability to create breadth and depth in a genre less familiar to him than fiction.

Allegory and Literary Journalism

Allegory and universal significance lie at the heart of literary journalism. Description, dialogue, and narration are its literary techniques, and

---

[14]Ibid.
[15]Grobel, *Conversations*, 90.
[16]Thomson, "Rereading."
[17]Ibid.

immersion is a way of being, a way of participating in the lives of one's sources. Allegory and universal themes are the motivation for literary nonfiction, they draw from the same reservoir, and they enhance one another. Where they are lacking, no amount of artistry can prevail.

Capote organized *In Cold Blood* into short sections that employ what Thomson calls "classic crime-genre techniques in order to create resonance and heighten suspense."[18] The decision creates a stylistic rhythm and fuels mystery and suspense. This technique—manipulative though it is—pales in comparison to the universal themes that drive the plot. For example, Thomson argues that Perry Edward Smith and Richard Eugene Hickock "symbolised the feckless, degenerate underbelly of the country, the absolute antithesis of Holcomb's God-fearing and law-abiding citizens."[19] Furthermore, their collision with the quiet, hard-working, God-fearing people of Holcomb is the stuff of allegory: "The murders represented a sudden, horrifying collision of two wildly divergent Americas,"[20] Thomson adds. Rather than oversimplifying the narrative, the "classic crime-genre techniques" complement what readers learn about chance, fate, and everything haphazard and uncontrollable. How did the murderers become who they were? What is their connection to one another? Why would they creep into the home of a Kansas family and, once inside, not realize there was nothing to steal—and flee? Why would Smith say he liked Herbert Clutter, all the way up to the moment that he cut his throat? What can readers learn from such sensational, disquieting tales? The reader enters the crime scene with Capote—in medias res—with corpses in the basement and on the second floor, with a church service in progress a few miles away. What is to be made of it all? One way to organize the chaos is to rely on allegory—to set up categories and correspondences and to believe in the power of a reader's curiosity about an unknown family, an unfamiliar region, and alien forensic and legal processes. What sense can we make of a collision between a quiet town and a focused, ruthless murderer? Most disturbingly, could it happen to anyone?

Hemingway and other giants of American literature believed in the power of writing to alter the world around them, they developed characters and themes that challenged the preconceptions of their readers, and they often struggled to make a living in order to pursue their art. One of the reasons literary journalism has become such a compelling and popular genre

---

[18]Ibid.
[19]Ibid.
[20]Ibid.

involves its headlong rush into phenomenological inquiry. Like those who chose to leave journalism and devote their lives to fiction, practitioners of literary journalism overwhelmingly consider their mission to be a search for meaning, for the deeper truth.

Even at the risk of being accused of didacticism, literary journalists often employ allegory, although it is doubtful that they sit at their computers and seek to introduce symbols and allegorical systems as manipulative tools or as artifice. Two articles, one by Roger Rosenblatt and the other by Joshua Hammer, illustrate the importance of allegory in contemporary newsgathering; however, they are only the tip of the iceberg. Scholars of American literature expect writers of fiction to employ symbolism and metaphor liberally; less expected is a journalist's devotion to telling the stories of ordinary people who find themselves in extraordinary circumstances. Their lives take on a significance not unlike the lives of fictional characters in works by Willa Cather, Stephen Crane, Theodore Dreiser, Upton Sinclair, and Ernest Hemingway.

An extended news feature and a news story that became a documentary illustrate how journalists and filmmakers use allegory to—as Flannery O'Connor wrote—command the attention of a reader by drawing "large and startling figures."[21] John Hellman argues that allegory is "a narrative made to develop some philosophical view."[22] While this may not always be the case, it is certainly true of literary journalists, who seek phenomenological significance and a higher truth and who devote themselves to conveying a kind of mythopoetic reality to readers. The language and techniques of literary journalism are those of literature, including description, dialogue, narration, point of view, stream of consciousness, and universal significance.

A news feature that illustrates the importance of an extended allegorical system is Roger Rosenblatt's 1994 article titled "The Killer in the Next Tent." The article deals with what the author in his subtitle calls the "surreal horror of the Rwandan refugees," opposing groups called Tutsis and Hutus—now refugees—who are forced to reside in the same camps. At the time Rosenblatt wrote his story, the Tutsi guerrillas of the Rwandan Patriotic Front had been fighting the Hutu government of Rwanda since 1990. Since the fifteenth century, Hutu tribespeople were dominated by the Tutsis, their

---

[21]Flannery O'Connor, "The Fiction Writer and His Country," *Mystery and Manners* (New York: Farrar, 1969) 34.

[22]John Hellman, *Fables of Fact: The New Journalism as New Fiction* (Champaign: Illinois University Press, 1981) 10.

feudal rulers. When the League of Nations turned over the country to Belgium in 1919, the Tutsis were the favored class, in part because they more closely resembled Europeans. But in 1959, 100,000 Tutsis were killed and another 200,000 forced to flee. Soon after, Belgium turned the country over to the Hutus.

Rwanda gained independence in 1962, but by 1973 the country was taken over by a military coup. By 1990, Tutsi rebels and Ugandans moved into Rwanda to remove the government. Of the raw violence that ensued, Rosenblatt writes, "Under certain circumstances, not always predictable, people will do anything to one another. Going by the descriptions of events in Rwanda, it is doubtful that the Hutu killers felt any twinge of conscience as they went about their torturing and murdering. The same is true of Americans, Europeans and Asians when they have been caught up in their own spasms of depravity."[23] Without announcing that he has moved into allegorical representation, Rosenblatt observes that one boy "saunters by wearing a San Francisco 49ers hat and a Nintendo T-shirt."[24] The symbol could refer to the political dominance of the United States, testify to the importance of American popular culture abroad, highlight children affected by the civil war, etc.

What Rosenblatt calls the "mixture of normal life and the presence of evil"[25] is most stunningly captured by a moment similar to a scene in George Orwell's journalistic short story "Shooting an Elephant." Rosenblatt writes compellingly (and horrifyingly) about the brutality of a crowd that encounters an African antelope that has been turned loose. The children "squeal with delight" and the women "begin to trill in a half-shriek" as they arm themselves with machetes:

> The waterbuck walks slowly at first in its normal dumb lope. Then, sensing danger, it quickens its pace to an awkward trot. A boy brings his machete down hard in its side. There is cheering. The animal bleats and runs uphill, its great body wobbling like a water bed, its horns thrust high in the air. Its eyes show white and terror. It moves as fast as it can now. But the crowd engulfs it—50, 60 people—hacking again and again at its rump, its legs and back, until the accumulation of the

---

[23]Roger Rosenblatt, "The Killer in the Next Tent," *The New York Times Magazine*, 5 June 1994, 41, web (accessed 3 August 2018).
[24]Ibid., 44.
[25]Ibid., 46.

blows cuts the animal in half. Then the crowd hacks at the two separate halves. They cut off the hooves, then the head. The trilling grows louder, then stops.

Now the pieces of the animal lie scattered on the road, wet with blood. Several hands grab hungrily at each piece, and there is nearly a fight. The people seem inches away from turning their machetes on one another but they do not. And no sooner has this moment occurred than it passes. The whole event, from the loosing of the waterbuck to the division of its body, has taken but half a minute. In a few more seconds, the pieces are gone and the people are back at their tasks. Only the bloodstains on the road testify to what happened here, and the rain will soon wash them away.[26]

This grisly event is Rosenblatt's parable about the mindless violence that lies at the root of the civil war and in the hearts of men, women, and children. Killing a sensitive creature with such brutality becomes the symbol of war itself, and after the short narrative, Rosenblatt's tale ends. What else is there to say about inhumanity and cruelty?

The second example first appeared in *Newsweek* April 15, 2002, and later became a documentary titled *To Die in Jerusalem*. On the cover of the magazine are two young women, Ayat al-Akhras and Rachel Levy, one a Palestinian suicide bomber and the other an Israeli casualty. The reader learns that Ayat al-Akhras, eighteen years old, secretly joined a martyr's brigade. Levy, a year younger than al-Akhras, was apolitical and is said to have "shrugged off the risk of suicide bombings."[27] Relying on symbolism, author Joshua Hammer writes the following introductory paragraph:

It was a typical Friday afternoon in the Kiryat Hayovel neighborhood of southern Jerusalem. At the Supersol market, the Sabbath rush was underway; shoppers pushed their carts past shelves stripped bare of bread and matzos for the weeklong Passover holiday. A line had formed at the delicatessen counter in the back, where Sivan Peretz wrapped chicken breasts and salmon steaks and made small talk with his customers. A middle-aged security guard stood poised inside the supermarket entrance, carefully searching bags. At 1:49 p.m., 17-year-old Rachel Levy—petite, with flowing hair and a girlish gap between

---

[26]Ibid., 47.
[27]Joshua Hammer, "How Two Lives Met in Death," *Newsweek*, 15 April 2002, 18.

her teeth—stepped off the bus from her nearby apartment block and strolled toward the market on a quick trip to buy red pepper and herbs for a fish dinner with her mother and two brothers. At the same moment, another girl—strikingly attractive with intense hazel eyes—walked toward the store's glass double doors. The teenagers met at the entrance, brushing past each other as the guard reached out to grab the hazel-eyed girl, whose outfit may have aroused suspicion. "Wait!" the guard cried. A split second later, a powerful explosion tore through the supermarket, gutting shelves and sending bodies flying. When the smoke cleared and the screaming stopped, the two teenage girls and the guard lay dead, three more victims of the madness of martyrdom.[28]

On the pages with this compressed narrative of senseless death are the photographs of suicide bombers and their victims. Editors included with an inset the following information: "Suicide bombings are now supported by 80 percent of the Palestinian population. At left, 20 of the 66 young Palestinian men and women who have blown themselves up since September 2000. At right, 150 of the 170 Israelis who died in the wave of bombings."[29] Staggering as the numbers might be, the story of al-Akhras and Levy is more powerful, more compelling, more focused, and infinitely more tragic than the numbers alone. By the end of the article, readers will know al-Akhras and Levy and their families and friends. Their tragedy is not soon to be forgotten.

Part of the reason the story of al-Akhras and Levy is so compelling is its reliance on the two central, tragic figures as representative. Their role in this particular horrific story of war suggests the power of fable, parable, and allegory on which journalists rely. Although allegory is in disrepute in some academic circles because it is considered too simplistic—in the way some scholars consider children's stories to be simplistic—it is too often misunderstood and misdefined.

Literary journalists dance along the border between nonfiction and fiction, provide the context often missing in straight news stories, and highlight the role of perception, vantage point, and authorial voice in newsgathering. Literary journalists also acknowledge their humanity, their biases, and their concern about particular issues in their work. They immerse themselves in places they describe; they shadow the people they portray. In addition—

---

[28]Ibid., 18-20.
[29]Ibid., 20.

perhaps as important as their challenge to the myth of objectivity—they remind us that the life of a "common" person engaged in an uncommon event can be the most compelling story of all. Finally, like the literary figures in John Bunyan's allegory *Pilgrim's Progress*, a literary journalist's characters may be both flesh and blood and grounded in place and time and still be richly suggestive. This portion of the study relies heavily on the work of numerous literary critics and journalism scholars, none more than John C. Hartsock and Norman Sims, who introduced the concept of the "borderlands between fact and fiction."[30] It focuses especially on a series of questions introduced by those who have just begun to ask important questions about the definitions, characteristics, contributions, and future of studies in literary journalism.

Literary journalism is often allegorical in the sense that it makes tangible an extended symbolic system. In "The Politics of the New Journalism," John J. Pauly suggests that literary journalism helped to resurrect the "romantic vision of the writer."[31] Pauly argues that two of the strengths of literary journalism are its attack on establishment journalism's "fact-fetish"[32] and its revelation that the "truth of all writing is a matter for social negotiation."[33] Like poet William Carlos Williams—who wrote that "it is difficult/ to get the news from poems,/ yet men die miserably every day/ for lack/ of what is found there"[34]—Pauly allows writers of nonfiction their place in a literary tradition that explores the depths and heights of human experience.

What is found in poetry, as Pauly and Williams both understand, of course, is an acknowledgment of the complexity of life and human society and a vivid and lyrical language with which to communicate it. In an essay titled "Historical Perspective on the New Journalism," Joseph M. Webb uses the terms "Romantic Reporter" and "Romantic Reporting"[35] repeatedly in his discussion of literary journalists and what he calls their focus on "internal,

---

[30]Norman Sims, ed. "Preface," *Literary Journalism in the Twentieth Century* (New York: Oxford University Press, 1990) v.

[31]John J. Pauly, "The Politics of the New Journalism," *Literary Journalism in the Twentieth Century*, ed. Norman Sims (New York: Oxford University Press, 1990) 119.

[32]Ibid., 121.

[33]Ibid., 122.

[34]William Carlos Williams, "Asphodel, That Greeny Flower," *Asphodel, That Greeny Flower and Other Love Poems* (New York: New Directions, 1994) 19.

[35]Joseph M. Webb, "Historical Perspective on the New Journalism," *Journalism History* 1/2 (1974): 40, 41, 42, 60.

rather than external, human processes and movements."[36] Webb suggests that literary journalists aspire to a purpose higher than entertainment or even the dissemination of facts in their work, and he suggests that literary journalism—with its focus on extended narratives, immersion, and the privileging of sources—is more consistent with Romanticism than Rationalism. Without taking too big a theoretical leap, Webb also may be suggesting that the intention of the language used by literary journalists is poetic rather than prosaic.

Literary scholars usually agree that allegory is extended metaphor; that it equates persons and actions with meanings that lie outside the text; that characters often are personifications; that events and settings may be historical or fictitious. What may be lost, however, is that allegory operates as much through tension and concealment as through equations and correspondences. Allegory is born when one recognizes the limits of realism. When writers have set out on a metaphysical quest—when their meaning lies beyond the familiar, common, recognizable patterns of reality—they move into allegory.

And finally, John C. Hartsock, too, suggests that the result of what he calls "narrative journalism" was "social or cultural allegory, with potential meanings beyond the literal in the broadest sense of allegory's meaning. Largely, although not exclusively, that allegory is about embracing an understanding of the social or cultural Other."[37] Speaking broadly, Hartsock writes that classics of literary journalism such as Capote's *In Cold Blood* and Mailer's *Executioner's Song* might be considered "allegories about the dark side of the American experience."[38] He draws this conclusion because of "their attempts to understand the subjectivities of convicted murderers"[39] in a new and dramatic way.

Allegory has been disparaged as a too-blatant system of correspondences that reduces the mysterious and profound to the concrete and simplistic. However, by studying the origin of allegory in American literature, one soon discovers that allegory is not reductive but expansive. Allegory does not provide tidy systems, although we may speak of an "allegorical system"; it is rather the product of oppositions and tensions that one must somehow hold in

---

[36]Ibid., 41.

[37]John C. Hartsock, *A History of American Literary Journalism: The Emergence of a Modern Narrative Form* (Amherst: University of Massachusetts Press, 2000) 22.

[38]Ibid., 78.

[39]Ibid.

balance. By understanding this, we begin to confront the violence or conflict inherent in allegory. Allegory has rich symbolic potential. When a writer such as Franz Kafka or Jorge Luis Borges changes men into insects or sets up hopelessly forking paths, respectively, he has stepped onto a plane that defies realism—has tapped into what the Transcendentalists knew as the unified world of Spirit behind the "thing." When one creates allegory—whether as a writer or reader—one moves into the realm of faith.

Yet one must not necessarily read for the moral or message within allegory—or even parable—for allegory points primarily to itself. Allegory builds upon contradiction and surprising reversals; through its employment of symbols, its significance approaches that of myth. As Angus Fletcher notes, allegories are not "dull systems" but "symbolic power struggles."[40] Allegories point both toward and away from themselves; they often point outside plot and character to a higher truth. To salvage allegory from the wastebin of second-rate fictional method, one must recognize that allegory can be nothing if not didactic. According to Fletcher, allegory "allows for instruction, for rationalizing, for categorizing and codifying, for casting spells. To conclude, allegories are the natural mirrors of ideology."[41]

Although critics have been loath to discuss news as allegory—in part because such a discussion suggests that news has a fictive element—they have addressed in great depth the role of mythology in newsgathering and news reporting. In fact, at least one issue of *Journalism and Mass Communication Quarterly* has been devoted to the topic. In the special issue, Jack Lule summarizes the role of myth in American culture by saying that "myth has provided the stories that make sense of a society, for a society"[42] and that "myth is essential social narrative."[43] He also highlights the role of myth in news by connecting mythology with storytelling and alluding to the history of news ("with roots in drama, folktale, and myth") until it was reconceptualized in the late nineteenth century to be "objective and scientific" rather than "dramatic and mythic."[44]

---

[40]Angus Fletcher, *Allegory: The Theory of a Symbolic Mode* (Ithaca: Cornell University Press, 1964) 23.

[41]Ibid., 368.

[42]Jack Lule, "Myth and Terror on the Editorial Page: *The New York Times* Responds to September 11, 2001," *Journalism and Mass Communication Quarterly* 79/2 (Summer 2002): 276.

[43]Ibid., 277.

[44]Ibid.

Certainly, allegory and mythology are closely related, although allegory is more didactic and less universal. Both derive from a society's need for stories that explain the inexplicable; both rely on symbols for their impact and cohesiveness; and both have a role in nonfiction, a genre that purports to be "true" while acknowledging its absolute reliance on the point of view of the storyteller.

At the center of many successful allegories is the quest. Hartsock discusses authors whose "mock heroic in the picaresque tradition" leads readers on a long pilgrimage in which they can identify with the hero or anti-hero. At the end of many examples of literary journalism that incorporate a journey, however, the "American dream is found to be empty."[45] In *The Orchid Thief: A True Story of Beauty and Obsession*, Susan Orlean departs on a literal quest through the swamps of Florida in search of a ghost orchid; on a symbolic level, she and those who people her nonfiction novel are on a quest for something more ephemeral than even the rare orchid. In *Loose Change: Three Women of the Sixties*, Sara Davidson writes a memoir of friendship, betrayal, and change at Berkeley in the 1960s, hoping, it would seem, to understand an entire generation by understanding herself and her two closest friends. In "Some Dreamers of the Golden Dream" and other essays in *Slouching Towards Bethlehem*, Joan Didion sets out on a journey to understand everything from middle-class America to the children of the 1960s. Like Roger Rosenblatt's "The Killer in the Next Tent" and Joshua Hammer's tale of suicide bombers and their victims, these nonfiction novels and collections of essays depend on extended symbolic systems for their impact.

As Capote conducted interviews for *In Cold Blood*, he moved further and further into allegory, which helped him transform one murder—after all, murders were and are all too common—into a narrative that would engage readers for decades. According to Thomas Fahy, between 1959 and 1965, *In Cold Blood* evolved into a "meditation on the impact of violence on a small community, an investigation into the psychology of two killers, a portrait of contemporary law enforcement, an indictment of capital punishment, and an examination of the pervasive fears defining 1950s America,"[46] a formidable achievement that guaranteed it a place among American literary classics.

---

[45]Hartsock, *History of American Literary Journalism*, 163.

[46]Thomas Fahy, *Understanding Truman Capote* (Columbia: University of South Carolina Press, 2014) 113-14.

An emphasis on representational systems in the nonfiction novel made it possible for a murder in the Midwest to appeal to an international audience. "Clutter's identity as a white, Christian, family man who had achieved economic and social success through hard work and with moral integrity reflected the best aspects of the American Dream," suggests Fahy. In Capote's rendering, the Kansas town of Holcomb embodied all small towns and all hard-working rural people of a particular generation: "It seems just another fair-sized town in the middle—almost the exact middle—of the continental United States,"[47] Fahy writes.

But there is no safety, no security, even for Herbert and Bonnie Clutter, who work from sunup to sundown, rear four children, attend church on Sundays, and treat field hands compassionately. In fact, one of the field hands—who confesses that he loved Nancy and Kenyon Clutter—will lie to a cellmate about money in a safe in a house on the Kansas plains, with no particular reason for doing so, and the fate of the Clutter family will be sealed. Without reason, purpose, or explanation, two men bound to one another in inexplicable ways will drive 400 miles across Kansas and, instead of realizing there is no point to the home invasion, will shoot four people at close range and destroy a family and a community. Two older sisters, who also planned to attend a Thanksgiving celebration, will be delayed. One of them will attend the funeral and a few days later marry her fiancé in the same church. By setting up correspondences and imposing order on crime that defies all ordering systems, Capote engages in allegory, explaining inexplicable events to himself and—perhaps—to us.

Truman Capote and Literary Journalism

In one of his most important contributions to the ever-controversial discussion about fiction, nonfiction, and the borderland between them, Capote said that the two genres are "coming into a conjunction like two great rivers": "The two rivers are going to suddenly flow together once and for all and forever. You see it more and more in writing,"[48] he said. Although Capote is correct about trends in literature and literary criticism, the experimentation and movement between boundaries does not suggest that the "rivers are going to suddenly flow together." Part of the necessary division between fiction and nonfiction is the issue of accuracy. Although few jour-

---

[47]Ibid., 125.
[48]Grobel, *Conversations*, 89.

nalists commit themselves to objectivity—understanding that reporting is dependent on one's acknowledged and unacknowledged biases, personal background, and vantage point—they define reportage differently from Capote and insist that no dialogue or description of an event be fabricated. In other words, with *In Cold Blood*, Capote claims to be part of a tradition in which newsgathering employs the techniques of fiction; however, he is not a journalist, was not trained in journalism, and is the target of journalists who do not support his claim that he could memorize hours of an interview and that making up the final scene of the nonfiction novel—and other violations of journalistic ethics—are appropriate.

According to many literary critics, Truman Capote claimed that he had contributed to a new literary form—the "nonfiction novel"—although in *Conversations with Capote*, Grobel sets the record straight:

> Capote never claimed—as many critics thought he did—that he invented narrative journalism or, as *In Cold Blood* came to be labeled, the nonfiction novel. He *did* consider it to be a serious new literary form and he did feel he had made a major contribution toward its establishment. And he also staked the claim to have undertaken the most comprehensive and far-reaching experiment in the medium of reportage.[49]

As Capote once explained, "Journalism always moves along on a horizontal plane, telling a story, while fiction—good fiction—moves vertically, taking you deeper and deeper into character and events. By treating a real event with fictional techniques (something that cannot be done by a journalist until he *learns* to write good fiction), it's possible to make this kind of synthesis."[50] *The Muses Are Heard*, which in 1956 preceded *In Cold Blood*, was a journalistic account of the Everyman Opera Company and its performances of *Porgy and Bess* in the Soviet Union. The next year, Capote published a profile of Marlon Brando, "The Duke and His Domain," in *The New Yorker*, further evidence that Capote wanted to try his hand at reportage and that he enjoyed elevating daily journalism to a new plane. Nonetheless, Capote was not a journalist and was not trained in newsgathering practices. He also disparaged the work of his contemporaries who employed literary journalism techniques; in doing so, he failed to understand that literary journalism—like fiction—"moves vertically" as well as horizontally. In short, Capote was

---

[49]Ibid., 109.
[50]Fahy, *Understanding Truman Capote*, 113.

not the first or last writer of nonfiction to exploit the narrative power of a true event.

Not surprisingly, the term "nonfiction novel" has been hotly debated since the book's publication. Many scholars have demonstrated that Capote was participating in a long tradition of historical fiction and literary nonfiction, including works such as Theodore Dreiser's *An American Tragedy* (1925), a crime story based on fact. Others consider *In Cold Blood* one of the first significant works in what Tom Wolfe called the New Journalism, which included writers such as Wolfe, Hunter S. Thompson, and Norman Mailer. Meanwhile, the very definition of New Journalism has been "contested,"[51] according to Fahy.

Describing Herbert, Bonnie, Nancy, and Kenyon Clutter as having been "murdered on a lonely wheat and cattle ranch,"[52] Capote understands how to employ fictional techniques. *In Cold Blood* was an experiment in writing creative nonfiction, although it was not Capote's only effort to explore another genre. For example, Capote told Roy Newquist that *The Muses Are Heard* was "the beginning of a long experiment":

> I've always had the theory that reportage is the great unexplored art form. I mean, most good writers, good literary craftsmen, seldom use this métier. For example, John Hersey is a very fine journalist and an excellent writer, but he's not an artist in the sense that I mean...I've had this theory that a factual piece of work could explore whole new dimensions in writing that would have a double effect fiction does not have—the very fact of its being true, every word of it true, would add a double contribution of strength and impact.[53]

One of the issues, of course, is that Capote does not clarify why Hersey, author of *Hiroshima*, is not an "artist" of Capote's caliber or type, and he does not admit that *In Cold Bood* is not, in fact, true in "every word."

Taking higher ground, Capote then explains how his immersion in a Kansas community and his conducting a series of interviews made him a stronger writer, giving him an understanding of diverse people and what they contribute. In this, Capote acknowledges his participation in a broader group of professionals committed to journalistic excellence:

---

[51]Ibid.

[52]Plimpton, "The Story," 51.

[53]Roy Newquist, *Counterpoint* (New York: Rand McNally, 1964) 78.

Now I feel capable of handling all sorts of new and different characters which I couldn't approach before, and I think reportage has helped me. I think it freed many things inside of me—this opportunity to work with real people, then using real people under their own names. It has freed or unlocked something inside myself that now makes it possible for me to return to fiction with the ability to use a far greater range of characters.[54]

In addition to interviews with people whom he did not know (and could not invent), Capote told Plimpton that he learned to empathize with those whom he described:

But, above all, the reporter must be able to empathize with personalities outside his usual imaginative range, mentalities unlike his own, kinds of people he would never have written about had he not been forced to by encountering them inside the journalistic situation. This last is what first attracted me to the notion of narrative reportage.[55]

As noted in chapter one, Capote praises a few literary journalists but claims he is engaged in producing art: "It seemed to me that journalism, reportage, could be forced to yield a serious new art form: the 'nonfiction novel,' as I thought of it,"[56] he tells Plimpton. True to form, Capote celebrates the nonfiction of Rebecca West, Joseph Mitchell and Lillian Ross but nixes James Breslin and Tom Wolfe: "It's useless for a writer whose talent is essentially journalistic to attempt creative reportage, because it simply won't work."[57]

In spite of his preference for some literary journalists over others, Capote provides an important opinion when he argues against the contemporary undervaluing of journalism itself:

Still, on the whole, journalism is the most underestimated, the least explored of literary mediums...Because few first-class writers have ever bothered with journalism, except as a sideline, "hackwork," something to be done when the creative spirit is lacking, or as a means of making money quickly. Such writers say in effect: Why should we trouble with

---

[54]Ibid., 83.
[55]Plimpton, "The Story," 48.
[56]Ibid., 47.
[57]Ibid., 50.

factual writing when we're able to invent our own stories, contrive our own characters and themes?—journalism is only literary photography, and unbecoming to the serious writer's artistic dignity.[58]

The idea that literary journalism is less dramatic because it is true and that its purpose is simply to describe what is right in front of us—without context or meaning—is an accusation that journalists continue to address. "When I first formed my theories concerning the nonfiction novel, many people with whom I discussed the matter were unsympathetic," Capote said. "They felt that what I proposed, a narrative form that employed all the techniques of fictional art but was nevertheless immaculately factual, was little more than a literary solution for fatigued novelists suffering from 'failure of imagination.' Personally, I felt that this attitude represented a 'failure of imagination' on their part."[59]

Truman Capote was not a journalist, nor was he primarily a writer of nonfiction, although he published crime stories, memoir, profiles, and travel pieces. Capote was not trained as a journalist, although, certainly, until after the Watergate scandal and the publication of *All the President's Men* and the film by the same title, departments and schools of journalism did not provide majors and minors in investigative journalism, media ethics, or all the areas of inquiry that now exist. But Capote was not one to underestimate himself, and after reading the story of the Clutter family murders in *The New York Times*, he put his formidable energies into an experiment, the nonfiction novel. Subsequently, he sought the support of his editor at Random House and convinced Nelle Harper Lee to accompany him to Kansas, which was both a foreign and familiar universe to two dislocated friends from the Deep South who understood small towns and their political and religious intricacies.

In "Master of His Universe," Tom Wolfe writes that he is a "journalist at heart," adding that "even as a novelist, I'm first of all a journalist." He believes that "all novels should be journalism to start, and if you can ascend from that plateau to some marvelous altitude, terrific. I really don't think it's possible to understand the individual without understanding the society."[60] With this statement, Wolfe celebrates extended nonfiction and underscores

---

[58]Ibid., 47-48.

[59]Ibid., 48.

[60]Tom Wolfe and Bonnie Angelo, "Master of His Universe," *Time* 133/7 (13 February 1989): 92.

the importance of journalism that clarifies and explains cultural phenomena. Wolfe's words about the definition and purposes of journalism and about literature as art lie at the heart of any study of Truman Capote's *In Cold Blood*. Closely connected to the distinctions we make between these literary enterprises is their role in describing the individual as a player in the larger society.

When scholars discuss literary journalism, they often do so by listing words and phrases that are sometimes synonymous and sometimes oppositional; furthermore, the terms are sometimes laudatory and sometimes tinged with contempt, depending both on the word choice and on the context. These words and phrases include "art-journalism," "artistic nonfiction," "creative nonfiction," "essay-fiction," "fact as fiction," "faction," "factual fiction," "immersion journalism," "intimate journalism," "journalit," "literary journalism," "literature as fact," "narrative nonfiction," "New Journalism," "new reportage," "nonfiction with a literary purpose," "the nonfiction novel," "novelistic journalism," "participatory journalism," "parajournalism," "personal journalism," "witness literature," and "writerly nonfiction."

As these phrases and terms might suggest, literary journalism has a great deal in common with documentary film, as we will explore in chapter seven. In *A History of American Literary Journalism: The Emergence of a Modern Narrative Form*, Hartsock says he prefers the terms "narrative journalism" or "narrative literary journalism": "Finally," he writes, "I prefer 'journalism' as the last element for three reasons. First, to define the form as a 'nonfiction' reinscribes its status as a 'nought,' thus reenacting an elitist literary conceit that has long consigned such writing as a 'non' 'essential' literature."[61]

The task involved in identifying and celebrating those we now call "literary journalists" has just begun. How convenient it would be if we could pretend that literary journalism is a genre that those in the news business, those in departments and schools of journalism and media studies, and those in departments of English debate good-naturedly. However, certain techniques employed in literary nonfiction raise doubt about accuracy among working journalists and scholars of journalism; these techniques include the revelation of interior states of mind, the recreation of a scene, manipulation of timelines, and other issues. Some journalism practitioners and scholars are put off by what they perceive to be a cavalier way of manipulating chronolo-

---

[61]Hartsock, *History of American Literary Journalism*, 12.

gy, dialogue, and character description by some literary journalists. Those in literary studies sometimes object to literary journalism's reliance on actual events and real figures. Fortunately for the scholarly pilgrimage itself, though, literary journalism texts provide those in both literature and journalism with a rich continuum for academic and personal inquiry.

Literary journalism *is* a borderland, and it is a borderland that makes the journalism establishment edgy. Literary journalism is not fiction—because the people are real and the events occurred—nor is it journalism in a traditional sense—because there is interpretation and a personal point of view and (often) experimentation with structure. Like Capote, not all of those considered literary journalists have written for or write for newspapers or magazines; they may use literary techniques, including stream of consciousness; they may experiment with chronology and rename sources, etc. Other characteristics of literary journalism concern literary scholars, most especially what they consider to be the secondary nature of nonfiction in literary studies (never mind the place of daily journalism in the estimation of some literary scholars).

In *Fables of Fact: The New Journalism as New Fiction*, Hellman introduces allegory. He argues that New Journalists and contemporary fiction writers share "an emphasis upon the perceiving consciousness as a transforming power, and desire to avoid the distortion caused by an attempt to disguise that power."[62] Literary journalists may frame their narratives with forewords, afterwords, and other devices; they often employ a conscious narrator or use first person; they alter punctuation and may experiment with composition; they use episodic structure; they introduce allegorical or mythic patterns; they use parody and satire; and they believe that the center of the work must be philosophical and should highlight social concerns.[63] An afterword might emphasize the factual nature of the piece and might draw attention to its "fictional shape" and to the author's "organizing consciousness."[64] Other characteristics, according to Norman Sims in "The Literary Journalists," include immersion in the story one is covering; thematic, not necessarily chronological structure; accuracy (no made-up dialogue, no composite characters, and evidence of the authority of the author's voice); personal voice (incorporating first-person perspective as opposed to the institu-

---

[62]Hellman, *Fables of Fact*, 13.
[63]Ibid., 13-14.
[64]Ibid., 14.

tional voice of newspapers); a sense of responsibility to the reader; and "symbolic realities" and resonance.[65]

News is not a collection of facts, no matter how finely arranged, and newsgathering is not merely the recording of a source's words or chronological events. Dismissing the importance of a writer's vantage point and personal perspective makes possible the false polarities of fiction and nonfiction on a complex continuum of storytelling. Within human events are meanings that sometimes propel those involved in them toward other events, toward a governing philosophy, or into a relationship with others in a particular community. External events contain images and symbols that participants and observers may transform into interior reality—into a personal and potentially self-orienting allegory. And if the events and people with whom we come in contact transform us, they most assuredly transform the reporters that cover the news.

In the postmodern universe, we need more than facts. Daily, there is evidence that human beings crave what Wallace Stevens called the "blessed rage for order"[66] in his poem "The Idea of Order at Key West." Readers want stories in which characters move from innocence to experience because readers themselves move from innocence to experience. Women and men in contemporary society do not cry out for press releases but for what Hellman calls the "penetration of mystery": "Almost by definition, new journalism is a revolt by the individual against homogenized forms of experience, against monolithic versions of truth,"[67] he writes. Hellman cites Robert Scholes, whom he calls "one of our most lucid theoreticians of narrative."[68] Scholes argues that the dichotomy between "fact" and "fiction" is artificial: the word "fact" comes from the Latin *facere*, meaning "to make or do," while "fiction" comes from *fingere*, meaning "to make or shape."[69]

Contributing to what many newspaper and news magazine readers want in order to make sense of their world is a mistrust of conventional journalism. What many perceive to be "corporate fiction,"[70] as Hellman sug-

---

[65]Norman Sims, "The Literary Journalists," *The Literary Journalists: The New Art of Personal Reportage* (New York: Ballantine Books, 1984) 8-25.

[66]Wallace Stevens, "The Idea of Order at Key West," *The Norton Anthology of Modern Poetry*, ed. Richard Ellmann and O'Clair, 2nd ed. (New York: W.W. Norton, 1988) 292.

[67]Hellman, *Fables of Fact*, 8.

[68]Ibid., 17.

[69]Ibid., 17-18.

[70]Ibid., 4.

gests, increases the distance between a reader's need for verifiable information on which to make life-altering decisions and the desire of owners of media outlets to survive economically and to make profits. For many Americans, the battle is not between objectivity and subjectivity or between fact and fiction but between a "disguised perspective and an admitted one," between a "corporate fiction" and a "personal one."[71]

One of the most important books to deal with the role of the reporter as "other" is Janet Malcolm's *The Journalist and the Murderer*. In it, Malcolm asks hard questions about the role of journalism and about the tendency of some reporters to manipulate their sources in order to get a story. The same issue is explored in the films *Capote* and *Infamous*, both of which deal with Capote's relationship with Perry Smith. One of Malcolm's most damning statements appears on the first page of the book. There, she focuses on the source, who must realize that the reporter's first obligation is to the story and not to the assumed relationship between the reporter and the source during the interview: "On reading the article or book in question, he has to face the fact that the journalist—who seemed so friendly and sympathetic, so keen to understand him fully, so remarkably attuned to his vision of things—never had the slightest intention of collaborating with him on his story but always intended to write a story of his own."[72]

Unlike corporate journalism and reporters who exploit their sources in order to get the story first, literary journalists immerse themselves in the worlds of those whom they cover. They build extended relationships with their sources, making it unlikely that they can avoid bias and making it even more unlikely that they would want to do so. They relay dialogue and use description in a way that makes it clear that they are a part of the world they describe. Does their work contain bias? Certainly. Do they write from their own point of view and "distort" the news by being too close to the events and sources? Most assuredly. But literary journalists count on readers to understand their vantage point and to trust their narrative precisely *because* they confess their preconceptions and their points of view.

Critics of literary journalism will continue to address the thin line between literature as art and journalism as practice. Ronald Weber titled his book *The Literature of Fact* but subtitled it *Literary Nonfiction in American*

---

[71]Ibid.

[72]Janet Malcolm, *The Journalist and the Murderer* (New York: Alfred A. Knopf, 1990) 3.

Writing. He describes the field as "nonfiction with a literary purpose."[73] Thomas B. Connery separates New Journalism and literary journalism in *A Sourcebook of American Literary Journalism*, but he defines the genres as "nonfiction printed prose whose verifiable content is shaped and transformed into a story or sketch by use of narrative and rhetorical techniques generally associated with fiction."[74] As noted earlier, Hellman's *Fables of Fact* provides a provocative discussion of a journalist's responsibility to provide a personal explanation for events instead of a corporate one and restates the impossibility of objectivity as the public and the media once understood it. His prose is clear and direct when he argues that New Journalism was forged in a revolution of individuals against what he calls "monolithic" institutions and established—and often unexamined—"versions of truth."[75]

Literary critics are profoundly aware of the borderland in which Willa Cather, Stephen Crane, Theodore Dreiser, Ernest Hemingway, Edgar Allan Poe, Katherine Anne Porter, Upton Sinclair, John Steinbeck, Mark Twain, Eudora Welty, Walt Whitman, and others lived and wrote. Their words remind us that the issues are not peripheral to our lives because distinguishing between truth and falsehood, between nonfiction and fiction, and between fact and inexactitude is at the heart of the decisions we make and the communities we build. Gary L. Whitby proudly summarizes the work of Truman Capote by writing, "What glitters most, perhaps, is Capote's remarkable memory for dialogue and scene. The former is rendered so convincingly as to make the reader believe that the author used a tape recorder. He did not."[76] However, if he did not use notes or a tape recorder, how much can we believe Capote's creation of scene in *In Cold Blood*? How much weight can we put on the stream of consciousness that pervades the nonfiction novel? How well can we know Perry Smith or Dick Hickock, the unlikely killers of a farm family in Kansas?

---

[73]Ronald Weber, *The Literature of Fact: Literary Nonfiction in American Writing* (Athens: Ohio University Press, 1980) 1.

[74]Thomas B. Connery, "Preface," *A Sourcebook of American Literary Journalism: Representative Writers in an Emerging Genre,"* ed. Thomas B. Connery (New York: Greenwood Press, 1992) xiv.

[75]Hellman, *Fables of Fact*, 8.

[76]Gary L. Whitby, "Truman Capote," *A Sourcebook of American Literary Journalism: Representative Writers in an Emerging Genre,* ed. Thomas B. Connery (New York: Greenwood Press, 1992) 241.

Other Authors Address the Borderland

The debate about the borderland between fact and fiction will continue as long as book stores and libraries shelve books, as long as *The New York Times* lists bestsellers as "fiction" and "nonfiction," and as long as readers want to know if the characters and settings are real or imagined (or something in between). Although the literary journalists writing extended nonfiction would be impossible to list, John Berendt and Sara Davidson surface in any conversation about the tenets of journalism and the techniques that have too long been considered the province of fiction. Berendt and Davidson are not only practitioners but also literary critics. As journalists and as nonfiction novelists, Berendt and Davidson are self-conscious about their published work and intensely self-aware as artists.

Davidson champions literary journalism without apology and without hesitation. In a 2002 lecture titled "Literary Journalism: What Are the Rules?" Davidson quoted Wright Morris, who said, "Anything processed by memory is fiction." She then introduced the history of literary journalism, suggesting that 1965 was the time of the New Left, the new woman, the new morality, and the New Journalism. Literary journalism "reached a swell" in the 1960s, she said, and was considered "bastard journalism." "The literati saw it as class warfare," said Davidson. The publication of *In Cold Blood*, which appeared first in *The New Yorker* in serial form, "helped legitimize what we were trying to do," Davidson said. Paying tribute to her colleagues in the field, Davidson listed Joan Didion, John Hersey, Tracy Kidder, Frank McCourt, Lillian Ross, Hunter S. Thompson, Mark Twain, and Tom Wolfe as preeminent examples of the tenets of literary journalism. Like other literary journalists whose work is featured in this chapter, Davidson believes the solution to the problem of trust between author and reader is complete disclosure by the author. During her lecture, she said that she measures her work by whether she has contributed to the "emotional bedrock of human truth" and has told a story so important that it "becomes a part of your inner life."[77]

One of Davidson's essays, "The Gray Zone," addresses directly the role of memoir, a particularly rich and problematic category of nonfiction, and provides a worthy introduction to a discussion of authorial identity and au-

---

[77]Sara Davidson, lecture, "Literary Journalism: What Are the Rules?" School of Journalism and Mass Communication, University of Colorado, Boulder, 22 November 2002.

thentic experience in both fiction and nonfiction. Although the essay does not address Truman Capote or *In Cold Blood*, it does explore the borderland between fact and fiction and the necessity for authorial disclosure. Among numerous magazine articles and books, Davidson also published bestsellers *Loose Change: Three Women of the Sixties* (1977) and *Cowboy: A Novel* (1999), which are both memoirs. In each, she protects the identities of her sources—often family members, friends, or partners—to a limited extent, but she also deals with the theoretical underpinnings of memoir itself. In "The Gray Zone," Davidson engages generally with the complexity of nonfiction and in particular with the difficulties she has encountered in writing about her own life.

Beginning with a reference to Patrick Hemingway, editor of his father Ernest Hemingway's *True at First Light*, and with Patrick Hemingway's decision to publish the work as "fictionalized memoir," Davidson asks the question that drives this study: "When a story has its wellspring in life—in actual events and real people—what constitutes a fictional rendering and what constitutes memoir?" In journalism, she suggests, the answer matters "absolutely" because reporters have a responsibility not to "invent, change or embellish the smallest detail." In the "gray zone" where she writes, however, the answer for her (and, presumably, for us) is not so clear:

> When a writer sets out to tell a true story, he immediately finds himself constrained by the fallibility of memory. No one can recall the exact words of a conversation that took place a few days ago, let alone years, even if the writer attempts to recreate the conversation faithfully. In addition, the very process of translating mood, nonverbal signals and emotions into words creates a reality on the page that does not exactly mirror the event in life. But beyond this, the writer makes a deliberate choice as to how much he will permit himself to take liberties.[78]

Ultimately, Davidson argues for what she calls "not a better system of classification" for nonfiction but "full disclosure"[79] by authors themselves.

Dealing with the difference between fiction and nonfiction and between the novel and memoir, Davidson writes in her introduction to *Cowboy* that "at one end of the spectrum are works that are entirely imagined, and at the other end, works that purport to be fact. Most, however, are a blend of

---

[78]Sara Davidson, "The Gray Zone," *Book* (July/August 1999): 49.
[79]Ibid., 50.

fact and imagination, and yet a line has been drawn to separate one from the other."[80] She adds:

> I have long worked in what I perceive as the slippery slope between the two poles, the terrain where we find such entities as the nonfiction novel and the imagined autobiography. In *Loose Change*, published as nonfiction, I wrote about real people and historical events, yet I used fictional techniques—inventing dialogue, rearranging time, and combining scenes for dramatic purpose.
>
> Then it came to me to write the story in my own voice, as I remembered it, which is not the same as the way it occurred. I tried to convey the experience as strongly as I could, and to that end, I began to add elements and imagine things I could not have known by any other means...What has resulted is a book that defies categories—a hybrid—and if that sounds like an elaborate dodge, what I can say is that I'm telling you this story in the best and perhaps the only way I can.[81]

As a journalist and media scholar, Davidson is comfortable working in several genres, including essays, extended nonfiction, screenplays, and other forms, and the more recent *Leap!: What Will We Do with the Rest of Our Lives?* (2007) is a tribute both to her ability to describe her own feelings and to her skills as a reporter. Davidson majored in English at the University of California at Berkeley and received a master's degree in journalism from Columbia University. By the age of twenty-six, she was a freelance magazine writer. Like many literary journalists trained in the study of journalism and literature, Davidson is self-conscious about her craft and deeply invested in conversations about the genre, which is also called the "new reportage," "personal journalism," "intimate journalism," "immersion journalism," etc.

Davidson understands firsthand the difficulties of writing memoir. In *Loose Change*, she writes about intimate aspects of her life. Two women and her ex-husband, who are central characters in her narrative, read the drafts. Although Davidson changed the names of some characters—including those of the two women—people knew who they were. "Suddenly, something that was all right as a manuscript was not all right when it was being read widely and people were responding to it," Davidson said. "There's one scene where

---

[80] Sara Davidson, "Introduction," *Cowboy: A Novel* (New York: HarperCollins, 1999) xi.
[81] Ibid., xii-xiii.

I had a fight with my husband and he slapped me. Well, he started getting crank calls from people who accused him of being a wife beater. It's true, he did slap me. But suddenly he was being vilified, publicly."[82] She adds:

> There were people who read it and thought he was a monster. One of the women would be walking down the street and someone would come up to her and say, "My God, I didn't know you had an abortion in your father's office when you were 16!" Relatives of the family would call in horror that she had exposed this kind of thing about herself and her family.[83]

The man with whom she had lived for seven years thought her descriptions violated his trust: "I wasn't living with you to have it become public knowledge," he said. "We weren't living our life as a research project."[84]

Because *Loose Change* was so hurtful to those portrayed in the novel (even though they had consented), Davidson moved into a kind of disguised memoir when she wrote *Cowboy*. Davidson said:

> What bothered me was that I had caused pain to other people, to my husband, to the women, who went through hell. People say knowing it was about real people heightened their appreciation and relationship to it. They preferred that it was nonfiction. But I do know I would never, never write again so intimately about my life because I can't separate my life from the people who have been in it.[85]

Acknowledging that the women in *Loose Change* had signed releases, Davidson said the fact made it legal for her to use the material, but "emotionally and morally, it's not always so clear cut."[86] Davidson altered her point of view and better protected her subjects by the time she wrote *Cowboy*. In *Cowboy*, she changed names and events to protect those about whom she wrote. Also, she included an author's note:

> This book is based on a true story—a love affair I've had with the character whom I call Zack. For reasons of privacy, however, I have placed

---

[82]Sims, "The Literary Journalists," 19.
[83]Ibid., 20.
[84]Ibid.
[85]Ibid.
[86]Ibid., 21.

this story in a fictional context. I've created imaginary characters for the heroine's extended family...No relationship should be inferred between these characters in the book and any living persons, nor should incidents about them be taken as fact.[87]

Like Davidson, John Berendt, author of *Midnight in the Garden of Good and Evil*, addresses the intrinsic perils of writing a nonfiction novel, although, unlike Davidson, his analysis does not involve memoir. Murder is at the center of Berendt's tale of Savannah, Georgia, as it is with *In Cold Blood*. The critics who reviewed *Midnight in the Garden of Good and Evil*—and later the film by the same name—struggled to find a category into which the two texts would fit neatly. The book has been called a travelogue, a travel book, a tale of real-life murder, a diary, a character sketch, a cultural study, and an allegory. One of the reviewers, Ken Ringle, cites both a library administrator and a relative of composer Johnny Mercer (Mercer was a Savannah native, and he and his music are prominent in the book and film). "Berendt acknowledges he changed some names for legal reasons and altered some sequences for readability, but that doesn't bother anyone here," Ringle writes. "They know he got things right." Ringle quotes Irma Harlan, the director of Savannah's regional library, who said, "In a strange way this book is a kind of celebration of Savannah. I believe he likes us." Elizabeth Mercer Hammond adds, "I want you to know I've enjoyed your book. I'd never heard that story about my brother's drinking, but then it might be true. I'm not one to spoil a story when the truth might be less amusing."[88]

Other critics and residents were not so lenient. Some were concerned that the book was neither fiction nor nonfiction. Others were concerned that Berendt treated some conversations and events as fact when they had simply been described to him by others. His contribution to the debate is in the form of an "Author's Note" at the end of the nonfiction novel. It reads:

All the characters in this book are real, but it bears mentioning that I have used pseudonyms for a number of them in order to protect their privacy. Though this is a work of nonfiction, I have taken certain storytelling liberties, particularly having to do with the timing of events. Where the narrative strays from strict nonfiction, my intention has

---

[87]Sara Davidson, author's note, *Cowboy: A Novel* (New York: HarperCollins, 1999) n.p.

[88]Ken Ringle, "Just Savannah Good Time," *Washington Post*, 24 February 1994, C1.

been to remain faithful to the characters and to the essential drift of events as they really happened.[89]

The debate about the veracity of *Midnight in the Garden of Good and Evil* and its nearly unprecedented "Author's Note" continue, but whatever its mixture of fact and fiction, Berendt's book brings to life a city of mystery and beauty. A Harvard graduate, Berendt has been an editor for *Esquire* and *New York Magazine*, and the fact that his bestseller about the Deep South was penned by a "Yankee" continues to intrigue his readers. Comparing *Midnight in the Garden of Good and Evil* to *In Cold Blood*, some critics challenge Berendt's description of his book as a nonfiction novel. *Midnight in the Garden of Good and Evil* is most certainly a murder mystery and what Justine Elias calls a "literary travelogue."[90]

Romping through the history of creative nonfiction illuminates the ways Capote participated in a tradition as old as Daniel Defoe and found himself—willingly or not—in the company of James Agee, Charles Dickens, Lillian Ross, John Steinbeck, Mark Twain, and others. Literary journalists from Willa Cather to Stephen Crane to Ernest Hemingway to Roger Rosenblatt share Capote's fascination with literature based on news events and the potential for making real life resonate for readers. If anything, Capote too often minimized the possibilities that daily events provide by treating journalism as a "horizontal form" and initially misunderstanding the ways in which it—like fiction—could go deeply into "context and behavior."[91] Like Sara Davidson, Joan Didion, Norman Mailer, Susan Orlean, Hunter S. Thompson, Tom Wolfe, and other giants in American literary journalism, Capote drew from and contributed to a genre far greater than he could have known at the time he published *In Cold Blood*.

Like those who came before him and those who would follow, Capote plumbed the depths of allegory and other signification systems long familiar to writers of fiction. Literary techniques such as description, dialogue, and narration never belonged exclusively to fiction, and with the 1973 publication of *The New Journalism*, Wolfe upended conventional notions about news-based storytelling. As Scholes suggests earlier in this chapter, "fact" and "fiction" are artificial constructs, part of a continuum of engaging narra-

---

[89]John Berendt, "Author's Note," *Midnight in the Garden of Good and Evil* (New York: Vintage, 1994) n.p.

[90]Justine Elias, "After Midnight," *US* (December 1997): 94.

[91]Thomson, "Rereading."

tive opportunities. Like Davidson, Capote lived and worked in "The Gray Zone," although he did not live long enough to continue his investigation into nonfiction or to know her work. Had he lived past the age of fifty-nine, he might have been more willing to consider himself part of a new movement—one that exploded in the 1970s—and was at least in part the result of *In Cold Blood* and the fires it ignited.

Ultimately, discussions about genres of literature pale in comparison to the experience of an evening in Bonaventure Cemetery—with the possibility of seeing ghosts and hearing tales told at twilight—or a visit to Holcomb, Kansas, surrounded by sky and endless fields of wheat. The ability to introduce thousands of readers to Savannah and Holcomb—and to hold their attention and encourage them to explore unfamiliar worlds—does not forgive a failure to adhere to the truth, to, in Berendt's case, change names and alter chronology and, in Capote's case, to create scenes and pretend to memorize hours of complex dialogue. Yet *Midnight in the Garden of Good and Evil* and *In Cold Blood* are American classics and tales of murder at the center of discussions about extended nonfiction, literary techniques, and the borderland between fiction and nonfiction. They are masterful works of creative nonfiction and literary journalism that lure readers into an imaginative universe they are unlikely to forget.

Chapter 3

In Cold Blood, Handcarved Coffins, and "Then It All Came Down"

Truman Capote published numerous examples of reportage, including novellas, profiles, and travel sketches. Although none of them gained the attention that *In Cold Blood* did, two—*Handcarved Coffins* and "The Duke in His Domain," a portrait of Marlon Brando—are widely anthologized. The challenges Capote encountered in writing and marketing *In Cold Blood* did nothing to dissuade him from continuing to explore nonfiction. *The Muses Are Heard*, first published in *The New Yorker* in 1956, immersed readers in the experience of the Everyman Opera Company as its members performed *Porgy and Bess* in the Soviet Union, and the piece established Capote's commitment to prose based on actual events. Published after *In Cold Blood*, the two texts at the heart of this chapter are based on true stories and actual people; furthermore, like Capote's magnum opus, they reflect his continued interest in murder.

As discussed in chapter one ("The Enduring Popularity of *In Cold Blood*") and chapter two ("*In Cold Blood* and American Literary Journalism"), Capote expressed an interest in nonfiction early in his career. In "The Shadows in Truman Capote's Early Stories," Hilton Als quotes the author, who kept a journal that included "descriptions of a neighbor" and "local gossip." Capote tells Als about "a kind of reporting, a style of 'seeing' and 'hearing' that would later seriously influence me, though I was unaware of it then," and adds that most of his work "was more or less fictional." Given the publication of *The Muses Are Heard*, *In Cold Blood*, and the pieces included in this chapter, Als finds Capote's "reportorial voice" especially significant:

> When Capote began publishing his nonfiction writing in the mid- to late 1940s, fiction writers rarely if ever crossed over into journalism—it was considered a lesser form, despite its importance to early masters of the English novel, such as Daniel Defoe and Charles Dickens, both of whom had started off as reporters.... In short, it was rare for a modern writer of fiction to give up its relative freedoms for journalism's strictures, but I think Capote always loved the tension inherent in cheating

the truth. He always wanted to elevate reality above the flatness of facts.[1]

The first chapters of this study take Als's perspective seriously, placing *In Cold Blood* into various historical, literary, and philosophical contexts in order to highlight its contributions. Chapter two locates *In Cold Blood* among classics in creative nonfiction, specifically literary journalism, suggesting that Capote had an uncomfortable relationship with facts—often compromising them in the interest of what he considered a larger truth. Most authors trained as journalists would, of course, argue that accuracy is essential to nonfiction; nonetheless, because Capote was a masterful stylist, it became difficult to discredit *In Cold Blood*, although most critics and readers—then and now—treat it as a novel based on fact. In other words, *In Cold Blood* remains an example of the possibilities of nonfiction at the same time that it is lambasted for its violations of the sacred tenets of journalism.

Unfortunately, unlike John Berendt, Sara Davidson, and other literary journalists whose work is explored in the previous chapter, Capote did not appear interested in disclaimers or full disclosure. His war with the facts is even more pronounced in *Handcarved Coffins: A Nonfiction Account of an American Crime*—a novella that was for many years on track to become a major motion picture—than it is in *In Cold Blood*. The fact that Capote was not a journalist and had not been trained in the ethics or history of journalism makes his reluctance to adhere to the truth understandable but, nonetheless, deeply disappointing. Even more disappointing is his lack of concern for truth-telling, his repeated avoidance of the issue, and his failure to adjust his perspective on the importance of facts. In one interview, Als asks Capote if he is a truthful person. Capote replies, "As a writer—yes, I think so. Privately—well, that is a matter of opinion; some of my friends think that when relating an event or piece of news, I am inclined to alter and overelaborate. Myself, I just call it making something 'come alive.' In other words, a form of art. Art and truth are not necessarily compatible bedfellows."[2] It is easy for Capote's admirers to view such statements as representative of the articulate charm that characterized him, but these statements also point to his discomfort with adhering to the truth when doing so might damage a good story.

---

[1] Hilton Als, "The Shadows in Truman Capote's Early Stories," *The New Yorker*, 13 October 2015, web (accessed 4 August 2018).
[2] Ibid.

First serialized in Andy Warhol's *Interview* magazine, *Handcarved Coffins* became part of the Capote collection *Music for Chameleons* in 1980. Over the years, according to Anthony P. Montesano in "The Film That Never Was," at least two teams showed an interest in making *Handcarved Coffins* into a film. One group included producer Lester Persky (*Taxi Driver, Shampoo*), director Hal Ashby (*Coming Home, In the Heat of the Night*), and actor Jack Nicholson (*As Good as It Gets, One Flew Over the Cuckoo's Nest, The Shining*); another, producer Dino De Laurentiis (*Hannibal, Serpico*) and directors Michael Cimino (*Deer Hunter*) and David Lynch (*Blue Velvet, Mulholland Drive*). As late as 2003, Montesano said film company Filmauro considered the novella for the big screen. British journalists Peter and Leni Gillman convincingly summarized the allure of *Handcarved Coffins*. The novella was successful, spending sixteen weeks on *The New York Times* nonfiction bestseller list, while the movie rights sold for $350,000. A review in *The Washington Post* called it "quite simply stunning." John Fowles said it was as "grippingly readable" as *In Cold Blood*. The *Tennessean* said Capote had "elevated reportage" to the level of "lyricism." The *San Francisco Chronicle* said he had reached the "peak of his creative and reportorial powers."[3]

This chapter confirms Capote's abiding interest in murders and the people who commit them. In both *Handcarved Coffins* and "Then It All Came Down," Capote revisits what drew him to the subject matter of *In Cold Blood* and to the criminal mind. By the time he published these works in 1979, however, his genius was in decline and a certain panic seemed to be setting in. He had not achieved with *In Cold Blood* what he had hoped—never winning the Pulitzer Prize—and his alcohol and drug use were escalating. In addition, after Capote's publication of several essays about the New York elite, some of his friends turned away from him. Lonely, angry, and determined to reestablish his literary presence, Capote turned his gaze toward murders in "a town in a small Western state"[4] and a series of murders in California in 1969, specifically a crime committed July 27, 1969, by a convicted murderer named Robert Kenneth (Bobby) Beausoleil. In the former, he played faster and looser with the truth than he had with *In Cold Blood*. In the latter, he seemed once again to fall under the spell of a convicted killer, although to a far lesser extent.

---

[3]Peter and Leni Gillman, "Hoax: Secrets That Truman Capote Took to the Grave," *Longform Reprints*, June 1992, web (accessed 4 August 2018).

[4]Truman Capote, *Handcarved Coffins*, in *Truman Capote: A Capote Reader* (New York: Penguin, 2002) 463.

As with *In Cold Blood*, the two texts included here appealed to a broad audience. *Handcarved Coffins* captivated readers, reassured Capote's editors, and appeared to be the antidote to Capote's fear of failure. Not everyone celebrated *Music for Chameleons*. An unnamed reviewer introduces his or her review of the collection by calling it a "distressingly thin and uneven new collection from a man who's clearly been having a terrible time at the type-writer," although the reviewer claims that *Handcarved Coffins* "rises above" the rest of the book, calling it a "ghoulishly outlandish (supposedly true) sto-ry."[5] Christopher Lehmann-Haupt, too, acknowledges *Handcarved Coffins* and "Then It All Came Down" as bright spots in the collection, calling the latter a "remarkable interview."[6]

The study of literary journalism in chapter two provides significant context for an exploration of *Handcarved Coffins* and "Then It All Came Down," which Capote considered nonfiction. Chapter three places *In Cold Blood* alongside a novella and an essay that Capote included in *Music for Chameleons*, a collection of fiction and nonfiction; in fact, in *Truman Capote: A Capote Reader*, both the novella and the interview are listed with *The Muses Are Heard* in a section titled "Reportage." Divided into three sections, *Music for Chameleons* begins with six short stories: "Music for Chameleons," "Mr. Jones," "A Lamp in a Window," "Mojave," "Hospitality," and "Dazzle." The second section includes only *Handcarved Coffins*, which Capote described in a subtitle as *A Nonfiction Account of an American Crime*. The connection of the novella to *In Cold Blood* is obvious, although the two works are distinctly different in style, purpose, and content. The third section, titled "Conversa-tional Portraits," highlights Capote's encounters and interviews with Willa Cather, Marilyn Monroe, and other well-known figures in entertainment, literature, and politics. Of particular interest in this section is Capote's inter-view with Beausoleil, who was a member of the Charles Manson crime family, although he was in prison before the horrific murder of pregnant actress Sharon Tate and four others at her home on August 9, 1969. The essays that make up "Conversational Portraits" include "A Day's Work," "Hello, Stranger," "Hidden Gardens," "Derring-do," "Then It All Came Down," "A Beautiful Child," and "Nocturnal Turnings."

---

[5]*"Music for Chameleons," Kirkus Reviews*, 10 October 2011, web (accessed 4 August 2018).

[6]Christopher Lehmann-Haupt, "Books of *The Times*," *The New York Times*, 5 August 1980, web (accessed 4 August 2018).

Handcarved Coffins: A Nonfiction Account of an American Crime *(1979)*

In the preface to *Music for Chameleons*, dedicated to Tennessee Williams, Capote clarified why he chose nonfiction and remained committed to resurrecting historical figures such as Perry Edward Smith and Richard Eugene Hickock of *In Cold Blood* and Robert Hawley (Bob) Quinn, a pseudonym for a suspected murderer in *Handcarved Coffins*. Discussing *In Cold Blood*, Capote said:

> For several years I had been increasingly drawn toward journalism as an art form in itself. I had two reasons. First, it didn't seem to me that anything truly innovative had occurred in prose writing, or in writing generally, since the 1920s; second, journalism as art was almost virgin terrain, for the simple reason that very few literary artists ever wrote narrative journalism, and when they did, it took the form of travel essays or autobiography. *The Muses Are Heard* had set me to thinking on different lines altogether: I wanted to produce a journalistic novel, something on a large scale that would have the credibility of fact, the immediacy of film, the depth and freedom of prose, and the precision of poetry.[7]

In Capote's novella *Handcarved Coffins*, Quinn, owner of the B.Q. Ranch, is an Ahab figure, obsessed by the river that irrigates his property and makes possible his wealth. Certain of his superiority and infallibility, Quinn becomes concerned about the townspeople who want to irrigate their own farms and ranches and water their livestock. Unwilling to share, Quinn begins to threaten his neighbors, anonymously mailing photographs of his intended victims inside small, handcarved, balsam coffins. After receiving a tiny coffin, the first two victims confront nine rattlesnakes in their car and die from the venom. Two others, who are trapped in their basement, are burned alive. Driving his Jeep near his house, a rancher is decapitated by a wire stretched across the road at neck height. The coroner is poisoned, and a teacher drowns mysteriously while her sister sits nearby. Another moves to Hawaii to avoid an attack. The final committee member, who had voted in Quinn's favor, survives. The two central characters in the short novel come together to solve the crimes: Detective Jake Pepper, a tragic hero reminiscent

---

[7]Truman Capote, "Preface to *Music for Chameleons*," *Truman Capote: A Capote Reader* (New York: Penguin, 2002) 719.

of Alvin A. Dewey in *In Cold Blood*, and "TC," who shares Truman Capote's initials.

Capote never wavered from his assertion that *Handcarved Coffins* was true. As the Gillmans reveal, he told one interviewer that the events were "exactly what happened" and that the novella was "one of my best pieces of reportage."[8] Journalist David Streitfeld's "Capote's 'Coffins'" is one of the most insightful essays about the novella. It begins, "There's always something delicious about the unmasking of a hoax." Streitfeld was responding to an article in London's *Sunday Times* and its claim that it had "unraveled a big one." At issue in the newspaper review and Streitfeld's essay was *Handcarved Coffins*, which Streitfeld described as the "centerpiece story" of Capote's 1980 collection, *Music for Chameleons*. Streitfeld quotes *The Times* review and then calls *Handcarved Coffins* "a bit of a fraud itself." *The Times* review states:

> Truman Capote's towering genius was the non-fiction novel, in which real-life events were religiously observed in molten narrative form...Or so the world believed. Capote's last great work was a stunning account of a series of bizarre and unsolved murders. But when the Sunday Times went in search of the killer, a literary lie born of torment and desperation was uncovered.[9]

Streitfeld then writes:

> Unfortunately, this story of Capote's fraud is a bit of a fraud itself. To discover that "Hand-Carved Coffins" [sic] is more creative than reportorial, you don't need to spend a couple of weeks in the Midwest searching for the windblown town that the writer (who died in 1984) hid under a pseudonym. Merely open Gerald Clarke's authoritative 1988 work, *Capote: A Biography*, to page 516. "Mostly fictional," Clarke writes of "Coffins," adding that Capote's "homespun detective was not a real person, but a composite of several lawmen he had known."[10]

In his article "In Search of the Real Truman Capote," Jonathan Russell Clark celebrates *Handcarved Coffins* as a "companion piece" to *In Cold Blood*

---

[8] Peter and Leni Gillman, "Hoax."

[9] David Streitfeld, "Capote's 'Coffins,'" *The Washington Post*, 19 July 1992, web (accessed 5 August 2018).

[10] Ibid.

and calls it a "fascinating yarn filled with mysteries." However, although Clark supports Capote's decision to create a narrator that makes it sound "as if the reader is right there in the room with him," he calls "TC" a "fictitious counterpart, a character of his own devising": "Capote is *performing* here," he writes, "presenting himself as a calm and collected sleuth, as if researching and writing *In Cold Blood* had made him an expert on crime." Clark is more forgiving than the Gillmans, certainly more forgiving than many scholars of literary journalism and the nonfiction novel. His compassion is rooted in his perspective on Capote himself, whom he perceives as a damaged artist desperate to save his literary legacy:

> He had become a pathetic figure in the years following the publication of *In Cold Blood*, and as his misery compounded, he sought to channel it by putting himself into his writing. Only in such a position—that is, writing himself into a narrative that was obviously fictional, somehow both inside the story and out of it—could Capote thrive and confront himself in a way he couldn't seem to in reality.[11]

To say that journalists do not create composites, make up facts, or violate the tenets of their profession would be ludicrous; however, when they are caught—and *The Washington Post* famously caught Janet Cooke; *The New York Times* caught Jayson Blair, Michael Finkel, Zachery Kouwe, and others; and the *New Republic* caught Stephen Glass—they are punished, usually losing any opportunity to return to their chosen career. In the case of Truman Capote, of course, his genius serves as his best defense, as does the fact that he was not trained as a journalist and did not practice journalism. However, his mere fascination with nonfiction, as we learned in chapter one, is not a compelling excuse for the shortcuts he took to pursue what he called reportage. As Streitfeld notes, biographer Gerald Clarke wasn't the first or only person to catch Capote in an exaggeration, fabrication, or lie. In 1981, David Lodge reviewed *Music for Chameleons* for the *Times Literary Supplement* of London, arguing that "no intelligent reader would believe that 'Hand-Carved Coffins' [sic] was a true story for a moment if it were not subtitled 'a non-fiction account of an American crime' and described as a 'true story' by its publishers."[12] In short, it is difficult to make public Ca-

---

[11]Jonathan Russell Clark, "In Search of the Real Truman Capote," *The Atlantic*, 10 September 2015, web (accessed 5 August 2018).

[12]Streitfeld, "Capote's 'Coffins.'"

pote's untrustworthiness while extolling the virtues of *In Cold Blood* and *Handcarved Coffins*, although this study, *Untold Stories, Unheard Voices*, walks that line.

Capote promised that *Answered Prayers* would surprise the literary world, although it was published posthumously and was incomplete. Instead of finishing *Answered Prayers*, Capote went back to Kansas for his subject matter, relying on a story Dewey once told him about one of his cases. Dewey consulted with Capote about compiling a book based on his lifetime of work in the sheriff's department and as a detective for the Kansas Bureau of Investigation. One of his stories involved a man named Richard J. Anton, who found a rattlesnake in his car and—after the police failed to charge anyone with this and several other crimes against him—was shot to death with his wife Clara Ann Anton in a barricaded basement. The couple and the house were then incinerated. Eventually, a man as different from Quinn as it was possible to be was interrogated about the crime, although he was not charged. "The suspect in the Anton case was not a vengeful rancher but Hilton Wade, a farmhand whom Anton senior had evicted and who was notorious for setting fires," writes Peter Gillman. "Wade denied killing the Antons and passed a lie-detector test. Any forensic evidence...had been obliterated by firefighters and although Dewey and his team spent a week sifting the ashes they found nothing."[13] Gillman concludes that Capote "elaborated" on the Anton case, "blending fact and fiction under the cloak of anonymity."[14]

Indeed, Capote edited the story for *Handcarved Coffins*—adding other victims of other crimes—and incorporated another story Dewey had told him about a small balsam coffin that was sent to frighten someone. Without flinching, Streitfeld writes:

> What should be made of all this? First, now that "Coffins" is no longer the piece of fine reportage many believed it was when it was first published, it's only a so-so piece of fiction. Contradictions and implausibilities that were acceptable because this was real life are now simply unbelievable. Second, Capote—a writer who always displayed more promise than achievement—seems even more pathetic.[15]

---

[13]Peter Gillman, "The Truth about Truman Capote," *The Sunday Times*, 17 February 2013, web (accessed 5 August 2018).

[14]Ibid.

[15]Streitfeld, "Capote's 'Coffins.'"

Streitfeld then quotes Capote biographer Gerald Clarke, who, after minimizing the charge of a "hoax," agrees with Streitfeld and others critical of the novella:

> Truman's mistake was claiming the story was totally accurate, which he felt he had to do. He claimed he had invented this new art form of the nonfiction novel, and then for the rest of his life felt he had to defend it. Whereas what he was doing was quite brilliant as fiction. He was doing what a fiction writer should do—bringing together various strains of truth and fancy and creating a work of art.[16]

Of particular interest is a 1992 *Sunday Times* article in which Peter and Leni Gillman reveal their conclusions about the authenticity of *Handcarved Coffins*. The two confirm that there was not a series of murders in any town in America that included the murderer sending small coffins or killing people by using rattlesnakes or other means described in the novella; however, they confirmed that the case strongly resembled one supervised by detective Dewey, whose role in investigating the Clutter murders is discussed at length in chapter one. The case involved the murders of Richard J. and Clara Ann Anton of Ensign, Kansas. The Gillmans conclude that the novella relates a compelling but fraudulent tale:

> It took me just a week in Kansas to prove that Capote's claims for *Hand-Carved Coffins* [sic] were false...The Anton case, it was clear, had merely served as the starting point for a blend of fact and fiction, reportage and fantasy...There was no decapitation, poisoning, or mysterious drowning; no rancher named Quinn or anything else, and no hand-carved coffins. Far from being "a non-fiction account of an American crime," as Capote claimed, it stood exposed as a literary hoax.[17]

Before the Gillmans left Kansas, Peter Gillman met with journalist Dolores Hope, who worked with Dewey and wanted to help him write a book about his most interesting cases, both solved and unsolved. She documented that in addition to the Anton murders, Dewey had investigated a case that involved sending "crude" small coffins. She suggested that Capote had "be-

---

[16]Ibid.
[17]Peter and Leni Gillman, "Hoax."

come unable to distinguish fact from fiction" and said Dewey told her, "Why didn't the little bastard say it was a story—why did he have to say it was true?"[18]

According to the novella itself, *Handcarved Coffins* is set somewhere in the American West in 1975. Asked directly on several occasions, Capote said the events in his novella had occurred in Nebraska. Although the ominous description of a nameless town is eerily reminiscent of Holcomb, Kansas, the actual town is Ensign, Kansas, only sixty miles away from River Valley Farm and the Clutter murders. Capote describes a place that is the "focus for the many large farms and cattle-raising ranches surrounding it," a town "with a population of less than ten thousand" that "supports twelve churches and two restaurants": "A movie house, though it had not shown a movie in ten years, still stands stark and cheerless on Main Street. There once was a hotel, too; but that also has been closed, and nowadays the only place a traveler can find shelter is the Prairie Motel."[19] The focal point of the ranch war that ensues is the Blue River, which forks into "Big Brother" and "Little Brother." Capote writes:

> The trouble started because of these tributaries. Many ranchers, who were dependent on them, felt that a diversion should be created in Blue River to enlarge Big Brother and Little Brother. Naturally, the ranchers whose property was nourished by the main river were against this proposition. None more so than Bob Quinn, owner of the B.Q. Ranch, through which the widest and deepest stretches of Blue River travels.[20]

Eventually playing chess with one another, Pepper and Quinn develop an uncomfortable relationship; in fact, the competition itself symbolizes the mind games that engage Pepper and Quinn. Quinn sits in his palatial home planning his next atrocity against his neighbors. Pepper makes his home at the Prairie Motel, "on the wintry, windblown outskirts of this forlorn little Western town," writes Capote. "Actually, the room was pleasant, cozy; after all, off and on, it had been Jake's home for almost five years."[21] Before Quinn's war concludes, George and Amelia Roberts, Roy Baxter, Clem and Amy Anderson, Ed Parsons, Tom Henry, Oliver Jaeger, and Addie Mason

---

[18]Ibid.
[19]Capote, *Handcarved Coffins*, 463.
[20]Ibid., 478.
[21]Ibid., 464.

will be dead: two are bitten in their automobile by rattlesnakes injected with amphetamines, two are incinerated with their houseguests in the basement of their home, and one is decapitated. As Capote notes, there are nine reptiles from a snake farm in Nogales, Texas, that attack Roberts and his wife, and, eventually, there will be nine dead townspeople. The coincidence would be fascinating if nine rattlesnakes—and the rest of the story—were true. Capote creates convincing detail in the course of perpetrating fraud. In his discussion of the characters George and Amelia Roberts, he adds a parenthetical note:

> (What I found inside the box was a miniature coffin. It was a beautifully made object, carved from light balsam wood. It was undecorated; but when one opened the hinged lid one discovered the coffin was not empty. It contained a photograph—a casual, candid snapshot of two middle-aged people, a man and a woman, crossing a street. It was not a posed picture; one sensed that the subjects were unaware that they were being photographed.)[22]

Capote's "melancholy village"[23] invites the reader into the text in the same way that the "village" of Holcomb on the "high wheat plains of western Kansas"[24] did in *In Cold Blood*. Quinn, a charming, narcissistic, powerful landowner, becomes an allegorical figure looming over the town. Quoting Mark Twain, Pepper makes clear his perspective on Quinn and much of humankind: "Of all the creatures that were made, man is the most *detestable*. Of the entire brood he is the only one, the solitary one, that possesses malice. That is the basest of all instincts, passions, vices—the most hateful. He is the only creature that inflicts pain for sport, knowing it to *be* pain."[25] In an interview with Lawrence Grobel, Capote said he agreed with Twain:

> I think it's true. There's no other living creature that's as wicked as man. I mean, animals never do the detestable, horrible things that human beings do. Can you imagine animals creating concentration camps and torturing people to death? Or, for that matter, can you imagine an-

---

[22]Ibid., 464.
[23]Ibid., 511.
[24]Truman Capote, *In Cold Blood: A True Account of a Multiple Murder and Its Consequences* (New York: Random House, 1965) 3.
[25]Capote, *Handcarved Coffins*, 471.

imals with a capital-punishment law running through the gorilla family?[26]

Like *In Cold Blood*, *Handcarved Coffins* relies on setting and a portrait of a murderer to engage the reader, although, obviously, Capote is more drawn to Perry Smith than to a wiser and more calculating Quinn. The fact that *Handcarved Coffins* is most decidedly not a "nonfiction account of an American crime"—any more than *In Cold Blood* is a "true account of a multiple murder and its consequences"—does not seem to affect Capote, whose focus appears to be on writing compelling tales about God-fearing people in the grip of a horror they cannot comprehend.

Unlike in *In Cold Blood*, Capote visibly intrudes in *Handcarved Coffins*, making himself a fictional character at the center of the tale of mayhem and murder. In doing so, he violates what had been one of his most sacred practices. In "Preface to *Music for Chameleons*," Capote explains his change of heart:

> From a technical point, the greatest difficulty I'd had in writing *In Cold Blood* was leaving myself completely out of it. Ordinarily, the reporter has to use himself as a character, an eyewitness observer, in order to retain credibility. But I felt that it was essential to the seemingly detached tone of that book that the author should be absent. Actually, in all my reportage, I had tried to keep myself as invisible as possible.[27]

Capote learned a few details while talking to Alvin A. Dewey about his cases, but he was no more present in the events in *Handcarved Coffins* than he was in the final scene of his earlier crime novel. Capote inserts a memory of being involuntarily baptized by a minister whom he clearly loathes: "(The kiss dissolved; the Reverend's face, receding, was replaced by a face virtually identical. So it was in Alabama, some fifty years earlier, that I had first seen Mr. Quinn. At any rate, his counterpart: Bobby Joe Snow, evangelist)."[28] The memory may or may not be true. If it is, then Capote has intruded upon a fictional tale. If it is not, then it is "TC" who remembers the baptism. Either way, the comparison between Quinn and Snow compels the reader to

---

[26]Lawrence Grobel, *Conversations with Capote* (New York: New American Library, 1985) 107.
[27]Capote, "Preface to *Music for Chameleons*," 722.
[28]Capote, *Handcarved Coffins*, 495-96.

trust the narrator and to accept his perspective on the crime, the perpetrator, and the townspeople.

Interestingly, Capote's descriptions of weather and the landscape both set the tone and reveal more about "TC" and his moods, again encouraging the reader to identify with the narrator. A few examples follow. Capote was not present, so the descriptions are fictional; however, the scenes are particularly potent:

> I remembered the last time I had traveled this territory: the full moon, the fields of snow, the cutting cold, the cattle banded together, gathered in groups, their warm breath smoking the arctic air. Now, in October, the landscape was gloriously different: the macadam highway was like a skinny black sea dividing a golden continent; on either side, the sun-bleached stubble of threshed wheat flamed, rippled with yellow colors, sable shadows under a cloudless sky. Bulls pranced about these pastures; and cows, among them mothers with new calves, grazed, dozed.[29]

In a series of descriptions set off by parentheses, the reader again learns what "TC" remembers. Each excerpt reveals not only an interior observation but an external vista that reinforces tone. In the first example, what might be a beautiful winter tableau is instead hideous and terrifying:

> (Outside, crusts of snow laced the ground; spring was a long way off—a hard wind whipping the window announced that winter was still with us. But the sound of the wind was only a murmur in my head underneath the racket of rattling rattlesnakes, hissing tongues. I saw the car dark under a hot sun, the swirling serpents, the human heads growing green, expanding with poison. I listened to the wind, letting it wipe the scene away.)[30]

Similarly, the next excerpt reveals a lonely town filled with people suspicious of one another, much like Holcomb, Kansas, after four shots rang out at the Clutter farmhouse in the middle of the night. In *Handcarved Coffins,* Pepper and "TC" maintain their silence, focusing on their own thoughts: "(It was a heavy snow, thick flakes too heavy to float...Main Street was gray and white

---

[29]Ibid., 511.
[30]Ibid., 465.

and empty, lifeless except for a solitary traffic light winking its colors. Everything was closed, even the Okay Café. The somberness, the gloomy snow-silence, infected us; neither of us spoke.)"[31] Later, Pepper, "TC," and two sisters enjoy each other's company, safe in a quiet house: "(In the distance the caged canaries sang, and snow, fluttering at the windows like torn lace curtains, emphasized the comforts of the room, the warmth of the fire, the redness of the wine").[32]

As in *In Cold Blood*, *Handcarved Coffins* hints always at what is to come. Death is as unexpected as it is inevitable, and no matter how many times Pepper says he will protect the woman he loves, the reader takes seriously the haunting scenes and the ruminations of the narrator and knows that things will not end well. Early in the murderous tale, the Andersons meet their demise: "And sometime just before dawn one humdinger of a fire broke out in that basement, and the four people were incinerated. I mean that literally: burned to ashes,"[33] states Pepper. Later, Capote describes the despair that envelopes envelops the town in the wake of the murders, suggesting that the "resumption of the snow had prompted thoughts of mortality, the evaporation of time."[34] Again, the entire quotation is enclosed in parentheses, suggesting that Capote is whispering a secret to the reader.

Before it was generally known that *Handcarved Coffins* was not true, literary critics struggled to explicate a story that seemed too strange to believe. In "'Handcarved Coffins' and the Nonfiction Novel," English professor Robert Siegle takes on the phrase "nonfiction novel," which he calls a "tautology," not an "oxymoron."[35] The first misstep may be using *Handcarved Coffins* (or, in fact, *In Cold Blood*) to represent a nonfiction novel. As noted earlier in the study, Capote was not a journalist charged with maintaining accuracy in reporting and writing. Siegle introduces his article by quoting William L. Nance, author of *The Worlds of Truman Capote*, and likens *In Cold Blood* to *Handcarved Coffins*:

> The nonfiction novel makes us uneasy by its apparently oxymoronic nature—its mixing of reality and fiction, of journalist and novelist, of fac-

---

[31]Ibid., 474.
[32]Ibid., 476.
[33]Ibid., 466.
[34]Ibid., 486.
[35]Robert Siegle, "Capote's *Handcarved Coffins* and the Nonfiction Novel," *Contemporary Literature* 25/4 (Winter 1984): 450.

tuality and imagination. Uncomfortable with so indiscrete a mixture, many writers on the subject resolve specific works back into either the novel or nonfiction. William L. Nance, for example, speaks of the "flaws" and "limitations...inherent in the very concept of a nonfiction novel" and concludes that *In Cold Blood* "falls back into a category which may as well be labeled 'documentary novel.'"[36]

Siegle then describes Pepper as the "hermeneutic investigator" and "sleuth"—much, it would seem, as C. Auguste Dupin serves Edgar Allan Poe in his detective stories—and "TC" as his "scribe." Herein, of course, lies one of the problems with any analysis that takes Capote at his word with respect to a "nonfiction account," a problem compounded by the fact that neither Siegle nor Nance is a media scholar. Analyzing Pepper as a fictional character who serves as a "sleuth"—without knowing that Pepper is a fictional representation of a living KBI detective—and regarding a fictional character with the initials "TC" as a stand-in for the author himself prevent Siegle and other critics from interpreting the tale as fiction, albeit fiction loosely based on fact. Therefore, readers see through a glass that is doubly dark: *Handcarved Coffins* depends on a story that law enforcement official Alvin A. Dewey told Capote, a story that at least two journalists who investigated the case suggest Dewey intended to include in a book of his own. Leni and Peter Gillman argue that Capote appropriated, fictionalized, and then—either straightforwardly or playfully—assembled facts from several of Dewey's cases into what is essentially a fictional whodunit. The subtitles of *In Cold Blood* and *Handcarved Coffins*—*A True Account of Multiple Murder and Its Consequences* and *A Nonfiction Account of an American Crime*, respectively—confuse both readers and critics such as Siegle and Nance and serve to protect Capote from charges of literary fraud.

In short, nonfiction does not allow for the appropriation of another person's story—wholesale or in parts—without crediting that person, nor does it move without consequence between what is imagined and what occurred. Professors of English may explore the role of Truman Capote as "TC" less judgmentally than practitioners of journalism, but ultimately, Capote is an illusionist—brilliant and seductive, yes, but an illusionist. As Capote constructs an outlandish but mesmerizing tale, he tricks a reader with promises of accounts that are "true" and that meet the standards of "nonfiction." Analyzing *Handcarved Coffins*, then, becomes a trip down a rabbit

---

[36]Ibid., 437.

hole. For example, Siegle takes "TC" to be Truman Capote himself, leading to unsupported statements: "Jake, a detective and a friend of Capote's, is one narrator worth comment," Siegle writes. "He selects the case for the character 'TC' as 'something that he thought might interest' a novelist, and he draws on his own literary tastes (Dickens, Trollope, Melville, and Twain are mentioned) to present matters to TC."[37] But, of course, the fictional detective in *Handcarved Coffins*, whose name is Jake, is not a "friend of Capote's," unless Jake is actually Alvin Dewey and "TC" is Capote.

Siegle then describes "TC" as the "ideal reader" for Jake, with "TC" "co-creating in his imagination the scene Jake outlines."[38] Creating a reliable reader or interpreter is a common and quite reputable fictional device, but, again, Capote makes such a connection problematic. In fact, neither Jake Pepper nor "TC" is an authentic narrator: "Lest we neglect our hermeneutic responsibilities, TC prods us from time to time by rendering facts as clues: 'There were nine snakes. And nine members of the Blue River Committee. Nice quaint coincidence.'"[39] Because Siegle appears unaware that "TC" is a creation, not Truman Capote himself, he inadvertently helps Capote get away with his literary scam. As we shall see in the analysis of the cases Alvin Dewey actually investigated, there were not nine snakes (only one), they had not been injected with amphetamines, and there were not nine members of a Blue River Committee; in fact, there was no such committee in a dispute that involved land, not water. Siegle argues correctly that "TC exploits fictional narrators too, as it turns out," adding:

> He paces his story as much like the omniscient novelist as Jake does; he finally remembers at one point of whom Quinn reminds him, but won't tell us until the time is ripe...And he makes good use of Dickensian dreams; he speaks of "Addie: her hair tangled in watery undergrowths, drifted, in my dream, across her wavering drowned face like a bridal veil...."[40]

Again, if "TC" is a fictional "scribe," to use Siegel's word, then it is irrelevant whether or not he creates Quinn in the image of a preacher he knew. If, however, "TC" is Truman Capote, then it matters very much indeed and

---

[37]Ibid., 442.
[38]Ibid.
[39]Ibid., 443.
[40]Ibid.

renders *Handcarved Coffins* exactly what it is—fiction that is based on a true story. Literary giant Capote freely appropriates allusions—such as the one suggested by Addie's description—for purposes of his engaging tale, but there was no Addie, and "TC" did not see her, except, perhaps, in a dream.

It is not fair to employ one critic to highlight Capote's journalistic lapses. The temptation results from Siegle's convincing argument, one that any reader who takes Capote at his word might make. If *Handcarved Coffins* is an example of a nonfiction novel—as Capote insists it is—then Siegle's insights are central to an understanding of authentic narrative voice. "But if Jake has indeed not described, but TC imagined, the details...then these cannot be external images at all," writes Siegle. "And if they are made by TC, then he is hardly the neutral, objective, crystal clear window upon them, but rather the opaque colorist or producer of them."[41] Of course, whether "TC" is a fictional character or Truman Capote himself, he is not a "neutral, objective, crystal clear window"; instead, he has accepted Jake Pepper's outlandish tale and retells it—with embellishment and the convenience of dream motifs—as a literary critic might do. To miss the fact that "TC" is not "neutral" or "objective" is to accept imaginary parameters of a fictional tale as fact—and why not? Capote provides a convincing subtitle and leads the reader and the critic into alluring quicksand.

Further complicating analysis is the fact that Capote may intermittently employ "TC" as an autobiographical prop: "Good novel reader that he is, TC keeps looking for the univocal 'key' to Quinn-as-character, finding it finally—or perhaps constructing it finally—by identifying him with a character in his own private psychodrama, the traumatically austere Reverend Snow,"[42] writes Siegle. "On the basis of this identification, TC finds Quinn guilty, seeing him as a sufficiently self-righteous monomaniac to perpetrate the crimes."[43] Employing Reverend Snow—who may be real or fictitious, given Capote's childhood spent in the land of Christian fundamentalism—to represent Quinn makes "TC's" conclusions about Quinn's guilt even more believable. The problem, of course, is that "Quinn" is a pseudonym, "TC" is a fictional character, and "Reverend Snow" may or may not be part of Capote's actual past. None of these issues matters if *Handcarved Coffins* is billed as fiction based on actual events, but it matters a great deal if it is perceived by Siegle and others to be a "nonfiction novel." (Not incidentally, Capote

---

[41]Ibid., 444.
[42]Ibid., 445.
[43]Ibid., 446.

uses a question-answer format in "Then It All Came Down," which is included in *Music for Chameleons*. In that interview, he identifies himself as "TC.")

In conclusion, to describe Capote "as sleuth, as novelist, as nonfiction chronicler, and as personally involved inquirer"[44] misses the point. In truth, he is all of these things. The problem in his assuming myriad shapes is that he employs them all to dupe the reader, to tell a story that did not happen to him—one that he appropriated from a friend who provided information during his research on *In Cold Blood*. Siegle's conclusion, which is that "we discover not the naïve realist's belief that fiction is adequate to reality, but the contrary, that nonfiction is never adequate to reality,"[45] is deeply troubling because it condemns an entire genre—the nonfiction novel—and those who devote themselves to it—with varying degrees of mastery—instead of looking deeply into one author's claims. Capote is, therefore, not held accountable for his ruse, for his disrespect of what is authentic experience, and for his appropriation of "nonfiction" intentionally to misdirect readers and critics and to mischaracterize his actual accomplishment.

There is no question that Joan Didion, Tom Wolfe, and the other masters of literary journalism impose a frame, look through their own interpretive lenses, and sometimes participate in their own stories. But Capote was not a literary journalist, and *In Cold Blood* is an only partially "true account," with *Handcarved Coffins* lagging light years behind it. *Handcarved Coffins* is a purloined tale loosely based on facts that Alvin Dewey shared with a novelist, although this fact does not necessarily discount *In Cold Blood* or *Handcarved Coffins* as literature that is worthy of one's time, even worthy of awe. "Capote's 'invention' of the nonfiction novel is both hoax and ingenious gathering of the full cultural resources into the act of narration,"[46] Siegle concludes. In this assertion, Siegle is entirely correct.

What follows is one of six stories posted on Kansas Trails, a website dedicated to helping genealogists, and excerpts from other news stories. Although all the stories are related to the June 30, 1974, murders of Richard J. and Clara Ann Anton, the first provides the background that inspired Dewey to consider a book about the cases he covered during his career and to discuss them with Capote. Two aspects of the story are especially important: first, the appearance of Dewey and other KBI detectives at the scene

---

[44]Ibid., 449.
[45]Ibid., 450.
[46]Ibid., 451.

of the Anton murders and, second, the similarities between the Antons and the Clutters. Both families were hard-working members of local Methodist churches and were invested in their communities and their families; in fact, in a *Salina Journal* story that appeared July 3, 1974, a woman in the town said of the Antons, "They were real nice ordinary type people. Those kinds of things happen in big cities. We just don't live that way around here."[47] The same might have been said about Herbert, Bonnie, Kenyon, and Nancy Clutter.

The following story from the *Salina Journal* published July 2, 1974, supports claims by the Gillmans that indicate how much Capote borrowed from Dewey while composing *Handcarved Coffins* (The story is presented here after being edited for capitalization, punctuation, and other inconsistencies. Content is not altered.):

ENSIGN—"I think we've got a dual murder," Gray County Attorney Jay Don Reynolds said as he probed for clues Monday in the deaths of a man and woman in a burned-out farm home 6 miles southwest of here.

The woman has been identified as Mrs. Clara Anton. The body of the man is presumed to be that of her husband, Richard. The farm home belonged to the Antons.

Earlier in the day, gunshot wounds had been discovered in the bodies, which were found in the rubble at the blaze scene.

Reynolds also disclosed that the victims had reported 3 mysterious incidents, including one involving a live rattlesnake.

The body believed to be that of Mr. Anton, 48, was shot twice in the chest, and Mrs. Anton, 47, was shot once in the heart, preliminary pathologists findings indicated.

According to the report the wounds would have been fatal even if the fire had not taken place.

"We are having an analysis made of blood to see if either one or both were alive after the fire started," Reynolds said.

The bodies were discovered early Sunday after a man driving north of the home on US-56 spotted the fire and notified the Gray County Sheriff's Office. The fire was extinguished early Sunday morning.

---

[47]"Sifting for Clues: KBI agents sift ashes of Richard Anton home near Ensign," *Salina Journal*, 3 July 1974, 13. See http://genealogytrails.com/kan/gray/anton.html.

Reynolds and agents from the Kansas Bureau of Investigation then sift-
ed through the debris. The search continued Monday.

Three incidents prior to the fire and shooting were mentioned by
Reynolds.

—On Feb. 1, of this year, the garage next to the Anton home was
destroyed by fire.

"We were never able to discover the origin of the fire," Reynolds
said.

—During the week of March 17 Mr. Anton discovered that all the
lug nuts except one had been removed from one of the front wheels of
his pickup, Reynolds said.

—April 6, Mr. Anton discovered a live prairie rattlesnake in his car
and alerted sheriff's officers who killed it. The rattle on the snake had
been removed, Reynolds said.

NOTHING CONCLUSIVE

After the snake incident, Anton talked with sheriff's officers. Reynolds said an investigation followed but nothing conclusive was established.

Reynolds said sheriff's officers told Mr. Anton to keep them ad-
vised on further developments.

KBI Agents Al Dewey and Jack Ford and Paul Beard from the
Kansas Fire Marshal's office were at the site of the home and will file
reports in the next few days, Reynolds said.

The first started between 11 p.m. Saturday night and midnight
Sunday and was discovered about 1 a.m. Sunday.

Reynolds said both bodies were found lying on their backs in the
rubble.

He said they were not found in bed but said the amount of debris
on the floor complicated the task of determining where the bodies had
been situated after they were shot.

Reynolds said the investigation of the fire and shooting "has not
centered on any one individual." He said all neighbors and close friends
will be questioned.

The only child who had lived at the home was John Anton, who
had been in Liberal with his girlfriend the night of the shooting. The
couple had 3 other sons and a daughter.

ACTIVE FARMER

Anton had farmed in the Ensign area since the family moved here
from Roeland Park in 1961. He was a member of the Farmers Home
Administration committee, had served on the Ensign Board of Educa-

tion and was vice-chairman of the Gray County Soil Conservation district board.

Mrs. Anton had been active in the Ensign United Methodist Church, and had formerly been organist at the church.[48]

Several differences and similarities between Ensign and Holcomb and between the Antons and the Clutters are apparent. Although Perry Smith and Dick Hickock were arrested, tried, and executed, the person who shot the Antons and set fire to the house was not convicted for the murders. A news story in the July 3, 1974, issue of the *Salina Journal* revealed that Anton "had enemies,"[49] an obvious difference between Richard Anton and Herbert Clutter, whose killers had never met him or his family. "Residents now find themselves wondering about each other,"[50] writes the reporter. The comment resurrects Capote's initial inclination to write about how a town— where residents rarely locked their doors—responded to the Clutter murders. Like the Clutters, the Antons were described in a July 11, 1974, story in the *Salina Journal* as "prosperous ranchers and landowners."[51]

The Garden City Telegram reported February 17, 1975, that the governor of Kansas was offering a $5,000 reward for information about the murder.[52] If the reference to the Garden City newspaper were not enough to conjure up images of the Clutter murders, a reporter alluded to them in a subsequent story published in the *Telegram* June 30, 1975: "Making the murder even more sensational in this farm belt county, only 50 miles east of where the famous Clutter killings took place, was the burning of the Anton farm house the night of the shooting." In the same story, Dewey is quoted as saying that he believes the murders will one day be solved: "We are still actively investigating this crime and have been since it occurred," Dewey said. "We had about seven agents on it for months after it happened. Now we have two to four working on it part or full time." The June 30, 1975, story continues:

> Dewey, who is credited with solving the Clutter murders, said an investigation of this magnitude "takes time."

---

[48]"Deaths of Ensign Man, Wife Were Dual Murder?" *Salina Journal*, 2 July 1974, 1.
[49]"Sifting for Clues," 13.
[50]Ibid.
[51]"Officers Question Man in Ensign Murder Cases," *Salina Journal*, 11 July 1974, 21.
[52]"Reward Offered in Anton Murders," *Garden City Telegram*, 17 February 1975, 3.

"We talk to everyone: friends, relatives, business associates, employees, former employees," Dewey said. "Because of his large holdings, he's had a lot of business contacts and we're leaving no stone unturned."

More than 500 interviews have been conducted in the investigation, Dewey said.

The interviews included all the people who lived within a 15-mile radius of the Anton home, Dewey said.

The fire is making the investigation especially difficult, Dewey said.

"That fire destroyed any evidence that might have been left at the scene of the crime," Dewey said. "We just don't have a bit of physical evidence."

However, Dewey believes the crime will be solved even though he will work on it only until he retires in December.

"I have the fullest confidence that these agents will find the answer," Dewey said.

Dewey said he did not believe a group, loosely tagged the Prairie Mafia, had anything to do with the murders or that it even existed.

"I just don't buy that theory," Dewey said. "Out here in western Kansas we just don't have organized crime as such."[53]

Years later on April 29, 1992, a *Lawrence Journal-World* story titled "Murder of Kansas Couple in 1974 Remains a Mystery"[54] said the investigation into the crime was still open. As of 2016, no one has been charged or convicted for the double homicide.

It is impossible to know what would have occurred if Capote had lived and had been interrogated about his research. Would Capote have confessed to the liberties he took with actual events? He remained staunchly determined to convince the reading public that *Handcarved Coffins* and *In Cold Blood* were factual. Interviewed about the veracity of *Handcarved Coffins*, Capote said without hesitation that Quinn was the killer, that Quinn never would have been indicted, and that he feared that Quinn would file a lawsuit against him: "He was never accused of anything. That's why I had to be so careful in the book. If ever I was going to have a lawsuit, that's where I was going to have a lawsuit. And I wasn't going to have a lawsuit."[55] Astonish-

---

[53]"Mysteries Hold Year After Anton Murders," *Garden City Telegram*, 30 June 1975, 3.

[54]"Murder of Kansas Couple in 1974 Remains a Mystery," *Lawrence Journal-World*, 29 April 1992, 2C.

[55]Grobel, *Conversations*, 155.

ingly, when Capote was asked if the coffins, the steel wire, the poison, and the rattlesnakes injected with amphetamines were accurate, he responded, "That's *exactly* what happened. That's one of my best pieces of reportage."[56] Even after *Handcarved Coffins* was published, Quinn vowed his innocence and expressed his hatred for Jake Pepper, whom this study establishes as a pseudonym for Dewey, the detective so central to *In Cold Blood*. Talking with the character "TC" about Pepper, Quinn tempts the wrath of God when he lies to "TC" (and to himself):

> "Well, I don't guess I'll ever see the old bastard again. Too bad. We could've been real friends. If he hadn't had all those suspicions. Damn his soul, he even thought I drowned poor Addie Mason!" He laughed; then scowled. "The way I look at it is: it was the hand of God." He raised his own hand, and the river, viewed between his spread fingers, seemed to weave between them like a dark ribbon. "God's work. His will."[57]

"Then It All Came Down" (1979)

Like *In Cold Blood* and *Handcarved Coffins*, "Then It All Came Down" highlights Capote's ability to create somber moods as he retells murder mysteries that occurred from Kansas to California. Describing his experience in a maximum-security prison before he begins his conversation with thirty-one-year-old convicted murderer Robert Kenneth (Bobby) Beausoleil, whom he calls the "real mystery figure of the Charles Manson cult," Capote writes, "But it is late on a winter afternoon, and in the air lingers a chill, even a hint of mist, as though fog from San Francisco Bay had infiltrated the prison itself."[58] Readers familiar with Capote's tales of murder and its aftermath read the somber description of San Quentin and know instinctively what lies ahead.

The interview titled "Then It All Came Down" is far less controversial than *Handcarved Coffins*, although it is similar to the novella in tone and purpose. Capote's conversation with Beausoleil appeared as a profile in *Music for Chameleons* (1980) and later was listed with *Handcarved Coffins* under "Reportage" in the first edition of *Truman Capote: A Capote Reader* (1987).

---

[56]Ibid., 156.

[57]Capote, *Handcarved Coffins*, 514.

[58]Truman Capote, "Then It All Came Down," *Truman Capote: A Capote Reader* (New York: Penguin, 2002) 455.

Not a fully developed essay, profile, or short story, it is best described as an interview that is especially important because of its historical significance and Beausoleil's well-publicized connection to cult leader and convicted murderer Charles Manson. The discussion of "Then It All Came Down" is less detailed than for *Handcarved Coffins* because the interview is relatively brief, because it is not controversial in content or format, and because—even years after the murder in question—several versions of the crime and the killer's motives are impossible to confirm or deny.

Speculation about how and why Beausoleil killed musician and student Gary Hinman is useful only to readers who desire a more thorough understanding of Beausoleil, his film and music career, his acquaintances, and his involvement in Hinman's death. Briefly, Beausoleil was and is a musician, having moved in his early twenties to Los Angeles and having played in several bands. Later, while in San Francisco, he met filmmaker Kenneth Anger, with whom he worked on *Lucifer Rising* (1972) as both an actor and composer. It was in the late 1960s that the lives of several people converged: the notorious Manson met Hinman, who introduced Manson to Dennis Wilson of the Beach Boys. Wilson in turn introduced Manson to record producer Terry Melcher, son of actress Doris Day. Melcher, who did not pursue a relationship with Manson, moved out of his home, which subsequently was leased to film director Roman Polanski and his wife, actress Sharon Tate. Eventually, Beausoleil would be convicted of murdering Hinman, and Manson and some of his followers would be convicted of murdering Tate and six other people in two separate events.

For purposes of this study, however, it is the text itself that matters. Although Capote's interview with Beausoleil was well received, one anonymous critic, who called *Music for Chameleons* a "distressingly thin and uneven new collection," is no kinder to "Then It All Came Down," describing it as "surprisingly tedious,"[59] especially given the sensational aspects of Hinman's death. Although Capote clearly is drawn to murders and the psychology of murderers, "Then It All Came Down" does not resemble interviews that Capote conducted with Perry Smith for *In Cold Blood*. It is different in at least two important ways: first, Capote expresses no affection for Beausoleil and does not defer to him in what was apparently only one conversation; second, although the interview follows a question-answer format, Capote

---

[59]"*Music for Chameleons*," *Kirkus Reviews*, 11 August 1980, web (accessed 6 August 2018).

belittles Beausoleil's belief that all that occurs is good and concludes the interview by implying how superficial he considers Beausoleil to be.

One of the most compelling aspects of *In Cold Blood, Handcarved Coffins*, and "Then It All Came Down" is Capote's obvious interest in outsiders, which Als argues obsessed Capote from the time he wrote *Local Color* (1950) and *The Muses Are Heard* (1956). "Most of his subsequent nonfiction work would be about outsiders, too," Als notes, "all those drifters and proles trying to make it in unfamiliar worlds."[60] From Perry Smith to Richard Hickock to the fictitious Robert Quinn to Bobby Beausoleil, Capote made clear his interest in people who live on the edges of society and whose deprivation and/or lack of empathy drive them to commit horrific crimes.

For those who are interested in Beausoleil and the Manson cult, "Then It All Came Down" is no more well known than A. L. Bardach's 1981 interview with Beausoleil published in *Oui Magazine*. In the interview that followed Capote's, Beausoleil admits to killing Hinman. When Bardach asks him about the day of the murder, Beausoleil responds in detail and addresses the two young women, part of the Manson "family," who accompanied him to Hinman's Topanga Canyon house near Malibu in the summer of 1969. For reasons that differ depending on the source, Mary Brunner and Susan (Sadie) Atkins accompanied Beausoleil: "I didn't go there with the intention of killing Gary," Beausoleil tells Bardach. "If I was going to kill him, I wouldn't have taken the girls...I was going there for one purpose only, which was to collect $1,000 that I had already turned over to him, that didn't belong to me."[61] In other news stories and interviews, sources describe other motives for Beausoleil's visiting Hinman (one suggests that Manson ordered the hit, another links the murder to a drug deal gone bad, another claims Manson himself killed Hinman, etc.). Beausoleil gives yet another explanation in his interview with Bardach: "Gary Hinman would not have died if he had not told me that he was going to blow the whistle as soon as I was gone...Up until that point I had assumed that everything was square between us."[62]

Whatever occurred, Hinman was terrorized and eventually stabbed to death, setting off a series of events that gripped Southern California and the nation. "He died immediately," Beausoleil said. "And it was a stupid deci-

---

[60]Als, "The Shadows in Truman Capote's Early Stories."

[61]A. L. Bardach, "Jailhouse Interview: Bobby Beausoleil," *Oui Magazine*, November 1981, web (accessed 6 August 2018).

[62]Ibid.

sion. I should have taken my chances with whatever he was going to do."[63]
According to Beausoleil, Atkins put a pillow over Hinman's face to "muffle
the sound" of what he called "death gasps" and a "death rattle."[64] In another
inconsistency in the widely divergent accounts of the Hinman murder, some
suggested that Atkins, not Beausoleil, killed Hinman, smothering him. Before leaving the scene, Beausoleil or one of the women scrawled "Political
Piggy" on the wall in Hinman's blood.

Motives for the July 27, 1969, murder and information about who actually was present are unclear; however, Beausoleil had spent the previous
evening with Manson and his followers at the cult's enclave called Spahn
Ranch. One theory revealed in Bardach's story is that Beausoleil bought
what he thought was mescaline and sold it to members of a motorcycle gang,
learning somehow that the drug actually was strychnine. The angry bikers
wanted their money back immediately, so Beausoleil drove to Hinman's res-
idence to confront him. On August 5, 1969, highway patrol officers found
Beausoleil sleeping in one of Hinman's missing cars. After trials in 1969 and
again in 1970, Beausoleil was convicted. When Bardach asked Beausoleil
why he drove Hinman's car and seemed to have no escape plan, Beausoleil
replied:

> I'm not sure that I was trying so desperately to prevent my apprehen-
> sion. I was kind of devastated by what I had done. I drove the car off
> on the pretense of ditching it somewhere. I picked up some hitchhikers
> and took them to where they were going and just continued north. In
> retrospect, it was definitely a stupid move...I think I wanted to pay for
> Gary Hinman's death. I think I owed Gary that. I've worshipped life
> my whole life. What's heartbreaking to me more than anything else is
> that killing Gary Hinman has negated all of my creative efforts. The
> world doesn't concentrate on anything other than that one mistake I
> made in my life. And it was a big mistake. You can't give a life back.[65]

What followed Hinman's death were the murders of seven more people. Calling Hinman's murder a "triggering effect,"[66] Beausoleil does not rule
out the possibility that Manson and his friends then went on a rampage in

---

[63]Ibid.
[64]Ibid.
[65]Ibid.
[66]Ibid.

order to convince the police to let Beausoleil go. In Manson's convoluted logic, if murders similar to Hinman's continued, then the judicial system might question Beausoleil's participation in the first murder and release him. Beausoleil explained:

> I don't think it was because of Charlie Manson's fondness for me, necessarily. I think that this was a justification—something that would give the whole episode a more noble cause...They were a bunch of people with their backs against the wall. This wasn't mere discontent. This was lunacy. At least in their minds, they were at the end corner of the world.[67]

In his interview with Capote, Beausoleil again seems to confirm the theory that the Manson cult committed the murders in order to free him: "If a member of our family was in jeopardy, we didn't abandon that person. And so for the love of a brother, a brother who was in jail on a murder rap, all those killings came down."[68]

After Hinman was killed, several events preceded other violent murders. Having married Roman Polanski on January 20, 1968, Sharon Tate moved the following year to a house in Benedict Canyon, an area northwest of Beverly Hills, where the couple hosted large gatherings—often without knowing all of the guests. In between lavish parties, the couple traveled to film sites on assignment—separately and together. On August 8, 1969, Tate was more than eight months pregnant and was spending an evening at home with friends. Polanski was abroad, planning to return to the U.S. before the birth of the child. Sometime after midnight on August 9, Manson and his followers murdered her, along with her friends, coffee heiress Abigail Folger, writer Wojciech Frykowski, and hairstylist Jay Sebring. The killers also murdered Steven Parent, a friend of the caretaker, who was shot in his car in the driveway.

In the aftermath of the grisly crime, shock reverberated throughout the country. Named for Tate's and Polanski's fathers, the unborn child, Paul Richard Polanski, died and was buried with his mother. Literary journalist Joan Didion wrote about the event in *The White Album*: "Many people I know in Los Angeles believe that the Sixties ended abruptly on August 9, 1969, ended at the exact moment when word of the murders on Cielo Drive

---

[67]Ibid.
[68]Capote, "Then It All Came Down," 461.

traveled like brushfire through the community, and in a sense this is true. The tension broke that day. The paranoia was fulfilled."[69] After a trial that lasted seven months, Manson and several of his followers were convicted of the murders that began at the Tate-Polanski home and continued the next day with the murders of Leno and Rosemary LaBianca, who owned a chain of grocery stores. The horror was memorialized in criminal prosecutor Vincent Bugliosi's *Helter Skelter: The True Story of the Manson Murders*. Like Beausoleil, Manson and his other followers are serving life sentences. In a summary of the events that preceded Beausoleil's conviction, Capote, too, writes in "Then It All Came Down" about the motives for the killing of Hinman and the subsequent murder of seven others:

> However, just a few days prior to the [Tate-LaBianca] slayings, Robert Beausoleil, caught driving a car that had been the property of the victim, was under arrest and in jail, accused of having murdered the helpless Mr. Hinman. It was then that Manson and his chums, in the hopes of freeing Beausoleil, conceived the notion of committing a series of homicides similar to the Hinman affair; if Beausoleil was still incarcerated at the time of these killings, then how could he be guilty of the Hinman atrocity? Or so the Manson brood reasoned. That is to say, it was out of devotion to "Bobby" Beausoleil that Tex Watson and those cutthroat young ladies, Susan Atkins, Patricia Krenwinkel, Leslie Van Hooten, sallied forth on their satanic errands.[70]

After completing his interview about the murder that set the others into motion, Bardach asked Beausoleil about his conversation with Capote. Beausoleil told Bardach he thought Capote was "trying to relive *In Cold Blood* or something."[71] He said that he and other inmates at San Quentin welcomed Capote because they thought he wanted to learn more about them in order to improve their lives. Instead, Beausoleil said that Capote "interviewed mostly murderers on death row" and claimed that he practiced "totally irresponsible journalism."[72] Showing his scorn for the famous author, Beausoleil said to Bardach, "And this guy is supposed to be somebody."[73]

---

[69]Joan Didion, *The White Album*, in *We Tell Ourselves Stories in Order to Live: Collected Nonfiction* (London: Knopf, 2006) 212.
[70]Capote, "Then It All Came Down," 456.
[71]Bardach, "Jailhouse Interview."
[72]Ibid.
[73]Ibid.

A few events have occurred in Beausoleil's life since the murder. Condemned to death, Beausoleil had his sentence commuted to life in prison when California temporarily banned capital punishment. Beausoleil regularly comes up for parole, although he has been denied more than fifteen times. (He will be eligible for parole again in 2027.) On October 19, 2012, Beausoleil's wife, whom he married while in prison, died. Barbara E. Beausoleil's obituary—datelined "Salem," the site of the Oregon State Penitentiary where he resided—mentions her notorious husband only in the list of survivors. With a bachelor of fine arts degree from Boston University, Barbara Beausoleil painted, played the guitar and piano, danced, and worked as a carpenter. The obituary identifies her as "a true Mother Goddess, treading softly yet powerfully upon this Earth" and does not disclose the cause of her death.[74]

Although Beausoleil, Manson, and Manson's followers committed their senseless and violent murders in California, Truman Capote might as well have been in Holcomb, Kansas, once more. Beausoleil asked Capote if he had ever seen a convicted person "gassed," and Capote responded by remembering Perry Edward Smith and Richard Eugene Hickock, who dominated his life for more than five years. He replied:

> Once. But he made it look like a lark. He was happy to go, he wanted to get it over with; he sat down in that chair like he was going to the dentist to have his teeth cleaned. But in Kansas, I saw two men hanged...But after the drop, they go on living—fifteen, twenty minutes. Struggling. Gasping for breath, the body still battling for life. I couldn't help it, I vomited.[75]

In "Then It All Came Down," Capote listens to Beausoleil as he thoughtlessly explains his crime and the crimes of the Manson cult: "If my brothers and sisters did it, then it's good. Everything in life is good. It all flows. It's all good. It's all music."[76] Possibly remembering the four gunshots that ended the lives of the Clutters and the hangman's noose that awaited Smith and Hickock, Capote responds, "War. Starving children. Pain. Cruelty. Blindness. Prisons. Desperation. Indifference. All good?"[77] If Capote did, in fact,

---

[74]Unger Funeral Chapel, "Barbara E. Beausoleil," web (accessed 6 August 2018).
[75]Capote, "Then It All Came Down," 457.
[76]Ibid., 461.
[77]Ibid.

say these words, then it might account for Beausoleil's more considered response when Capote asks if he would kill again. Reminiscent of the vague sense of inevitable disaster that characterizes *In Cold Blood*, Beausoleil tells Capote, "It depends. I never meant to...to...hurt Gary Hinman. But one thing happened. And another. And then it all came down."[78]

As the first three chapters of this study illustrate, contexts matter. They suggest which texts might belong in particular literary frames, intensify the reading experience by suggesting new ways of locating familiar texts, and allow for specialists in journalism, literature, media, psychology, sociology, women's studies, or another field to draw from their own expertise. Contexts are enlivening. They allow us to break down assumptions that may predate our own engagement with a text. They make reading an art form, an act of will, and an act of defiance in the face of previous ways of seeing. So much depends on the desire to break down or to reestablish paradigms. From the historical, literary, and sociological contexts in chapter one, journalistic and literary contexts in chapter two, and the other Capote tales about murder here in chapter three, we now explore in chapter four the doppelgänger and its relevance to crime in American film and literature.

---

[78]Ibid., 462.

Chapter 4

In Cold Blood, the Doppelgänger, and Murder

Murder and other sensational crimes have captivated readers for centuries. In *The Invention of Murder: How the Victorians Revelled in Death and Detection and Created Modern Crime*, Judith Flanders discusses the allure of murder, writing that "crime, especially murder, is very pleasant to think about in the abstract: it is like hearing blustery rain on the windowpane when sitting indoors. It reinforces a sense of safety, even of pleasure, to know that murder is possible, just not here."[1] Victorians, according to Flanders, attended funerals "out of curiosity"[2] and frequented executions in order to watch people die and then to view their bodies in the "anatomy theatre" after the autopsies.[3]

One corpse in Flanders's historical survey drew 30,000 views, and one of the diary entries reads, "Burke's body was lying stretched out on a table in a large sort of lumber or dissecting room, quite naked. The upper part of the skull had been sawn off and the brain extracted, but in other respects he was untouched, except, indeed, that the hair had been shaven off his body."[4] In her analysis of the portrayals of the ultimate crime, Flanders focuses on the works of Charles Dickens, Sir Arthur Conan Doyle, Edgar Allan Poe, Robert Louis Stevenson, Oscar Wilde, and others, whose work preceded Truman Capote's *In Cold Blood* but was familiar to him.

For this study, the most important theme in *The Invention of Murder* is the "double nature of the killer that made it possible for him to escape detection":[5] "Perhaps, though, the strongest [Jack the Ripper] element was another entirely unspoken one, that of doubling, the man who presents two faces to the world."[6] In this chapter, we encounter protagonists—some of whom are mentally unstable—who compromise their values and sense of self when confronted by a person who is charming or persuasive or threatening (or all

---

[1] Judith Flanders, *The Invention of Murder: How the Victorians Revelled in Death and Detection and Created Modern Crime* (New York: St. Martin's, 2011) 1.

[2] Ibid., 5.

[3] Ibid., 41.

[4] Ibid., 68.

[5] Ibid., 435.

[6] Ibid., 455.

three). Mirrors are among the symbols that represent our desire to see ourselves clearly, but from *The Talented Mr. Ripley* (1955) to *True Story* (2015), no one and no place is what it appears to be, and mirrors reflect distorted images.

Several flawed characters are introduced in this chapter, including two of the ones created by the prolific mystery writer Patricia Highsmith. Tom Ripley (*The Talented Mr. Ripley*) and Chester MacFarland (*The Two Faces of January*) are seemingly rational—even likable and intelligent—agents of death. The murders they commit are not always premeditated, seeming to occur in slow motion outside their own will, which makes them highly unreliable narrators of their own stories. Another fictional narrator follows analysis of Tom Ripley and Chester MacFarland, Stephen King's Mort Rainey. The novella *Secret Window, Secret Garden* is a labyrinth of miscues. Those who enter find it impossible to ascertain what is real and what is imagined. Similarly, Edward (Teddy) Daniels, a U.S. marshal, discovers in Dennis Lehane's *Shutter Island* that he has committed an especially gruesome murder and later realizes with horror that he is losing his mind. The final narrator in this study is not fictional, not a composite, and not based on a historical person. Instead, Michael Finkel, who enjoyed his rising stature in the journalistic community before *The New York Times* fired him, is an actual person who produced a nonfiction novel about his interviews with a convicted murderer. Finkel—in a real-life nod to *In Cold Blood*—develops and sustains a relationship with Christian Longo, who kills his family and subsequently appropriates Finkel's identity. Finkel assumes authorial control; however, the reader soon discovers that as Finkel relates his story, he does not entirely understand himself or his sources.

Before exploring these novels that became films—as did *In Cold Blood*—it is important to understand why a study of popular culture from 1955 to 2015 is pertinent to a better understanding of Capote's 1965 nonfiction novel. As noted in chapter one, Capote did not immerse himself in nonfiction broadly defined. He sought a particular crime with a long shelf life, settling on the Clutter murders. It might have been any other topic. In an interview with Roy Newquist, Capote said:

> I didn't know what the theme was going to be, but I knew it would be reportage on an immense scale...I suddenly realized that perhaps a crime, after all, would be the ideal subject matter for the massive job of reportage I wanted to do. I would have a wide range of characters, and,

most importantly, it would be timeless. I knew it would take me five years, perhaps eight or ten years, to do this, and I couldn't work on some ephemeral, momentary thing. It had to be an event related to permanent emotions in people.[7]

After four members of the Clutter family died, residents of Holcomb, Kansas, began to lock their doors and to suspect and fear one another. Capote's initial goal was to reveal the deep and pervasive changes in the community after the murders, to tell a story of a village under siege; ultimately, though, he developed a friendship with a murderer, penned a polemic about capital punishment, and captivated the nation with the publication of *In Cold Blood*.

With his immersion into local life and law enforcement procedures, Capote initially maintained a reporter's detachment. With his immersion into the lives of Perry Edward Smith and Richard Eugene Hickock, Capote demonstrated artistry, heightened perception, and empathy, all of which affected the course of the narrative. Capote revealed the mind of a killer, grieved his death, and sparked a debate about objectivity in nonfiction that has yet to subside. "For all his technical accomplishment," writes Rupert Thomson, "Capote's campaign to remove himself from the text was only partly successful":

> In his deft manipulation of the facts and impressions that he had gathered, Capote's hand is there for all to see. But there is another deeper and more troubling level on which he achieves a kind of visibility—namely, in his covert yet increasingly palpable identification with the criminals themselves, in particular with Smith.[8]

Persuasively, Thomson and others—in varying degrees—critique Capote's claims that everything in *In Cold Blood* is true and that he maintained journalistic objectivity and produced what he states in his subtitle, *A True Account of a Multiple Murder and Its Consequences*.

Chapter two dealt with *In Cold Blood* as part of the tradition of literary journalism, in which first-person point of view and the beliefs and predispositions of an author help to drive the narrative. Therefore, the intent of this chapter is not to demean Capote for investing himself in the life of another

---

[7]Roy Newquist, *Counterpoint* (New York: Rand McNally, 1964) 79.

[8]Rupert Thomson, "Rereading: Truman Capote's *In Cold Blood*," *The Guardian*, 5 August 2011, web (accessed 6 August 2018).

human being—an occurrence that may be inevitable if one subscribes to the tenet of immersion in literary journalism—or for allowing his feelings to shape his nonfiction novel. Instead, the immediate goal is to explore how Capote's increasing awareness about the people of Holcomb and Garden City and how his evolving consciousness about crime are made visible in the text. At the center of the discussion is the relationship between Capote and Smith, which may or may not have been sexual but which changed Capote forever. Thomson emphasizes the connections between Capote and Smith, suggesting that they represent "echoes" of Capote's "past life":

> They both had promiscuous, alcoholic mothers and incompetent, large-ly absent fathers; they were both brought up in foster-homes; they were both ridiculed as children—Capote for his effeminacy, Smith for his Cherokee blood and his bedwetting...As Gerald Clarke, Capote's bi-ographer, puts it: "In Perry he recognised his shadow, his dark side, the embodiment of his own accumulated angers and hurts." Though he prized coolness and objectivity, Capote found it impossible not to re-veal where his sympathies lay. When he claimed that Smith could have stepped right out of one of his stories, it was because Smith resembled Capote's imaginative projection of himself: they were both outsiders, freaks.[9]

Just as important, Thomson writes that what makes *In Cold Blood* "un-forgettable" is the "portrait it paints of the eerie, unspoken contract that ex-ists between the observer and the observed, and the trade-off that can occur when the two become too intimate, a Faustian pact in which they both ulti-mately stand to lose as much as they have gained."[10] Whether or not the re-lationship was "too intimate" is a matter best left to readers and critics. The focus of this chapter—about a nonfiction novel, doppelgängers, and mur-der—is to place *In Cold Blood* into a broad, unfamiliar context that makes it richer and more evocative. Although it is impossible to improve on Thom-son's analysis of the central theme of *In Cold Blood*—the undeniable relation-ship between Capote and Smith—this chapter addresses the ways in which Capote's identification with Smith is itself a literary device. The concept of the doppelgänger—characters that are complementary, even mirror images of one another—is well known to readers. In numerous works in American

---

[9]Ibid.
[10]Ibid.

and British literature, the image of the doppelgänger persists. As we will explore in chapter seven ("*In Cold Blood* in Documentary and Film"), screenwriters exploited the literary construct in both *Capote* (2005) and *Infamous* (2006), building on the not-so-subtle references that Capote provides in *In Cold Blood*. The portrayal of a criminal with a tortured past will reappear in several of the relevant texts in this chapter, making a final appearance in Michael Finkel's *True Story* (2005).

Although *True Story* does not equal the achievement of *In Cold Blood*, it is another example of a murder mystery in which the author is invested in understanding the criminal mind and in which the author and the murderer develop a close and—at least occasionally—a-mutually sustaining relationship. It also is an example of the challenges implicit in literary journalism—with its reliance on a true story that employs literary images and techniques. In "The Worthy Elephant: On Truman Capote's *In Cold Blood*," David Hayes and Sarah Weinman argue that one of Capote's achievements was to "harness the techniques of fiction and journalism to document a crime, effectively inventing the modern true crime genre." Given the extraordinary English novels and plays from which the American crime novel emerged, it is difficult and perhaps unnecessary to analyze whether or not Capote helped to "invent" the "true crime genre" or simply sustained it in a grand manner. "As long as there has been crime there have been town criers or writers telling people about it," Hayes writes. "Some of the most interesting early newspaper work of the 19th and 20th centuries was accounts of crimes and disasters. A crime has built-in drama, notoriety, and an opportunity to reveal aspects of a society at that particular time, so that would make it a natural subject for ambitious writers."[11] The two revisit themes from the first three chapters of *Untold Stories, Unheard Voices* when they highlight how *In Cold Blood, Handcarved Coffins*, and other reportorial work began to overshadow Capote's fiction, in large part because the author repeatedly chose to submerge himself in stories based on fact. Hayes writes:

> Oddly, I think Capote's reputation rests almost entirely on *In Cold Blood*. But I'm sure Capote wanted his fiction to be what he would be remembered for. In Ralph Voss's book, *Truman Capote and the Legacy of* In Cold Blood, he argues that Capote was always an accomplished stylist but a second-rate writer of fiction. *In Cold Blood*, though, repre-

---

[11]David Hayes and Sarah Weinman, "The Worthy Elephant: On Truman Capote's *In Cold Blood*," *Hazlitt*, 27 January 2016, web (accessed 6 August 2018).

sented in the '60s the possibilities of writing about crime. That reportage could also be artful.[12]

Several texts that deal with murder and introduce the image of the doppelgänger are explored in this chapter. The purpose is to place *In Cold Blood* into a genre of literature that includes the classics that precede and follow it. Capote did not plan to have an obsessive and disquieting relationship with Perry Smith—no one accuses Capote of having exploited a premeditated event. Instead, he was taken by surprise, and his relationship with a killer who probably murdered four people without empathy or explanation ultimately affects both his emotional health and his ability to publish. The unanticipated connection between Capote and Smith suggests the importance of reviewing the role of the doppelgänger in twentieth-century American literature and film. In short, *Untold Stories, Unheard Voices* focuses on a famously flamboyant American writer who meets two murderers and befriends one of them. Capote recognizes in the soft-spoken Perry Smith an artistic sensibility. In spite of the comparisons he draws between himself and Smith, the relationship he pursues is so disruptive that Capote loses his creative edge and sinks into depression. The nonfiction novel that Capote hoped would lead to a Pulitzer Prize instead broke him and made it impossible for him to publish another book.

One of the most in-depth studies of Truman Capote's connection to and need for Perry Smith is *Tiny Terror: Why Truman Capote (Almost) Wrote Answered Prayers*. In this book, William Todd Schultz combines literary criticism with psychoanalytic criticism and discusses the doppelgänger motif as it pertains to *In Cold Blood*. Alluding often to Swiss psychiatrist Carl Jung, Schultz suggests that a better term for the doppelgänger is a "shadow—that side of ourselves we don't dare express": "Forbidden impulses, rejected thoughts and feelings, repellent fantasies—all get exiled to a shadowland where they form a virtually ancestral personality-in-waiting."[13] Schultz continues:

> The shadow self has to be known; it has to be acknowledged and assimilated. It cannot be held at bay forever. If we ignore it or deny it, it only agitates more restively. It whispers, then speaks out loud, then

---

[12]Ibid.

[13]William Todd Schultz, *Tiny Terror: Why Truman Capote (Almost) Wrote Answered Prayers* (New York: Oxford University Press, 2011) 95.

howls till we hear. It might appear in dreams, it might appear in art, it might appear in symptoms, but most commonly it shows itself in relationships. We get to know the shadow by projecting it on other people, who then mirror it back to us.[14]

According to Schultz, who argues that Smith was Capote's "projected shadow," when Smith was executed, Capote was once again bereft: "Yet another lost love, another abandonment, another punishment for misdirected intimacy."[15] Capote's relationship with Smith is significantly present in the book and the film *In Cold Blood* in 1965 and 1967, respectively, and in the films *Capote* and *Infamous*. In *Infamous*, Capote and Smith are involved with one another sexually, although *In Cold Blood* and *Capote* are far more subtle in portraying the men's affection for one another.

Detailing Capote's time in Kansas after the murder of four family members, *In Cold Blood* became a film in 1967, two years after the serialized version of the novel appeared. Starring Robert Blake as Perry Smith, the film features a reporter, played by Paul Stewart, in Capote's stead. Directed by Richard Brooks, the film reenacts the crimes and the arrests of Smith and Richard Eugene Hickock, who is portrayed by Scott Wilson. It also explores the reason for the murders and the executions of the perpetrators—both of which, according to Capote, occurred in cold blood. This film was the precursor to *Capote* and *Infamous*, which depict the relationship between Capote and his "research assistant," the Pulitzer Prize-winning author Nelle Harper Lee, played by Catherine Keener and Sandra Bullock, respectively. All three films highlight and seek to explain Capote's relationship with Smith and are explored at length in chapter six ("Nelle Harper Lee and *In Cold Blood*") and chapter seven ("*In Cold Blood* in Documentary and Film").

For now, we will focus on familiar literary and psychological concepts such as doppelgängers, alter egos, and narcissists; trace themes such as madness, creativity, and obsession; and question the reliability of narrative constructs in well-known tales of murder. Exploring the interconnectedness of these terms, themes, and narrative devices, this chapter addresses real and imagined relationships in six novels that became films. Each of the books and films relies on two characters that subsume one another, define each other, and/or destroy one another. Certainly, fragmented identities emerge often in film and literature. Four of the most famous examples of doppel-

---

[14]Ibid., 96.
[15]Ibid.

gängers, alter egos, and narcissists are those in Joseph Conrad's *The Secret Sharer*, Edgar Allan Poe's "Wilson Williams," Robert Louis Stevenson's *The Strange Case of Dr. Jekyll and Mr. Hyde*, and Oscar Wilde's *The Picture of Dorian Gray*. Stevenson's masterpiece is addressed in some detail here. These texts provide historical context for this study and a paradigm with which to address the ways we struggle to understand ourselves and to deal with the shifting identities of the people around us. Whom do we trust? Do we depend on our own perceptions? If so, what if we are so wrong that it costs us our lives? If not, on whose perception *can* we depend? Madness often is implicit in stories of creativity and obsession. What is the line between insanity and genius? Can such a line be discerned? How does obsession inform conversations about madness? And, finally, might obsession drive one mad, as well as provide focus and order?

This study explores doppelgängers in film from 1967 to 2015 and literature from 1955 to 2005. Film texts include *The Talented Mr. Ripley*, *The Two Faces of January*, *In Cold Blood*, *Secret Window*, *Shutter Island*, and *True Story*. Patricia Highsmith, Truman Capote, Stephen King, Dennis Lehane, and Michael Finkel create doppelgängers, alter egos, and narcissists. Like the characters in Franz Kafka novels and other labyrinthine tales, the protagonists in novels by Highsmith, Capote, King, Lehane, and Finkel may lose their sanity or their direction and sense of self when they begin to lose confidence in their perceptions and interpretations of the signs and symbols that surround them. Tom Ripley immerses himself in the passionate life of Dickie Greenleaf; Chester MacFarland dies in the streets of an unfamiliar city, having believed foolishly that he could manipulate the younger and more strategic Rydal Keener; Perry Smith, having been convicted of shooting four people at close range, convinces author Truman Capote that he deserves the compassion afforded to a stray cat in Garden City, Kansas, since he, too, survives as best he can; John Shooter destroys Mort Rainey, the writer who created him; Andrew Laeddis, an anagram for Edward (Teddy) Daniels, is so deranged that he is destined to spend the rest of his life in an asylum; and Christian Longo, who murdered his wife and children, fools a former *New York Times* reporter who desperately wants to believe that his charming and childlike friend is innocent of unspeakable crimes.

Before engaging with the texts that encompass sixty years, it is instructive to focus on the 1980s, a decade during which a notably large number of films about our duplicitous nature were released. We will explore the correlation between a fragmented self and a predisposition to violence in film and literature. The focus here is on the films themselves, rather than a critical analysis of American society during this period, although it is impossible to accomplish the former without at least alluding to the latter.

Changing Faces: Dr. Jekyll, Mr. Hyde, and Films of the 1980s

The 1980s in particular were littered with the broken reputations of those who fell from national grace. Americans watched as Oliver North, accused of deceiving the country about the Iran-Contra scandal, became a hero with fan clubs from the Midwest to the Deep South to the West Coast; they became familiar with the trial of Jim Bakker, who was convicted of breaking tax laws and who bilked viewers of Praise the Lord (PTL) out of millions; and they saw televangelist Jimmy Swaggart weep with remorse and publicly address charges of immorality. Americans dropped off their children at day care centers staffed by people they hoped they could trust; they listened to reports of government spokespeople claiming that it was safe to eat most fruits and vegetables and to live in the shadow of a nuclear plant; and they read statistics claiming that most rape victims knew their assailants.

In the midst of the decade of distrust, Americans frequented movie theaters and screened films that allowed them a temporary sense of control over their lives. While Americans lost their confidence in their ability to determine the moral character of national figures like Gary Hart, they turned to themes of betrayal and contested loyalty in the popular arts—perhaps to reassure themselves that they could spot fraud and deception when they encountered them. Films of the decade mesh themes of betrayal and the failure of perception with what writers and critics often have identified as the highest purpose of art: to transform the familiar. In her well-known essay, "The Fiction Writer and His Country," Flannery O'Connor says that a writer must "make [one's] vision apparent by shock—to the hard of hearing you shout, and for the almost-blind you draw large and startling figures."[16] In an essay titled "A Gossip on Romance," Stevenson, likewise, emphasizes the artist's responsibility to jolt the reader or viewer out of complacency:

This, then, is the plastic part of literature: to embody character, thought, or emotion in some act or attitude that shall be remarkably striking to the mind's eye. This is the highest and hardest thing to do in words; the thing which, once accomplished, equally delights the

---

[16]Flannery O'Connor, "The Fiction Writer and His Country," *Mystery and Manners* (New York: Farrar, 1969) 34.

schoolboy and the sage and makes, in its own right, the quality of epics.[17]

Little is more striking or startling than the characters in 1980s films such as *Still of the Night* (1982), *Sophie's Choice* (1982), *Betrayal* (1983), *Jagged Edge* (1985), *The Morning After* (1986), *Black Widow* (1987), *No Way Out* (1987), and a battery of 1988 films such as *Dangerous Liaisons, Masquerade, Betrayed,* and *Criminal Law.* Films that followed—including *Music Box* (1989), starring Jessica Lange, and *Bad Influence* (1990), starring Rob Lowe—also dealt with the con artist and human duplicity and promised a continued interest in these particular themes well into the 1990s.

The films in this study may be grouped into four categories: (1) plots in which a rogue is taught a lesson and alters his or her ways, usually after much suffering and often only before an untimely death; (2) plots in which an immoral and vicious character persists in wreaking violence and havoc and must be stopped (usually killed); (3) plots in which the inner worth of a person long suspected of evil is revealed to the viewer and, thankfully, the main character; and (4) plots in which the trickster escapes pursuit and asserts that evil (or at least deception) will triumph. The prototype for the plots of 1980s films about changing faces is Robert Louis Stevenson's novel *The Strange Case of Dr. Jekyll and Mr. Hyde.* More than a precursor to the modern mystery tale, the book also epitomizes a theme that has obsessed the reading public since the earliest days of American literature.

Ever obsessed with the villain, the seductress, the rogue, and the trickster, American audiences are never more captivated with evil than when a character is both cruel and cryptic. From the Bible to early American literature to music videos and song lyrics, we engage texts in which forces of good and evil clash, but we feel vindicated only if the knaves get their due. One of the most representative myths, of course, is the biblical story of Jesus, who is betrayed by Judas Iscariot:

> Now the betrayer had arranged a signal with them: "The one I kiss is the man; arrest him."
> Going at once to Jesus, Judas said, "Greetings, Rabbi!" and kissed him.
> Jesus replied, "Friend, do what you came for." (Matt. 26:48-50)

---

[17]Robert Louis Stevenson, "A Gossip on Romance," *Memories and Portraits,* in *The Works of Robert Louis Stevenson,* vol. 6 (New York: Greenock Press, 1906) 123.

Justification, more difficult to achieve in life, is gained when Judas, "seized with remorse" (Matt. 27:3), hangs himself. In Acts, biblical writers are even more graphic: "With the reward he got for his wickedness, Judas bought a field; there he fell headlong, his body burst open and all his intestines spilled out" (Acts 1:18). Scripture is only the starting point in the study of themes of betrayal and dual personalities.

Two of the most effective warnings against the sinister confidant appear in nineteenth-century American literature; both Nathaniel Hawthorne's *The Scarlet Letter* and Herman Melville's *The Confidence-Man: His Masquerade* draw heavily from the Bible. In *The Scarlet Letter,* Arthur Dimmesdale, a minister who has fathered a child by Hester Prynne, is befriended by a physician, Roger Chillingworth. Eventually freed from Chillingworth's clutches, the Rev. Dimmesdale says of his cunning adversary, "He has violated, in cold blood, the sanctity of a human heart."[18] Melville portrays Christ himself as a con artist who dons disguises in order to trick both his enemies and his friends in *The Confidence-Man.* Alluding to the New Testament, which urges the followers of Christ to strengthen their confidence in their savior, Melville creates a microcosm aboard the steamer *Fidele* (the Faithful) and allows travelers to be conned by the greatest fraud of them all. Asking in succession, "Is he or is he not, what he seems to be?"[19] those who populate the novel give way to his charms one by one. The theological implications of Melville's piece are not under scrutiny here; we must, however, understand the significance of the ironies in the text and even the subtitle, *His Masquerade.*

Historically notable music and videos, such as "Thriller" by Michael Jackson and "The Wall" by Pink Floyd, emphasize seemingly trustworthy individuals who change before one's eyes. Even song lyrics from musicals such as *Sweeney Todd* portray demons "prowling everywhere" and demons that will "charm you with a smile, for a while."[20] Contemporary media reenact that which the culture most seems to fear: the individual allowed into the deepest emotional sanctuary, who then will betray or fool the unsuspecting.

---

[18]Nathaniel Hawthorne, *The Scarlet Letter* (New York: New American Library, 1959) 186.

[19]Herman Melville, *The Confidence-Man: His Masquerade* (New York: New American Library, 1954) 36.

[20]Stephen Sondheim, "Not While I'm Around," *Sweeney Todd,* lyrics available online.

Examples of popular television series that employ duplicity as a theme include *Damages* (2007–2012) and *House of Cards* (2013–2018).

The Strange Case of Dr. Jekyll and Mr. Hyde

The novel that best depicts the formula for deception employed by the filmmakers that follow is *The Strange Case of Dr. Jekyll and Mr. Hyde*. In the novel, Stevenson explores the trials and eventual annihilation of Henry Jekyll, a London physician and chemist, through the perspective of several characters, primarily Gabriel John Utterson. The portrait of Jekyll is in Stevenson's words certainly one "striking to the mind's eye."[21] In an introduction to the novel, Vladimir Nabokov reveals the Danish origins of the names of the primary character(s), Dr. Jekyll and Mr. Hyde. "'Hyde,'" he writes, "comes from the Anglo-Saxon *hyd*, which is the Danish *hide*, 'a haven.' 'Jekyll' comes from the word 'Jökulle,' which means an 'icicle.'"[22] Both names, of course, reverberate with meaning, for Hyde hides his monstrosity as best he can, and he hides literally in an apartment that Stevenson locates in a "district of some city in a nightmare."[23] Hyde and Jekyll unsuccessfully hide Hyde's crimes, and Jekyll hides for a time from his dual nature. Jekyll, too, lives down to his name, as an icy, detached physician akin to Roger Chillingworth, as he concocts a potion that will alter his nature and as he wallows in Chillingworth's greatest sin—pride.

For purposes of this study, the centrally important line in *The Strange Case of Dr. Jekyll and Mr. Hyde* is a description of Dr. Jekyll as his friend, Dr. Hastie Lanyon, watches him change into Mr. Hyde: "His face became suddenly black and the features seemed to melt and alter."[24] How reassuring it would be if faces literally changed into something we could recognize as evil. Nabokov records in his introduction to the novel the ironic connection between Stevenson's own life and his creation of Dr. Jekyll. In Samoa in 1894, Stevenson died from a blood vessel that burst in his brain: "He went down to the cellar to fetch a bottle of his favorite burgundy," writes Nabokov, "uncorked it in the kitchen, and suddenly cried out to his wife: what's the matter

---

[21]Stevenson, "A Gossip on Romance," 123.

[22]Vladimir Nabokov, "The Strange Case of Dr. Jekyll and Mr. Hyde," in *The Strange Case of Dr. Jekyll and Mr. Hyde,* by Robert Louis Stevenson (New York: New American Library, 1987) 9.

[23] Robert Louis Stevenson, *The Strange Case of Dr. Jekyll and Mr. Hyde* (New York: New American Library, 1987) 62.

[24]Ibid., 101.

with me, what is this strangeness, has my face changed?—and fell on the floor."[25]

Nabokov then repeats the line, "What, has my face changed?"[26] as he refers to what Stevenson describes in his novel as "Satan's signature upon a face"[27]—the mark of Cain on Hyde. Who, as a child, has not been startled or frightened by the face of someone familiar and trusted who alters his or her expression unexpectedly and without explanation? Stevenson and others play upon that universal fear and need—the need to have the people close to us behave consistently with our expectations and desires. Fortunately, as Richard Enfield observes, Hyde is recognizable as evil:

> There is something wrong with his appearance; something displeasing, something downright detestable. I never saw a man I so disliked, and yet I scarce know why. He must be deformed somewhere; he gives a strong feeling of deformity, although I couldn't specify the point. He's an extraordinary looking man, and yet I really can name nothing out of the way.[28]

In *The Strange Case of Dr. Jekyll and Mr. Hyde*, Stevenson describes Hyde as someone meriting fear, using phrases such as "pale and dwarfish": "[Hyde] gave an impression of deformity without any nameable malformation, he had a displeasing smile, he had borne himself to the lawyer with a sort of murderous mixture of timidity and boldness, and he spoke with a husky, whispering and somewhat broken voice."[29]

Dr. Jekyll looks down from a window in his home to converse with two of his trusted friends. He seems happy and safe, when suddenly, his face changes: the "words were hardly uttered, before the smile was struck out of his face and succeeded by an expression of such abject terror and despair, as froze the very blood of the two gentlemen below."[30] What has caused the change in his features? Obsessed with the "duplicity of life"[31] and "man's dual nature,"[32] Dr. Jekyll has made a fatal discovery: "With every day, and

---

[25]Nabokov, "The Strange Case," 34.
[26]Ibid.
[27]Stevenson, *The Strange Case of Dr. Jekyll and Mr. Hyde*, 52.
[28]Ibid., 43-44.
[29]Ibid., 52.
[30]Ibid., 77.
[31]Ibid., 103.
[32]Ibid., 104.

from both sides of my intelligence, the moral and the intellectual, I thus drew steadily nearer to that truth, by whose partial discovery I have been doomed to such a dreadful shipwreck: that man is not truly one, but truly two."[33] Later in the tale, Jekyll expresses what he calls "horror of my other self,"[34] a horror we shall find mirrored in film, and Jekyll literally changes faces:

> I began to be aware of a change in the temper of my thoughts, a greater boldness, a contempt of danger, a solution of the bonds of obligation. I looked down; my clothes hung formlessly on my shrunken limbs; the hand that lay on my knee was corded and hairy. I was once more Edward Hyde. A moment before I had been safe of all men's respect, wealthy, beloved—the cloth laying for me in the dining-room at home; and now I was the common quarry of mankind, hunted, houseless, a known murderer, thrall to the gallows.[35]

"Without bowels of mercy,"[36] Hyde tramples a child and then kills Sir Danvers Carew, a local nobleman, with unusual brutality:

> The old gentleman took a step back, with the air of one very much surprised and a trifle hurt; and at that Mr. Hyde broke out of all bounds and clubbed him to the earth. And next moment, with ape-like fury, he was trampling his victim under foot and hailing down a storm of blows, under which the bones were audibly shattered and the body jumped upon the roadway. At the horror of these sights and sounds, the maid fainted.[37]

The irony here, which Stevenson may or may not have intended, is that apes do not demonstrate the kind of unprovoked rage exhibited by Mr. Hyde. Only—as we shall see in a study of films that feature other doppelgängers and other murders—do humans.

---

[33]Ibid.
[34]Ibid., 122.
[35]Ibid., 118-19.
[36]Ibid., 49.
[37]Ibid., 60.

Films of Initiation

The first category of films involves a plot in which a duplicitous or cruel person learns something essential about himself or herself at great cost. Often, the initiation is paid for by his or her death or the death of someone important to him or to her. Films from the 1980s that meet this criterion include *Dangerous Liaisons* and *Masquerade*. In *Dangerous Liaisons* (1988), a film based on the often-banned 1782 novel *Les Liaisons Dangereuses*, the Viscount of Valmont (John Malkovich) is challenged to a love duel by the Marquise of Merteuil; before the contest of power is over, Valmont has fallen in love with the woman he was challenged to seduce, Madame de Tourvel (Michelle Pfeiffer). His feelings and her predicament eventually cause their deaths. In *Masquerade*, Tim Whalen (Rob Lowe) falls in love with Olivia Lawrence (Meg Tilly) in a scam to take her money. In the end, he dies a death intended for her, and she understands for the first time his commitment to her.

The brutality of *Dangerous Liaisons* is subtle though immediately evident in the first scene, in which the Marquise hails Valmont with "love and revenge, two of your favorites." She reminds Valmont that his intended lover believes in God and virtue and the sanctity of marriage. He agrees but responds, "I want the excitement of watching her betray everything that's most important." As the two lean toward each other and plot their vengeance, their voices take on the "hissing intake of breath"[38] that Stevenson attributes to Hyde. One also remembers Stevenson's warning that Hyde "enjoys the inflicting of pain."[39] The Marquise promises to sleep with Valmont if he accomplishes his cruel mission. Much to his surprise, Valmont ultimately falls in love with the Madame de Tourvel, and the Marquise, who secretly is attracted to him, is devastated. Eventually, the two declare war on each other when the Marquise refuses to keep her end of the bargain, and Valmont dies in a duel she arranges. Degraded and weeping, the Marquise sits alone in her dressing room, symbolically removing her mask as she takes off her makeup. As Valmont dies, he tells his adversary to take a message to Madame de Tourvel: "Tell her love was the only real happiness that I have ever known." The theme of the film is uttered by the conniving Marquise, who says, "Illusions, of course, are by their nature sweet," while reality proves to be torment. When the illusions die, so does the hope of the contestants.

---

[38]Ibid., 50.
[39]Ibid., 24.

In *Masquerade,* Tim Whalen teams up with a former high school friend of Olivia Lawrence and with Lawrence's stepfather in a plan to kill her and take her money. Whalen argues with the stepfather about the necessity of killing her, and when her stepfather breaks into the house one night to attack her, Whalen kills him instead. Lawrence claims she killed him, and Whalen sets up his alibi. After numerous twists and turns, Whalen and Lawrence marry, she becomes pregnant, and Whalen finds he cannot hurt her. Mike McGill, a high school friend, plans to kill Lawrence aboard a boat before a sailing trip, but when Whalen races to the dock to warn her, crying, "Olivia, get off the boat!" he is himself killed in the propane explosion. In the end, standing in the graveyard, an attorney tells Lawrence, "He loved you, Olivia. However it started, he came to love you."

The triumph of love over cruelty and immorality is evident in both films, but one can hardly call the conclusions optimistic; in both films, the characters pay for their newly found compassion and empathy for another with their lives. However, both Valmont and Whalen look into their dark side and would say with Dr. Jekyll, "This, too, was myself."[40]

Films of Murder and Destruction

In the second set of films (*Jagged Edge, Fatal Attraction, Betrayed, Black Widow,* and *Criminal Law*), a vicious character wreaks violence on his or her fellows and must be stopped—killed or imprisoned—in the end. This category is most closely linked to the formula of *The Strange Case of Dr. Jekyll and Mr. Hyde,* although Hyde is "restrained" only by illness and not by forces from outside himself. In three of the films—*Jagged Edge, Betrayed,* and *Criminal Law*—the deceiver is male; in the other two, female.

Jagged Edge opens with the brutal death of Page Lofton Forrester, wife of *San Francisco Times* editor Jack Forrester, who is then charged with his wife's murder. Teddy Barnes (Glenn Close) steps in as his reluctant attorney and, much against her will, falls in love with him. Thomas Krasny (Peter Coyote), district attorney prosecuting the case, believes in Forrester's ability to deceive. When asked, "Do you really think he could have done that to his own wife?" he replies that Forrester committed the crimes in precisely such a way as to make them look like a "Charlie Manson did it."

But in spite of such warnings, point of view dominates, as the viewer sees Forrester despondent and alone after his wife's death, throwing her ash-

---

[40]Ibid., 108.

es (along with roses) into the sea. Nonetheless, the dual nature of human-kind is obvious from the beginning, as Barnes's perceptive abilities (and ours) are called into question. Barnes talks with a colleague, who says, "What if he passes the polygraph test? How are you going to know if he's lying to you?" She responds confidently, as do we all, "I'll know." He says, "A guy like him? You'll never know." After Forrester passes the polygraph, Barnes's assistant tells her that the "machine loves him." Then the assistant says, "He's telling the truth—or, he's the kind of ice cube even the machine can't melt."

A psychiatrist called in to advise the defense attorney tells Barnes that Forrester is not psychopathic but that he is manipulative. Yet the audience is set up to hope with Barnes that her opening statement in the trial is true: "He is an innocent man unjustly accused." We then wait to watch her prove it. Barnes's objectivity is called into question soon after by her colleague, Sam Ransom (Robert Loggia), who tells her, "He killed her." Barnes later tells him, "Sam. He didn't do it." "Yeah?" he says. "Is that your head talking or another part of your anatomy?" During the trial, Krasny claims Forrester planned the murder for eighteen months: "He is not a psychopath. He is an ice man. He is a monster."

Found innocent by the jury, Forrester sleeps with Barnes at his opulent home; she wakes to sunlight and chirping birds in a reconstituted Garden of Eden. Looking in the closet for clean sheets, Barnes finds a typewriter that was used to type notes giving her anonymous tips about the murder. Her reaction is much like Utterson's in *The Strange Case of Dr. Jekyll and Mr. Hyde*, when he sees the weapon Hyde used to kill Carew: "When the stick was laid before him, he could doubt no longer; broken and battered as it was, he recognized it for one that he had himself presented many years before to Henry Jekyll."[41] Since Forrester cannot be tried again for the same crime, Barnes does not call the police. She flees, locks herself in her house, showers, and refuses to take his calls. As Forrester breaks into her house and creeps into her bedroom, Barnes says softly, "I need to see your face, Jack. I could have loved...." She shoots him with a gun she has hidden under the covers when the masked man, carrying a knife and rope, moves toward her without speaking. Sam, suspecting something is wrong, drives to her house, goes upstairs, and removes the mask. Forrester dies, and the mask takes on a symbolic significance as Barnes sees him realistically for the first time.

---

[41] Ibid., 61.

Betrayed, too, opens with a murder, this time of a Jewish talk show host known for his candor and thinly suppressed rage. Sent to investigate those whom the government believes to be guilty is federal agent Catherine Weaver (Debra Winger). As in *Jagged Edge*, where Forrester's position, wealth, seeming sincerity, and tearful reaction to his wife's death are placed in direct contrast to those warning Barnes of Forrester's ability to deceive, *Betrayed* sets Midwestern culture (with its families, farms, "USA" baseball caps, and churches) against the suspicion that some of the residents "go hunting," a euphemism for chasing blacks in the woods and shooting them with semi-automatic weapons. The whites, assisted by dogs, give the blacks thirty seconds and ten bullets and make statements such as "gonna get some black stuff" and "coon in a trap." The murders are in horrible contrast to the simple country life portrayed in the film. When a grandmother says, "There's filth and trash everywhere," she means blacks and Jews. When the local minister preaches, "Our schools can teach that we came from apes but can't teach we are created by God," the viewer must understand that being "created by God" is a distinction reserved for whites, the chosen people.

However, as Weaver tracks down the murderers, she understands the ironies in the lives of the community residents, and she realizes the irony in her own life as well: she, too, is not what she seems. Love soon enters the plot in *Betrayed* when Weaver begins to fall in love with Gary Simmons, a farmer who adores his two children and seems moral and compassionate. His words after a "hunt" shake Weaver to the soul: "Just a nigger. Don't make too much out of it. There's plenty more where he came from." She continues her pursuit of the members of the Zionist Occupation Government (ZOG), a group dedicated to ridding the country of Jews and blacks. In the end, Weaver must kill Simmons and leave the FBI in order to regain her own integrity and to eliminate the part of her that could love a man capable of racism and murder.

In the unfocused and plodding *Criminal Law*, the words of Friedrich Nietzsche precede the film: "Whoever fights monsters should see to it that in the process he does not become a monster. And when you look too long into an abyss, the abyss also looks into you." After Dr. Lanyon of *The Strange Case of Dr. Jekyll and Mr. Hyde* looks into Dr. Jekyll's face when he drinks the potion that will transform him, Lanyon is never the same again. In *Criminal Law*, Ben Chase (Gary Oldman) believes his old college friend incapable of the rape and mutilation of a woman. He defends his friend in court, and when he learns his friend is guilty, his faith in his own judgment is shaken forever. For both Lanyon and Chase, association with evil calls their own character into question.

Black Widow and *Fatal Attraction* are films that feature women as detached and vicious killers. In *Fatal Attraction*, Alexandra Forrest (Glenn Close) meets Dan Gallagher (Michael Douglas) and becomes obsessed with him. Married, he has a weekend affair with her before she begins a series of bizarre acts guaranteed to preserve monogamy: she rips his shirt, kicks him, slits her wrists, tells him she's pregnant, pours acid on his car, kills a family pet, kidnaps his daughter, and breaks into the house to kill his wife. Gallagher's stereotypical happy life—with a wife and daughter whom he adores and a new house complete with a white picket fence—intensifies the viewer's horror at (1) the underlying violence of which Forrest is capable and (2) Gallagher's inability to remain faithful to Beth (Anne Archer).

Of course, Forrest is killed, as is the alluring enchantress-murderer of *Black Widow*, Catherine (Theresa Russell). Seductive and beautiful, Catherine murders her wealthy husbands and inherits their money. Alexandra (Debra Winger) is again a federal investigator who must confront her own masquerade as she pursues a woman engaged in an illegal one. Brought under Catherine's spell, Alexandra must ask herself why she, too, is obsessed with the black widow. Giving Catherine a spider pin on the day of her most recent wedding, Alexandra is startled to hear Catherine say, "Black widow. She mates and she kills. Your question is: Does she love? It's impossible to answer that unless you live in her world. Such an intriguing gift." The suggestion of lesbianism is intensified when Catherine kisses Alexandra on the mouth at the wedding reception, but the film skirts the issue of sexual orientation and honesty with oneself and plays instead on Catherine's ability to seduce those around her. Caught in the end in dependable Hollywood fashion, Catherine goes to jail, and Alexandra walks out into the sunlight.

Films of Individual Vindication

Those identified as evil or potentially evil early in a film often are vindicated later, as the person who suspects them initially later discovers they are trustworthy. Films in this third category are *Still of the Night*, *Sophie's Choice*, and *The Morning After*.

In *Still of the Night*, Meryl Streep plays Brooke Reynolds, an art curator accused of murdering a man with whom she had an affair. The film opens with the discovery of his body, and flashbacks involve sessions between the man and his psychiatrist, Sam Rice (Roy Scheider). Reynolds is a lovely, flustered, and frightened woman whose eyes mingle pain and innocence. Warning her son about the mystery woman he has described to her, Rice's mother (Jessica Tandy) says, "We're probably dealing with a woman who on the surface seems childlike and innocent, but underneath is capable of extreme violence." Heeding his mother's words, Rice flinches when Reynolds approaches him in her office; she realizes he is enamored of her but does not trust her. In the end, the real murderer is apprehended, Rice saves Reynolds's life, and the mother is proven wrong.

In *Morning After*, the viewer deals with a similar plot, in which Alex Sternbergen (Jane Fonda) awakens to find herself in bed with a corpse. Turner Kendall (Jeff Bridges), an ex-policeman, ultimately saves her from her husband, a man who has set her up to protect an heiress he plans to marry. When the film came out on video, promoters enticed the customer with the slogan, "Nothing is as it seems," and that reminder bears more notice in an analysis of *Sophie's Choice*.

In a decidedly more noteworthy film, *Sophie's Choice*, William Styron's novel is turned into a screenplay by Alan J. Pakula. In the film, Stingo (Peter MacNicol) travels to Brooklyn, sets up an office in a boardinghouse, and begins to write a novel. One night he meets a couple named Sophie and Nathan and hears Nathan verbally abusing Sophie on the stairwell before leaving the house. Sophie immediately says to Stingo, "I'm very sorry. That's not the way he really is, you know." What follows are days of dancing, laughter, and carnivals, as Stingo is jolted out of innocence and learns that cruelty and madness often lurk beneath a smile. As Jekyll says in Stevenson's novel, "My devil had been long caged, he came out roaring."[42] Remembering Nathan's voice raised against Sophie, Stingo says, "Suddenly, I shivered violently." Capable of emotional and physical brutality, Nathan nonetheless once rescued Sophie, a Polish survivor of Auschwitz, when she, exhausted and malnourished, collapsed in a library. Tending gently to her as the two read Emily Dickinson poetry and shared an apartment, Nathan won her love. So warm and loving is he when sane that Sophie continually comes to his rescue after his explosions of rage: "But, you know, you don't understand Nathan. You don't know," she tells Stingo. Stingo learns from Nathan's brother that Nathan was "born the perfect child" but that he is a chronic liar, a paranoid schizophrenic, and a drug user. Ultimately, Stingo cannot save the people he loves, and Nathan and Sophie commit suicide. Having grown into a writer

---

[42]Ibid., 115.

with a message, Stingo crosses the Brooklyn Bridge and ends his "voyage of discovery," weeping for the "butchered, betrayed, and martyred children of the earth."

The Triumph of Evil

The final category in the review of 1980s films involves a main character who is so intelligent and deceptive that he or she escapes detection and continues to deceive others. Two very different films comprise the section: one is a Soviet-American spy thriller, and the other is a sensitive, understated screenplay written by dramatist Harold Pinter.

In the first film, *No Way Out*, Kevin Costner plays Tom Farrell, an American war hero who seduces Susan Atwell (Sean Young) at a party and lures her away from her lover, Secretary of Defense David Brice (Gene Hackman). Although he is married, Brice supports Atwell financially and demands monogamy from her. Brice learns of her infidelity, and with a "Listen, damn it. I pay the rent," throws her against a railing. The railing breaks, and she plummets to the floor below and dies. Brice then must place the blame on someone else; he and his chief adviser elect a Soviet spy already sought by their office. Brice begins seeking the KGB agent in earnest, hoping to find and kill the agent before he can deny that he killed Brice's girlfriend. Because the office needs a front man, Brice and the aide select Naval Commander Farrell. While looking in a file in Brice's office, Farrell learns that Atwell is dead and crumbles in grief when out of Brice's view.

The audience sympathizes with Farrell throughout the film, hoping he will evade his pursuers, avenge the death of Atwell, and implicate Brice. The final scene, however, shows Farrell talking with Soviet agents in Russian. The viewer then learns that Farrell is the missing KGB agent but is never sure if he loved Atwell or fooled her, since he was assigned to seduce her and learn more about Brice. Were his actions throughout the film designed to implicate Brice, or was he merely protecting himself? Farrell escapes, Brice is caught, and the plot remains unresolved, perhaps a more realistic ending than identifying someone as purely good or consummately evil. Certainly, this film is more true to the Jekyll-Hyde formula, in which elements of trust and deception are commingled in one person.

In Pinter's *Betrayal*, deception occurs in a romantic triangle, with Jerry (Jeremy Irons) and Emma (Patricia Hodge) carrying on an affair for seven years. Robert (Ben Kingsley), who is Emma's husband and Jerry's best friend, does not initially suspect them. The film begins in the present and moves backwards in one- and two-year intervals to the day when the two first confess attraction for one another. The confusion of the three (Jerry's wife is never introduced) is symbolized by an interchange between Robert and Jerry in which Jerry learns that Robert has known about him and Emma for some time; the dialogue is typical of Pinter's style, as the two struggle to understand, repeating themselves and confusing each other:

> Robert: She didn't tell me about you and her last night. She told me about you and her four years ago. I thought you knew.
> Jerry: Knew what?
> Robert: That I knew. That I've known for years—I thought you knew that.

Much of the dialogue is cold and ruthless, as evidenced by Robert as he seeks to force Emma to tell him the truth about her affair. After seeing a letter from Jerry addressed to her, Robert says, "What do you think of Jerry as a letter writer? You're trembling. Are you cold? ...Well, we're still close friends...He wasn't best man at our wedding, was he? ...Was there any message for me in his letter?" Emma responds carefully, "No message." Robert smiles brutally and says, "No message? Not even his love?" She replies, "We're lovers." He moves in for the kill: "Ah, yes. I thought it might be something like that, something along those lines." Robert then says, "I've always liked Jerry. To be honest, I've always liked him rather more than I've liked you."

The cost of dishonesty and miscommunication lies at the heart of the film. Pinter peppers the script with references to truth: the phrase "to be honest," when no one is; a reference to a character whom he calls a "brutally honest squash player"; the memory of a conversation between the two couples about a novel that is "dishonest," etc. The theme of the film is the failed communication that results from an inability to be honest; that failure is captured in Jerry's plaintive words, "What are you talking about?" In one of Pinter's brilliant uses of irony, Emma and Jerry even talk about faithfulness to one another, when both are betraying their spouses. Very drunk and a little in love, Jerry says to Emma late in the film that if she refuses him, she will be "banishing" him "to the land where the Prince of Emptiness reigns." Pinter and the audience know, of course, that the couples—trapped in their own selfishness and inability to commit themselves—already live there.

Reflections of Cultural and Personal Fears

The concentration of films about deception in one decade testifies to our need to discern the truth about each other. *No Way Out* is frustrating, for we are duped as we watch the film in the same way we are duped in life. In *Jagged Edge*, we are at least prepared for the possibility that Jack Forrester may be a murderer, even though—if the film succeeds—we hope with his love-struck attorney that he is not.

Television Westerns, situation comedies, and other genres prevail because conflict is resolved in an expected way and in an allotted time, when the incidents of our days are much less reassuring. In *The Strange Case of Dr. Jekyll and Mr. Hyde*, we are at least assured that Mr. Hyde is dying and can no longer wreak his rage upon the world. We also know that his evil nature is the product of a potion that concentrated the evil already present in Dr. Jekyll, and we reassure ourselves that evil is rarely that potent. We also are reassured by the fact that Hyde is so physically repulsive; we are not as sure that we can identify evil when confronted with someone as attractive as Catherine in *Black Widow*, as seductive as Alex Forrest in *Fatal Attraction*, or as charismatic as Jack Forrester in *Jagged Edge*.

Melville writes in *The Confidence-Man* that the appearance of truth can destroy and that ignorance is no excuse for blunders. The difficulty of maintaining compassion and love in the face of distrust is illustrated by the following dialogue between two acquaintances in *The Confidence-Man*:

> "He's a rascal," I say.
> "But why not, friend, put as charitable a construction as one can upon the poor fellow?" said the soldier-like Methodist, with increased difficulty maintaining a pacific demeanor towards one whose own asperity seemed so little to entitle him to it: "he looks honest, don't he?"
> "Looks are one thing, and facts are another," snapped out the other perversely.[43]

In short, the films in this study allow us to discover if our heroes on the screen and our perception of them are to be trusted. Outside the darkened theater, of course, we are less sure of ourselves.

---

[43]Herman Melville, *The Confidence-Man*, 20.

Faces in a Mirror

This chapter, the last in the first of two sections of *Untold Stories, Unheard Voices*, explores adaptation from novel to film and pays tribute to American and British literary traditions that are familiar to scholars and general readers, relying on our fascination with alter egos, the god Narcissus, the fine line between madness and creative genius, the role of obsession in art and literature, and the unreliability of point of view. Literary studies of the doppelgänger—defined as a shadowy or mirror image of a protagonist or other character—are plentiful, as are studies of madness and artistic genius. What follow are six highly successful films that illustrate the role of the alter ego, that employ the theme of the artist as a madman, and that challenge the authority of the narrative voice in fiction and nonfiction.

Although they feature murder and doppelgängers, some films such as *Mr. Brooks* (2007), starring Kevin Costner, are mentioned only briefly because they are not adapted from literature. In the film, Earl Brooks is named the "Man of the Year" by the Portland Chamber of Commerce. His alter ego (William Hurt) and he adhere to a set of rules for the murders they commit ("Don't keep photos," "Never kill someone you know," and others). Brooks looks into his rearview mirror as his doppelgänger encourages him to kill and suggests ways for him to avoid detection, saying, "Remember if you die, I go with you. And I like being alive."

Analysis of murder and the doppelgänger begins with Tom Ripley, Dickie Greenleaf, and *The Talented Mr. Ripley* (1955). Patricia Highsmith's novel became a 1999 film starring Matt Damon as Ripley and Jude Law as Greenleaf. Directed by Anthony Minghella, *The Talented Mr. Ripley* explores Ripley's homoerotic desire to lose himself in his friend. When Greenleaf rejects him, Ripley destroys what he loves and, in the process, annihilates everything he values in himself. "He was himself and yet not himself,"[44] writes Highsmith in what is no doubt her most provocative line in a novel that would launch a series about the alluring and tormented Tom Ripley.

More Highsmith characters follow, with Chester MacFarland and Rydal Keener at the center of *The Two Faces of January* (1964), which became a film with the same title in 2014. Directed by Hossein Amini, the sensuous and suspenseful film stars Viggo Mortensen as Chester McFarland, who trusts a seductive but dangerous man named Rydal Keener (Oscar Isaac) to

---

[44]Patricia Highsmith, *The Talented Mr. Ripley* (New York: W.W. Norton, 2008) 130.

help him escape his crimes. McFarland deftly manipulates his new acquaintance but in the end underestimates his opponent's intelligence and humanity and fails to understand the increasingly intense relationship between them.

In a Stephen King tale of mayhem and madness, Mort Rainey (Johnny Depp) meets John Shooter (John Turturro) near his cabin in upstate New York. Tormented by visions, voices, and writer's block, Rainey goes slowly insane. Directed by David Koepp, *Secret Window* was released in 2004, more than a decade after King published *Secret Window, Secret Garden* in a collection titled *Four Past Midnight* (1990). Shooter pursues Rainey, and in an explosion of violence, the two break mirrors that splinter and project distorted images of themselves.

One of the most harrowing tales in this study, *Shutter Island*, drawn from a 2003 Dennis Lehane novel with the same title, was released in 2010. Directed by Martin Scorsese, the film introduces U.S. Marshal Edward (Teddy) Daniels (Leonardo DiCaprio) and his new partner Chuck Aule (Mark Ruffalo). Viewers who watch the film a second time will discover that it tells an entirely different story from the one they first believed was true. They discover that Daniels's alter ego is Andrew Laeddis, a mentally ill patient being treated at the facility, and that neither Ashecliffe Hospital, an asylum on the island, nor its inhabitants are what they appear to be.

The Talented Mr. Ripley *(1955) and* The Two Faces of January *(1964)*

Patricia Highsmith's novels *The Talented Mr. Ripley* and *The Two Faces of January* became films with the same titles in 1999 and 2014, respectively. *The Talented Mr. Ripley* stars Matt Damon as Tom Ripley; Gwyneth Paltrow as Marge Sherwood; Jude Law as Richard (Dickie) Greenleaf; Philip Seymour Hoffman as Freddie Miles; Cate Blanchett as Meredith Logue; James Rebhorn as Herbert Richard Greenleaf Sr.; and Jack Davenport as Peter Smith-Kingsley.

Lies and disguised identities drive the plot, as Ripley, who works part time as an accompanist, a piano tuner, a men's room attendant, and in other occupations, pays his way through college. Ambitious but destitute, Ripley meets a businessman, who is impressed with his energy and work ethic, comparing him favorably to his son Dickie Greenleaf, who is living abroad and spending money he does not earn. Here begin the lies, as Ripley tells Dickie's father that he went to Princeton and has a girlfriend. Conversely, after Ripley meets the younger Greenleaf, he tells him the truth, but the truth is so inappropriate that no one believes him: "Everyone should have one talent," Greenleaf tells Ripley. "What's yours?" Ripley responds, "Forging signatures, telling lies, impersonating practically anybody." Greenleaf laughs at what he thinks is a clever joke.

Ripley is enamored of Greenleaf, who is everything he isn't. In one scene in the film, he asks to get into a bathtub with his friend, who exits rapidly. Ripley gazes longingly at Greenleaf as he gets out of the water, and later, stares at gay male couples in Rome, making it clear to the viewer that he is gay. Hiding his sexual identity provides another layer of duplicity. In another scene in the film, Ripley fingers Greenleaf's jewelry, mimics his voice, and stares into a mirror, pretending to be Greenleaf himself. The music changes from bright to dissonant, as Greenleaf enters the room and catches him. When Ripley hurries to take off the clothes, Greenleaf says, "Would you get undressed in your own room?" Later, on a train to San Remo, Ripley leans his head against Greenleaf's shoulder, pretending to be asleep. Like many of the mirrored images in the six films highlighted in this study, the men's reflection appears prominently in the window of the train car.

In both the book and the novel, the relationship between Tom Ripley and Dickie Greenleaf turns dark and terrifying and culminates in Ripley's killing the object of his affection. On a boat together off the coast of Italy, Ripley murders Greenleaf after Greenleaf tells him that their time together is over. As Greenleaf bleeds to death, Ripley lies down next to him in the boat. On shore, he weighs down the boat and the body, watching as they sink, and steals Greenleaf's identity. At one point, he tells Marge Sherwood, Greenleaf's girlfriend, "When Dickie does something wrong, I feel guilty." This and similar statements underscore his confusion about the line between himself and Greenleaf.

Early in the narrative, Sherwood is kind to Ripley, understanding his obsession with Greenleaf and his desire to be closer to him: "The thing with Dickie," she says empathetically, "it's like the sun shines on you, and it's glorious. And then he forgets you, and it's very, very cold…When you have his attention, you feel like you're the only person in the world. That's why everybody loves him." Later, though, Sherwood rejects Ripley as he begins to try to impersonate Greenleaf.

To hide his string of lies, Ripley kills Freddie Miles, a friend of Greenleaf's who is relentless in his desire to learn what really happened to Greenleaf. Those who know Ripley refer to his looking more and more like his friend: "The only thing that looks like Dickie is you," Miles tells Ripley before he dies. "Whenever I look for Dickie, I find you," says Sherwood, who is beginning to realize something is profoundly wrong.

Little by little, Ripley disappears, becoming Greenleaf and being happy for the first time in his life. His contentment cannot last. Dodging and evading, Ripley is confronted on a steamer bound for the United States by an acquaintance named Meredith Logue, who believes him to be Dickie Greenleaf. Because he is traveling with Peter Smith-Kingsley, with whom he is involved, he must kill Smith-Kingsley to protect his new identity and avoid making Logue and her family suspicious.

The Talented Mr. Ripley is a compelling tale of murder and mistaken identity, a provocative look into the mind of a criminal staying one step ahead of law enforcement. For our purposes, the novel and film are important because of Highsmith's reliance on the doppelgänger. Excerpts from the novel suffice: "Dickie had long, bony hands, a little like his own hands, Tom thought."[45] Later, Highsmith also writes, "It seemed to Tom that he was looking in a mirror when he looked at Dickie's leg and his propped foot beside him. They were the same height, and very much the same weight, Dickie perhaps a bit heavier, and they wore the same size bathrobe, socks, and probably shirts."[46] In a similar but more methodical description, she writes:

> There was a freshly pressed, new-looking gray flannel suit that he had never seen Dickie wearing. Tom took it out. He took off his knee-length shorts and put on the gray flannel trousers. He put on a pair of Dickie's shoes. Then he opened the bottom drawer of the chest and took out a clean blue-and-white striped shirt.
>
> He chose a dark-blue silk tie and knotted it carefully. The suit fitted him. He re-parted his hair and put the part a little more to one side, the way Dickie wore his.[47]

Subsequently, Ripley observes how much he looks like Greenleaf when he dons a hat: "It was a little gray Tyrolian hat with a green-and-white feather in the brim. He put it on rakishly. It surprised him how much he looked like Dickie with the top part of his head covered."[48]

---

[45]Ibid., 49.
[46]Ibid., 65.
[47]Ibid., 75.
[48]Ibid., 76.

On occasion, Ripley talks to himself while staring into a mirror, imagining what it would be like to leave the identity he loathes and become his dead friend. Ripley also reveals his internalized homophobia, although Highsmith uses Ripley's desire for Greenleaf as a way to emphasize his wish to be someone else, not to investigate what it was like to be gay in the 1950s. In one scene, Ripley pretends to be Greenleaf and talks to himself, acting as though he is addressing Sherwood:

> He wiped his forehead the way Dickie did, reached for a handkerchief and, not finding any, got one from Dickie's top drawer, then resumed in front of the mirror. Even his parted lips looked like Dickie's lips when he was out of breath from swimming, drawn down a little from his lower teeth. "You know why I had to do that," he said, still breathlessly, addressing Marge, though he watched himself in the mirror. "You were interfering between Tom and me—No, not that! But there *is* a bond between us!"[49]

One conversation between Ripley and Greenleaf makes Ripley's desire for his friend even more clear. Rather than suggesting that Highsmith is ahead of her time in creating a gay protagonist, it is more likely that Ripley's identity as a gay man is simply further evidence of his role as an outsider. Highsmith relays a conversation between Greenleaf and Ripley:

> "Another thing I want to say, but clearly," he said, looking at Tom, "I'm not queer. I don't know if you have the idea that I am or not."
> "Queer?" Tom smiled faintly. "I never thought you were queer."
> Dickie started to say something else, and didn't. He straightened up, the ribs showing in his dark chest. "Well, Marge thinks you are."
> "Why?" Tom felt the blood go out of his face. He kicked off Dickie's second shoe feebly, and set the pair in the closet. "Why should she? What've I ever done?" He felt faint. Nobody had ever said it outright to him, not in this way.
> "It's just the way you act," Dickie said in a growling tone, and went out of the door.[50]

---

[49]Ibid., 75-76.
[50]Ibid., 77.

Ultimately, Ripley's transitions between his own identity and that of his friend (and murder victim) are deeply disturbing and amplify his self-loathing. He is most happy when he is Greenleaf, desperately unhappy and fearful when he must inhabit his own persona. "He had done so little artificially to change his appearance, but his very expression, Tom thought, was like Dickie's now. He wore a smile that was dangerously welcoming to a stranger, a smile more fit to greet an old friend or a lover,"[51] writes Highsmith. Later in the novel, however, Ripley realizes that he must become himself again in order to survive. He must begin to acknowledge to himself that the object of his affection is dead because of his own rage: "He felt sad. He was not afraid, but he felt that identifying himself as Thomas Phelps Ripley was going to be one of the saddest things he had ever done in his life."[52]

The Talented Mr. Ripley and *The Two Faces of January* resemble *Mr. Brooks*, especially as Earl Brooks tells his alter ego, "You have no idea what I am thinking." His doppelgänger replies, "Yes, I do. And it's wonderfully twisted." Highsmith not only tells riveting stories about crime and subterfuge but her work contains compelling psychological drama. In "'The Two Faces of January': Holding a Mirror to Mr. Ripley," Ty Burr links *The Talented Mr. Ripley* and *The Two Faces of January*, suggesting that the title of the latter novel and film is never explained in the "crisp, minor, sometimes intensely pleasing psychological thriller" but that the "dueling antiheroes of 'January' are stand-ins for young Tom and his older self, each sizing up the other and wondering what he can get away with."[53]

Burr also refers to "two Toms," describing not Tom Ripley and Dickie Greenleaf but the central characters in *The Two Faces of January*. Burr suggests that Chester MacFarlane and Rydal Keener represent an older Tom Ripley and his younger self. "In between is a scene of nearly perfect tension, set at a passport checkpoint in which our two Toms, Chester and Rydal, are forced by circumstance to assume the father-son bond they both crave and dread,"[54] writes Burr. The film, Burr argues, is a "movable character study" that "never reaches a boil,"[55] although the relationship between MacFarland

---

[51]Ibid., 119.
[52]Ibid., 187.
[53]Ty Burr, "'The Two Faces of January': Holding a Mirror to Mr. Ripley," *Boston Globe*, 9 October 2014, web (accessed 8 August 2018).
[54]Ibid.
[55]Ibid.

and Keener is a compelling study of an older man and a young grifter. The film may not reach a "boil" if the viewer is hoping for a rapidly developing plot, but it succeeds if the viewer appreciates the meticulous description of an older man without a son and a young man whose father—from whom he is estranged—recently died.

Set in Greece in 1962, the film begins with scenes of the Parthenon, where Keener leads tours, or, as one film critic writes, spends his time "pontificating about Theseus's tumultuous relationship with his father."[56] According to Odie Henderson, the mythological allusion suggests the father-son rivalry that will develop between Keener and MacFarland, who resemble one another, both "dangerously sexy and morally dubious" con artists. *The Two Faces of January* diverges from Highsmith's series of Tom Ripley novels (*Ripley Under Ground, Ripley's Game, The Boy Who Followed Ripley*, and *Ripley Under Water*) but employs familiar images of Gemini and Janus, symbols that increase dramatic tension. The word "January" derives from "Janus," a Roman god of beginnings, passages, transitions, and endings. He has two faces, looking to the past and the future. Even now, the word "Janus" is linked to contrasts, polarities. In a less complimentary way, it is also employed as an adjective, especially in political discourse. Here, "Janus-faced" suggests more than viewing the past and the future. The term signifies deceptiveness, operating as a double agent or traitor and taking on a role as a two-faced person unworthy of trust.

In "The Janus-Faced Novel," Franz Kuna discusses Joseph Conrad, Robert Musil, Franz Kafka, and Thomas Mann, arguing that the opposites they employ—such as ecstasy and horror and a "dual vision of life"[57]— dominate their best work. Basing his research on Friedrich Nietzsche's interest in the "Janus face of the Aeschylean Prometheus,"[58] Kuna relies on the myth of Prometheus, a god who defied Zeus and provided humankind with fire. Both divine and human, Prometheus wants to preserve his place among the gods but empathizes with humankind and, at the risk of his own happiness, provides it with something both helpful and forbidden. Of course, the Promethean legend and the derivation of the words "Janus" and "January" fit

---

[56]Clayton Dillard, "The Two Faces of January," *Slant Magazine*, 20 September 2014, web (accessed 8 August 2018).

[57]Franz Kuna, "The Janus-Faced Novel: Conrad, Musil, Kafka, Mann," in *Modernism: A Guide to European Literature (1890-1930)*, ed. Malcolm Bradbury and James McFarlane (New York: Penguin, 1991) 445.

[58]Ibid., 452.

into a larger discussion about the doppelgänger in film and literature. The "other"—the person who is separate from us but who, by virtue of his or her very existence, defines us—may exhibit itself in external form, as it does with Dickie Greenleaf and Tom Ripley. The "other" also can manifest itself in a person who experiences warring internal impulses, as it does with Ripley.

The Two Faces of January alludes both to Chester MacFarland's alter ego, Rydal Keener (Oscar Isaac), and to a battle that rages within himself. Intensely confident, yet immobilized by fear, MacFarland (Viggo Mortensen) depends on and needs his wife, yet he seems unable to love her selflessly. Drawn to and repelled by Keener, MacFarland is forced to depend on his guide even as he watches his wife Colette (Kirsten Dunst) grow closer and closer to Keener. At one point, MacFarland discovers that Keener's father is dead, and he finds a letter revealing that Keener failed to attend the funeral. MacFarland, it turns out, reminds Keener of his father, although neither one of them seems able to understand why they are drawn to and repulsed by one another.

The Two Faces of January is a character study of two men who are complicit in covering up a murder and a woman who knows more about her husband's activities than she discloses. As members of different social classes, MacFarland remembers his father, who drove a truck, and Keener tells him about his own father, a professor of archaeology at Harvard. In spite of these differences, however, MacFarland has achieved financial success, although he is on the run from people whom he cheated. Keener seems bent on becoming just like him, a fact MacFarland mentions: "I don't expect you to understand now, but one day you're gonna wake up and you're gonna look in the mirror, and you're gonna see someone who's not all that different from me." At the end of the film, the adversaries make peace with one another as MacFarland dies. While law enforcement officers listen, McFarland confesses to murder, telling them that Keener "had nothing to do with it." "I framed him," he tells the officers. MacFarland then whispers to Keener, "Sorry I disappointed you," words that express his own regret and the words he suspects that Keener wishes he could say to his own father. MacFarland's death provides absolution—for himself and for Keener. The young man reciprocates by visiting MacFarland's gravesite, something he could not bring himself to do for his father.

Secret Window, Secret Garden *(1990)*

"You stole my story," the man on the doorstep said. "You stole my story and something's got to be done about it. Right is right and fair is fair and something has to be done."[59] The first paragraph of the novella *Secret Window, Secret Garden* is vintage Stephen King. Who could possibly stop reading without learning who stole the story? And what story? And who is the man on the doorstep? And if something has to be done, what is that something (and who will do it)?

Secret Window, Secret Garden—which became the 2004 film *Secret Window*, starring Maria Bello, Johnny Depp, Timothy Hutton, and John Turturro—explores how authors may appropriate the ideas of others and how the characters they create may come alive, seeming at times to move and breathe on their own. With Mary Wollstonecraft Shelley's *Frankenstein: or, The Modern Prometheus* (1818) as the most compelling example, fictional characters may become more real than we dreamed and may dominate our consciousness in ways we could not, quite literally, have imagined.

Secret Window, Secret Garden poses seductive questions about the production of narrative. In "A Note on 'Secret Window, Secret Garden,'" King expresses his longtime interest in the impact of fiction, his desire to engage questions about plagiarism broadly defined, and his focus on why authors create particular characters. (The note, which is both autobiographical and critical, precedes the short novel *Secret Window, Secret Garden* in the collection *Four Past Midnight*). He writes:

> A few years ago, I published a novel called *Misery* which tried, at least in part, to illustrate the powerful hold fiction can achieve over the reader. Last year I published *The Dark Half*, where I tried to explore the converse: the powerful hold fiction can achieve over the writer. While that book was between drafts, I started to think that there might be a way to tell both stories at the same time by approaching some of the plot elements of *The Dark Half* from a totally different angle. Writing, it seems to me, is a secret act—as secret as dreaming—and that was one aspect of this strange and dangerous craft I had never thought about much.[60]

---

[59]Stephen King, *Secret Window, Secret Garden*, in *Four Past Midnight* (New York: Penguin, 1990) 253.

[60]Ibid., 250.

This study addresses the creative process by acknowledging the impossibility of articulating entirely new thoughts or producing wholly original texts. According to Ecclesiastes 1:9, "What has been is what will be, and what has been done is what will be done; there is nothing new under the sun." William Shakespeare makes the same argument in the first five lines of "Sonnet 59," as he wonders if there is anything original left to find. A more recent example from popular culture is Led Zeppelin's 1999 album *There Is Nothing New Under the Sun*, which was reissued in 2007 by Missouri band Coalesce, a group of musicians fully aware of the ironies in their project.

In addition, this study addresses comments by King and film director David Koepp about the role of the author. In the film *Secret Window*, John Shooter (John Turturro) says to his own Victor Frankenstein, Morton Rainey (Johnny Depp), "I exist because you made me. Gave me my name. Told me everything I wanted me to do. I did them things so you wouldn't have to." But why do authors develop certain characters? Are those characters reflections of themselves? Do characters act out in ways the author fears to behave? Do some characters—such as Anton Chigurh in *No Country for Old Men* or Joe Christmas in *Light in August* or The Misfit in "A Good Man Is Hard to Find"—so dominate the narrative that they haunt both the authors who gave them their existence and the readers who encounter them?

Finally, *Secret Window, Secret Garden* is at home in the gothic tradition of literature popular in Germany, Russia, the American South, and elsewhere. Although the doppelgänger is not exclusive to gothic literature, authors as diverse as Joseph Conrad, Herman Melville, and Robert Louis Stevenson have created characters who do not exist fully without their double; in the case of the reclusive writer Morton Rainey and his violent visitor from Mississippi, however, Rainey is complicit in his own fate, having created the agent of his own demise. Stark differences exist in the adaptation of the novella into the film, and although this study stops short of detailed aesthetic analysis, some of Koepp's decisions—especially with respect to the ending of the dark tale—are more artful, less manipulative, and significantly more realistic than Stephen King's.

Six months after he discovers his wife Amy Rainey (Maria Bello) making love to another man, Mort Rainey sits alone and disoriented in his lakeside cabin. A stranger appears, introducing himself as "John Shooter" and accusing Rainey of having stolen his story. In the novella, Shooter tells Rainey that he wrote "Sowing Season," which Rainey published as "Secret Window, Secret Garden" seven years before and asks, "How in hell did a big money scribbling asshole like you get down to a little shit-splat town in Mississippi and steal my goddam story?" In King's fictional universe, plagiarism may be defined as the theft of another's intellectual property or, more broadly, as participation in a free-flowing marketplace of ideas, a theme that lies at the heart of the novella *Secret Window, Secret Garden* and the film *Secret Window*.

Without making excuses for those who deliberately steal another person's work and publish it as their own—as central character Mort Rainey most assuredly does—King and Koepp explore the ways in which the truths of human experience inevitably repeat in film, literature, music, television, and other creative projects. "When two writers show up at the same story, it's all about who wrote the words first," Mort Rainey tells his alter ego, John Shooter, who comes from Mississippi to Tashmore Lake in upstate New York to reclaim his stolen story. The seriousness of the duel is obvious later in the film when Shooter tells Rainey that their war will not end "until one or the other of us is dead." In an even more sinister statement, Shooter tells Rainey, "I will burn your life like a canefield in a high wind."[61]

In the novella *Secret Window, Secret Garden*, Rainey is tortured by the memory of having stolen a short story by fellow student John Kintner in a creative writing class at Bates College. Confronting the dissolution of his marriage and his sudden inability to write, Rainey begins to question whether any of the work that followed his misappropriation of Kintner's short story is authentically his own. King writes:

> ...Had he *ever* stolen someone else's work?
>
> For the first time since Shooter had turned up on his porch with his sheaf of pages, Mort considered this question seriously. A good many reviews of his books had suggested that he was not really an original writer; that most of his books consisted of twice-told tales. He remembered Amy reading a review of *The Organ-Grinder's Boy* which had first acknowledged the book's pace and readability, and then suggested a certain derivativeness in its plotting. She'd said, "So what? Don't these people know there are only about five really good stories, and writers just tell them over and over, with different characters?"
>
> Mort himself believed there were at least six stories: success; failure; love and loss; revenge; mistaken identity; the search for a higher power, be it God or the devil. He had told the first four over and over, obses-

---

[61]Ibid., 361.

sively, and now that he thought of it, "Sowing Season" embodied at least three of those ideas. But was that plagiarism? If it was, every novelist at work in the world would be guilty of the crime.

Plagiarism, he decided, was outright theft. And he had never done it in his life. *Never.*[62]

Losing both his marriage and his sanity, Rainey eventually confronts the reality of his crime against the profession he reveres, on which he has based his identity, and from which he derives his self-esteem. In part to address his guilt, Rainey creates a dark figure who stalks him and carries out the crimes that ordinarily would make him recoil with horror.

Mort Rainey and John Shooter are two of the most compelling doppelgängers in a chapter full of mirror images. *Secret Window, Secret Garden* introduces the mysterious John Shooter, a dairy farmer with a southern accent, a distinctly gothic sensibility, and a stubborn claim that Mort Rainey has stolen his intellectual property. Suffice it to say that overt plagiarism rarely ends well, and Rainey begins a voyage into his past that will culminate in his own annihilation.

Murder and psychosis collide in a screenplay adapted by Koepp (whose work also includes *Jurassic Park, Mission: Impossible, Panic Room, War of the Worlds, Ghost Town, Jack Ryan,* and other films). Given the intricacies of the creative process that King and Koepp seek to unravel, one wonders if they discussed the "plagiarism" involved in adapting King's story into a screenplay and, ultimately, into a film; the final project results from not solely the desire of the original author, director, and scriptwriters but also from decisions made by actors such as Johnny Depp, known for his extemporization on the set, and by casting directors, marketing executives, and others committed to an artistic and commercial success.

Koepp is no stranger to nightmares, during which his characters are not certain whether they are awake or asleep as they seek to survive, among other things, alien attacks, a bizarre invasion of a four-story brownstone on the Upper West Side of New York City, and an amusement park filled with cloned dinosaurs. In the haunted universe of *Secret Window*, people and pets die and a betrayed husband goes quietly insane. Darkness, doppelgängers, horror, and romance identify the film as part of the southern gothic tradition and propel viewers into a world in which they must identify with a man who is either a victim or a monster—or both. In "Gothic Fiction Tells Us the

---

[62]Ibid., 335-36.

Truth about Our Divided Nature," Alison Milbank argues that by the nineteenth century, attention had shifted from concerns about the value of religious belief in gothic fiction to "the horrors that lurk in our own psyche."[63] Citing Robert Louis Stevenson's *The Strange Case of Dr. Jekyll and Mr. Hyde* and quoting Sigmund Freud, Milbank writes:

> Although the haunting by a second self may appear to confirm the existence of the supernatural, ever since Freud this apparition has been understood not as a true spiritual presence but as a figure of repression. The eeriness of two selves where there should only be one is, Freud argued, an irruption of disquiet caused by our separation from our origin in our mother's womb.[64]

The relationship between authors and their characters is central to the film *Secret Window*, as voices take over Mort Rainey's mind. One voice says, "There is no John Shooter. There never has been. You invented him." Rainey yells back, "Leave me alone!" The voice whispers, "You are alone." Wearing John Shooter's black ten-gallon hat, Rainey gazes at himself in the mirror and asks, "What is happening to me?" To save himself, Rainey tells Shooter, "You don't exist." Shooter assures Rainey that he most certainly does exist and, more important, that Rainey created him and keeps him alive.

The foray into what Koepp calls "dual identity" becomes far more than an exploration of an author's divided self. In the film, as Koepp states in the documentary short *Secret Window: From Book to Film*, there is a "dark awful part" of each person, and Mort Rainey imagines this part of himself as a "wholly separate person" with the ability to kill. Depp himself suggests that mirrors and windows in the film are portentous and deeply symbolic, providing glimpses into the multiple facets of our essential selves. Hutton alludes to the phrase "keep passing the open windows," which he interprets to mean that we should take seriously our choices. (Interestingly, Hutton incorrectly attributes the phrase to a novel by William Faulkner instead of the film *Hotel New Hampshire*, which is based on John Irving's novel with the same title. The band Queen, too, produced an album titled *Keep Passing the Open Windows*. Here again, it is appropriate to understand that artists borrow ideas,

---

[63]Alison Milbank, "Gothic Fiction Tells Us the Truth about Our Divided Nature," *The Guardian*, 27 November 2011, web (accessed 8 August 2018).
[64]Ibid.

methods, and perspectives during the creative process, often prohibiting general consensus about what constitutes an act of plagiarism.)

As Rainey loses his grasp on his marriage and his sanity, the home he created with his wife burns—the result of arson—and dire events become the rule of the day. In the novella, Bump, a friendly cat beloved by the couple, is killed, his neck broken before he is nailed to the roof of the garbage bin "with a screwdriver from Mort's own shed."[65] Rainey becomes less able to manage his rage, displacing it and becoming more and more agitated. For example, as the phone rings, Rainey gives a "screaky little cry" and falls backwards, "dropping the telephone handset on the floor" and almost tripping over "the goddam bench Amy had bought and put by the telephone table, the bench absolutely no one, including Amy herself, ever used."[66]

Clearly, it is his wife—not the bench—whom Rainey would like to hurt; her betrayal and the relentless pain that followed precipitate Rainey's mental collapse. Ironically, Rainey talks to himself about the way people try to shield themselves from loss. King writes:

> Mort didn't believe that people—even those who tried to be fairly honest with themselves—knew when some things were over. He believed they often went on believing, or trying to believe, even when the handwriting was not only on the wall but writ in letters large enough to read a hundred yards away without a spyglass. If it was something you really cared about and felt that you needed, it was easy to cheat, easy to confuse your life with TV and convince yourself that what felt so wrong would eventually come right...probably after the next commercial break. He supposed that, without its great capacity for self-deception, the human race would be even crazier than it already was.
>
> But sometimes the truth crashed through, and if you had consciously tried to think or dream your way around that truth, the results could be devastating: it was like being there when a tidal wave roared not over but straight through a dike which had been set in its way, smashing it and you flat.[67]

Rainey's loss of his wife and home prevents him from attaining self-awareness. There is no longer a window through which he can see himself

---

[65] King, *Secret Window, Secret Garden*, 291.
[66] Ibid., 294.
[67] Ibid., 309-10.

clearly, as he grows increasingly disassociated from his essential nature. Intellectually, he understands; emotionally, he is distraught and immobilized. "It was over," King writes. "Their lives together were history. Even the house where they had shared so many good times was nothing but evilly smouldering beams tumbled into the cellar-hole like the teeth of a giant."[68] As Rainey's mind unravels, he remembers in particular his wife's love for a room in the house, a room that becomes symbolic and the basis for the title of the film and novella:

> The room was well away from the main house and she liked the quiet, she said. The quiet and the clear, sane morning light. She liked to look out the window every now and then, at her flowers growing in the deep corner formed by the house and the study ell. And he heard her saying, *It's the best room in the house, at least for me, because hardly anybody ever goes there but me. It's got a secret window, and it looks down on a secret garden.*[69]

Rainey's descent into madness becomes more and more obvious. Even when Amy Rainey is with him in the actual moment, he confuses "her real voice with her voice in his mind, which was the voice of memory. But was it a true memory or a false one? ...Wasn't it at least possible that he was having a...well, a recollective hallucination? That he was trying to make his own past with Amy in some way conform to that goddam story where a man had gone crazy and killed his wife?"[70] Later, King describes Rainey as he pursues and confronts the hallucination he calls "John Shooter":

> He turned the knob of the bathroom door and slammed in, bouncing the door off the wall hard enough to chop through the wallpaper and pop the door's lower hinge, and there he was, *there he was*, coming at him with a raised weapon, his teeth bared in a killer's grin, and his eyes were insane, utterly insane, and Mort brought the poker down in a whistling overhand blow and he had just time enough to realize that Shooter was also swinging a poker, and to realize that Shooter was not wearing his round-crowned black hat, and to realize it wasn't Shooter at all, to realize it was *him*, the madman was *him*, and the poker shattered the mirror over the washbasin and silver-backed glass sprayed

---

[68]Ibid., 310.
[69]Ibid., 315-16.
[70]Ibid., 316.

every whichway, twinkling in the gloom, and the medicine cabinet fell into the sink. The bent door swung open like a gaping mouth, spilling bottles of cough syrup and iodine and Listerine.[71]

Madness does not protect Rainey entirely from the gradual realization that he is violent. By the end of the macabre tale, Rainey cannot avoid looking into a mirror and taking on the identity of his nemesis:

> He stood in the front hallway, not sure what he wanted to do next...and suddenly, for no reason at all, he put the hat on his head. He shuddered when he did it, the way a man will sometimes shudder after swallowing a mouthful of raw liquor. But the shudder passed.
> And the hat felt like quite a good fit, actually.[72]

As "dark horror stole over his brain,"[73] Rainey rejects his role in the arson, in the killing of his pet, and in the murder of Tom Greenleaf, but his denial is short lived. King writes:

> ...Would you like to do something that does make sense? Call the police, then. That makes sense. Call the police and tell them to come down here and lock you up. Tell them to do it fast, before you can do any more damage. Tell them to do it before you kill anyone else.
> Mort dropped the pages with a great wild cry and they seesawed lazily down around him as all of the truth rushed in on him at once like a jagged bolt of silver lightning.[74]

Eventually, even Rainey must confront his demon, the part of himself that can maim and kill and bury the bodies of his wife and her lover—and then calmly go to the market, chat with other customers, and complete a manuscript.

Commonly accepted characteristics of the gothic tradition, according to Robert Harris, include (1) a mansion, or in the case of the novella *Secret Window, Secret Garden* and the film *Secret Window*, an old cabin, in which shadows create a "sense of claustrophobia and entrapment"; (2) fear, mystery, and inexplicable events; (3) dreams and other portents; (4) highly dramatic

---

[71]Ibid., 328.
[72]Ibid., 349.
[73]Ibid., 382.
[74]Ibid., 380.

occurrences; (5) "anger, sorrow, surprise, and especially, terror" ("Characters suffer from raw nerves and a feeling of impending doom," Harris writes); (6) women in peril; (7) and a mood of "gloom and horror."[75] Like Edgar Allan Poe, whose gothic characters often slip into madness ("The Fall of the House of Usher" and "The Pit and the Pendulum," for example), other authors introduce dark and mysterious settings and create characters who are in the throes of confusion and loss. Examples include the Brontë sisters (*Jane Eyre* and *Wuthering Heights*), Charles Dickens (*Bleak House, Great Expectations, Oliver Twist,* and other novels), Oscar Wilde (*The Picture of Dorian Gray*), Bram Stoker (*Dracula*), Daphne du Maurier (*Rebecca*), and novels and short stories by William Faulkner, Harper Lee, and Flannery O'Connor that are too numerous to mention.

Similarly, in *Secret Window, Secret Garden* and *Secret Window,* we encounter yet another dark and isolated figure struggling to deal with a fragmented identity in a frightening universe. Mirrors in the cabin suggest the distortions between real life and fiction, between sanity and madness. In the film, townspeople tell Rainey, "I don't think you're really all that well" and "You really don't look well at all." But Rainey continues his dialogue with himself, even when Shooter tells him that if he himself is wrong about the author of his story, he'll turn himself over to authorities: "Then I'd turn myself in. But I'd take care of myself before a trial, Mr. Rainey, because if things turn out that way then I suppose I am crazy. And that kind of crazy man has no reason or excuse to live."

Mort Rainey's inability to separate dreams from reality becomes apparent in *Secret Window, Secret Garden* and underscores his connection to characters in stories by Charles Dickens, Edgar Allan Poe, and others. King describes a nightmare from which Rainey cannot escape:

> He dreamed he was lost in a vast cornfield. He blundered from one row to the next, and the sun glinted off the watches he was wearing—half a dozen on each forearm, and each watch set to a different time.
> *Please help me!* he cried. *Someone please help me! I'm lost and afraid!*
> Ahead of him, the corn on both sides of the row shook and rustled. Amy stepped out from one side. John Shooter stepped out from the other. Both of them held knives.

---

[75]Robert Harris, "Elements of the Gothic Novel," *VirtualSalt,* 22 November 2011, web (accessed 10 August 2018).

I am confident I can take care of this business, Shooter said as they advanced on him with their knives raised. *I'm sure that, in time, your death will be a mystery even to us.*

Mort turned to run, but a hand—Amy's, he was sure—seized him by the belt and pulled him back. And then the knives, glittering in the hot sun of this huge secret garden—[76]

The novella *Secret Window, Secret Garden* is different from the film *Secret Window* in significant ways, including the reader's introduction to the story, John Shooter's corporeal presence, and the fate of Amy Rainey and her lover Ted Milner (Timothy Hutton). Some of the changes make little difference at all. For example, in the novella, it is a cat named Bump who dies; in the film, it is a dog named Chico. In the novella, two townspeople, Tom Greenleaf and Greg Carstairs, die; in the film, Detective Ken Karsch (Charles S. Dutton) and Greenleaf (John Dunn-Hill) die.

Secret Window opens with a snowstorm, as Mort Rainey flees a motel in which his wife Amy Rainey and Ted Milner are making love. As the wipers thump across the windshield, Rainey sits behind the wheel of his Jeep and argues with himself: "Don't go back. Do not go back there." The cacophony of voices begins, but we do not yet understand their significance. Rainey ignores his own warning, takes a key from the front desk, enters the couple's room, points a gun at them, screams, and leaves, his SUV careening away from the scene of his humiliation. But the debilitating pain that follows such a discovery has just begun. Only later do we learn that Rainey's voices are evidence of separate identities that are beginning to manifest themselves as he goes slowly and privately insane. The snowstorm heightens the intensity of the scene, as wind and snow reflect Rainey's own swirling emotions. The initial moment in *Secret Window, Secret Garden*—the instant when John Shooter appears at Mort Rainey's front door—is equally powerful but less dramatic for a medium that relies on visual impact.

From the moment in the film that Tom Greenleaf claims he sees Mort Rainey alone by the side of the road—not with Shooter, as Rainey claims—there are inklings that Rainey is losing his battle against his baser self. King writes, "'I am *not* having a nervous breakdown,' he whispered to the little voice, but the little voice was having none of the argument. Mort thought that he might have frightened the little voice. He hoped so, because the little

---

[76]King, *Secret Window, Secret Garden*, 268.

voice had certainly frightened *him*."[77] In the novella, Greenleaf looks in the rearview mirror and sees "another man with Mort, and an old station wagon, although neither the man nor the car had been there ten seconds before. The man was wearing a black hat, he said...*but you could see right through him, and the car too*."[78] Koepp deletes the ghostly presence of John Shooter, making the film more believable than the story (in Koepp's version, Shooter exists only in Rainey's mind).

In both the film *Secret Window* and the novella *Secret Window, Secret Garden*, Amy Rainey drives to Tashmore Lake to ask her husband to sign divorce papers. As she gets out of the car, King writes, "The hand pulled the shade in Mort's head all the way down and he was in darkness."[79] The man in the black hat—who is and isn't her husband—tells her Mort Rainey is dead, that he died by his own hand, and then comes after her with scissors, on which the sun "sent a starflash glitter along the blades as he snicked them open and then closed."[80] In both texts, when Amy Rainey visits the cabin, she discovers the word "Shooter" ("Shoot Her") etched into and painted on-to walls. Perhaps her surprise and terror mirror her husband's on the night when he found her and Milner in a motel room.

The final scenes differ in each medium. In the novella, Amy Rainey understands the meaning of the word "Shooter," but she survives the attack. In the film, viewers learn the meaning of the word moments before Mort Rainey murders Amy Rainey and her lover. In neither text does Amy Rainey immediately believe that her husband will kill her, thinking that if he were capable of murder, he would have killed her at the motel when he found her with Milner. Even after the murder attempt that occurs in the novella, Amy Rainey attributes her husband's violence to the madman who seems to pos-sess him. As Rainey comes after his wife, she realizes she is dealing with someone she no longer recognizes—"But this wasn't him,"[81] she thinks. Suddenly, Fred Evans, an insurance investigator, appears at the cabin at the last moment and shoots and kills Mort Rainey. He and Amy Rainey explain her husband's behavior as a "schizophrenic episode":

---

[77] Ibid., 374-75.
[78] Ibid., 398.
[79] Ibid., 383.
[80] Ibid., 386.
[81] Ibid.

"He *was* two men," Amy said. "He was himself...and he became a character he created. Ted believes that the last name, Shooter, was something Mort picked up and stored in his head when he found out that Ted came from a little town called Shooter's Knob, Tennessee. I'm sure he's right. Mort was always picking out character names just that way...like anagrams, almost."[82]

In King's version, Amy Rainey and Fred Evans deal for many years with the events at Tashmore Lake: "Both he and the woman who had been married to Morton Rainey woke from dreams in which a man in a round-crowned black hat looked at them from sun-faded eyes caught in nets of wrinkles. He looked at them with no love...but, they both felt, with an odd kind of stern pity."[83] In a startling twist, Shooter leaves a conciliatory note for Amy Rainey, which she retrieves from inside the black hat he left behind.

Viewers who like Amy Rainey or who simply prefer a happier ending will appreciate King's denouement more than Koepp's. Those who understand that every destructive action prompts an even more devastating reaction are more likely to appreciate Koepp's tidy (albeit horrific) finale. In both texts, of course, the function of the ending is to explain the doppelgänger and the hold that fiction can have over us. Both the novella and the film include references to Shooter's demand that Rainey "fix" his story. However, fixing the story does not mean resetting the clock to the moment before Rainey appropriates and publishes Shooter's work. Instead, it means correcting the ending, tying up loose ends by meting out a punishment that (more than) fits the crime, and preserving the integrity of the events as Shooter understands them. To "fix" Shooter's story, Amy Rainey and Ted Milner should die, although in the novella, Mort Rainey dies before he can kill them. In the film, their deaths are the price for their thoughtless cruelty and their own particular duplicity. The two people who set disastrous events in motion die, and the end to Mort Rainey's story—or is it John Shooter's?—is a calm writer back at his computer, eating an ear of corn near an open window that looks out upon a secret garden. Beneath the garden—and feeding the cornstalks—are the still-recognizable decaying corpses of Amy Rainey and Ted Milner. "I know I can do it, [he] said, helping himself to another ear of corn from the steaming bowl," reads the narrator at the end of the film. "I'm sure that in time her death will be a mystery, even to me."

---

[82]Ibid., 395.
[83]Ibid., 399.

This study relies on comments by William Faulkner—whose strongest connection with the wildly popular Stephen King may be his gothic sensibility—and on statements by King himself. In fact, King refers to Faulkner multiple times in his novella. For example, in Sec*ret Window, Secret Garden*, King describes the reaction Mort Rainey has to John Shooter: *"This man doesn't look exactly real. He looks like a character out of a novel by William Faulkner."*[84] Later, Rainey tells a detective that Shooter "didn't strike me as the house-burning type," and Rainey's estranged wife Amy Rainey surprises him with her literary acumen:

> "You mean he wasn't a Snopes," Amy said suddenly.
> Mort looked at her, startled—then smiled. "That's right," he said. "A Southerner, but not a Snopes."
> "Meaning what?" [the detective] asked, a little warily.
> "An old joke, Lieutenant," Amy said. "The Snopeses were characters in some novels by William Faulkner. They got their start in business burning barns."
> "Oh," [the detective] said blankly.[85]

And still later in the novella, Rainey shares what he tells students in creative writing classes when he is asked to talk about his work, a responsibility he does not enjoy: "Get a job with the post office," he'd say. "It worked for Faulkner."[86]

But it is not the allusions to Faulkner or his characters that most interest King (or the readers of *Secret Window, Secret Garden*). While speaking to a class on American fiction at the University of Virginia in 1958, Faulkner told students that his work "begins with a character, usually, and once he stands up on his feet and begins to move, all I can do is trot along behind him with a paper and pencil trying to keep up long enough to put down what he says and does." During the same occasion, Faulkner advises the students to "get the character in your mind": "Once he is in your mind, and he is right, and he's true, then he does the work himself."[87] The same year, this time at Washington and Lee University, Faulkner talks about his characters

---

[84]Ibid., 254.
[85]Ibid., 313.
[86]Ibid., 367.
[87]William Faulkner, presentation, University of Virginia, 21 February 1958, web (accessed 10 August 2018).

in a similar fashion: "Then they all stand up" and "begin to move," and "all you've got to do…is to trot along behind them and put down what they do and say."[88]

Mort Rainey and John Shooter are larger-than-life figures that draw from the gothic tradition so familiar to Faulkner. As Rainey's creation, Shooter overtakes, usurps, and ultimately destroys his master. The characters reign over a universe that is unmerciful and unyielding. In short, artistic production can be a process both fascinating and terrifying. Characters take over our imaginations, sometimes surprising even their creators. "I think there *was* a John Shooter," Amy Rainey tells Evans at the end of the novella. "I think he was Mort's greatest creation—a character so vivid that he actually *did* become real."[89] In fact, John Shooter was so real that he destroyed the author that made him possible.

The profession that obsessed and sustained Mort Rainey became his undoing. "In tough times—up until the divorce, anyway, which seemed to be an exception to the general rule—he had always found it easy to write. Necessary, even," King writes. "It was good to have those make-believe worlds to fall back on when the real one had hurt you."[90] But clearly, as writers themselves, King and Koepp understand what occurs when the make-believe world, too, turns on us. "The writer's job is to gaze through that window and report on what he sees," King writes. "But sometimes windows break. I think that, more than anything else, is the concern of this story: what happens to the wide-eyed observer when the window between reality and unreality breaks and the glass begins to fly?"[91]

Other questions arise, as well: Is our intrusion into other people's lives prompted by an interest in alternative ways of being, or something far more sinister? Like talk show audiences, do we feel better about ourselves if we see the conundrums and frailties of others? Do we need film, literature, and television to entertain us, or do we need to escape from our own empty spaces? If the answers to these questions—and others like them—are complex, would it be wise to account for the duality of our own nature? Just as Mort Rainey stares into a mirror and confronts a startling image of himself, are we

---

[88]William Faulkner, speech, Washington and Lee University, 15 May 1958, web (accessed 10 August 2018).

[89]King, *Secret Window, Secret Garden*, 398-99.

[90]Ibid., 323.

[91]Ibid., 251.

prepared to face our secret selves? And where is the line between imagination and action? Of what are we capable?

Writers create characters who do "them things" so they don't have to. They live vicariously through their creations and allow their readers to do so as well. However, where an author takes us may or may not be where we want to go. Like the unborn boy in the book *Widow for One Year*, which became a 2004 film titled *The Door in the Floor*, do we really want to be born into a world in which there is a door in the floor? Do we really want literature to take us there?

Shutter Island *(2003)*

Ominous clouds droop low over the ocean. An island rises out of the fog ahead. Winds slash trees and slam into the windows of Ashecliffe Hospital. Lavish lawns and bright gardens are juxtaposed with frozen corpses in a winter tableau. And dread is the mood of the day.

Although previews of *Shutter Island* depict spiral staircases, candlelight, mist, and other gothic portents of doom, Martin Scorsese's 2010 film is not a horror film in the traditional sense. Instead, the dark and twisting hallways of a mental institution and the paths along the bluffs of the island represent the labyrinths of the human mind. With water that drips hauntingly on the stone walls of the hospital wards and an eerie light that illuminates the faces of those trapped within, *Shutter Island* elicits a different kind of terror.

The film and the book on which it is based trade on dreams, hallucinations, and delusions. There are no vampires or rivers of blood on Shutter Island; instead, living people wander alone in ghostly silence. Author of *Gone, Baby, Gone* (1998) and *Mystic River* (2001), Dennis Lehane has perfected a mood of gloom and apprehension. His 2003 novel *Shutter Island* is no different. "The dark trees on the other side of the wall had begun to sway and whisper,"[92] he writes. Similar descriptions of nature as a menacing force permeate the film as well.

Reminiscent of the endlessly twisting tunnels of Franz Kafka's *The Trial*, the dank catacombs of Edgar Allan Poe's "The Cask of Amontillado," and the evocative bell tower of Alfred Hitchcock's *Vertigo*, the images that characterize both the novel and the film include barbed-wire fences, a cemetery, jagged cliffs, and a Civil War fortress that stands watch over the resplendent (and incongruous) flower gardens below. Drawing us into a mi-

---

[92]Dennis Lehane, *Shutter Island* (New York: HarperTorch, 2003) 68.

crocosm of human cruelty and depravity, Scorsese creates an allegory of despair.

From our first glimpse of a ship moving slowly toward the forbidding island to Dinah Washington's singing "This Bitter Earth" during the final credits, we understand that we have entered a baffling but self-contained and carefully choreographed universe. Washington's lyrics—"This bitter earth/ What a fruit it bears"—provide the thematic center for this strange new world. In his *Wall Street Journal* review, John Anderson notes "the film's ever-present cigarette smoke and mood of anxiety."[93] Similarly, Roger Ebert describes the film with characteristic attention to its place among other narratives: "In its own way it's a haunted house movie, or make that a haunted castle or fortress."[94]

Scorsese's allegory is a finely hewn narrative, and, in fact, effective storytelling lies at the heart of the film, as character after character tells his or her own somber tale. Throughout the novel, Lehane employs numerous synonyms for narrative, reminding us that—wisely or not—human beings are doomed to talk about themselves and their individual realities. Lehane writes about the "late-night boogeyman story,"[95] the fairy tale that develops in a "boo-ga-boo-ga-boo-ga kind of way,"[96] "tall tales,"[97] "yarns,"[98] "a handsomely mounted stage play,"[99] and a "masquerade."[100] In the novel, protagonist Edward "Teddy" Daniels accuses his wife of having filled their children's heads with "dreams" and "fantasies" and of having taken them too often to the movies.[101] In a film in which memory and the impossible borderland between truth and fiction are at stake, there are sure to be surprises.

Shutter Island is two films in one, and its startling twists encourage a second (and third) viewing. It is and is not about World War II, the Holocaust, and the dead victims and their oppressors at Dachau. It is and is not

---

[93]John Anderson, "Scorsese Rules This 'Island,'" *Wall Street Journal,* 19 February 2010, web (accessed 10 August 2018).

[94]Roger Ebert, *"Shutter Island," Chicago Sun Times,* 17 February 2010, web (accessed 10 August 2018).

[95]Lehane, *Shutter Island,* 252.

[96]Ibid., 253.

[97]Ibid., 286.

[98]Ibid.

[99]Ibid., 348.

[100]Ibid.

[101]Ibid., 354.

about the thin line between sanity and madness: "Sanity is not a choice," Dr. John Cawley (Ben Kingsley) tells Daniels.

The film is set in 1954 in the Boston Harbor Islands of Scorsese's imagination. Taking place in three days, *Shutter Island* opens with Daniels (Leonardo DiCaprio), a U.S. marshal, retching in a lavatory on a ship that carries him to his current assignment. Perhaps his nausea is related to seasickness; perhaps it is the result of something more sinister ("It's just water. It's a lot of water," Daniels says. "I just can't stomach the water"). Critic Anthony Rainone notes that in *Shutter Island*, "water is as dangerous as acid."[102] Anderson concurs: "The heaving water on Boston Harbor looks as welcoming as a grave."[103]

The ocean, the waves, the rain, and the impenetrable fog are central to the plot. Unlike bodies of water in *The Adventures of Huckleberry Finn*, *A River Runs Through It*, or other masterpieces of American literature, water in *Shutter Island* is sinister. Instead of giving life, it threatens those who live on the island and hints at the trauma that torments Daniels. Water is often central to Daniels in his dreams and in his waking moments. Telling Daniels "I'm just bones in a box, Teddy," his wife turns to ashes in his arms as water runs off his hands. A mother drowns her three children after going for a "long swim in the lake."

Before long, we understand that in this fictional universe, little is as it appears, and music and setting are nearly as important as character or plot. The ship captain—anxious to deposit his cargo before the impending storm engulfs the island—maroons us along with marshals Daniels and Chuck Aule (Mark Ruffalo). We are left with the doctors, guards, inmates, nurses, and orderlies who populate a seemingly corrupt mental institution at the height of the Cold War. As if the post-World War II anxiety, the uneasy relationship between the U.S. and Russia, and the proliferation of nuclear weapons aren't enough, we are witnesses to escalating debates about psychopharmaceutical drugs and surgical procedures that are used to treat the criminally insane.

A patient, Rachel Solando, is missing. She has escaped from her cell, although everyone agrees it is impossible for her to get past the guards or to survive outside the facility. Having relinquished their weapons, Daniels and Aule begin to interview doctors and patients and to search the wards and the

---

[102]Anthony Rainone, "Island of No Return," *January Magazine*, web (accessed 10 August 2018).
[103]Anderson, "Scorsese Rules This 'Island.'"

rest of the island for her. But soon Scorsese makes it clear that all is not as it seems. Cawley tells Daniels that Solando created an "elaborate fictional structure" and gave all those on Shutter Island parts in the play she wrote. She enlisted others in her story in order to avoid facing the truth about her past. "The greatest obstacle to her recovery was her refusal to face what she had done," Cawley says to Daniels.

Unsurprisingly, Rachel Solando is not the only one who has created an intricate fiction, and we soon begin to understand how Daniels is connected to the escapee he has been assigned to locate. Driven mad by the traumatic events of war and by guilt for his complicity in the deaths of his wife and children, Daniels confronts his family in a dream. "You should have saved me," his daughter tells him. "You should have saved all of us." Later, covered in blood, Solando (played in this particular scene by Emily Mortimer) stands above three dead children who are lying at her feet. Daniels lifts one of the children, who is his daughter, and says, "I'm so sorry." Again, the child asks, "Why didn't you save me?" Slowly and with the atrophied movements of someone trapped in a dream, Daniels puts the body of his daughter in the water with the other children. "See? Aren't they beautiful?" Solando says to him.

Like Solando, Daniels has reinvented reality in order to save himself. In the novel, Cawley tells Daniels, "You've created a dense, complex narrative structure in which you are the hero."[104] To cope with the unalterable pain of guilt and loss, Daniels has redefined himself as a brilliant, caring U.S. marshal and has displaced his darker side onto a character named Andrew Laeddis. As Daniels and Aule investigate odd occurrences on the island, Aule says cryptically, "Maybe we'll run into Andrew Laeddis." And later, Daniels says, "He's here. Laeddis. I can feel him."

The conclusion of the film resolves some mysteries and highlights others. As Daniels runs into a room in the lighthouse, gun drawn—ostensibly to put an end to lobotomies that he believes are taking place—he is drenched from swimming to the promontory. Cawley is alone in the room. In an allusion to Daniels's past, he says, "Why are you all wet, baby?" He then shows Daniels his intake form, and Daniels reads that in two years of treatment on the island, he has denied that the murder of his children and the death of his wife ever took place and has created "highly developed and fantastical narratives" about his life. In the novel, Lehane includes a lengthier report: "Pa-

---

[104]Lehane, *Shutter Island*, 331.

tient is highly intelligent and highly delusional. Known proclivity for violence. Extremely agitated. Shows no remorse for his crime because his denial is such that no crime ever took place. Patient has created a series of highly developed and highly fantastical narratives which preclude, at this time, his facing the truth of his actions."[105]

We then learn that Daniels also has invented anagrams: His wife Dolores Chanal (Michelle Williams) is Rachel Solando. Edward Daniels is actually Andrew Laeddis. As we learn that Daniels has hidden his violent past from himself, we begin to understand that he in fact might not be allowed to leave. From the way Daniels describes his passion for his wife, we know the depths of his loss and his inability to deal with the manner in which she died. Throughout the film, Scorsese visually suggests the deep love Daniels has for his wife, but Lehane also powerfully evokes the torment of his separation from her as she sinks further and further into madness: he "wanted to ask her what sound a heart made when it broke from pleasure, when just the sight of someone filled you the way food, blood, and air never could, when you felt as if you'd been born for only one moment, and this, for whatever reason, was it."[106]

Little by little, we understand more about the convoluted but intriguing plot. Manic-depressive and suicidal, Chanal and Daniels had three children—Simon, Henry, and Rachel, according to the novel. As his wife sank into madness, Daniels ignored the severity of her condition, even after she set their apartment on fire. Having moved the family to a lake house, Daniels returns from a trip one day in 1952, pours himself a drink, and goes outside to greet his family. Rising from a backyard swing, Chanal is drenched. "Baby. Why are you all wet?" Daniels asks. Seeing the bodies of his children in the water, Daniels throws himself into the lake. Lifting each of them, he screams his grief to the heavens and lays the bodies in a row and folds their arms. As Chanal begs him to set her free, Daniels then cradles his wife in his arms and shoots her. Later, in a rare moment of self-awareness, Daniels tells Cawley, "I killed them because I didn't get her help."

As Cawley talks with his most challenging patient, we learn that at one point during his treatment, Daniels acknowledged his guilt, and the doctors began to hope for a breakthrough; however, as Cawley explains, Daniels "reset." Throughout the carefully monitored role-play during his three days as a marshal, Daniels is again brought into consciousness of his past. However,

---

[105]Ibid., 326.
[106]Ibid., 242.

as we witness his conversation with Aule, who is actually psychiatrist Lester Sheehan, Daniels drifts back into his other persona and calls Sheehan "Chuck." Sheehan nods to Cawley and Jeremiah Naehring (Max Von Sydow), indicating to them that the role-play therapy did not succeed. Although the words do not appear in the novel, Daniels then asks the man he believes to be his partner, "Which would be worse? To live as a monster? Or to die as a good man?"

Scorsese's allegory is part thriller, part psychological drama, and part tormented love story. His analysis of human violence and of the ability of the mentally ill to deny their crimes by creating alter egos and writing their own stories is masterful. Dr. James Gilligan, author of *Violence: Reflections on a National Epidemic*, served as the psychiatric consultant on *Shutter Island*. An expert in dissociative identity disorder, Gilligan addresses the ways people avoid treatment by creating an imaginary world or meta-reality. According to Gilligan, in the final seconds of the film, Daniels chooses symbolic suicide by agreeing to a lobotomy.[107] After interviewing Gilligan, David Cox writes, "According to Gilligan, those cryptic last words mean: 'I feel too guilty to go on living. I'm not going to actually commit suicide, but I'm going to vicariously commit suicide by handing myself over to these people who're going to lobotimise me.'" He adds that if people do not know what they're doing at the time they commit violence—and if psychiatric treatment "returns them to their senses"—then "guilt may overwhelm them" and be too much to bear.[108]

However, horror reverberates far beyond Shutter Island. Even the inmates are terrified of what lies across the ocean, a reminder to viewers that madness has many forms. For example, one patient who killed her spouse with an ax tells the marshals she doesn't know what she would do if she were released, especially now that bombs can "reduce whole cities to ash." And later, as Daniels subdues a violent patient in Ward C, the man cries out, "I don't want to leave here. All right? I mean why would anybody want to? We hear things here. About the outside world...Do you know how a hydrogen bomb works?...Get it?...Do you?"

Three other scenes suggest Scorsese's desire to make Shutter Island a microcosm of a dangerous and violent world. When he is invited to talk with Cawley and Naehring after he disembarks on the island, Aule asks if the

---

[107]David Cox, "*Shutter Island's* Ending Explained," *The Guardian*, 29 July 2010, web (accessed 10 August 2018).
[108]Ibid.

music playing in the mansion is Brahms. Daniels responds, "No. It's Mahler." In the room with Cawley and Naehring, Daniels flashes back to his time as a soldier in Germany and to the suicide of a Nazi commander. The commander was playing Mahler as he slowly bled to death and as Allied troops outside faced the horrors of Dachau. Bodies were frozen to the ground—"too many to imagine," Daniels says. When prison guards were executed, Daniels tells Aule, "It wasn't warfare. It was murder."

In another scene, Daniels finds the woman he believes is Rachel Solando (played in this scene by Patricia Clarkson). She is hiding in a cave at the far reaches of the island and tells him she was never a patient but a psychiatrist. She calls the surgical procedures in use on the island "barbaric" and "unconscionable." She says the doctors are creating ghosts, people "who can't be interrogated because [they have] no memories to confess." "You can never take away all man's memories," Daniels says. "Never." He then asks her, "Who knows about this? On the island, I mean. Who?" "Everyone," she tells him. Solando talks about North Koreans, Nazis, Soviets, and Americans, all of whom prey upon one other and create chaos and death, she says. There is no "moral order" on the island—or anywhere else.

When Daniels leaves the cave, a menacing warden offers him a ride. The warden identifies with Daniels's violent nature and issues a short soliloquy as he drives: "God loves violence…Why else would there be so much of it? It's in us. It's what we are. We wage war, we burn sacrifices, and pillage and plunder and tear at the flesh of our brothers. And why? Because God gave us violence to wage in his honor." He ends their conversation by suggesting that he and Daniels are very much alike: "We've known each other for centuries."

Lehane placed his novel in the tradition of paranoid political thrillers and set out to create an unreliable narrator, and screenwriter Laeta Kalogridis honored his vision. Daniels is or isn't a marshal. Sheehan did or did not leave the island while the marshals searched for Solando. The lighthouse is either a sewage treatment plant or a hospital annex in which lobotomies are performed. Reality depends on which story we believe: a U.S. marshal's tale of a missing patient or psychiatrist's tale of an intricate role-play designed to bring a patient back to his senses.

Naehring, who early in the film identifies Daniels and Aule as "men of violence," tells Daniels he has "outstanding" and "very impressive" defense mechanisms, but it is not until the end of the dark tale that we understand what he means. Listing *Kudun*, *The Age of Innocence*, and *Raging Bull* as three other Scorsese films about "psychological or physical cruelty," Lawrence Toppman writes in the *Charlotte Observer* that the "consequences of violence" in *Shutter Island* are "inescapable guilt, fruitless denial, pathetic justification."[109] Certainly, his assessment is true of Daniels, whose defenses prohibit him from integrating his two selves.

In his novel, Lehane explores the manner in which we write our own fictions and maintain what we need to believe about ourselves. "You surfaced without a history, then spent the blinks and yawns reassembling your past, shuffling the shards into chronological order before fortifying yourself for the present,"[110] he writes. In the film, we realize that when Cawley describes Solando, he is talking not only about her but also about Daniels and—to a lesser extent—all human beings who engage in self-delusion. Describing Solando in the novel, Cawley says, "To sustain the structure, she employs an elaborate narrative thread to her life that is completely fictitious."[111] But, of course, instead of simply describing one troubled woman, Cawley refers to us all.

In its first week, *Shutter Island* opened at number 1 and netted $41 million. Still number 1 during the second week, it earned $22.2 million. Like other Scorcese films starring DiCaprio (*The Aviator*, *The Departed*, and *Gangs of New York*), *Shutter Island* is also a critical success. However, *Shutter Island* is unlike anything that came before. Anderson calls it Scorsese's "most enigmatic" film: "*Shutter Island* requires multiple viewings to be fully realized as a work of art. Its process is more important than its story, its structure more important than the almost perfunctory plot twists it perpetrates. It's a thriller, a crime story and a tortured psychological parable about collective guilt."[112]

Anderson predicted that *Shutter Island* would have limited popular success, as much because of its topic as its meandering plot line: "It won't be a beloved movie. It will inspire doctoral dissertations." He celebrates Scorsese's having "turned a death camp into a frozen tableau of permanently lovely children," another suggestion that the dark tale might appeal to critics more

---

[109]Lawrence Toppman, "*Shutter* Yields Shudders—and Ideas," *The Charlotte Observer*, 18 February 2010, web (accessed 1 August 2018).

[110]Lehane, *Shutter Island*, 20.

[111]Ibid., 50.

[112]Anderson, "Scorsese Rules This 'Island.'"

than to the American public. "Not since *Raging Bull* has Mr. Scorsese so brazenly married brutality to beauty,"[113] he writes.

Certainly, *Shutter Island* is a contribution to film noir, but it is also a narrative that comments on the nature of storytelling. And if the story isn't compelling enough, Ebert argues that the film is notable for other reasons:

> And that's what the movie is about: atmosphere, ominous portents, the erosion of Teddy's confidence, and even his identity. It's all done with flawless directorial command...
> This movie is all of a piece, even the parts that don't appear to fit...What if there were things about Cawley and his peculiar staff that were hidden? What if the movie lacks a reliable narrator? What if its point of view isn't omniscient but fragmented? Where can it all lead? What does it mean? We ask, and Teddy asks, too.[114]

Shutter Island challenges our conclusions about mental illness as it introduces us to a Kafkaesque universe in which nothing is what it seems to be. What do the multiple narratives mean? Which characters may we trust? Why do we so readily privilege Daniels's version of reality? Ultimately, making sense of the macabre allegorical tale is as rewarding as it is challenging.

True Story: Murder, Memoir, Mea Culpa *(2005)*

Like *Shutter Island*, the story of Michael Finkel begins innocently enough. As a contributor to *The New York Times Magazine* and other publications, Finkel established himself as a committed interviewer and engaging writer. In 2001, his story "Is Youssouf Malé a Slave?" was published. The piece, which dealt broadly with slavery in West Africa, enhanced a reputation that included nine cover articles in three years. Finkel was on his way to a staff position at a major American newspaper or magazine. The article begins:

> A man came to the village on a moped. Youssouf Malé watched him. A man on a moped was unusual. When visitors did come to Nimbougou, deep in the hill country of southern Mali, they were almost always on foot, or on bicycle. The man on the moped had come to sell fabrics, the

---

[113]Ibid.
[114]Ebert, "*Shutter Island.*"

flower-patterned kind from which the women in Youssouf's village liked to sew dresses. Youssouf sat beneath a palm tree and watched.[115]

There was only one problem with the colorful, detailed scene, a problem repeated throughout the compelling piece of what the writer considered literary journalism: the reporter was not present, did not hear the conversation that follows this particular descriptive passage, and used Youssouf Malé, a real person, as a composite. Editorial comments that now appear at the end of *The New York Times Magazine* story confirm the ethical violations, ending with the statement: "The Times's policies prohibit falsifying a news account or using fictional devices in factual material" ("Editor's Note").[116]

"Is Youssouf Malé a Slave?" featured photographs, including one that purportedly showed Malé himself. A representative of Save the Children contacted the editors of *The New York Times* and questioned the identity of the person in the photograph. After an investigation, editors learned that in order to personalize the interviews Finkel conducted with multiple sources, he had created a composite character and given him a fictitious name. In other words, Finkel violated journalistic principles by merging several interviews and inventing a source He was fired. In "The Return of Michael Finkel," Jack Shafer provides details:

> Although Youssouf Malé actually exists, Finkel created the Youssouf of the article by combining the stories of several boys. The real Youssouf spent less than a month at the plantation, not a year as Finkel reported. Youssouf's return to his home and his parents, of which Finkel wrote, was told to him by another boy. A scene from the article in which a psychologist interviews Youssouf never took place.[117]

Finkel returned to his home in Montana, received a call from a reporter at *The Oregonian*, and learned that a man accused of murdering his family was using the name "Michael Finkel" in Mexico while he evaded U.S. law enforcement. David Wiegand, who interviewed Finkel in 2005, said the reporter's call was "divine intervention": "When Finkel heard the story, he wanted to know more, initially just about why Longo decided to pretend to

---

[115]Michael Finkel, "Is Youssouf Malé a Slave?" *The New York Times Magazine*, 18 November 2001, web (accessed 10 August 2018).

[116]Ibid.

[117]Jack Shafer, "The Return of Michael Finkel," *Slate Magazine*, 27 July 2007, web (accessed 10 August 2018).

be Michael Finkel. Something told him that there was a story here and perhaps a way to redeem his career."[118] Finkel called the man, Christian Michael Longo, who had been arrested, brought back to the U.S., and charged with the murder of his wife and three children, MaryJane Longo and Zachery, 4; Sadie, 3; and Madison, 2. What followed were years of communication—in person, by phone, and in letters—between a disgraced journalist and an accused murderer. After Longo was found guilty, he admitted to Finkel that he had committed the murders. Until the trial, Finkel had held out hope that he might be innocent.

This study is not the first to link *In Cold Blood*—and the 1967 film with the same title—to *True Story*—and the 2015 film with the same title. In fact, prominent *New York Times* film critic A. O. Scott "attests to the strong, often uncomfortable affinity between reporters and killers":

> Truman Capote's "In Cold Bood" is perhaps the supreme example, and one that has inspired several movies over the years. Neither Michael Finkel's book "True Story" nor Rupert Goold's film adaptation is anywhere near as accomplished as Capote's book or Bennett Miller's movie "Capote." The new film is of interest mainly because it demonstrates just how difficult it can be to map the queasy moral territory where crime and journalism intersect.[119]

Scott's comparison of the films *In Cold Blood* and *True Story,* as well as his reference to journalists who cover murderers, makes his review especially significant to a discussion of the texts in this chapter. Especially relevant in the analysis of books separated by fifty years—and the films adapted from them—is Scott's acknowledgment of the "queasy moral territory"[120] and the often complicated relationships that develop between journalists and the criminals whom they cover.

Another astute analysis of novels, films, and the relationship between murderers and journalists appears in Garrett Epps's "The True Story Behind *True Story.*" In his review, Epps describes the connection between Finkel and Longo. Epps accurately states that Finkel's interest in the killer is intensified

---

[118]David Wiegand, "After Getting Fired by the *New York Times* for Lying in Print, a Reporter Stumbled on the Story of His Life," *SFGate,* 11 June 2005, web (accessed 10 August 2018).

[119]A. O. Scott, "'True Story' Stars Jonah Hill and James Franco," *The New York Times,* 16 April 2015, web (accessed 10 August 2018).

[120]Ibid.

"because Longo is a liar: both the film and the book are framed as parables about truth and lies." However, Epps subsequently discounts Finkel's concern about whether or not Longo tells the truth: "A man who murders his wife and children doesn't become a worse man because he lies about it afterwards. The two sins are simply incommensurable: one is a character deficiency, the other is an open doorway into Hell." Interestingly, Epps describes Longo's life in a way that conjures up images of Perry Smith; until he kills his family, Epps argues, Longo's "life was a grim pageant of failure, betrayal, and petty crime."[121]

Finally, another critic underscores similarities between *In Cold Blood* and *True Story* and further justifies the inclusion of both nonfiction novels in this study. Michael Cieply calls Longo a "creepy doppelgänger" and says the film *True Story* reveals a "hint of something new and slightly chilling: journalistic horror." Not a fan of the relationship that develops between Finkel and Longo, Cieply describes it as "a mutually exploitive relationship—mixing friendship, journalism and some bizarre exploration of shared reality."[122] The same, of course, might be said about Capote and Smith.

Directed by Rupert Goold, the film derived from Michael Finkel's novel begins with a stuffed teddy bear falling into a suitcase. In flashback, viewers learn about Finkel's breach of journalistic ethics and hear the editor tell him, "You have a great future ahead of you, Mike. But not here." After he establishes a connection with Longo, we learn that his humiliation has devastated him. "At the very same time that you were using my name, they stripped me of it," Finkel tells Longo. Spending much of his time "soul searching," Finkel says to Longo, "I thought maybe you could tell me what it's like to be me." Although the two are drawn to one another, Finkel vacillates in how he feels about Longo, sometimes expressing compassion for his difficult life, as Capote did with Smith, and sometimes describing Longo as a "narcissist who resents every single second of attention" not given to him: "I'm here to tell you whatever else is coming to you, you will never—ever—escape what you are."

One of the numerous interviews between Longo (James Franco) and Finkel (Jonah Hill) is particularly revealing. We learn that Longo is desperate to be heard and understood, while Finkel focuses, appropriately enough,

---

[121]Garrett Epps, "The True Story Behind *True Story*," *The Atlantic*, 24 April 2015 web (accessed 10 August 2018).

[122]Michael Cieply, "Telling a True-Life Story, Following a 'True-Film' Style," *The New York Times*, 17 April 2013, web (accessed 10 August 2018).

on the story he thinks might resurrect his career. In the film, Finkel transcribes the conversation this way:

> Longo: ...the way you stand up for people that don't have voices...I guess I felt like I knew you...
> Finkel: I needed the story to be ahead of the game.
> Longo: I know I'm very valuable to people like you...Most journalists are only interested in writing what their readers want to hear. They don't want to take the time to find out the truth about what really happened...You know, when I was being you was the happiest I've been in a long tine. Do you think you could ever imagine being me?
> Finkel: This is a once-in-a-lifetime story.

After he was accused and banished from the newspaper, Finkel defended himself, but his argument is not compelling. "I hope readers know that this was an attempt to reach higher—to make something beautiful, frankly," Finkel said, adding, "In the article, there's no question of the quality of reporting, just in the journalistic techniques employed."[123] Of course, "journalistic techniques," as Capote discovered, are no small consideration when writers commit themselves to nonfiction. Continuing his futile attempt to link his work to the best in literary journalism, Finkel said, "In my writing, I try to combine all my favorite elements of journalism—accuracy, real characters that exist on this planet—with all my favorite elements of literature: a sense of flow, of propulsion, of wanting to read every sentence."[124] Again, while it is important to acknowledge that no one doubts Finkel's use of the techniques that characterize literary journalism, what leads to his public disgrace is his invention of a name and his use of a composite character. Journalists such as Janet Cooke of the *Washington Post* were guilty of similar journalistic overreach long before Finkel, although he appears not to have learned from her. In fact, Cooke never found a way back into the profession after being fired and having to relinquish a Pulitzer Prize for a 1981 story titled "Jimmy's World." In it, she creates a composite character to represent child heroin addicts. Reporters discovered lies on her résumé at the same time that government officials tried to locate a child that did not exist: both investigations led to her exposure and censure.

---

[123]Robert Kolker, "The Great Pretender?" *New York Magazine*, 9 March 2013, web (accessed 10 August 2018).
[124]Ibid.

Linking Finkel's story to Capote's is somewhat risky because Capote was not a journalist, was never trained as a journalist, and was not writing for a publication dedicated to accuracy and committed to fact checking. However, both writers succumbed to arrogance and a desire to be famous, and they employed several questionable newsgathering techniques. In "The Great Pretender," Robert Kolker details Finkel's 2002 fall from grace, writing that Finkel's "methods were, to say the least, unorthodox, and far from *Times*ian: spending hours with sources without a notebook, writing epic-length articles with barely a quotation in them."[125] Similarly, as explored in chapters one and three, Capote believed he could memorize hours of interviews, he relied on quotations that preserved what he considered to be the essence of what actually occurred, he invented scenes, he changed names, and he committed other violations of journalistic ethics in both *In Cold Blood* and *Handcarved Coffins*.

Like Capote, Finkel is drawn to a story with multiple murders and hopes to build his reputation on his retelling of the events that preceded and followed the crime. Calling Longo's story "tragic, creepy and compelling,"[126] Finkel is nonetheless flattered when Longo tells him that he chose to appropriate the name "Michael Finkel" because he was familiar with his work. In *True Story*, Finkel describes Longo's interest in journalistic techniques: "'You're probably writing your first impressions,' he said. I confessed I was. 'I'd be doing that, too,' he added knowingly, as if he were also a journalist, swapping tricks of the trade with a colleague."[127] Later, Longo speculates in a letter about how his life might have been different if he had made the same choices Finkel did: "'I sat there...half daydreaming of what the real life of Michael Finkel must be like,' he wrote. 'I've learned enough in life to realize that no life or career is as fantastic as you might imagine, but I couldn't help picturing how my life would have been if I had taken whatever steps the real Mr. Finkel took to attain the position that he now held.'"[128] Finkel is disturbed when he reads the letter and imagines that their roles are in some way reversed: "As I read, I was struck by an odd feeling of detachment, thinking of Longo thinking of me. It was both riveting and uncomfortable; I imag-

---

[125]Ibid.

[126]Bruce Fretts, "A Writer Watches His Life Unspool on Film," *The New York Times*, 14 April 2015, web (accessed 10 August 2018).

[127]Michael Finkel, *True Story: Murder, Memoir, Mea Culpa* (New York: Harper Perennial, 2005) 58.

[128]Ibid., 71.

ined it might be something like viewing an unauthorized, low-budget movie of your own life."[129]

The doppelgänger motif so central to this chapter is more pronounced in the autobiographical novel than in the film. Finkel reveals at length the connection he feels to Longo:

> I sustained the patter by asking the most basic, blind-date sort of questions, then exclaiming eagerly about any similarity I uncovered. For example: We both had January birthdays! Longo had recently turned twenty-eight, two weeks after I'd turned thirty-three. Neither of us was a native of the West—he'd grown up in suburban Indianapolis; I was from suburban Connecticut. He's been a Jehovah's Witness but had been kicked out of the organization. I was a lapsed Jew.
>
> He told me that he felt battered by the media's coverage of his case. "There's no way you can know me from reading the papers," he said. I told him I understood exactly what he meant. He said he had never written anything for publication but had once worked for a company that handled home delivery of the *New York Times*. "I was always proud to say I worked for the *Times*," he told me. I was always proud of that too, I said.[130]

In fact, what develops in *True Story* is a relationship that profits Finkel professionally and Longo personally. After he is tried and convicted, Longo calls Finkel in 2009 and confesses that "he had indeed killed his entire family—strangling MaryJane during lovemaking, and throwing all of his children into the water while they were still breathing,"[131] writes John Calhoun in "The True Story Behind 'True Story.'" Capote's relationship with Smith obviously ended when Smith was executed, but as of 2014, Finkel and Longo remained in touch. Finkel says:

> He calls me the first Sunday of every month…There's always this internal tug of war over whether I should pick up the phone or not, but I usually do…Despite the fact he's a sociopath and a quadruple murder-

---

[129]Ibid., 72.
[130]Ibid., 53.
[131]John Calhoun, "The True Story Behind 'True Story,'" *Biography*, 16 April 2015, web (accessed 10 August 2018).

er, Longo is also insanely perceptive and eloquent, and his descriptive abilities are amazing. So yes, I pick up the phone. I'm a journalist.[132]

In conclusion, it is important to note two allegorical moments in the film. In one, Finkel describes a courtroom scene in which the judge involved in Longo's case shows off during a break in the trial, solving a Rubik's Cube for the jury "with practiced precision." However, after viewing and hearing what are—even for the judge—horrifying crime photos and forensics, he is unable to repeat his success with the puzzle. The judge—who tells Finkel that Longo's crimes were "wholly inexplicable" and a "mystery"—sits "fiddling with a Rubik's Cube," distracted and sad and unable to complete what once had been a simple task. "Quite frankly," the judge tells Longo, "you are a mystery to me, and God willing, you will remain so." Nonplussed, Longo replies, "I'm the most important thing that ever happened to you. From now on, you'll just be the guy who talked to the guy who killed his wife. And that's it." The judge and the Rubik's Cube challenge our belief that we can determine what is true and suggest the myriad ways we may be fooled even by those who presume to tell a "true story." In short, the Rubik's Cube symbolizes the challenges we face in interpreting the world and the people who might cause harm. Given the reality of fragmented identities—and our own inconsistencies and indecisions—how can we know or disseminate truth, and who is at risk when we are most certain of ourselves and our own narrative constructions? Who can really solve the Rubik's Cube?

The second allegorical and evocative scene in the film involves Jill Barker (Felicity Jones), who plays "If You Crave My Death" ("Se La Mia Morte Brami") for Longo. Having talked with the killer by phone, Finkel's partner (later wife) wants to meet Longo and tell him what she thinks of him and his horrific crime against his family, so she travels to the prison to meet him. Written by Carlo Gesualdo da Venosa (1566–1613), an Italian composer and musician known for writing madrigals and sacred music, the composition she plays is hauntingly beautiful. However, the viewer learns that Gesualdo da Venosa was as well known for cruelty and the murder of his first wife Donna Maria d'Avalos and her lover as he was for his music. As a nobleman, he did not face prosecution for the murders. He doubted the paternity of one of his children. He also is rumored to have killed his father-in-law and his second son by d'Avalos, who, incidentally, was also his first cousin. "The music is almost beautiful enough to make me forget I'm listen-

---

[132]Fretts, "A Writer Watches."

ing to something written by a man who broke his baby's skull on a piece of furniture. But not quite," Barker tells Longo.

As with Truman Capote and Perry Smith in *In Cold Blood*, the unusual connection between the journalist and the murderer is a destabilizing one, gradually growing more and more difficult to sustain. In the book *True Story*, an attorney, Steven Krasik, suggests to Finkel that he and Longo "were linked before you even knew each other."[133] During times when Finkel wants to believe his source, he tries to justify the crime he suspects Longo may have committed, writing that "classic familicide" can be a "form of murder in which a father kills his family members not out of hatred, but because he feels unable to adequately care for them."[134] In Finkel's desperate desire to reconcile his relationship with Longo with what he concedes Longo may have done, he tries to believe that grief may have driven Longo to kill his family in order to protect them. Finkel begins to detach himself from Longo in much the same way that Capote seeks to control his correspondence with Smith and minimize prison visits. "We'd now been in contact for six months, and Longo marked the occasion with a letter expressing his feelings about our relationship," Finkel writes. "It was a manifesto of sorts, by turns perceptive and preachy, one that I ended up reading numerous times in the following months, as the link between us grew stranger and ever more troubling."[135]

Again similar to Capote's experience, Finkel's health begins to suffer from his inability to extricate himself from his relationship with a murderer. "And I wasn't crazy. I could not plead insanity," Finkel writes. "The pressure, the amphetamines, the sleeping pills, and the pot are merely excuses. I knew what I was doing. I had the power to stop myself at any time, but I decided not to."[136] There remained an unmistakable, deeply felt connection between the men, and severing the relationship would take time. Finkel writes:

> He [Longo] felt like he was becoming a real writer. If he'd only made a couple of different decisions in his life, he added, and had been blessed with a little more luck, it's a career that could have been his from the start. "We were just separated at birth is all it was," he said. I laughed at

---

[133]Finkel, *True Story*, 122.
[134]Ibid., 101.
[135]Ibid., 143.
[136]Ibid., 181.

this comment, we both did, but I sensed it wasn't meant entirely as a joke.[137]

Finkel appears to be less devastated than Capote was: his relationship with Longo changes, but in Capote's case, Smith is dead. After Smith is executed, Capote is unable to maintain his reputation. Finkel, on the other hand, published *True Story* and subsequently won a national award for a co-written 2007 *National Geographic* story about malaria. He also has been published in *The Atlantic, Backpacker, Men's Journal, Runner's World, Skiing, Sports Illustrated*, and other publications. Shafer writes:

> The short autobiographical note about Finkel in *National Geo* names *True Story* as one of his works but does not mention his *Times Magazine* disgrace. The 600-word author bio on *National Geo's* Web site is also silent on this score. Most readers of *National Geo* won't get a chance to forgive Finkel because they won't know that he ever did anything wrong.[138]

Perhaps Finkel's professional resurrection is linked to his ultimate ability to let go of his obsession with Longo, rebuild a relationship with Barker, and establish new professional connections. Perhaps he's simply more adept at denial. In *True Story*, as Finkel begins to pull away, he understands more about himself and about the man whom he met by chance:

> I had been fascinated by Longo. I'd also been fooled by him. As he was led out of court for the final time, he seemed to me not much different than the day he'd first called. He left as a liar and con man and definite killer. He was gone, condemned to die, and I had this sense of having survived something—a storm of sorts, and here I was on the back end, alive and intact, though in many ways not the same person at all.[139]

At the end of the book that reignited his career, Finkel acknowledges that Longo is the "most dangerous kind of man—a man who can fool even his own wife into thinking he's not dangerous at all."[140] Ultimately, though,

---

[137]Ibid., 157.
[138]Shafer, "The Return of Michael Finkel."
[139]Finkel, *True Story*, 294.
[140]Ibid., 305.

what may haunt readers of both *In Cold Blood* and *True Story* is the doppel-gänger, the fragmented image of the men in a mirror. Finkel writes:

> And as much as I'd like to deny it, the truth is that I saw some of my-self in Longo. The flawed parts of my own character—the runaway egotism, the capacity to deceive—were mirrored and magnified in him. All the time I spent with Longo forced me to take a lengthy and un-comfortable look at what I'd done and who I had become.[141]

Ultimately, though, what concerns journalists is not Finkel's ability to move on emotionally and professionally. It is Shafer who probably speaks most eloquently for newsgatherers who care about the ethics of their profession:

> If I had the constitution of a hanging judge, which I don't, I'd have sent Finkel directly to the gallows for his Youssouf lies. He deliberately wrote things that were not true and called the work journalism. If that doesn't constitute a professional death wish, I don't know what does. He filed his lies in a fact-checked magazine that is read by knowing eyes around the world, the equivalent of robbing a camera-filled bank while wearing no mask. Finally, he violated the extreme bond of trust that readers and editors must invest in foreign correspondents. Distance, language, and culture make double-checking the truthfulness of stories reported from overseas difficult.[142]

Comments Finkel made since the misguided story about slavery also "indicate something less than complete remorse,"[143] Shafer adds. As a writer for *Slate Magazine*, known for its coverage of politics, business, technology, and the arts, Shafer advocates for his profession and reminds us of the retaliation Capote faced after the publication of *In Cold Blood* and *Handcarved Coffins*. Time has dimmed some of the anger toward Capote—a writer, not a journalist—but Finkel's 2005 novel and the 2015 film with the same title make conversations about verisimilitude and prevailing definitions of nonfiction again salient.

---

[141]Ibid., 307-308.
[142]Shafer, "The Return of Michael Finkel."
[143]Ibid.

PART TWO

VOICES

Chapter 5

Starling Mack Nations and *High Road to Hell*

On November 15, 1959, Herbert and Bonnie Clutter and two of their four children were terrorized and murdered in a farmhouse in the small town of Holcomb, Kansas. Bonnie Clutter and her daughter Nancy were shot in their upstairs bedrooms. Herbert Clutter and his son Kenyon were killed in the basement, Kenyon on a couch and his father on the floor. Both were shot. Herbert Clutter also had his throat cut. Three family members listened while Herbert Clutter was killed, two listened while Kenyon was killed, and Bonnie Clutter heard Nancy, who was not gagged, as she begged for her life before she, too, was shot. Friends found the bodies later that morning before church services.

The murders immobilized, shamed, and shattered a close-knit community that—until the deaths occurred—had lived and worshipped together as friends in a close rural neighborhood. Their social interactions were characterized by church gatherings, farming and ranching organization events, school functions, sports competitions, and other activities in Holcomb and nearby Garden City. After gunshots shattered the town in which many residents previously did not lock their doors, no one knew whom to trust. The world they had known was gone.

Author of *Other Voices, Other Rooms* (1948), *A Tree of Night and Other Stories* (1949), *The Grass Harp* (1951), *The Muses Are Heard* (1956), and *Breakfast at Tiffany's* (1958), Truman Capote read a short newspaper article about the murders in *The New York Times* and became obsessed with their context and aftermath. Eventually, the title *In Cold Blood* would refer broadly to the murders in the Clutter home, the executions of those responsible, and, according to some critics, the techniques Capote used while writing his magnum opus. In hindsight, it is no surprise that a famous gay author from New York would be fascinated by a story about death in a peaceful locale known for its white, heterosexual, religious population, nor is it strange that the nation itself would be drawn to an allegory about the presumed end of American innocence.

By the time readers engaged Capote's masterpiece, they already were familiar with the news stories about the event and the investigation, arrests, and executions that followed; however, they were interested in learning how Capote would describe a series of events that absorbed more than five years of his life and produced several file cabinets of research. What could possibly explain the deaths of four family members who kept no money on the premises? How could a strong and healthy farmer accustomed to physical labor allow two invaders to bind him and his family? Why would he believe the promises to set the family free after the robbery? And why would anyone kill a family for a pair of binoculars, a transistor radio, and about forty dollars in cash? (Convicted murderer Richard Eugene Hickock would later claim that he and his partner took $1,000; most sources set the amount at between forty and eighty dollars—for consistency, this study settled on "forty.") Such a crime might occur in New York City, residents told themselves, but how could it happen in the rural Midwest?

Eventually, two men who had previously served time were apprehended, tried and found guilty, and sentenced to death by hanging. First, however, Hickock and Perry Edward Smith would spend years in prison in Lansing, Kansas, with few visitors except Capote himself. Capote and his childhood friend Nelle Harper Lee, celebrated author of *To Kill a Mockingbird* (1960), came to Holcomb to investigate the murders. Capote intended to write a book about what he called a "village"[1] and its shattered innocence. *In Cold Blood* became that and more. Ultimately, the narrative struck the heart of a nation and highlighted issues including the death penalty, justice, violence, and the very nature of humankind. Having befriended and identified with one of the murderers, Capote shocked and engaged his readers, creating a masterpiece that would eclipse his previous work.

Part two of *Untold Stories, Unheard Voices* deals with the events and people that Truman Capote left out of his 1965 nonfiction novel. This portion of the study relies on the last line of *In Cold Blood*. In the final scene of the landmark novel, Alvin A. Dewey, who investigated the murder of the Clutter family for the Kansas Bureau of Investigation, meets a friend of the late Nancy Clutter in the cemetery near the four Clutter graves. According to Capote's description of what was an imaginary encounter, Dewey considers how Susan Kidwell is the age Nancy Clutter would have been if she had lived. He chats with her for a few moments: "Then, starting home, he

---

[1]Truman Capote, *In Cold Blood: A True Account of a Multiple Murder and Its Consequences* (New York: Random House, 1965) 3.

walked toward the trees, and under them, leaving behind him the big sky, the whisper of wind voices in the wind-bent wheat."[2]

Because previous chapters of this study address the lack of ethics reflected in inventing the scene, the focus here is on the "voices" themselves. No one would suggest that Capote should have included every voice—every interview and every source—in his final product. The title *Untold Stories, Unheard Voices* is not a condemnation of Capote but a reminder that any revelation of contexts and absent voices enriches the reading experience. Capote made strategic decisions when he composed *In Cold Blood*, and few take issue with the short chapters that alternate between the murders and Holcomb, Kansas, and the killers themselves. However, he did not and could not include all perspectives.

There is no doubt that when a novel, for example, is adapted into a screenplay, characters are redefined and may even disappear. Aunt Alexandra Finch, so central to the novel *To Kill a Mockingbird*, for example, vanishes from the screen version, and the Academy Award-winning film is none the poorer for it. However, just as the first part of *Untold Stories, Unheard Voices* mentions contexts that readers might not have considered, the second half of the study suggests narratives that enhance the nonfiction novel, contributing nuanced and sometimes controversial perspectives. The voices in part two include those of Starling Mack Nations, a longtime newspaper reporter, editor, and publisher and executive secretary for a Kansas governor; Nelle Harper Lee, Pulitzer Prize-winning author and Capote's childhood friend; the screenwriters, directors, and producers who collaborated on the films *In Cold Blood* (1967), *Capote* (2005), and *Infamous* (2006); and residents of Holcomb and Garden City, Kansas, and their descendants, etc. Only in Lee's case is there an implicit criticism of Capote, who dedicated *In Cold Blood* to her and to his long-time partner Jack Dunphy, a gesture that does not adequately acknowledge Lee's commitment to the project. (Lee herself did not criticize Capote.)

As noted in part one, *In Cold Blood* remains one of the 100 greatest novels of the twentieth century, an extensive study of a particular crime, a psychological analysis of the criminal mind, and a polemic against capital punishment. *In Cold Blood* was one of the first nonfiction novels that helped to usher in the era of New Journalism, as defined by Tom Wolfe. It also was the catalyst for a century of crime reporting in America, and since crime cov-

---

[2]Ibid., 343.

erage is by definition popular—involving heightened dramatic conflict, human interest, and issues of morality—*In Cold Blood* maintains high readership and has elicited significant critical attention into the twenty-first century.

In order to move forward, it is helpful to review part one and to understand how its themes are interwoven with what follows in the remaining chapters of the study.

Briefly, the introduction to *Untold Stories, Unheard Voices* places *In Cold Blood* into historical context and provides a chronological summary of the events that led to its publication. It also relies on biographical information about Capote, his insecurities, his reputation among the New York literati, and his childhood, including his relationship with Harper Lee. The section reveals both the timeline for and the significance of Capote's most well-known work.

Chapter one ("The Enduring Popularity of *In Cold Blood*") addresses the allure of *In Cold Blood* without ignoring the well-documented inaccuracies in what Capote considered to be a true story. It begins to answer this question: Why is *In Cold Blood* a landmark work in an interdisciplinary genre?

Chapter two ("*In Cold Blood* and American Literary Journalism") continues the goal of part one—unveiling contexts—and considers the place of *In Cold Blood* among other classics of literary journalism, a subset of creative nonfiction.

Chapter three ("*In Cold Blood*, *Handcarved Coffins*, and "Then It All Came Down"") deals with the allegorical nature of certain American crime stories, exploring the universality of particularly compelling narratives and the popularity of stories about crime. It addresses these questions: Why does the murder of a farm family in 1959 hold such a powerful sway? What is the history of sensationalism—both in extended nonfiction and daily journalism—and what role does it play in Capote's novel?

Just as important, the chapter locates *In Cold Blood* among other Capote tales of murder based on fact. *In Cold Blood*, *Handcarved Coffins*, and "Then It All Came Down" attest to Capote's fascination with nonfiction, to his artistry, and, sadly, to his inadequacy as a journalist and his unwillingness to subject himself to accuracy and the methodical gathering of facts required by the genre that drew him.

Chapter four ("*In Cold Blood*, the Doppelgänger, and Murder") situates *In Cold Blood* among other popular tales of murder and mayhem in American film and literature; specifically, it introduces the long-familiar figure of the doppelgänger as it appears in literature from 1955 to 2005 and film from 1967 to 2015. Rounding out the sections of part one of the study titled "Contexts," the chapter introduces several flawed characters, including Tom Ripley (*The Talented Mr. Ripley*) and Chester MacFarland (*The Two Faces of January*). Others are Mort Rainey, the protagonist in *Secret Window, Secret Garden*, and Edward (Teddy) Daniels, a U.S. marshal, who discovers in *Shutter Island* that he has committed an especially horrific crime. The final narrator in the study is the one who most closely resembles Capote, both in his motives for writing nonfiction and in his intimate connection to a murderer. Through a series of coincidences in a tale ironically titled *True Story*, journalist Michael Finkel meets Christian Longo, who murdered his family and—while on the run—appropriated Finkel's identity.

As noted earlier, part two ("Voices") introduces chapter five ("Starling Mack Nations and *High Road to Hell*") and the late newspaper reporter, editor, and publisher who interviewed Richard Eugene Hickock at length and wrote his own unpublished book-length account of the Clutter family murders. Michael Nations provides biographical information about his father, who served in the governor's office in Kansas and who was at the time of his death a Colorado newspaper publisher. He also provides correspondence between his father and Hickock. How was Capote able to exclude Kansas journalists, gain the trust of local law enforcement officials, and become friends with one of the convicted killers? Could he achieve the same access today?

Chapter six ("Nelle Harper Lee and *In Cold Blood*") deals at length with the role of celebrated author Harper Lee in producing *In Cold Blood*. Lee maintained her privacy and her silence on the matter until her death in 2016. What did Harper Lee actually provide Capote? Did he take some of her advice and dismiss the rest? More important, is Lee's sister Alice Lee correct when she argues that Capote's rejection of his childhood friend was part of his undoing and a possible explanation for his alcoholism and death at age fifty-nine?

Chapter seven ("*In Cold Blood* in Documentary and Film") analyzes *In Cold Blood* (1967), *Capote* (2005), and *Infamous* (2006) and documents the ways in which a new generation of readers and filmgoers learned about Truman Capote, Harper Lee, *In Cold Blood*, and *To Kill a Mockingbird*. Portrayals of Capote differ greatly in *Capote* and *Infamous*, and rather than trying to reconcile them, this chapter seeks to account for the fact that—in spite of two lengthy and methodical biographies—Capote is less well understood than one might expect.

Questions that drive the chapter include these: Why did the creative teams involved with *Capote* and *Infamous* select different Capote biographies as sources for their film projects? Are the films accurate? Should they be? What does scholarship about film adaptation suggest? The chapter argues that all three films enhance our understanding of *In Cold Blood*, even if they leave us questioning what we actually know about the author. In the Academy Award-winning film *To Kill a Mockingbird* (1962), we meet Charles Baker (Dill) Harris as a bright, curious, intelligent, likable, precocious child. Modeled after Truman Capote, Dill is the fictional character who delighted and engaged Harper Lee. What happened to their friendship between 1962 and 1984? Given the silence of Capote and Lee on the matter, what might literary historians deduce?

Chapter eight ("River Valley Farm and Beyond") addresses questions unanswered by several decades of scholarship about *In Cold Blood*. Who were the Clutters? Why did Capote all but ignore their lives in telling his extraordinary tale? Why did he portray Bonnie and Herbert Clutter in the way he did, ignoring or mischaracterizing information from the surviving Clutter sisters and other residents of Holcomb and Garden City? Did Capote's narrative goals determine his caricature of a farm family? Why does the novel begin in medias res—like *The Scarlet Letter* and other "crime stories"—and what does his emphasis on the forensic study, the trial, and Perry Smith tell us about his objectives in documenting the crime?

Questions that drive the chapter include the following: Why do so many visitors descend upon Garden City and Holcomb to this day? Why are so many residents willing to talk with them? Why did some of the central figures in the novel—including Bobby Rupp, who was Nancy Clutter's boyfriend—remain in their hometown following the murders, the trial, and the executions? What are Garden City and Holcomb, Kansas, like today—after more than fifty years since *In Cold Blood*? What memorials have been established and what tributes document the lives of Herbert, Bonnie, Nancy, and Kenyon Clutter? Where are their gravesites?

As noted earlier, with the exception of one interview with a Kansas newspaper, the surviving Clutter sisters refused to talk with reporters since they believed Capote betrayed them more than a half-century ago. The chapter updates readers about the sisters and their husbands. It also takes readers into the former Clutter home that was advertised for sale and then taken off the market, and it features one homeowner who gave tours of the house and farm.

Starling Mack Nations and High Road to Hell

In addition to his lifelong quest to believe in himself and to be the center of every party, Truman Capote was determined to best his friend Harper Lee and her unprecedented success after the publication of *To Kill a Mockingbird*. The films *Capote* and *Infamous*, drawn from two biographies about Capote, are among the texts that testify to his unrelenting desire to make *In Cold Blood* his greatest work. In achieving his goal, Capote bitterly attacked those he saw as threats to his genius; made up dialogue and scenes; misrepresented facts; manipulated local law enforcement officers, FBI investigators, and killers Hickock and Smith; and alienated some of the Kansas residents most affected by the murders. Capote's obsession with the events of November 15, 1959, came at a terrible personal cost. Critics argue that after the nonfiction novel appeared, Capote had a breakdown from which he never recovered; in fact, until his death in 1984, he never published another book. In *Chronicling Trauma: Journalists and Writers on Violence and Loss*, Doug Underwood suggests that *In Cold Blood* may have been largely responsible for Capote's "physical and emotional decline."[3] Capote died at the home of Joanne Carson, ex-wife of talk show giant Johnny Carson, after years of abusing his body with alcohol and drugs.

At least thirty researchers have produced studies that deal with the shortcuts Capote took in writing *In Cold Blood*, a book that some of them consider to be fiction. This study necessarily refers to that body of literature, all secondary sources, in part one, "Contexts"; however, the current chapter introduces an unpublished manuscript titled *High Road to Hell* that—had Random House been more interested—would have predated *In Cold Blood* and might, in fact, have stolen some of the fanfare that Capote craved. Although *High Road to Hell* was lost, a condensed version of the novel, "America's Worst Crime in 20 Years," was published in the December 1961 issue of *Male* magazine. In it, Mack Nations reveals Hickock to the reader in much the same way that Capote delves into the character and motivations of Smith.

---

[3]Doug Underwood, *Chronicling Trauma: Journalists and Writers on Violence and Loss* (Urbana: University of Illinois Press, 2011) 173.

One of the voices omitted from *In Cold Blood* belongs to Mack Nations. His youngest son Michael Nations provided biographical information about his father, who served in the governor's office in Kansas and at the time of his death was a Colorado newspaper publisher. He also made available correspondence between his father and Hickock. Much of his documentation now resides in the Kansas Historical Society. An adult probation officer for the Harris County Community Supervision and Corrections Department, Michael Nations confirms that Capote scorned Nations, whom he viewed as a competitor, even celebrating the fact that Nations spent eight years defending himself against tax fraud allegations, although he was acquitted. He also makes clear that Nations was no admirer of Capote, either.

The feud is documented in various places, including a letter to Alvin A. and Marie Dewey dated February 29, 1962, where Capote writes, "Was much amused by Marie's letter today—especially the Mack Nations news! *Do* tell me more. Is it serious? Will he go to jail? I certainly hope so...."[4] Relaying the information about Mack Nations to Bennett Cerf on March 4, 1962, Capote describes the plight of Hickock and Smith, demonstrating no concern for them, and then again lambasts Nations:

> First off, some Kansas news. It is now quite definite that the Kansas Supreme Court will reject the appeal for a new trial. The hearing was a fiasco as far as Smith and Hickock are concerned. I understand their lawyer never intended appealing directly to the U.S. Supreme Court. Isn't it absurd? Oh yes—one very amusing item: Remember Mack Nations, the newspaper bastard who has caused me so much trouble? The one who said Random House was publ. [sic] his book? Well, he has been *arrested* for income tax evasion![5]

As is obvious, this side of Capote did not endear him to members of the Nations family.

Born December 6, 1919, in Baxter Springs, Kansas, Starling Mack Nations married Bernita Jean Weikal in 1942, and the couple had three children before their divorce in 1965. He served in the U.S. Navy from 1941 to 1945. In the winter of 1961, Mack Nations went to the penitentiary in Lansing to interview several killers for a Wichita newspaper for which he also

---

[4]Gerald Clarke, *Too Brief a Treat: The Letters of Truman Capote* (New York: Random House, 2004) 342.

[5]Ibid., 343.

covered the courts and the state legislature. According to Michael Nations, his father spent six months and engaged in extensive correspondence in order to help write and edit Hickock's life story, which would be titled *High Road to Hell*. Michael Nations said Hickock's initials appeared on each page of the manuscript. For many years before he was forced to acknowledge that it was destroyed or lost, Michael Nations sought the manuscript, which was, fortunately, condensed and published as "America's Worst Crime in 20 Years." Leaving to visit their mother for the holidays, Michael Nations and his older brother last saw the manuscript and their father on December 24, 1968. When Mack Nations died in an automobile accident outside of Walsenburg, Colorado, later that day, his desire to convey another side of the 1959 murders died, too.

Scholars have neglected to pursue research about the rivalry between the Kansas journalist and the New York City celebrity novelist and did not until recently know about the letters and other documents that Michael Nations preserved. Murderer Richard Hickock talked extensively with Nations, not Capote, and the dramatic monologues Nations captured illustrate the depths of Hickock's depravity and sociopathic disorder. In the only article Nations published about the events in Holcomb, he describes Hickock as wishing the judge and jury had been at the Clutter house on the night of the murders: "I would have found out how much God they had in them!" Hickock told Nations. "If they had been there and had any God in them I would have let it run out on the floor...When the jury filed out of the courtroom not one of them would look at me...I looked each one in the face and I kept thinking, Look at me, look at me, look at me! But none of them would."[6] Here, readers encounter a man who sounds as though he believed he was fated to do what he did and who was desperate to be noticed: "To some degree I've always had the feeling that things would happen no matter what I did or where I was," Hickock said. "I knew I couldn't control them if I tried. And I never tried."[7] Later in the same interview, Hickock said, "At the time, though, I thought a person could get a lot of glory out of killing...All my life I had been told that nothing I would ever do would amount to anything. Well, this is my chance, I thought. I'm going to do it. Then nobody will be able to say Dick Hickock didn't do anything worth while [sic]."[8] Hickock

---

[6]Mack Nations, "America's Worst Crime in 20 Years," *Male* 11/12 (December 1961): 83.
[7]Ibid., 77.
[8]Ibid., 79.

describes in horrifying detail how he helped to kill Herbert Clutter, who was a strong man desperate to save himself and his family, and how he laughed uncontrollably during and after the murders.

One of the most important contributions of this study is its revelation of another manuscript about the murders in Holcomb, Kansas, by someone other than Truman Capote and featuring interviews with someone other than Perry Smith. At the same time that Capote was beginning *In Cold Blood*, Nations finished and submitted his manuscript to Random House. Eventually, Capote's was accepted, becoming what many consider to be the greatest American nonfiction novel. However, Random House editors rejected the other manuscript, and the author died before he could find another publisher or safely entrust the book to the care of an agent or members of his family. No one knows what happened to *High Road to Hell*. Its production predated computers during a time when retyping and/or mimeographing were the ways authors preserved even one additional copy. Michael Nations remembers seeing the manuscript next to his father's typewriter at his newspaper office in Walsenburg, Colorado, 165 miles south of Denver, but he was only thirteen years old when his father died. Michael Nations's searches among his father's papers and his numerous inquiries into the fate of the manuscript failed (as did mine).

Much of what we know about the life of the late Mack Nations is the result of more than a decade of his son's research. A reporter, editor, and publisher for newspapers in Kansas and Colorado, including the *Wichita Eagle and Beacon* and what is now the *Huerfano World Journal*, Mack Nations was at one time a court and political reporter who covered the state legislature in Topeka. In 1961, Richard Hickock and Mack Nations exchanged handwritten letters; in fact, Nations spent more than six months that year interviewing Hickock, who was housed on Death Row at the state penitentiary in Lansing, Kansas. In an e-mail message to the author of this study dated April 11, 2011, Michael Nations shared a portion of what he knows about his father's interviews with Richard Hickock:

> My father had written several articles for the *Wichita Eagle and Beacon* on "Death Row" inmates while he was a correspondent in Topeka, Kansas, covering the 1961 Kansas legislative session for the newspaper. The drive to Lansing took less than an hour for my father to make. He met Richard Hickock at this point in time. Hickock was a talker, and was open to visiting with my father as were many of the killers there...

Perry Smith did not trust anyone. He had learned from an early age to become detached from the world and depend solely upon himself. My father concluded early on that Smith would resent his approach to interview him, and Hickock was just the opposite. Hickock's father had died not long after he was sentenced for the Clutter murders, and Hickock was interested in trying to find a way to help his mother financially, before his own death, so that she wouldn't lose the family's tiny farm near Olathe, Kansas.

Michael Nations is convinced that after his father sent *High Road to Hell* to Random House, the editors shared it with Capote. In a March 3, 2012, telephone interview, Nations said, "He took my father's book. He used it as a blueprint." Michael Nations believes that Capote grew to hate his father because, as he said in the same conversation, the article that Mack Nations wrote for *Male* magazine preceded *In Cold Blood*. After Random House rejected *High Road to Hell*, Mack Nations condensed the book and published it in article form as "America's Worst Crime in 20 Years." It is not clear whether he planned to place the book with another publishing house.

According to Michael Nations in a June 8, 2015, telephone interview, Capote "despised" Hickock in part because he gave his story to Mack Nations, adding that Capote "hoodwinked" his father with the help of Random House, cheating him of the opportunity to publish *High Road to Hell*. One of the derogatory references Capote makes to Mack Nations appears in *Too Brief a Treat: The Letters of Truman Capote*. In a letter to agent Dewey and his wife dated November 21, 1961, Capote writes, "I wanted at once to thank dear Alvin for the detective information and also for sending me that extraordinarily vulgar magazine containing the preposterous Hickcock [sic] Nations contribution. Dear God!—and to *think* that I was worried about Mr. Nations...I would certainly be interested to see the original Hickcock [sic] mss. before Nations tampered with it."[9]

Understandably defensive of his father, Michael Nations said in a June 8, 2015, telephone interview that his father was not a "stylist" or an "artist": "He wrote like a sledgehammer. He was a journalist." While Capote spent five years researching and writing, "my father had the story in four months," Michael Nations added. According to him, Capote called his father at the *Wichita Eagle and Beacon* at least once. His father and Mr. Capote had "words" about their intentions to have their respective stories published first,

---

[9]Clarke, *Too Brief a Treat*, 331-32.

and both men despised each other, Nations said. "My father is mentioned very unfavorably in both Capote's biography by Gerald Clarke and in his personal letters. There is no doubt that my father's finished book posed a very real threat to Mr. Capote and his plans for fame" (telephone interview, April 10, 2011). Michael Nations claims that Hickock wanted his father to attend the execution in Lansing, Kansas, on April 14, 1965, but Mack Nations had no interest in doing so.

As mentioned earlier, Starling Mack Nations died December 24, 1968, after hitting a bridge while driving from Aguilar to Gulnare, Colorado. "My father was co-owner and publisher of the *Huerfano World* newspaper located in Walsenburg, Colorado, at the time of his death," Michael Nations said in an interview March 3, 2012. "The last time I saw the manuscript was inside the newspaper office on his desk." After his death, the manuscript was either destroyed or misplaced, Michael Nations said, and certainly, no one at that time could have understood its historical significance. Mack Nations was buried in Greensburg, Kansas, after a funeral service that drew many of his family and friends: "The chapel in that blizzard was full," said Michael Nations in telephone interview June 8, 2015.

Aside from his investigation into the Clutter murders, Mack Nations is worth remembering, having become executive secretary to Frederick (Fred) Hall, the governor of Kansas; having worked as a reporter, editor, and publisher until his death at age 49; and having been beloved by his son Michael Nations. "He was a man's man, who understood people...He could talk with a janitor just as easily as he could interview a condemned killer like Richard Hickock or Lowell Lee Andrews feet away from their Death Row cells," Michael Nations said in an April 17, 2012, e-mail interview. "I guess like many kids my age, I didn't think there was much that my Dad couldn't do."

Michael Nations's searches among his father's papers and his numerous inquiries into the fate of the manuscript have failed, although his life is not defined by his father's newspaper career. Michael Nations was born in Topeka, Kansas, on April 23, 1955, during the time his father was executive secretary to Governor Hall from 1955–1957. "He was a handsome man and could be very charming and funny," Michael Nations said in an e-mail message April 17, 2011. A graduate of Wichita State University, Michael Nations now has made available all the documents he can locate that testify to his father's research into the murders in Holcomb, Kansas. He loves his father deeply, having lost him when he was barely a teenager. He vividly remembers swimming, fishing, and working in the office together: "I played on the typewriter, fetched coffee, swept the office...He wanted me with him," said Michael Nations in a telephone interview June 8, 2015.

When Starling Mack Nations died, his correspondence with one of the killers and an article he published about his interviews with that killer were all that were left. Until 2015, no one had access to the papers and interviews, and no one had succeeded in interviewing the surviving members of the Clutter family. Because of missing or lost primary materials, scholars have relied for much of their information about the murders and their aftermath on biographies about Capote written by Gerald Clarke and George Plimpton and a biography about Harper Lee by Charles J. Shields in which Capote and Holcomb, Kansas, figure prominently.

In addition to "America's Worst Crime in 20 Years" in the now extant *Male* magazine, the unpublished letters between Mack Nations and Hickock and the notes the newspaperman took during prison visits are grisly treasures. For example, Hickock told Mack Nations in horrifying detail how he helped to kill the Clutters, although he denied his confession during a clemency hearing on April 6, 1965, a few days before his execution. According to the "Summary of Clemency Hearing Held at Kansas State Penitentiary," the three committee members wrote a formal report, including the following paragraph:

Hickock explains his entering into a contract with Mack Nations to publish his life story as a means of receiving money to carry on his fight for life, that in order to make his story have sales appeal he fabricated his part in the murders, declaring there was no truth whatever in the copy he prepared for his ghost writer, Nations. (Kansas Historical Society, Perry Edward Smith Inmate Case File No. 629)

What follows is the condensed version of *High Road to Hell*, which is based on interviews Mack Nations conducted with Richard Hickock and letters they exchanged in 1961. The chronological tale is made more horrifying by the fact that—although Mack Nations edited it for grammar and style—he preserved the story as stream of consciousness. Unlike *In Cold Blood*—which Capote and editors at Random House edited—"America's Worst Crime in 20 Years" takes readers into the mind of a murderer who, although conscious that he is being interviewed, has no idea how amoral he is or how despicable are his crimes.

No one knows how much of Hickock's story is true, of course. Even after reading *In Cold Blood*, the reader has no idea who actually killed the

Clutters, why Hickock and Smith did not wait until no one was home to seek the nonexistent safe, or why they left behind boot prints and other clues. No one will ever know why Hickock spent so much time talking with Nancy Clutter—if he did—nor will we know whether he or Smith experienced empathy for their victims. Mack Nations's article, printed in its entirety below, is an account far darker than *In Cold Blood*, forcing readers to consider the unimaginable events that occurred after Bobby Rupp left his girlfriend's home and after the hired man and his family, who lived only a few yards away, extinguished their lights.

"America's Worst Crime in 20 Years"

Editors of the defunct *Male* magazine describe "America's Worst Crime in 20 Years" as a way of "perhaps understanding better the workings of the criminal mind." They published what they called a "mass killer's own story—in his own words—the most hair-raising expose ever to appear in an adventure magazine."[10] The article—introduced with the words "By Richard Eugene Hickock, as told to Mack Nations"—follows. Nations wrote the preface, included here and in the original publication in italics.

> *This is a story of sheer depravity. It is so amoral that upon first recital I could not believe it in spite of 25 years spent viewing the worst in people in my capacity as a working newspaper reporter.*
>
> *It is the story of Richard Eugene "Dick" Hickock who at 29 years of age has been on Death Row at the State Penitentiary, Lansing, Kansas, for a year and four months. With average luck he will be there another 10 or 12 months before he is hanged.*
>
> *Dick Hickock was the instigator of four of the most brutal murders ever committed in the modern history of this country. The slayings were carefully premeditated, intricately planned and mercilessly executed. Only a threat by his partner in the crime prevented Hickock from raping one of his victims— an attractive teen-age girl with whom he spent 30 minutes discussing her church and school activities—before blasting her and three members of her family into Eternity.*
>
> *Every word of his story was written by Dick Hickock and his vivid description of the emotions he experienced in planning, executing and trying to escape the consequences of murder is without precedent. Following scores of*

---

[10]Nations, "A Condemned Killer," 31.

visits with him in the Death House, as well as an exhausting six-month in-
vestigation, I am convinced he believes every word he wrote is true.

In this story, Dick Hickock reveals—without reservation—every
thought, emotion, action and reaction he encountered during the plotting and
execution of the murder of four members of a western Kansas family. The
victims were 48-year-old Herbert Clutter, a moderately wealthy farmer and
cattleman; his 45-year-old wife, Mrs. Bonnie Clutter; and his two children,
Nancy, 16, and 15-year-old Kenyon.

Shortly after midnight on November 15, 1959, these four were methodi-
cally and ruthlessly beheaded by a close-range shotgun blast while bound
hand and foot in their farm home at the outskirts of Holcomb, Kansas. In
addition the throat of Herbert Clutter was "sawed on" with a knife by both
of his assailants prior to his being shot. The bodies were not discovered for
some eight hours after commission of the murders.

Because of the unbelievably brutal method used in slaying the family, law
enforcement officers assumed the murderer was a psychopathic killer who had
quenched the thirst of a long-standing grudge against the Clutters. So con-
vincing was this evidence that officers at first refused to believe the man who
gave them the names and motives of the killers. The story came from a con-
vict in the State Penitentiary who had at one time worked for Herbert Clut-
ter. That man was also a former cellmate of Dick Hickock and was present
when Hickock first conceived his plan for killing four persons he had never
seen.

This story has been supplemented with considerable testimony from the
trial of Dick Hickock and his partner, Perry Edward Smith, both of whom
were convicted on four counts of first degree murder. The material from the
trial was taken directly from the official trial transcripts.

You will observe glaring discrepancies in the story of Dick Hickock and
you will be shocked by his brilliant description of the ugly, brutal and stupid
crimes he committed.

But in the end you will undoubtedly conclude, as I did, that Richard
Hickock is a product of your society and mine. He is responsible for his deeds.
We are responsible for understanding what he did and why he did it—in the
hope that someday, we can help his kind to rid themselves of the black desires
that torment them.

As my partner and I turned west into the road leading to the Clutter house I turned off the lights. I figured there was no need to an-
nounce our arrival if we didn't have to.

There was a bright moon that night and I could see the roadway well. The first building I saw was the Clutter house. It was a large two-story affair and it appeared to be fairly new. What next took my eye was a building some distance to the west of the main house. There was a light burning in the second building.

My buddy Perry said he didn't like the setup. I didn't either but we had gone too far to back out now. I knew from the diagram that the house with the light belonged to the hired man and his family. But it was closer to the Clutter house than it was supposed to be. I turned the car around and drove back down the roadway. I told Perry that this guy must really be loaded. He was supposed to be wealthy and from the looks of his place, the house, barns, and such, I was certain that he was.

We drove back down the road and I asked Perry if he had the cord and tape ready. He said that he did. I had already loaded the shotgun, so we parked the car to see if the lights would be turned out. We couldn't see the light from where we were, which meant we would have to again run the risk of being spotted when we returned to the house. We didn't know if we had been seen the first time but it was a risk we had to face if we were going through with it. Perry told me he didn't want to go through with it and said we should leave. In fact he continued to be reluctant until we got into the house.

A few minutes later we returned to the vicinity of the house and the light was out. We decided to go on with it. I turned the car around in the driveway and backed it up beside the west entrance of the house. I drove as carefully as possible. I told Perry that I would check and see if the light in the hired man's house had been turned on again. We couldn't see it from where we were because a shed blocked our view.

I eased the car door open and slipped over to the shed. I worked my way to the corner where I could see and had my look. It was all clear. There was no light burning. I retraced my steps to the car where I told Smith it looked like clear sailing for us. As we sat in the car Perry again told me he thought we'd better get out of there. I told him that I had far too much at stake to back out now and I was going to do the job alone if necessary. With that I got back out of the car.

I closed the door of the car and moved as silently as possible toward the west door of the Clutter home. The moon was shining with great brilliance and illuminated the house in every detail.

I knew I would have to gain the house as quickly as possible because anyone looking out a window would certainly have no trouble seeing me.

As I approached the house a multitude of thoughts raced through my mind. I had a feeling of suspense, then fear. Most of all, though, the experience was a thrill. I had never done anything like this before and I wondered if I could carry it out. I reached the door and my heart was hammering with such intensity that it felt like it was going to burst. I made up my mind to one thing. When I got into that house I was going to show them who was boss. Although my partner had never said so I knew he was thinking I didn't have the guts to go through with it. But I would show him who had guts.

I pressed against the door and gently turned the knob. We were in luck! It was unlocked. I left the door standing ajar a couple of inches and retraced my steps to the car as quickly and quietly as possible. I reported my find to my partner and we quickly put our plan into action.

I armed myself with a long thin-bladed hunting knife that had been used on my hunting trip the weekend before. It had been left in the car. I also took a flashlight which belonged to my partner. Perry took the shotgun and followed me back to the house.

As I felt the knife in my hand I felt excitement, a thrill. I was going to kill a person—maybe more than one. Could I do it? Maybe I'll back out, I thought. What if they are not home? I hope they're not, I thought, but if they are I can't back out. What would my partner think if I chickened out? These thoughts raced through my mind.

A slight breeze swept across my face and I thought, what am I worrying about? Things like this happen every day. Other guys do it, why can't I? Of course I can. All I've got to do is put my mind to it. Actually there is nothing to it. It'll only take a minute and then it will be all over. All over, God. I'll be glad when it's all over!

The door was still standing ajar and when I tried to see inside a breath of warm air hit me in the face. I couldn't suppress a shiver, though I tried. It left me with a feeling of weakness in my legs. I shoved the door slowly inward until I could slip through. The inside of the house was extremely dark. The only light was filtering in past the blinds on the windows. The November moon was really bright and there were no clouds to dull its brilliance. As my eyes became accustomed to the dark, different objects came into view.

As I began to recognize these objects I experienced the strangest feeling I've ever had. It seemed that everything that was happening was taking place regardless of whether I put forth any effort. It seemed to me that I was viewing a movie in which I appeared.

But that doesn't quite explain my feeling. It was more like an incident was taking place and all I needed to do to become part of it was sit back and wait. To some degree I've always had the feeling that things would happen no matter what I did or where I was. I knew I couldn't control them if I tried. And I never tried.

We had entered the room Clutter used as an office and I noticed a fairly large desk on my left. According to the information I had a safe was located directly behind it. I turned the flashlight toward the wall and flicked on the switch. In the beam of light I saw a panelled wall of some kind but no safe. I quickly switched off the light and was immediately sorry I had turned it on. What if the light had been seen, I thought. Boy, am I stupid! It was really dark then.

If the diagram a convict buddy had made for me was correct the bedroom of Mr. Clutter was on the left side of a hallway that ran to the left of the office which we were in. As I started toward the inner doorway the floor gave some protesting sounds that sounded loud enough to wake the dead. Every step I took seemed louder than the one before! We moved forward as quickly as possible, but no matter how hard I tried, I couldn't stop the floor from squeaking.

They hear it, I thought, I know they do. I've got to hurry! I'll bet they're getting out of bed right now, I thought. But then another thought hit me. Maybe they aren't home. All of a sudden I wished with all my might that they were not at home. Suddenly I was convinced that there was no one home and I hurried—almost ran—toward the place where Clutter would be sleeping if he were there.

Just as the diagram showed, a hallway led to the left and on the left of this was the bedroom. I flashed the light on as I entered the bedroom and I could hardly believe it. They were home! A man sat up in bed and said, "Is that you, dear?" That made me mad because I had been so sure they were not there. Controlling myself as best I could I told him, "Just take it easy pop, don't do anything foolish and everything will be okay."

I was thinking about the way to handle this. I wanted to do it the way I had read about it being done. I wanted to handle it the way a real pro would. Like a torpedo from Detroit or some place. It was very important to me that I made a good impression on my partner. I also wanted Clutter to think that he was facing a hood who knew what was what. Maybe the most important thing to me at that time was that I suddenly felt like I really was a big shot. I remember thinking I wish I had worn a trench coat. Sounds foolish, I know, but it was important enough to me at the time that I still remember it.

"Come on, get up," my partner said. "You got a safe?" I asked. I hadn't seen one when I had the light on in the west room. Of course I didn't look good. Clutter said he had no safe. When he got out of bed we escorted Clutter back into the office and I began to question him in regard to the safe. A warm comfortable feeling had come over me, once I got over the shock of finding him at home. It was a feeling of power, of being boss. How many times in my life I had wished to be boss! A dozen, a hundred! Always before somebody was giving me orders. But not now!

Clutter kept telling me there was no safe and turned on the light in the office to prove it. By this time I knew there wasn't any safe. But I didn't care. I had never experienced this feeling before and I wouldn't trade it for anything.

My thoughts were interrupted when my partner informed me that some one had come down the steps from upstairs. I didn't see anyone, but I knew we were in trouble if there was a phone up there. I asked Clutter, "Where are your phones?" He said that there was one in the kitchen and one in the room where we were. My partner handed me the shotgun while we went to the kitchen to take care of the telephone.

I leaned against the wall and thought about how simple it would be to blow Clutter's hair all over the wall. The power of life and death was in my hands. The blood was pounding in my ears to such an extent that I put my hand to the side of my head to see if any was running out. Then my stomach seemed to tie into a knot and I got the shakes. I noticed Clutter was staring at me with his mouth open. He didn't say anything, he just stared. I broke out in a sweat and yelled at Clutter to get back in his bedroom just as my partner started back in the kitchen. Thank God I at least had sense enough to get out of that lighted room before my partner saw me!

When we got back in the bedroom I told Clutter to give me his wallet, which he did. It contained about $30 and some travel checks. I left the wallet lying on the bed. My partner had found some binoculars and he took these to the car. While my partner was gone I was told by Clutter that the rest of his family was sleeping upstairs. I knew that Clutter had a daughter and maybe two. I believe he said that only one girl was home and never did say that he had any other children. I wondered what his daughter would look like. Was she good looking? How old was she?

When my partner returned I left him to guard Clutter while I want [sic] back to the office to look again for the safe. While I was gone Mr. Clutter offered my partner a check for $200 if we would leave. Of course this was refused. When I couldn't find a safe I returned to Clutter's bedroom and we escorted Clutter upstairs.

We were going to have to do something about the rest of the family. If we were to cut Clutter's throat and leave him downstairs the family would come down as soon as we left and the heat would be on. We had to at least tie them up. But, I thought, they would see us and that wouldn't do. Oh well, I would cross that bridge when I came to it. Clutter lead [sic] the way upstairs and Perry took the shotgun and followed him. I suddenly felt weak again and climbed the stairs very slowly.

When I got to the top of the stairs in the Clutter house I heard Perry asking Clutter where the rest of the family was. Before he could answer my partner told him to get them up. Mrs. Clutter, who was a frail sort of woman—not so much in stature, but in the way she carried herself—got up first. We told her to go into the bathroom. Next to get up was the daughter. When I saw her I thought, not bad, not bad at all. She was not very tall and had dark hair and eyes. I found out later that she was 15. I told her to go into the bathroom, along with her dad, and my partner and I went into the boy, Kenyon's room to get him up.

At first the boy didn't want to get up. I guess he was scared but my partner hit him on the back with the flat of his hand, not hard, but enough to let him know we meant business. Kenyon said, "All right, I'm getting up." He was a strapping kid for no older than he was. When he got up he just had on his shorts and we put him in the bathroom that way. About 10 minutes later we let him go to his room to put on his trousers.

With the family in the bathroom we continued our search for the safe. I looked upstairs and my partner looked downstairs. The only thing we took of any value from the second floor was a portable radio from the boys [sic] room.

While we were looking through the house I had considerable time to do some thinking. This was easy, I thought, but these people were being too meek. I didn't like it. I wanted to be able to show them who was boss but they were actually letting me do whatever I wanted. Here we were, picking them like chickens and they weren't even raising a beef of any kind. How could I be tough if there was no reason to be.

It was then that I started thinking about the girl again. She looked pretty nice. I wondered what she would be like in bed. I made up my mind to find out before I left. And then it started. The same old thing. I could picture myself in bed with her. Not doing what everybody else does, but different. I've got to be different, I thought. I'm going to be different. Everything I do has to be different. In my mind I could visualize each and every detail of the intimate relationship I was planning for that night. My thoughts were interrupted by the return of my partner upstairs.

It was almost 2:00 o'clock in the morning and we decided we had better discontinue our search. We decided to tie the family up with me standing guard at the bathroom door while Perry did the tying. I thought that was a good set-up because it fit right in with my plans. I told my partner I planned to rape Nancy and he threw a fit. He looked at me and said, "If you do you and I are going to have one helluva fight." I didn't say anything but I thought to myself, I could slap you down with one hand and you say you want to fight. It wouldn't be much of a fight! I was mad and I decided I'd do as I damned [sic] well pleased.

Prior to this time my partner and I had discussed what we should do with the family. We know [sic] that if we killed the old man and left the rest of the family alive we were going to leave a bunch of witnesses. So we decided we would tie them in separate rooms and cut their throats. That way no member of the family would know what was going on until their throat was cut. That would avoid a ruckus. We knew we had to tie them up so that one of them didn't make it outdoors some way or another. We didn't want to shoot them because it would be too noisy with all the shooting and screaming going on.

By this time the Clutters seemed convinced that we were just robbing them and none of them put up any fight when we took them out of the bathroom one at a time. Little did they know what was in store for them! Mr. Clutter was the first to be tied. Just where this was I didn't know at the time. I stayed upstairs and looked through the rooms again.

I started thinking, I should have pulled this myself. It would have been impossible to do but at the time I reasoned that if I killed them I could have handled the job by myself. The more I thought of the idea the better I liked the thought of killing them. Now that is doing something, I thought. When you bump somebody off you are really in the big time.

It happens every day and I don't know why I thought it would amount to so much. There really is nothing to killing a person. It's easy to do. A lot easier than committing a burglary or cashing checks or stealing a car. At the same time, though, I thought a person could get a lot of glory out of a killing. The word "glory" seemed to keep going through my mind.

All my life I had been told that nothing I would ever do would amount to anything. Well, this was my chance, I thought. I'm going to do it. Then nobody will be able to say Dick Hickock didn't do anything worth while. I'll have to tell them I did it, I thought, or how else will they know it was me? But that will take the fun out of it. No really big time operator would do that. No, I decided, I'll wait until they catch me—if they do—and then I can tell them. But what if nobody cares who did it? What then? That's ridiculous, I thought. Naturally they will care who did it. But that's in the future. What I care about is now.

The boy was next to be tied. Perry was taking the men downstairs so I supposed it was in the cellar. I supposed right. While the boy was being tied I told the girl to come out of the bathroom to answer some questions about money. When she came into the hall I lost all desire to do anything to her at all. I don't know why. I could feel the blood rush to my head when she looked at me. It seemed she was reading my mind. All of a sudden I was ashamed of what I was thinking.

We went into the boy's bedroom which was directly across the upstairs hall from the bathroom. Nancy and I talked about various things such as why I did things like this, where I was from, if I had any parents or brothers or sisters. I tried being gruff when I talked to her but it didn't come out right. My voice sounded like my throat was full of water and it gurgled. I don't remember all the answers I gave her but I did tell her I was from Chicago. Why I told her this I'll never know. Maybe I was trying to impress her with the idea that I was a tough guy from the Windy City. But I was failing miserably and I knew it.

I asked her if there was any more money in the house, and she said, no. I then told her I had no parents and that my brother was dead. I told her my sister lived with a man who was not her husband. I asked her about school, boy friends and some other things. She told me about her church activities and I got to thinking that she was a pretty good kid.

It was about this time that Mrs. Clutter opened the bathroom door and saw us talking. Nancy went over to her mother who said she was worried about what was going on. She also said she was tired. I asked her if she wanted to go and lie down and she refused. She said she was afraid that I was going to hurt someone. I told her I had never hurt anyone before and that I wasn't going to start then.

I wondered to myself if I was. I had just about given up the idea of trying to be tough. I remember that I thought I ought to be real proud of myself, wanting to be tough and impress some one [sic] when all I had to be tough with was an elderly woman and a young kid. A feeling of reproach came over me. Then I thought to myself, why lie about it? Am I the one who is boss or not?

It was at this time that my partner returned from downstairs. If he had been gone another 10 minutes Mrs. Clutter might have talked me into leaving right then. Of course I can't be sure about that but as I look back on it I know it wouldn't have taken much to have induced me to have walked out. I was getting pretty soft-hearted.

I went to the basement with my partner, where Clutter and the boy were tied. I thought to myself, the time is getting close. My heart was pounding and I broke out in a sweat. My hands were trembling with excitement. I was going to show them. I was going to show everybody. All my life I had heard I wasn't ever going to do anything that amounted to much. But wait until they find these people, I thought, and they will know!

After the family had been tied, but before Mr. Clutter and Kenyon were moved from their first position in the furnace room, I was looking around on the first floor of the house when I came across a purse that I learned belonged to Nancy. I discovered it lying on a shelf fairly close to the first floor entrance to the basement steps. It contained several dollars. As I was looking through it I heard Mr. Clutter talking to Kenyon.

Mr. Clutter asked his boy if he could hear us. His boy said no. Clutter said, "I wonder if they have left yet." Kenyon said he didn't think so. Clutter then muttered something I couldn't make out. I then went down the steps, leaving the girl's purse on the floor. I went down to look at the north wall of the recreation room to see if the safe was located down there. As I passed the furnace room door Mr. Clutter asked me if the women were all right. I told him that they were both in bed and all right. He then told me his wife was sick and had been taking treatments from a doctor in Garden City. He asked if I had found what I had been looking for. I told him, "never mind," and went back upstairs.

Perry and I then went back to the cellar where I helped my partner move the kid into another room. I looked at him and thought, I'm doing you a favor kid if you only knew it. Just think, it won't be long and your troubles will be over. And I smiled to myself, and thought, I'll be famous! My only regret at the time was that I'd have to share my glory with my partner. But I didn't really mind because he was a good guy.

We tied the kid on a couch and put old man Clutter on a big cardboard box in the furnace room. My partner and I then discussed who was going to do it. At first I revolted. Then, I thought, it was my idea. I became infuriated—I think at myself for being weak. If it is going to be done, I thought, I want to do it. I want the glory. I want to get into the big time! I had given no thought of how I was going to do it. I guess I never really thought I would go through with it. It had just seemed like a good idea.

The boy must have heard us talking because he started struggling as if he was trying to get loose. I walked over to where he was, out of the furnace room, and flashed the light on him. He was still tied.

It was then that I heard it! It sounded like someone trying to scream with a mouth full of water, a gurgling half scream. I thought, he has done it!

At the time I was still carrying the shotgun that my partner had handed me when he was tying Clutter. With the flashlight in one hand and the shotgun in the other I rushed into the furnace room. In the beam of the flashlight I saw my partner sawing on Clutter's throat. Clutter had come out of his ropes and was fighting for his life.

My heart was ready to pound itself out of my chest, my body was ready to explode! This isn't the way I planned it, I thought. I felt like I was being cheated.

Clutter was kicking and screaming out through his throat. Blood was everywhere. Clutter was still fighting, even with his throat cut.

I dropped down and tried to hold him but he had the strength of 10 men. I'm a weightlifter and definitely no weakling but I couldn't hold him. I was getting madder all the time and on top of that I was hurt. I was hurt to think that I had planned it all and now was being cheated out of what was really mine.

By this time my partner had quit sawing on Clutter's throat. He handed me the knife and picked up the shotgun. I was still trying to hold Clutter when Perry said, "Cut him, I can't keep hold of the knife."

At first I didn't pay any attention. I was heartbroken and infuriated because I wasn't the one to cut Cutter's [sic] throat. I believe I was actually on the verge of tears.

I laid the knife down and Smith handed it back to me and said, "Stick him. It'll make you feel better."

I don't remember whether I grabbed the knife in a rough manner or not but I think I did. I thought, there is no use of my doing anything to Clutter because Smith has already done it. I thought I should use the knife on Smith! But then Clutter almost jumped straight up. I raised the knife and plunged it into his throat. It went in real easy and it surprised me. I twisted it real good once then I pulled it back out. Clutter was still for a second and I thought, that did it.

But then he started kicking even harder than ever. I was furious! I dropped the knife and hit Clutter in the head as hard as I could with my fist. It made no difference. He kept right on fighting.

I jumped up and yelled to Smith, "Shoot him! I'll hold the light!" My partner stopped Clutter's kicking. He blew his head off!

Suddenly I laughed. It was funny, very funny! Clutter wasn't ever going to give anyone a hard time again!

Perry pumped the shotgun and told me to pick up the shell. I did. I thought, why can't it go the way I planned it? Why I kept thinking this I don't know because I hadn't made any actual plans for the killings. Or had I? At the time I am writing this I can't remember all my thoughts. But I do remember that I was disappointed, very disappointed.

The boy was next. And he was having a fit. I held the flashlight and watched the kid struggle to get loose. I'm sure he had heard everything that had happened. He got it right in the face. I thought at the time that my partner was a lousy shot. He just caused the undertaker a lot of unnecessary work. Now the kid would need a facial. But I would like to have seen the embalmer fill that hole!

I had seen a lot of embalmers work when I drove an ambulance in Kansas City and I knew how much work there was on a guy that a shotgun was used on. A 12-gauge shotgun is really nasty and all the undertakers cuss and go on when they have to work on someone who has been hit with one. I knew we were causing somebody a lot of work and I still think it is funny.

Suddenly, I thought that the hired hand had probably heard the shots and might foul things up. I made up my mind that if he tried it I would kill him too. As we left the basement and went up the stairs— after I had picked up the shells—I had three different emotions. I was mad. I felt cheated, and I thought the shootings were the funniest things I had ever seen.

We ran up the stairs and headed for the girl's room. She was tied in bed in her room at the top of the stairs on the second floor. My partner was ahead of me with the shotgun and I thought, there is a solid boy. Nerves of steel. I never gave any thought to what he was thinking but I imagine he was like me, having a swell time.

As I think about it now I realize it was fun. Nobody was telling us what to do. We were boss in that house. It felt good to be able to do as I damn well pleased. No orders, no bosses, no nothing. The thought went through my mind that it would really be fun to do this to my in-laws. I'd heard a lot of guys say they'd like to but they were cowards. It took guts to do what we were doing, but it was so simple I was really surprised.

The girl was next. She said something just before the shotgun went off. She was the only one that wasn't gagged. Whatever she was saying was cut off by the roar of the shotgun as Perry pulled the trigger. It hit her in the back of the head I think.

That just proves, I thought, that all women aren't hard-headed. Which made me laugh. But then I felt a little sick. I'd liked her. I'll say this for her, she knew how to die. She didn't even kick. She knew how to go. But it is possible she didn't know what was going on.

She had said something but I don't remember what it was. It might have been her prayers and she might not have finished. I worry about that. But I pray for her so she is okay.

But Mrs. Clutter knew what was going on. She was almost out of her ropes. She was really struggling—I think even harder than the old man before he was shot. But her struggles soon stopped. I don't know where she was shot. The side of the head I think. At any rate she quit kicking.

The only fear I had at this time was that the hired man had heard the shotgun going off. He is liable to come running in the front door at any time, I thought. It would have been too bad for him if he had.

I picked up the last of the shells and we ran down the steps and out to the car.

It was over. We had killed four people. I didn't time it but it couldn't have taken long. Everything happened in the space of about 10 minutes, or even less, from the time we killed the first one (Mr. Clutter) to the time of the last one (Mrs. Clutter).

Boy, that fresh air felt good when we got out of the Clutter house! My ears were ringing from the noise of the shotgun so that I could hardly hear. When we got in the car my partner asked me what I thought about the hired hand. I told him I didn't think he had seen anything. The light wasn't on so we drove on down the road.

I felt as if a big weight was off my shoulders. But I was disappointed. It didn't go like I expected it to at all. I couldn't help but feel cheated.

All at once I knew I was scared. Just what I was scared of I don't know. I remember that I was breathing real hard and I had a tight feeling in my chest as if I had run a long distance. I was real nervous. I tried, did light a cigarette and I noticed that my hands were shaking. I know I thought at the time I didn't want my partner to see it. But above all else I was disappointed.

In fact it looks to me now as if I was just like a kid getting ready to throw a fit. I felt like I wanted something but had been denied it. I felt almost exactly as I used to feel when I had to give up something to my brother. I kept thinking, over and over, why did it happen this way? And for the life of me, even as I write this, I can't think of any other way I wanted it to happen.

After we drive several miles I said to my partner, "I guess you know we've stirred them up like a hornet's nest around here." I felt a little resentment toward my partner. But other than that I felt good. I felt like a big load had been lifted from my shoulders. For a while I enjoyed a feeling of exhilaration. But then I began getting tired and suddenly I was hungry. Boy, was I hungry!

Most of our conversation driving away concerned our going to Mexico the next weekend. We thought we'd stay there a couple of weeks then head on south, probably to Brazil. I told Perry I would write all the checks I could before we left Kansas City for Mexico. We planned for me to work the following week as if nothing had happened. We were to leave Kansas City the following Saturday. I told Perry it would be best if he went to Kansas City to stay and that we shouldn't be seen together around Olathe. I knew a lot of people around town and my parole officer also lived there.

We decided that when we got back to Olathe my partner would register in a hotel until Monday night when I would take him to Kansas City. Perry sort of thought we ought to head for Mexico right then but I told him, no, that might put the heat on us.

After I left Perry Smith off at an Olathe Hotel I happened to look at the floor of my car opposite the driver's seat and thought, good God! The floor had blood all over it. I hadn't noticed it before but I certainly did now! Smith must have stepped in the blood because it was all over the floor where his feet had been. I knew I had to clean it up but I didn't know where I could do it. I couldn't do it at home without the folks seeing me. Maybe I can do it after dark, I thought. So I decided that as soon as it was dark I would wash it off, or try to.

It was pretty close to 12:00 o'clock noon when I drove into the yard at the farm. As I parked the car I looked in the kitchen window and saw that my folks were eating dinner. I decided to leave the shotgun in the car until later when I would give it a good cleaning.

Mom asked me if I was hungry and I told her, yes. She set a place at the table for me and I found that I was real hungry. During dinner Dad and I talked about first one thing and then another—mostly about work that needed to be done around the farm. When we finished eating Dad asked me if I was going to watch the ball game on television with him. I told him I would a little later. There was no one at the farm except my parents and myself all that day.

I went to the car and got the shotgun and brought it in the kitchen to clean it. I knew the folks wouldn't give a thought to the gun because around our house a gun was common and I was always hunting. I never left a gun lying around without cleaning it from time to time. I wanted to make sure it didn't rust. Also, I never handled a gun without wiping it off with an oiled rag. So I knew my cleaning of the gun would cause no comment.

While cleaning the gun I noticed that there was blood along the ventilated rib and in the cracks around the trigger guard. It took me about 15 minutes to clean it. After putting the gun in its case I went into the living room to watch television with my Dad.

I don't remember who was playing but it was a professional football game. I lay on the couch and Dad asked me if I was tired. I told him I hadn't got much sleep the night before and was a little tired. I told Mom to be sure and wake me when supper was ready if I happened to fall asleep. I don't know how long I watched television but it was only a few minutes before I dropped off to sleep. It was Dad who awakened me and said supper would be ready in a few minutes.

I had just finished washing when I heard a newscast start. I didn't want to appear overly interested in it but I watched the whole broadcast. Nothing was mentioned about any killing and I wondered if I had only dreamed about the Clutters. Maybe, I thought, I hadn't been involved in killing anyone at all. Then, I thought, maybe it won't even be on television. I had felt quite excited at the prospect of it being mentioned.

While I was eating supper I thought about the blood on the floor of my car. If I had dreamed about the Clutters there definitely wouldn't be any blood in my car. I wanted to hurry and finish eating so I could inspect the floor-boards of my car. I must have been eating real fast because my Dad asked me if I was going to a fire. I said, "No, why?" He said, "You're shoveling your food in as fast as you can work your elbow."

I thought, I better slow down, I don't want to do anything to make my folks think something is wrong. But I could hardly wait to get out to the car. Then I thought, I wonder if Dad has seen the blood. Surely he hasn't or he would want to know where it came from. Maybe there isn't any. I just couldn't wait to find out!

Finally supper was over and I told my folks I was going out to get some fresh air. I took a rag which I found on the back porch. I wet it in the rain barrel. I had also taken a flashlight with me. I opened the car door on the side that my partner had sat. When the dome light came on I saw the blood. I got busy with the wet rag wiping Clutter's blood off as fast as I could. I wondered if they had been found yet. There was the possibility that no one had discovered the bodies.

After cleaning the knife and washing the floor mat as good as I could I shoved the rag down in some trash I knew would be burned in a couple of days. I put the knife in a green fishing tackle box and headed for the house. I made up my mind that the first thing I was going to do when I got to work the next morning was give the car a good bath—inside and out...

I seriously thought about leaving Smith shortly after we returned to the States from Mexico. We crossed the border at Tia Juana on December 7, 1959. Prior to our leaving Mexico City we had a wild fling which included wine, women but no song. Even without the music our last two days in Mexico City were costly ones.

I found that my partner never had any respect for a dollar and he threw money around more than I did. When we arrived in California we had less than $100 between us. Our only hope for future resources lay in using pistols.

We finally ended up in Kansas City, my home town, and our only purpose for returning to the U.S. was to pull a score big enough to finance a trip to South America. Our proposed destination was Brazil where they couldn't extradite us back to the States if they ever caught onto who pulled the Clutter deal.

During our 2,004 mile bus trip back to the States we had agreed that we were not going to stay for any length of time. As quick as a score could be set up and pulled, we were heading back across the border.

I started on one of the most cautious check passing sprees that part of the country had ever seen. I couldn't be sure but I had an idea we were hotter than a pistol because of the checks we'd passed before. I found out later that we were also wanted for the Clutter case. Every law enforcement agency in 17 states was on the alert for us and there I was in Kansas City, my home town, hanging paper!

I cashed over $500 worth of checks. I got a set of tires, a wrist watch, two television sets and some other stuff. I also managed to get some cash. About everything we got with the checks was sold later in Florida for about a fourth of what I had paid for it.

How I ever managed to cash the checks without getting busted I can't imagine. But I guess I really didn't get away with it because it was the purchase of one of the television sets which led to our eventual arrest in Las Vegas.

I used my own name in cashing the checks and the owner of one of the places where I bought a television set took down the license number of the car I was driving. He wrote the number on the check I gave him. I didn't know about that at the time or I could have very easily switched plates. But Perry told me when we were in jail waiting trial for the Clutter case that he saw him do it, but didn't think about telling me about it. Can you imagine being so stupid? But that's just how much help he was to me all the way through. I not only had to do all the work, I also had to do all the thinking!

Anyway, after we were under arrest one of the policemen told me the reason we were picked up was that when the check for the television set bounced, the number of our license tag was circulated all over the country. That is why the Las Vegas police picked us up while we were sitting in a car.

Our trial was more like a circus than anything else. It took only one day to choose the jury. The way the feeling was running around town I figured it would take at least three or four days for this. But the whole trial didn't last much longer than that.

The courtroom overflowed with spectators and the halls were lined with photographers and newspaper reporters. Every exit was covered by a pair of highway patrolmen. Extra deputy sheriffs were brought in from neighboring counties. I couldn't tell whether this was done to prevent our escape or to protect us. It could have been both, or more likely it was just for show.

I never did think much of the Finney County Attorney and I sure liked him less after our first day in court. He kept pointing his finger at me and telling the jury how no good I was. I resented it. It wasn't so much what he was saying but how he was saying it and who he was saying it in front of.

I looked at my Mom and Dad and I saw my Mom was crying. It was worse on her, I think, than anybody. I didn't care what the rest of the people thought but I did my Mom and Dad. Also, my Aunt and Uncle were sitting there and some friends from Hutchinson, Kansas. One was an old girl friend of mine.

Every time the county attorney pointed his finger at me I wanted to hit him. He was making a lot of statements that were not true and I certainly didn't like it. Things were bad enough without him telling a lot of lies. When he first started waving his finger at me I saw red.

I looked at my Dad and he knew what I was thinking because he shook his head and motioned to me to keep my seat, so I did. But I'd really like to get a crack at that boy in the free world!

I wasn't surprised when the State asked for the death penalty. I had been told by the County Attorney over a month before the trial that he was going to ask for it. I don't know how my buddy Smith felt about it because we were kept in separate cells and weren't allowed to talk until after the trial was over.

When the jury started to deliberate I was taken back to my cell on the top floor of the courthouse. Taking into consideration the type testimony that was given and the attitude of the court I knew that the State was going to get just what it asked for. My only hope, I figured, was with the Judge.

As these thoughts went through my mind I began to have hopes of getting a break from the Judge. I knew that I wouldn't be sentenced for three or four days and I was determined to find out just what kind of a Judge this one was. He looked to me to be the type that would turn down any request that a man made. I had heard he was a friend of the Clutters and he would probably have a personal interest in the case that would make him biased toward me.

I decided that I wouldn't ask for anything unless I had a 50-50 chance of getting what I wanted. I had asked a favor of the police and had been turned down so I knew it was no use to ask them. I decided that when they took me down for sentencing I would have my lawyer enter a plea for parole. I had so many other charges against me that I figured if I entered a plea of guilty to them the Judge might give me a parole on the Clutter deal.

I had tried to work a similar deal in Johnson County once before but the Judge wouldn't go for it. I knew I didn't have much hope of getting it here because the State was asking the death penalty and the people were really stirred up.

I only had one real good argument and that was the fact that this was the first time I had ever been involved in murder and first time offenders in a lot of cases get a parole or probation. I figured it was worth a try. I had nothing to lose. The law didn't have much to lose by going along with it. I had enough other stuff against me to do 50 years in the penitentiary.

There was another guy in jail and since he might know the Judge I thought I would ask him if he thought I might swing a parole. But then I got to thinking this guy might say something to the FBI and they would queer the deal because they sure didn't like me.

I knew the jury would bring in a verdict of guilty when I returned to the courtroom and I told the guy in jail so. He asked me if I thought they would give me the death sentence. I told him probably, but I didn't know if the Judge would go for it.

I asked him what kind of a guy the Judge was and if he knew him. He said he did and added, "He would send his own mother to the gallows. If that jury brings in a guilty verdict you are in a world of trouble." I said, "The Judge won't deal, huh?" And he said, "In your case? You nuts? Why the people would run him out of town on a rail."

I thought, just as I figured. He can go to and stay put for all I care. I'll never ask him for a favor. But if he doesn't give me a parole on his own hook I'll file to the Supreme Court on it. I was supposed to get another lawyer when I got to the penitentiary and I was determined to let him know all about it. He is one of the best lawyers in the state and I figured it would be no sweat for him to get me out.

It was about this time that I was taken down to the courtroom. The jury had only taken about 25 minutes to deliberate. But the Judge was out feeding his horses and we had to wait until he got back.

Every other time I was taken to the courtroom the handcuffs were taken off. But this time they stayed on and I was kept cuffed to the undersheriff. When the verdict was given and the jury said the punishment was to be death I wasn't surprised. I leaned over to the undersheriff and I couldn't help laughing when I told him it was what I expected.

When the Judge was telling the jury what a good job they had done I thought that these pompous old ginks were the lousiest looking specimens of manhood I had ever seen; old cronies that acted like they were God or somebody.

Right then I wished every one of them had been at the Clutter house that night and that included the Judge. I would have found out how much God they had in them! If they had been there and had any God in them I would have let it run out on the floor.

I thought, boy, I'd like to do it right here. Now there was something that would have really stirred them up!

When the jury filed out of the courtroom not one of them would look at me. I looked each one in the face and I kept thinking, Look at me, look at me, look at me!

But none of them would.[11]

Conclusion

In addition to "America's Worst Crime in 20 Years," the unpublished letters between Mack Nations and Richard Hickock; notes from the prison visits; correspondence between Capote and prison officials; signed visitation logs, where Capote's and Lee's signatures appear; a list of items for the prisoners' last meal, etc., join other documents in various collections and exhibits at the Kansas Historical Society. Some of the materials are restricted in how they may be used, but most are available online or on site and provide invaluable resources for the public and the scholarly community.

Michael Nations said he has read *In Cold Blood* "more than once," calling it a "masterpiece in storytelling" but arguing in an e-mail message April 17, 2011, that Capote's claim of accuracy is "simply absurd." Having devoted much of his life to providing journalists, scholars, and readers with information about his father, Michael Nations summarizes his contribution de-

---

[11]Ibid., 30-31, 76-83.

scriptively in a June 8, 2015, e-mail message: "I feel like a guy with a flashlight giving tours. My dad died with a head full of secrets. Dick Hickock took his secrets to the gallows. Mack Nations took his to the grave."

Starling Mack Nations's voice is not the only one Capote omitted. Beverly Clutter English and Eveanna Clutter Mosier gave interviews to Capote with the promise that he would let them read the story about them before he published it in *The New Yorker*. Stunned that he did not keep his word (and devastated by his negative portrayal of their mother), the sisters refused all subsequent interviews with the exception of a 2005 news article in which they explain their desire not to share their story. In the story by Patrick Smith, the Clutter sisters describe their commitment to collecting material about their parents and brother and sister for the scrapbooks they planned to give their grandchildren. Interested in their parents' lives—not their deaths—the two of them compiled "three thick red binders" of family documents, Smith said.

This study gives expression to some of the narratives omitted from *In Cold Blood*, which Capote wrote during his whirlwind race to an imaginary finish line. In addition to craving external validation in order to fill a deep emotional void, Capote was determined to compete with his childhood friend Harper Lee and her success after the publication of *To Kill a Mockingbird* (1960) and the release of the film by the same title (1962). The book would win a Pulitzer Prize, and the film starring Gregory Peck as Atticus Finch would garner three Academy Awards and be nominated for eight more. The films *Capote* and *Infamous*, drawn from two biographies about Capote, testify to his unrelenting desire to make *In Cold Blood* his most widely celebrated work. Although Capote did not win a Pulitzer Prize, *In Cold Blood* remains one of the 100 greatest novels of the twentieth century, a study of crime and a polemic against capital punishment that is without equal. It helped to usher in the era of New Journalism and was the catalyst for a century of crime reporting in America, which drew from popular narratives about heightened human conflict in England, France, and Italy.

Ultimately, of course, *In Cold Blood* is not about Capote and his desire for recognition, nor is it about Perry Smith, Capote's alter ego, or Alvin A. Dewey, the hero of the nonfiction novel. Although *In Cold Blood* provides nail-biting realism, it is at heart only one thing—the story of the last moments in the lives of four people who, as Capote reminds his readers, had no idea that it would be their last day. They left the door unlocked. They went to bed in safety, expecting to join members of the community at church in the morning. They looked forward to Thanksgiving, when they would reunite with the rest of their family. For no reason—based on a lie told by a convict—Richard Eugene Hickock and Perry Edward Smith entered through an unlocked door and did not leave until they had fired "four shotgun blasts, that, all told, ended six human lives."[12]

---

[12]Capote, *In Cold Blood*, 5.

Chapter 6

Nelle Harper Lee and *In Cold Blood*

Nelle Harper Lee's contribution to *In Cold Blood* has never been fully explored, in part because she herself remained largely silent on the topic. Her sister spoke out, albeit briefly and rarely. Biographers of Truman Capote and Lee address her commitment to the project. As we shall see, a recent dissertation purports to go more deeply into the issue. The fact remains that *In Cold Blood* as we know it might not have existed if Lee had not made possible interviews with skeptical Holcomb and Garden City residents, if she had not softened Capote's aggressive and often brash approach, and if she herself had not been fascinated by crime stories.

A study of documents housed at the Kansas Historical Society provides a sometimes humorous but always accurate sense of Lee's involvement in the research for the nonfiction novel. A letter from an attorney representing Capote to the director of penal institutions in Topeka is but one of numerous documents suggesting her investment:

> Miss Nelle Harper Lee, the novelist, who accompanied Mr. Capote on his visit, has advised that Perry Smith indicated that he would like to correspond with her. I trust that this privilege could not be granted unless Smith himself would make a request for it. I understand Miss Lee's letters have been returned undelivered. It would be very much appreciated if you could advise as to the proper procedure in this regard. (Perry Edward Smith Inmate Case File, No. 96)

Although the request was not granted, Lee remained deeply invested in the fates of Richard Eugene Hickock and Perry Edward Smith. More amusing excerpts from the case files include messages among prison officials, such as: "Confirming our telephone conversation of this morning, Mr. Truman Capote and his associate, Mrs. Nellie Lee Harper, will be at KSP on Monday" (No. 298), "This is to inform you that Mr. Truman Capote and his assistant, Mrs. Harper, interviewed Hickock and Smith" (No. 142), and "Mr. Capot [sic] and lady friend will be here approximately 11:00 a.m." (No. 376). Records that list visitors to Hickock and Smith repeatedly reveal Lee's name, her signature, and her New York address. Like Capote, she is listed as a "friend" (No. 441, No. 512, and others).

Truman Capote and Nelle Harper Lee were friends. Reliable information about the fluctuations of their friendship is not part of the public domain. Speculations about whether or not they broke off their relationship after the publication of *In Cold Blood* and whether they eventually reconciled are pointless. Storytelling giants of the American South, Capote and Lee live on in film and literature and in the hearts of millions of readers. Played by Catherine Keener (*Capote*) and Sandra Bullock (*Infamous*), Nelle Harper Lee—whose parents chose to name her "Ellen," spelled backwards, after her grandmother—is as beloved as Capote is scrutinized.

As children, Capote and Lee were neighbors in Monroeville, Alabama, and their collections now share physical space in the Monroe County Heritage Museum. No doubt Capote would be irritated by having to share space with someone who was both one of his closest and most loyal friends and, at least briefly, his literary nemesis. Two permanent exhibits grace the museum, "Truman Capote: A Childhood in Monroeville" and "Harper Lee: In Her Own Words." Poetically and insightfully, Ralph F. Voss writes that when Capote and Lee began their illustrative careers, the "literary stars were falling on Alabama." He calls their friendship "rich in imagination."[1]

William T. Going's article "Truman Capote: Harper Lee's Fictional Portrait of the Artist as an Alabama Child" is especially helpful in an assessment of their relationship. As noted earlier, Truman Streckfus Persons was born in New Orleans in 1924. His Alabama parents were Lillie Mae (Nina) Faulk and Archulus (Arch) Persons. Unprepared to be a parent, Faulk sent her son to live with her cousins in Monroeville in Monroe County northeast of Mobile. Capote lived there until he was ten and spent summers there until he was about fifteen. When his mother divorced, she married Joseph Garcia Capote, who adopted Truman Capote and appears to have loved him. Citing several sources, Going reveals that Lee and Capote played with an old typewriter in their "office" and wrote stories. Monroeville residents remember Capote as a "brilliant little boy 'with yellow hair in his eyes—talking incessantly and using big words most people never heard.'"[2]

---

[1] Ralph F. Voss, *Truman Capote and the Legacy of* In Cold Blood (Tuscaloosa: University of Alabama Press, 2011) 24.

[2] William T. Going, "Truman Capote: Harper Lee's Fictional Portrait of the Artist as an Alabama Child," *Alabama Review* 42/2 (1989): 138.

Going adds that Capote was bullied by other children and felt "isolated and unwanted."[3]

Capote's deep friendship with Lee enriched his life and provided comfort and refuge. It is during this time, too, that we begin to see Capote's gift for the dramatic: "Thus the summer came to an end, thus an adventure got under way, and thus the tiny quixotic Dill began to dominate the Finch children's lives," Going writes. "He began by telling Jem and Scout fanciful tales about himself: his father was taller than theirs, he was president of the [Louisville and Nashville] Railroad, his grandfather was General Joe Wheeler."[4] Going continues:

> When Dill returns to Maycomb for the summer of 1935, he does it with a flourish. The children find him hiding, dirty and exhausted, under Scout's bed. After a bath and food he recounts his harrowing escape from the basement in Meridian, where his new father had bound him. Kept alive by raw field peas from a passing farmer who heard his cries, he finally works free of his wrist manacles. He joins a small animal show (his job being to feed the camels), and then he gradually finds his way to Abbott County across the river from Maycomb. Actually, of course, Dill has stolen money from his mother's purse and walked to the Finch house from the train station at Maycomb Junction.[5]

Lee died in 2016 without disparaging Capote or releasing details about the status of their friendship. Quiet, humble, unassuming, and private, Lee was nothing if not the antithesis of Truman Capote, who craved external affirmation, competed with other successful writers, and made himself the center of every gathering. If one is to trust the portrayals of Jean Louise (Scout) Finch and Charles Baker (Dill) Harris in the novel and film *To Kill a Mockingbird*, then theirs is a relationship for the ages. In *To Kill a Mockingbird*, Lee's affection for her friend is obvious. As Going notes, she creates a character named Dill who demonstrates "sympathy for both victim and perpetrator,"[6] as Capote will do again with the Clutter family and Perry Smith. In the novel, as Going notes, Lee discloses Capote's "agility of mind, his inventiveness, his concern for the underdog, his love of mystery and

---

[3] Ibid., 139.
[4] Ibid., 145.
[5] Ibid., 146.
[6] Ibid., 148.

gothic shadows, his longing for a place called home, and his veneration for the written page."[7]

This chapter explores Lee's contributions to *In Cold Blood*, which were and are underestimated and may never be fully recognized, but it is also a testament to a passionate relationship between two people who would live in New York City, would embrace film versions of their most popular novels, and would choose markedly different ways of engaging with the world. The depth of their connection is illustrated in *Counterpoint*, where Lee tells Roy Newquist about a childhood spent with Capote:

> We had to use our own devices in our play, for our entertainment. We didn't have much money. Nobody had any money. We didn't have toys, nothing was done for us, so the result was that we lived in our imagination most of the time. We devised things; we were readers, and we would transfer everything we had seen on the printed page to the backyard in the form of high drama.[8]

When Capote was confident and ebullient, he claimed Lee and showered her with praise. When he wasn't feeling good about himself or his work, he withheld his affection. Either way, there is little doubt about his love for her. As he said to Lawrence Grobel, "Harper Lee was my best friend. Did you ever read her book, *To Kill a Mockingbird*? I'm a character in that book, which takes place in the same small town in Alabama where we lived. Her father was a lawyer and she and I used to go to trials all the time as children. We went to the trials instead of going to the movies."[9] Capote's memories are sometimes more bawdy than the soft-spoken Miss Harper Lee might prefer: "That's been the story of her life—that I spent my childhood asking her to marry me," Capote said about his friend. "I spent my childhood asking her to keep her hands out of my pants...There's more truth than fiction in that."[10]

Hoping to be considered the "Jane Austen of south Alabama,"[11] Lee remained compassionate about and empathetic toward her friend Truman. For example, having seen Richard Eugene Hickock and Perry Edward

---

[7]Ibid., 149.

[8]Roy Newquist, *Counterpoint* (New York: Rand McNally, 1964) 407.

[9]Lawrence Grobel, *Conversations with Capote* (New York: New American Library, 1985) 53.

[10]Ibid., 66.

[11]Newquist, *Counterpoint*, 403.

Smith for the first time January 6, 1960, Lee said in a *Newsweek* interview, "I think every time Truman looked at Perry he saw his own childhood."[12] Others responded to Lee's generous spirit, especially in Holcomb and Garden City, Kansas, where Capote's brash otherness alienated some of the residents. Bobby Rupp, Nancy Clutter's boyfriend, for example, gave an interview only because Lee solicited it.[13] Lee exhibited "graceful charm and friendliness"[14] while in Kansas, Voss said, and "made the crucial difference"[15] in Capote's success.

Like *To Kill a Mockingbird*, Capote's magnum opus also would deal with alienation and violence—but without the point of view of children struggling to make sense of the world around them. Unlike Scout in Lee's novel, there were no sympathetic, trustworthy characters who could serve as the primary narrative voice in *In Cold Blood*. At almost midnight on November 14, 1959, Hickock and Smith—acting on an inaccurate tip from an inmate named Floyd Wells—rolled into Holcomb, Kansas, population 270. After driving to River Valley Farm, they parked and walked into an unlocked house belonging to Bonnie and Herbert Clutter. Failing to locate what was in fact a nonexistent safe, Hickock and Smith confronted the parents and their two youngest children, bound them with rope, and killed them, leaving the scene with about forty dollars, a pair of binoculars, and a transistor radio. Friends found the bodies of Bonnie and Herbert Clutter and their children, Kenyon Neal Clutter and Nancy Mae Clutter, on the morning of November 15, 1959. The oldest children, Beverly Jean Clutter English and Eveanna Marie Clutter Mosier, were not at their parents' home.

As noted in previous chapters, Capote read about the crime in *The New York Times*, and, deeply affected by the story, made plans to travel to Garden City and Holcomb to conduct research with Lee. Having completed the final draft of *To Kill a Mockingbird*, Lee enthusiastically agreed. The daughter of an Alabama attorney, Lee was interested in crime and legal processes, as her novel about Atticus Finch and a devastating rape trial in Maycomb, Alabama, suggests. Arriving in Kansas, Capote and Lee began to gather information and set up interviews. On January 6, 1960, Capote and Lee caught their first glimpse of Hickock and Smith, and five years later, their efforts culminated in the nonfiction novel *In Cold Blood*.

---

[12]Phillip K. Tompkins, "In Cold Fact," *Esquire* 65/6 (June 1966): 170.
[13]Voss, *Truman Capote and the Legacy of* In Cold Blood, 195.
[14]Ibid., 5.
[15]Ibid., 37.

For far too many reasons to explore here, the murders in Holcomb, Kansas, have captured the international imagination for decades. In 2005 and 2006, respectively, the films *Capote* and *Infamous* introduced a new generation of moviegoers to a tragic tale in the American heartland. Since then, news stories related to the murders have multiplied: one suggests that Hickock and Smith might have killed a family in Florida (DNA eventually disproved this suspicion); another explores materials discovered at the family home by the son of Harold R. Nye, a former Kansas Bureau of Investigation official, and the KBI's claim to those documents; another features the Kansas Historical Society and its impressive holdings related to the case; and still others discuss the surviving Clutter sisters and their reluctance to provide interviews.

Although the murders, subsequent trial, and executions lie at the center of the public fascination with *In Cold Blood*, one of the most compelling aspects of the larger historical narrative is the friendship between Capote and Lee, which resulted in their collaboration on one of the most riveting crime stories in American literature. The Southern Literary Trail lauds Capote and Lee as "America's most famous pair of childhood friends,"[16] and in *Capote in Kansas: A Ghost Story*, Kim Powers invents a story to answer his own questions about the relationship between these literary giants. Accusing Capote of calling Lee his "assistant"[17]—which he did—and giving Lee *"half* a dedication"[18] (she is listed with Capote's partner Jack Dunphy)—Powers makes up dialogue, even adding a scene in which Capote writes a conciliatory message to Lee about *To Kill a Mockingbird*: "It's the book I wish I could have written."[19] Powers explains his purpose for writing the novel in the "Author's Note": "After a childhood of broken arms, an absent father, and terrors both imagined and real and only partially glimpsed, I wanted, somehow, to live inside that story."[20] His motivation for writing *Capote in Kansas* may be shared by some readers of *To Kill a Mockingbird*, although this fact does not mitigate the harm his novel does in contributing to the rumors about the relationship between Capote and Lee.

---

[16]"Monroeville: Truman Capote and Harper Lee," *The Southern Literary Trail*, web (accessed 11 August 2018).

[17]Kim Powers, *Capote in Kansas: A Ghost Story* (New York: Carroll and Graf, 2007) 13.

[18]Ibid., 24.

[19]Ibid., 245.

[20]Ibid., 252.

Biographers, journalists, and literary critics argue that collaborating on *In Cold Blood* cost Capote and Lee their close and trusting relationship, although this essay raises questions about what we actually know and seeks to dispel the proliferation of rumors and wishful thinking to which they have resorted. Understandably, much has been made of Capote's competitiveness, which some suggest precipitated a loss of affection between the childhood friends. Of all those who have weighed in on the friendship, Lee's sister Alice Lee speaks with the most authority. Characteristically, Harper Lee herself never addressed the issue.

At one point, when asked if Lee contributed to the reporting that made *In Cold Blood* possible, Capote emphatically replied, *"No.* She was just there."[21] As we shall see, this inaccurate and demeaning comment does not represent how Capote ordinarily described Lee's contributions to their collaborative research. For her part, Lee always was gracious, celebrating Capote as the more experienced and well-known writer, praising *In Cold Blood* as Capote's "long piece of reportage" and saying publicly, "Capote, I think, is the greatest craftsman we have going."[22] As Charles J. Shields writes in his biography of Lee, "Harper Lee had a way of smiling as she explained in her soft drawl, 'Well, Truman is a genius, you know. He really is. He's a genius.'"[23]

Relying on archived material, biographies of Capote and Lee, and the films *Capote* and *Infamous,* this chapter and the one that follows focus on one of the most famous literary relationships of all time and separate evidence from impassioned speculation. Lee kept her own counsel about her relationship with Capote. Whether or not her sister and friends represent Lee's perspective accurately, whatever reactions she might have had to Capote's well-documented slights remain hers alone—and Lee was nothing if not private about her personal life. As indicated by Lee's response to a memoir by Marja Mills titled *The Mockingbird Next Door: Life with Harper Lee,* the author had no plans to tell all. When Penguin Press said it was publishing a book that was "written with direct access to Harper and Alice Finch Lee and their friends and family," Lee responded through her sister Alice Lee's law office: "Contrary to recent news reports, I have not willingly par-

---

[21]Charles J. Shields, *Mockingbird: A Portrait of Harper Lee* (New York: Henry Holt, 2006) 240.

[22]Newquist, *Counterpoint,* 409.

[23]Shields, *Mockingbird,* 156.

ticipated in any book written or to be written by Marja Mills. Neither have I authorized such a book. Any claims otherwise are false."[24]

Although it was futile to wait for Lee to address her feelings about her old friend Capote, we can learn a great deal about their reliance on one another from the literature they produced. Furthermore, close attention to historical detail might defuse some of the impassioned rhetoric about their fractured relationship. For example, although some argue that Capote and Lee were estranged after their collaboration on *In Cold Blood*, the two often were shown together in photographs, including one in 1966 in which Capote signs copies of his book as Lee looks on. It is important to pay tribute to the time during which the two were devoted to one another, a time that began in a "tired old town" where "streets turned to red slop"[25] when it rained, as Lee writes in *To Kill a Mockingbird*.

Capote and Lee as Childhood Friends

For those who remember the Academy Award-winning film *To Kill a Mockingbird*, the young Nelle Harper Lee and Truman Capote may always evoke memories of Mary Badham and John Megna, who played Jean Louise (Scout) Finch and Charles Baker (Dill) Harris in the film. Lee documented her friendship with Capote in her affectionate portrayal of Dill. Just as Dill is based on Truman Capote, tomboys Idabel Thompkins of Capote's *Other Voices, Other Rooms* (1948) and Ann (Jumbo) Finchburg of "The Thanksgiving Visitor" (1967) are based in part on Lee. Charles J. Shields aptly describes how two of the greatest writers in American literary history met and helps to explain the public obsession with their relationship as they grew older:

Nelle was going on five years old the summer she became acquainted with Truman, who was almost six and living with his aunts, the Faulks. Barefoot, Nelle enjoyed teetering along the top of the low rock wall that separated the Lee and Faulk properties. Next to the wall grew a twin-trunk chinaberry tree supporting a tree house. From this outpost, Nelle could spy on Truman ambling among the lilacs and azaleas. "Beautiful things floated around in his dreamy head," she would later write of him, when Truman became Dill, the lonely boy next door in

---

[24]Patricia Cohen, "'To Kill a Mockingbird' Author Repudiates Journalist's Memoir About Her," *The New York Times*, 27 April 2011, web (accessed 11 August 2018).
[25]Harper Lee, *To Kill a Mockingbird* (New York: HarperCollins, 1999) 5.

To Kill a Mockingbird. "[He] preferred his own twilight world, a world where babies slept, waiting to be gathered like morning lilies."[26]

As noted earlier in this chapter, Capote was born in New Orleans but grew up in Monroeville, now called "Alabama's Literary Capital." His parents are said to have neglected Capote, who in 1930 went to live with extended family in Monroe County, Alabama. As fate would have it, Nelle Harper Lee was the youngest daughter of the family that lived next door to the Faulk house on South Alabama Avenue. Just as Monroeville was the inspiration for Maycomb in *To Kill a Mockingbird*, Capote, too, chose a small southern town as the setting for several short stories and novels, including "My Side of the Matter," "A Tree of Night," "Children on their Birthdays," "A Christmas Memory," "The Thanksgiving Visitor," *Other Voices, Other Rooms,* and *The Grass Harp.*

In the film and novel *To Kill a Mockingbird*, Scout Finch and Dill Harris provide accurate portrayals of Harper Lee and Truman Capote, one in overalls and scuffed tennis shoes and the other in pressed white shirts and shorts. As Capote biographer Gerald Clarke writes, Lee was the "tomboy on the block, a girl who...could beat the steam out of most boys her age, or even a year or so older, as Truman was...Neither had many other real friends. Nelle was too rough for most other girls, and Truman was too soft for most other boys."[27] Although the gendered descriptions may or may not be accurate, they are most certainly reinforced in the 1962 film *To Kill a Mockingbird.* Alice Lee, who was fifteen years older than the sister she called "Nelle Harper," said her sibling was athletic and enjoyed football and baseball.[28] Like Scout, "Nelle Harper grew up quite the little tomboy,"[29] Alice Lee said.

Capote seemed especially proud to be reincarnated in the Pulitzer Prize-winning novel *To Kill a Mockingbird*, based largely on Lee's memories of Monroeville in the 1930s; in turn, Lee wanted to be an investigator for *In Cold Blood.* In a letter to David O. Selznick and Jennifer Jones in early June 1960, Capote asks the Hollywood icons to host Alvin and Marie Dewey on a tour of Los Angeles, calling Alvin Dewey the "hero of my book." The

---

[26]Shields, *Mockingbird*, 34.

[27]Gerald Clarke, *Capote: A Biography* (New York: Simon and Schuster, 1988) 22.

[28]Alice Finch Lee, interview, *Scout, Atticus & Boo: A Celebration of Fifty Years of* To Kill a Mockingbird (New York: HarperCollins, 2010) 122.

[29]Ibid., 121.

postscript reads, "On July 11th, Lippincott is publishing a delightful book: TO KILL A MOCKINGBIRD by Harper Lee. Get it. It's going to be a great success. In it, I am the character called 'Dill'—the author being a childhood friend."[30] Soon after, in an August 12, 1960, letter to the Deweys—who established a friendship with both Capote and Lee during their visits to Kansas—Capote wrote, "Nelle's book is high on the best-seller list...And yes, my dear, I *am* Dill."[31] According to The Library of America, Lee was enthusiastic about accompanying Capote to Kansas: "The crime intrigued him, and I'm intrigued with crime—and, boy, I wanted to go. It was deep calling to deep,"[32] Lee said.

Shields suggests that early and frequent interaction and the obsession the children had with a reclusive man in Monroeville—a man who inspired the character Boo Radley in *To Kill a Mockingbird*—linked Capote and Lee as they set out for River Valley Farm. Looking through the crime scene at the Clutter house, Capote and Lee "were embarking once again on a hunt for something monstrous."[33] The dark and brooding story about attempted murder, ignorance, poverty, prejudice, and rape in Monroeville, Alabama, set the stage for a tale of horror in another small town.

Collaboration on In Cold Blood

Several literary critics and a few sources that appear in *In Cold Blood* make Lee the central cog in the success of the nonfiction novel, suggesting reasonably enough that Capote gained a great deal from his friend's interpersonal skills and research ability. Dewey of the Kansas Bureau of Investigation described Lee as "unaffected" and "charming," "never attempting to upstage or interrupt"[34] Capote. Shields is quick to agree with Dewey: "It was the synergy of two writers at work in Garden City that gave *In Cold Blood* such verisimilitude,"[35] he writes, adding that Nelle's "gift for creating character sketches turned out to complement Truman's ability to recall remarks."[36]

---

[30]Gerald Clarke, ed., *Too Brief a Treat: The Letters of Truman Capote* (New York: Random House, 2004) 284.

[31]Ibid., 290.

[32]"Truman Capote and Harper Lee: Immortalizing Each Other in Fiction," The Library of America, 1 October 2010, web (accessed 11 August 2018).

[33]Shields, *Mockingbird*, 146.

[34]Ibid., 156.

[35]Ibid., 163.

[36]Ibid., 140.

Lee ran interference for Capote until he established his own connections and became a familiar face among the residents of Garden City and Holcomb. Even in the film *Capote*—a decidedly fictional recreation of Capote's life and the time he spent in Kansas—Capote (Philip Seymour Hoffman) says, "People here won't talk to me." In *Infamous*, Capote (Toby Jones) tells his partner Jack Dunphy (John Benjamin Hickey) that he and Lee will have to stay in Garden City during Christmas "because no one will talk to me." In *Mockingbird: A Portrait of Harper Lee*, Shields suggests that Kansans couldn't relate to Capote, but Lee understood farmers and other rural residents. "Truman didn't fit in, and nobody was talking to him," wrote KBI investigator Nye to Shields in 2005. "But Nelle got out there and laid some foundations with people. She worked her way around and finally got some contacts with the locals and was able to bring Truman in."[37]

In fact, Lee was the antithesis of Capote, who thrived in the spotlight. She listened more than she talked. She helped the wives of Capote's sources in the kitchen. She admired family photos. She played "Chopsticks" with the children whom she and Capote encountered. She and Capote left bottles of Scotch and small gifts to thank the Deweys and others for their hospitality. Shields accurately describes the benefit Lee provided Capote and emphasizes the relationship she facilitated with the Deweys in particular:

> Nelle scoured the town for information that might be useful to Truman, applied the eye of a novelist to identify elements of drama, and opened doors of homes for him…And now, in early January 1960, with the killers caught and soon to be returned to Garden City, Truman was about to come into a windfall of privileged information, as a result of the friendship that Nelle had nurtured with the Deweys.[38]

A highly dramatic and emotional person, Capote assessed his friend in different ways at different times. In his biography of Lee, Shields writes that Capote called Lee an "assistant researchist,"[39] although he acknowledges that Capote relied on her. For example, according to Shields, Capote often wrote "See NL notes" as reminders to himself.[40] In the film *Capote*, Capote says Lee is the only person he knows with the qualifications to be both his "re-

---

[37]Ibid., 157.
[38]Ibid., 163-64.
[39]Ibid., 139.
[40]Ibid., 140.

search assistant" and "personal bodyguard," although there is no evidence he actually described her in this way. Lee seemed content in an ancillary role, spending two months in Kansas during the initial portion of their research, returning to Kansas at least two more times to conclude interviews, and sitting with Capote through the trial of Hickock and Smith. There is no record of her losing her temper with Capote or demanding more credit for her work. In fact, the two were quite successful as an interviewing and writing team. When Capote and Lee first arrived in Kansas and began to make progress in their investigation, they worked during the day and went to the Warren Hotel at night to type what they had learned. In a conversation with biographer George Plimpton, Capote praised Lee:

> She is a gifted woman, courageous, and with a warmth that instantly kindles most people, however suspicious or dour...She kept me company when I was based out there. I suppose she was with me about two months altogether. She went on a number of interviews; she typed her own notes, and I had these and could refer to them. She was extremely helpful in the beginning, when we weren't making much headway with the town's people, by making friends with the wives of the people I wanted to meet.[41]

There is little doubt that Lee contributed enthusiastically to the interviews and other research that would become *In Cold Blood* and helped to ensure its literary legacy.

When literary critics and others assess Lee's state of mind during her collaboration with Capote, they often fail to acknowledge her own meteoric rise during the early research on *In Cold Blood*. In 1960, when Capote and Lee were working together on the nonfiction novel, *To Kill a Mockingbird* was named the Literary Guild Selection, the Book-of-the-Month Club Alternate, a *Reader's Digest* Condensed Book, and the British Book Society Choice. A year later, the novel won the Alabama Association Award and the Brotherhood Award of the National Conference on Christians and Jews, and Robert Mulligan and Alan J. Pakula purchased film rights. When Lee said "no" to writing the screenplay, Horton Foote stepped forward, later winning an Academy Award for his adaptation. Although the novel has more characters and a more intricate plot, Foote focused on Boo Radley and

---

[41]George Plimpton, "The Story Behind a Nonfiction Novel," *Truman Capote: Conversations*, ed. M. Thomas Inge (Jackson: University Press of Mississippi, 1987), 51-52.

the trial of Tom Robinson, contributing cohesion to a film that did justice to Lee's novel. By 1962, 4.5 million copies of *To Kill a Mockingbird* had sold, and Lee was named a consultant on the film, which was nominated for eight Academy Awards, winning three, including one for best actor (Gregory Peck). In time, *To Kill a Mockingbird* would win a Pulitzer Prize and be translated into almost fifty languages. In short, although Capote might have considered Lee his assistant, she collaborated willingly on *In Cold Blood* and had a sense of her own value and burgeoning success. The year before Lee's death in 2016, *To Kill a Mockingbird* had sold more than fifty million copies internationally and had been translated into more than forty languages. It sells more than one million copies per year.[42]

Although Lee appeared to be far less self-assured about her abilities than did the flamboyant Capote, both she and Capote were aware that they were becoming well-known literary figures. If *Capote* and *Infamous* are accurate, Capote's jealousy fueled his desire to consider Lee his protégé, research assistant, and secretary, but Lee seemed confident enough to correspond independently with Hickock and Smith, explore the murder scene, interview law enforcement officials, and otherwise contribute to a book unlike anything either she or Capote had contemplated fully.

The biographers, journalists, literary critics, and friends and family members who are protective of Lee question whether or not she was acknowledged appropriately for her contributions to *In Cold Blood*. Lee is the only entirely reliable source on this particular topic, and she did not discuss her relationship with Capote during or after their adventures in Kansas. The concerns seem to center on (1) the amount of work Lee produced without compensation or recognition, (2) the number of Lee's suggestions that Capote dismissed, and (3) Capote's extensive use of Lee's notes. According to Shields, Lee wrote 150 pages of notes, which she gave to Capote in the spring of 1960. In Shields's opinion, this work was never sufficiently acknowledged. One reason, he suggests, might have been Capote's jealousy of his friend, although the lengthy quotation that follows simply does not provide evidence for this argument:

Truman Capote, who craved winning the Pulitzer or the National Book Award, and hoped he would with *In Cold Blood*, wrote to friends

---

[42]Alexandra Alter, "Harper Lee, Author of 'To Kill a Mockingbird,' Is to Publish a Second Novel," *The New York Times*, 3 February 2015, web (accessed 16 August 2018).

in Kansas: "Well, and wasn't it fine about our dear little Nelle winning the Pulitzer Prize? She has swept the boards."

Despite Capote's casual tone, he no doubt resented this turn of fortune in his friend's life. After all, when they were children, he had been the one to urge her to write stories (he later revised the nature of their partnership, telling the *Washington Post*, "I got Harper interested in writing because she typed my manuscripts on my typewriter. It was a nice gesture for her, and highly convenient for me"). Moreover, Lee tended not to put the emphasis on winning the Pulitzer Prize that Capote would have. "The Pulitzer is one thing; the approval of my own people is the only literary reward I covet," she wrote to a friend. It was gall that Truman had to swallow, as gracefully as he could, but his cousin Jennings Faulk Carter recalled, "The only time I've ever heard him say anything about Nelle's book was that he remarked, 'She got the Pulitzer, and I've never, never done that.' I forget how he put it, but you could tell he was hurt badly. That as much writing as he had done, he had never won it, but Nelle had."[43]

However, complimenting Lee on sweeping the literary awards might be entirely heartfelt. Furthermore, Capote's expressed disappointment in failing to win a Pulitzer Prize for *In Cold Blood* is quite different from begrudging Lee her success. Shields even argues that Capote had difficulty understanding how "his protégé—which is how he regarded Nelle—had written a publishable novel in which he was an important character."[44] Unfortunately, Shields does not quote sources or cite other primary material: Capote does not use the word "protégé," and surely he can be forgiven for celebrating his inclusion as a character in *To Kill a Mockingbird*.

For Shields and others, the sizable amount of material that Lee produced merits more than a dedication. In its entirety, the dedication reads, "For Jack Dunphy and Harper Lee, with my love and gratitude." The Library of America concludes that Lee was angry that she shared only a brief dedication with Jack Dunphy, Capote's partner: "When Lee saw the first edition of *In Cold Blood*, she was shocked that she shared the dedication with Capote's lover, her contributions acknowledged as 'secretarial help.' Their friendship would never be the same."[45] It is unclear how writers for The Li-

---

[43]Shields, *Mockingbird*, 200-201.
[44]Ibid., 180.
[45]"Truman Capote and Harper Lee," The Library of America.

brary of America know Lee was "shocked," although the website might be referring to Shields's biography in which he uses the same word to describe Lee's reaction. Shields writes a scathing attack on Capote for his apparent insensitivity:

> So when, in January 1966, she opened the first edition of *In Cold Blood*, she was shocked to find the book dedicated to her, a patronizing gesture in light of her contribution—"With Love and Gratitude," it said. And, out of the blue, she found she had to share Capote's thanks with his longtime lover, Jack Dunphy.
>
> Nelle was not a woman who was quick to anger or demanding of attention. Still, "Nelle was very hurt that she didn't get more credit because she wrote half that book. Harper was really pissed about that. She told me several times," recalled R. Philip Hanes, who became friends with her later that year. She was "written out of that book at the last minute," maintained Claudia Durst Johnson, a scholar who has published extensively about *To Kill a Mockingbird*. Not even the perfunctory acknowledgment page paid tribute to Nelle's large and important contribution.
>
> Truman's failure to appreciate her was more than an oversight or a letdown. It was a betrayal. Since childhood, Truman had been testing their friendship, because perhaps, deep down, he believed that no one, including Nelle, really liked him—not since his parents had withdrawn their love. He was constantly showing off to get people's attention and approval, all the while gauging their response. But hurting her so gratuitously, perhaps to see what she would do, spoke volumes about whether she could trust him. She would remain his friend, but their relationship had suffered its first permanent crack.[46]

Although anger toward Capote would be an entirely reasonable response to a significant slight, neither Shields nor The Library of America offers evidence that Lee was "shocked" or that the publication of *In Cold Blood* led to a lessening of affection or contact between Capote and Lee. Similarly, Shields's analysis of Capote's insecurities is interesting but speculative, and he does not cite the source for Johnson's opinion. Hanes's allegation that Lee wrote half of *In Cold Blood* is not supported by any primary or secondary source.

---

[46]Shields, *Mockingbird*, 253-54.

Speculation by others also appears to be problematic. For example, in a review of *Capote in Kansas*, Bob Minzesheimer states, "Something happened in Kansas, or shortly after, that chilled their friendship,"[47] but, of course, Powers's novel is fiction, based only loosely on fact. Writer and documentary filmmaker Mary McDonagh Murphy joins those who believe the relationship between Capote and Lee was strained after the publication of *In Cold Blood*. Her assertions are more valid than others because she cites Alice Lee, both in her book and her documentary. One presumes that the sisters discussed the relationship Harper Lee had with Capote:

The childhood friendship would not survive. According to Alice Lee, Capote's envy over *To Kill a Mockingbird* winning the Pulitzer Prize consumed him. "Truman became very jealous because Nelle Harper got a Pulitzer and he did not. He expected *In Cold Blood* to bring him one, and he got involved with the drugs and heavy drinking and all. And that was it. It was not Nelle Harper dropping him. It was Truman going away from her."[48]

This study concludes that whatever break Capote and Lee suffered in their relationship probably was due to a disagreement about truth-telling, not about who most deserved a Pulitzer Prize. In the film *Infamous*, Capote and Lee discuss the fact that *To Kill a Mockingbird* is fiction and that since *In Cold Blood* is nonfiction, it should be entirely truthful. Capote and Lee argue about the difference between the genres, creating what Voss calls "a possible fault line" between them, "a line of potentially seismic sensitivity in their longtime friendship."[49] In the film, explaining that he would like to "bring fictional techniques to a nonfiction story," Capote argues with Lee:

Lee: The truth is enough.
Capote: I must say I don't appreciate this lecture from you of all people. *Mockingbird* was based on true things, and you sure improved that.
Lee: Right. It's a novel. Reportage means recreating, not creating.

---

[47]Bob Minzesheimer, "'Kansas' Imagines Truman Capote-Harper Lee Rift," *USA Today*, 18 December 2007, web (accessed 12 August 2018).
[48]Mary McDonagh Murphy, "Part I: Scout, Atticus, and Boo," in *Scout, Atticus & Boo: A Celebration of Fifty Years of How to Kill a Mockingbird* (New York: Harper Collins, 2010) 25.
[49]Voss, *Truman Capote and the Legacy of* In Cold Blood, 179.

Capote: This is a new kind of reportage.
Lee: I'll say…Fine, it's your book.
Capote: Yes. My seventh.

In *Capote*, Truman Capote also behaves especially badly and "sulks at the bar, downing martinis" and muttering that he does not "see what the 'big deal' is about her book."[50] However, Lee herself said the conversations portrayed in *Capote* and *Infamous* never occurred.[51] In addition, the film is not a documentary and cannot be considered evidence that such conversations ever occurred. Although it is fiction based on fact, *Infamous* quotes Capote as saying, "Thanks to Nelle, who has been a gift from heaven." Perhaps this is a more accurate assessment of his gratitude to her, even though it, too, is undocumented.

Whether or not Lee's suggestions were incorporated into *In Cold Blood* is the second major concern. According to The Library of America website, Capote ignored her recommendation to make the victims "more complex,"[52] and Shields believes that Capote missed an opportunity for character development: "The Clutters were an emotionally troubled family, and Nelle wrote pages of notes providing evidence of it. But in the end, Capote barely used her insights in the final version of what would become *In Cold Blood*."[53] It may be that Capote missed an opportunity to improve his book; it may also be that he preferred to focus on the aftermath of the crime.

Third, Lee's contributions to *In Cold Blood* went far beyond her ability to engage potential sources, and her devotees want her to be recognized. For example, in a description of Hickock's face, Lee wrote in her notes that it appeared "as if someone cut it down the middle, then put it back together not quite in place." Capote altered her phrase to read, "It was as though his head had been halved like an apple, then put together a fraction off center."[54]

Certainly, no one should presume that Lee was content in the shadows; however, she was not hungry for fame and seemed surprised when it came her way. Paul Harris suggests that the "instant success" that followed the publication of *To Kill a Mockingbird* "terrified" Lee: "In one of her few detailed interviews, given in 1964 to author Roy Newquist, she offered an in-

---

[50]Ibid., 171.
[51]Ibid., 174.
[52]"Truman Capote and Harper Lee," The Library of America.
[53]Shields, *Mockingbird*, 152-53.
[54]Ibid., 169.

sight into the impact of instant fame, for someone who had been seen as a sidekick to the more glamorous Capote." The quotation to which Harris refers follows: "I sort of hoped that maybe someone would like it enough to give me encouragement. Public encouragement. I hoped for a little, as I said, but I got rather a whole lot, and in some ways this was just about as frightening as the quick, merciful death I'd expected."[55] In a letter to Shields in 2002, Dolores Hope, who befriended Capote and Lee in Kansas, provides even more evidence of Lee's humility and desire to maintain a private life:

> She was always very protective of Capote and made sure the limelight was on him most of the time. She was quick to divert mention of the Pulitzer prize back to Capote. She also gave him credit for his help and encouragement. My impression of the Pulitzer time is that people who had come to know Truman here in Kansas just had a gut feeling that he would have his nose out of joint about it. Nelle knew him so well and she was anything but an attention-getter herself. In fact, she shunned it. She was the exact opposite of Truman, being more interested in others than she was in herself.[56]

Hope's description of people who knew Capote and who had a "gut feeling" about him is secondhand. No one is cited, and impressions—no matter how well founded—simply are not fact. It is, however, quite clear that Lee was sensitive to Capote's insecurities and did what she could to support him.

As recently as 2011, two Kansas residents who knew Capote and Lee remembered their time in Garden City and Holcomb. At the Lawrence Public Library, Garden City residents Kay and Bob Wells discussed their relationship with the two authors. When they first learned that Capote was coming to Garden City, they heard that the famous author was arriving with his "secretary." "First of all, we had no idea that Capote's secretary was Harper Lee," Kay Wells said. Wells described Lee as "warm" and as a person who "says it like it is." She noted especially Lee's sense of humor and her ability to make friends easily.[57] For Kay and Bob Wells, as for many others, Lee provided Capote with a significant entre into Kansas society and was most decidedly not his "secretary."

---

[55]Newquist, *Counterpoint*, 405.

[56]Shields, *Mockingbird*, 209-10.

[57]"Garden City Couple Recount Friendship with Truman Capote, Harper Lee," *Lawrence Journal-World*, 15 April 2011, web (accessed 12 August 2018).

Capote and Lee after In Cold Blood

Clearly, it was neither kind nor accurate for Capote to describe Lee's contributions to *In Cold Blood* by saying, "She was just there."[58] Fortunately, this comment is not representative of the statements Capote made in other conversations and in letters. Perhaps their relationship dimmed after the publication of *In Cold Blood*. Certainly, Capote's depression after the execution of Hickock and Smith is well documented, and it would be reason enough for him to withdraw from Lee in the same way that he withdrew from others.

In her dissertation, *A Well-Hidden Secret: Harper Lee's Contributions to Truman Capote's* In Cold Blood, T. Madison Peschock draws important conclusions, although she bases some of them on her own speculation or the speculation of others. Nonetheless, her determination to learn what happened to the friendship between Capote and Lee after the publication of *In Cold Blood* is a worthy goal. In her summary, Peschock argues that Capote failed to disclose the major role that Lee played in the research for *In Cold Blood*. She concludes that Lee took on most of the interviews with townspeople and that Capote spent most of his time talking with Hickock and Smith. Her suggestion that Capote's treatment of Lee contributed to Lee's failure to publish anything between *To Kill a Mockingbird* (1960) and *Go Set a Watchman* (2015) cannot be confirmed.

Importantly, Peschock cites sources who confirm Lee's contributions to *In Cold Blood*. Lee's friend Wayne Greenshaw told Peschock that Capote got to know the killers well but "not the neighbors, the farmers, shopkeepers, even the policemen, all of whom talked to her": "Even the investigators talked mostly to her,"[59] Greenshaw said. Wayne Flynt was stronger in his statements to Peschock: "More important than even the copious notes she took, was her common background as a Methodist girl from a small town, which Truman had long since jettisoned but which in many ways she retained...She was in every sense a [co-author of *In Cold Blood*, whereas he was in no sense a co-author of *To Kill a Mockingbird*]. Dedicating the book to her hardly compensated for his use of her notes."[60] Finally, Alan Gurganus said *In Cold Blood* profited from having the "benefit of her extraordinary

---

[58]Shields, *Mockingbird*, 240.
[59]T. Madison Peschock, "A Well-Hidden Secret: Harper Lee's Contributions to Truman Capote's *In Cold Blood*," diss., Indiana University of Pennsylvania, 2012, 35.
[60]Ibid., 36.

legwork, her extraordinary political sense, her finesse in covering for [Capote]."[61]

Peschock draws persuasive conclusions from her perusal of Lee's research notes, which are housed with Capote's papers, and other documents: Lee typed and transcribed the notes that she and Capote took; she interviewed the townspeople, often without Capote; she drew diagrams; she studied the history of the town; she researched where Hickock passed bad checks; she drew up a travel itinerary for Hickock and Smith; she attended the trial; she disagreed with Capote on his assessment of the Clutters (she thought some of Bonnie Clutter's issues might be due to menopause and believed that the Clutters were not the perfect Midwestern family that Capote wanted them to be); and she proofread galleys for the book.[62] In summary, as Shields suggests, "Not even the perfunctory acknowledgment page paid tribute to Nelle's large and important contribution."[63]

Peschock believes that *In Cold Blood* took a toll on Capote's health and on his relationship with Lee. According to Peschock, Lee did not attend Capote's famous "Black and White Ball" in 1966 to celebrate the novel, nor did she attend a private screening of the film *In Cold Blood*.[64] On the other hand, Peschock suggests that Lee attended Capote's funeral in Los Angeles and a memorial service in New York. The dissertation is important for two reasons: one, because it provides interviews with sources who knew Capote and/or Lee, and two, because it signals an ongoing interest in the relationship between Capote and Lee that was so crucial to the production of *In Cold Blood*.

Like Capote, Lee was deeply invested in the events in Kansas and involved with the people whom she met there. She stayed for two months on her first visit to Kansas, returned several times, and attended the trial of Hickock and Smith in March 1960. Hickock and Smith asked Capote and Lee to attend the execution April 14, 1965, and Capote asked Lee to accompany him. Although Lee told Capote and the prison warden that she would not be there, just hours before his execution, Smith wrote to both Capote and Lee. Not knowing that Capote was planning to attend, Smith wrote what Shields calls a "hasty note" at 11:45 p.m. (the execution was set for sometime between midnight and 2 a.m.):

---

[61]Ibid., 37.
[62]Ibid., 39-41.
[63]Shields, *Mockingbird*, 253.
[64]Peschock, "A Well-Hidden Secret," 266.

I want you to know that I cannot condemn you for it & understand. Not much time left but want you both to know that I've been sincerely grateful for your friend[ship] through the years and everything else. I'm not very good at these things—I want you both to know that I have become very affectionate toward you. But harness time. Adios Amigos. Best of everything. Your friend always, Perry.[65]

Capote and Lee are two of the most respected writers in American literary history. The old courthouse in Monroeville now houses the Monroe County Heritage Museum, which exists in large part as a tribute to Capote and Lee and to her novel that originally was titled *Atticus*. More than 20,000 people visit the museum each year. Former news anchor Tom Brokaw is among those devoted to Lee's novel, suggesting that it succeeds because of its "absence of piety"[66] and because Scout is "irresistible."[67] *To Kill a Mockingbird*, writes Voss, is "arguably the most popular, most accessible, and most entertaining Southern Gothic novel ever published."[68] Oprah Winfrey calls *To Kill a Mockingbird* "our national novel,"[69] and Andrew Young suggests that Lee wrote it as "an act of protest" and an "act of humanity."[70]

Because of the positions Capote and Lee hold in the esteem of the international literary community, the obsession with what did and did not occur between these two literary giants continues. Only those in a relationship know what actually happens between them, and even then, it can be difficult to understand all the nuances involved. Relationships experience power struggles, require patience, and have moments of ecstasy and despair. If Lee was furious with Capote for slighting her or if Capote drew away from Lee because of her success, only they knew. To suggest that the two maintained a warm relationship until Capote died in 1984 is as unwise as to suggest that the two severed their relationship at some point and never spoke again.

---

[65]Shields, *Mockingbird*, 245.

[66]Tom Brokaw, interview, in *Scout, Atticus & Boo: A Celebration of Fifty Years of* To Kill a Mockingbird (New York: HarperCollins, 2010) 64.

[67]Ibid., 63.

[68]Voss, *Truman Capote and the Legacy of* In Cold Blood, 48.

[69]Oprah Winfrey, interview, in *Scout, Atticus & Boo: A Celebration of Fifty Years of* To Kill a Mockingbird (New York: HarperCollins, 2010) 202.

[70]Andrew Young, interview, in *Scout, Atticus & Boo: A Celebration of Fifty Years of* To Kill a Mockingbird (New York: HarperCollins, 2010) 209.

Truman Capote as Charles Baker (Dill) Harris

After they screen *Capote* and *Infamous* or read analyses by Peschock and others that point to Capote's inadequacies—whether those inadequacies are well documented or not—readers and moviegoers wonder why Lee would want to be friends with Capote. The arrogant, narcissistic, sometimes cruel person portrayed in the films and other popular texts suggests that Capote got what he deserved after his five years researching and writing *In Cold Blood*. If he struggled with addiction, so be it. If he was drunk while on live television, so be it. If he died relatively young without the support of a life partner, so be it.

However, these conclusions are too strident and simplistic. In fact, Capote also was a bright, charming, well-read, and witty man, often the center of attention, often an engaged and responsive listener. There were causes about which he cared—such as capital punishment—and his genuine affection for Alvin Dewey, Perry Smith, and others in Kansas and New York was intentional and heartfelt. Because this portion of the study addresses *In Cold Blood* and Harper Lee, it is important to consider the person whom Lee and her family came to love. Who was the lost boy who appeared in Monroeville in the summer, who loved his aunts, who enjoyed the affection and warm welcome of Amasa Lee and his family? It is the fictional *To Kill a Mockingbird* that provides a glimpse into what Lee remembers and the characteristics she might well have continued to see in her childhood friend. Letters from Lee to Capote would provide stronger documentation, but, for now, her semi-autobiographical novel and the film derived from it will have to do.

Whether in the novel *To Kill a Mockingbird* or the film based on it, Jean Louise Finch and Jeremy Atticus Finch remain two of the most well-known and beloved characters in twentieth-century American literature. Foote's adaptation of the novel is a memory play in which a mature narrator remembers life in 1930s Maycomb, Alabama. The novel itself is a mockingbird's song—innocent, melodic, resplendent. In the midst of the wonder the novel and film convey—even now—there is a little boy named Charles Baker (Dill) Harris: "Thus we came to know Dill as a pocket Merlin, whose head teemed with eccentric plans, strange longings, and quaint fancies."[71] In spite of the prominence of the Finch children, Dill is the conscience of the community, the first person to see injustice and the last person to forget it. His position as an outsider—a child without any desire to be masculine, to con-

---

[71]Lee, *To Kill a Mockingbird*, 9.

trol others—makes him especially empathetic to Arthur Radley, Raymond Adolphus, and Tom Robinson.

The "tired old town"[72] of Monroeville, Alabama, on which Maycomb is based, was home to Nelle Harper Lee. The success of the novel and film dramatically enlarged her literary and social sphere, and an international audience joined her on a nostalgic journey into another time and place. The Great Depression and racial and gender inequality unsettled the Deep South financially and socially, although white residents in the novel and film appear content to live in a town where only the Radleys lock their doors. The black experience, represented by Tom Robinson and Calpurnia, was decidedly different.

In both the book and the film titled *To Kill a Mockingbird*, it is the children—Jeremy Atticus (Jem) Finch, Jean Louise (Scout) Finch, and Charles Baker (Dill) Harris—who embody a sense of ethics. It is especially the Truman Capote character, Dill, who illustrates Isaiah 11:6: "The wolf also shall dwell with the lamb, and the leopard shall lie down with the kid; and the calf and the young lion and the fatling together; and a little child shall lead them." The well-known verse is important for at least two reasons: first, it highlights the roles that Scout and Jem Finch play in the novel, screenplay, and film; second, it addresses the central theme of all three texts—the significance of moving from innocence to experience (and, as much as possible, back again). Dill's amusing and incisive declaration—"I'm little but I'm old"[73]—both points to childhood as a central theme and suggests the inherent wisdom of the young. At the end of the novel, Scout, too, acknowledges weariness far beyond her years: "As I made my way home, I felt very old."[74] The world of children dominates the film musically, thematically, and visually; for example, in the introductory montage of crayons and children's toys—overlaid with the sounds of a child humming—lies the promise of uncorrupted, unscripted insight.

When Foote transformed Lee's coming-of-age novel into an award-winning screenplay, he necessarily omitted certain characters and scenes. Not only does adaptation demand focus—often making it necessary to abbreviate the narrative and/or eliminate or combine characters—but in the case of *To Kill a Mockingbird*, which is more than 300 pages, Foote's task was to produce a screenplay that was less than one-third of Lee's Pulitzer

---

[72]Ibid., 5.
[73]Ibid., 7.
[74]Ibid., 322.

Prize-winning book and preserved the dramatic intensity and suspense of the original. His success is evident in the fact that the 1962 film, nominated for eight Academy Awards, won for best screenplay based on material from another medium. (It also won for best actor with Gregory Peck as Atticus Finch and best art direction and set decoration. The film itself lost best picture to *Lawrence of Arabia*.)

However, in addition to omitting certain characters and events, Foote added a few scenes to provide cohesiveness and dramatic power, and he altered chronology. Noticeable differences between the novel and screenplay include modifying the timeline; amplifying, changing, or omitting the roles of Alexandra Finch Hancock, Jem, Scout, and Dill; altering the first-person point of view; abbreviating trial scenes; and adding references to Atticus's wife and Tom Robinson's children and father. In all of his alterations, Foote remained focused on the role of the children and longed for his screenplay to help "discover the evil and hypocrisy in this small southern pastoral town along with and through the eyes of the children."[75]

Although Lee applauded Foote's work, not all critics or viewers were as enthusiastic. Robert Mulligan, the director, worried about the fact that Atticus Finch overshadowed the children in the screenplay. Discussing his concerns with producer Alan J. Pakula, Mulligan said, "You know what your problem is—too often you lose the point of view of the children."[76] At the heart of Bosley Crowther's notable 1963 *New York Times* review is a concern about what he considers the loss of the child's perspective in the screenplay, which led to a film that Crowther considered only partially "rewarding." Crowther writes:

> And for a fair spell it looks as though maybe we are going to be squeezed inside the skin of Scott [sic] and Jem as they go racing and tumbling around the neighborhood, shrieking with childish defiance at crusty old Mrs. Dubose, skirting with awe around the dark house where the mysterious Boo Radley lives…
>
> It is when the drama develops along the conventional lines of a social crisis in the community—the charging of a Negro with the rape of a white woman—that the children are switched to the roles of lookers-on…

---

[75]Horton Foote, "Foreword," *Three Screenplays by Horton Foote* (New York: Grove Press, 1989) xiii.

[76]Shields, *Mockingbird*, 206.

While this still permits vivid melodrama and some touching observations of the children, especially in relations with their father, which is
the crucial relationship in the film, it leaves the viewer wondering precisely how the children feel. How have they really reacted to the things
that affect our grown-up minds?[77]

This study addresses Crowther's concerns at some length and explores
the artistic journey from novel to screenplay to film, noting especially Lee's
enthusiasm for the Foote masterpiece. It explores the coming-of-age narratives, the place of didacticism and point of view in the novel and film, and
other literary techniques. It focuses on the film as a memory play and on the
children's emerging consciousness, which takes them from the trivial events
of the everyday—such as wondering whether or not Atticus will play football
for the Methodists—to an expansive awareness of social justice.

The children's evolving consciousness culminates in a loss of innocence,
as Scout, Jem, and Dill pay the price for living in a world both miraculous
and violent, both bathed in soft morning light and haunted by shadows. Of
course, Lee, who is writing a largely autobiographical tale, understands
clearly the cost of the trio's newfound awareness; however, she also wants for
them to remain open and childlike (as "harmless as doves") as they move
into adulthood, where, according to Matthew 10:16, they soon enough will
have to be as "wise as serpents." Lee's desire to hold innocence and experience in balance is evident even in the epigraph: "Lawyers, I suppose, were
children once [Charles Lamb]." What follows Lamb's statement are questions: "Is the world all grown up? Is childhood dead? Or is there not in the
bosoms of the wisest and the best some of the child's heart left, to respond to
its earliest enchantments?"[78] Both Lee and Foote emphasize the "child's
heart," although Foote chooses to compress the timeline—which provides a
smaller window into the children's development—and lets Atticus take center stage.

Adaptation of To Kill a Mockingbird

Offered the opportunity to write the screenplay for her novel, Harper
Lee declined. Pakula then selected Horton Foote, a southerner whose own
plays, such as *Tender Mercies* and *The Trip to Bountiful*, are character based.

---

[77]Bosley Crowther, "'To Kill a Mockingbird': One Adult Omission in a Fine Film,"
The New York Times, 15 February 1963, web (accessed 16 August 2018).
[78]Charles Lamb, *Essays of Elia* (Paris: Baudry's European Library, 1835) 93.

Foote loved and, more importantly, understood life and relationships in a small town because of his own time in Wharton, Texas. He was perhaps the perfect screenwriter to adapt a novel he appreciated by a fellow southerner whom he respected. In the foreword to his screenplay, Foote writes about his affinity for all things southern and his respect for particular writers of the Deep South:

> For me to have any chance of successfully dramatizing the work of another writer, I have to choose material that I respect and that I am in sympathy with, that deals with people and a world I understand. Whenever I've done that with Faulkner, Flannery O'Connor, or Harper Lee, I have felt a real satisfaction in the work; when I haven't, I've felt lost and confused. I felt I understood the world of Harper Lee's novel and its people. The town of the novel was not unlike the town I was born and brought up in, and the time of the novel, the depression era of the 1930s, was a period I had lived through.[79]

However, his affection for the novel and its creator is precisely the reason he delayed accepting Pakula's offer, fearing he might like the novel too much to recreate it effectively. According to the documentary *Fearful Symmetry*, Foote met Lee for the first time at his home in Nyack, New York. "It was love at first sight on my part," said Foote. "And I just somehow felt that we were members of the same family." Alice Lee (Boaty) Boatwright, who cast the children in the film, said Foote was the "perfect person" to adapt the novel. Lee and Foote "became the closest and the best of friends and stayed totally, completely in touch" until Foote died in 2009. Of his ability to transform the novel set in Monroeville, Boatwright said, "He was a poet, and he understood those people."[80]

After Foote agreed to take on the project, Pakula suggested that Foote write a screenplay that compressed the action into a year instead of three and that he consider the similarities between Scout Finch's experiences and those of Huckleberry Finn and Tom Sawyer. When Foote complied, Scout joined the legendary company of children in celebrated American novels. In the documentary, Pakula said that Foote wanted to "honor the book and be true to the book," and he thought Foote achieved that goal. Foote and Pakula

---

[79]Foote, "Foreword," xii.

[80]Alice Lee (Boaty) Boatwright, interview, in *Scout, Atticus & Boo: A Celebration of Fifty Years of* To Kill a Mockingbird (New York: HarperCollins, 2010) 55.

collaborated easily because Pakula, too, is known for his character-oriented adaptations, such as *All the President's Men* (Bob Woodward and Carl Bernstein) and *Sophie's Choice* (William Styron).

The novel *To Kill a Mockingbird* and the film provide both the sense of a mature narrator looking back on her life and a child experiencing for the first time the adult world (with all of its conflict, inequalities, and mysteries). However, less is explicit in the film, in part because children cannot fully understand the events that affect their family and community and in part because Foote expects the viewer to understand that what is portrayed on screen is no more potent and metaphorical than what remains in the shadows. For example, the audience does not need for Mayella Ewell's rape to be reenacted; the horror of her life and her father's assault are perhaps even more disturbing if her abuse occurs off screen.

Casting in the film contributed mightily to its reception and to Foote's success. In an essay about the impact of the film, actress and media celebrity Oprah Winfrey praises both the novel and the film, especially the actors:

> I loved it from the beginning, and like a lot of people, I get the lines blurred between the movie and the book. The movie is very distinct for me because the reading experience comes alive for me in a way that my imagination cannot. In the history of filmmaking I have never seen a book really live its essence through film like this one, and that is because of the casting of Scout and Atticus, and all of them, really.[81]

When Mary Badham left her fellow students in her fourth-grade classroom in Birmingham, Alabama, to audition for the role of Scout Finch, she could never have imagined the unparalleled success that she and the film would achieve. Little did she know that she would be nominated for an Academy Award in what would become an American film classic. In fact, the film mirrors some of Badham's life, making the child actor even more determined to bring Scout Finch to life. For example, two black women, Beddie Harris and Frankie McCall, helped to raise Badham, and she rebelled against sitting away from them in the front of the bus when one of them accompanied her around town. "I would love to have included the parts of the book that talked of our relationship with Calpurnia, for it was so

---

[81] Oprah Winfrey, interview, in *Scout, Atticus & Boo: A Celebration of Fifty Years of To Kill a Mockingbird* (New York: HarperCollins, 2010) 201-202.

close to my relationship with the ladies who raised me,"[82] she said. Badham developed a close and sustaining relationship with Gregory Peck, who played Atticus Finch, and remained in contact with him until his death in 2003. "He was my other daddy," she said. "He really was Atticus: fine, firm, and gentle."[83]

Other relationships developed from the experiences on the set of the film and facilitated the adaptation and the film that followed it. Lee and Peck liked one another immensely, and many years later, Peck's daughter would name her son "Harper."[84] Lee and Foote, too, liked and respected one another. "If the integrity of a film adaptation is measured by the degree to which the novelist's intent is preserved, Mr. Foote's screenplay should be studied as a classic,"[85] Lee said. Later, she observed, "I can only say that I am a happy author. They have made my story into a beautiful and moving motion picture. I am very proud and grateful."[86]

In *Fearful Symmetry*, Pakula said he believes the "triumph" of the film *To Kill a Mockingbird* is that it captures the "soul" of the novel. However, although what adaptation scholars call "fidelity" is one of the ways of assessing a film's success, it is far from the only one. Furthermore, some scholars of adaptation history and practice now diminish the importance of faithfulness to the original text in order to highlight other methods of analysis. In the introduction to *Now a Major Motion Picture: Film Adaptations of Literature and Drama*, Christine Geraghty encourages film critics to focus on more than fidelity and suggests that other approaches employed in film criticism might be similarly shallow. She challenges several common assumptions:

> So, it is ruled that, among other things, novels are verbal and use words while films are visual and rely on images; novels can express internal knowledge of a character, but screen adaptations have to imply feelings or motivations from a character's actions since the camera is best suited to the objective recording of physical appearances; films can only use

---

[82]Mary Badham, interview, in *Scout, Atticus & Boo: A Celebration of Fifty Years of* To Kill a Mockingbird (New York: HarperCollins, 2010) 46.

[83]Sandra McElwaine, "'To Kill a Mockingbird' Makes Its Mark, 50 Years After the Film's Release," *The Daily Beast*, 31 January 2012, web (accessed 12 August 2018).

[84]Ibid.

[85]Shields, *Mockingbird*, 206.

[86]Kerryn Sherrod, "To Kill a Mockingbird," Turner Classic Movies, web (accessed 12 August 2018).

the present tense; voice-overs are noncinematic; and cinema and television rely on realism while literature requires the reader's imagination.[87]

Geraghty also opposes what she calls the prevailing "hierarchy of judgment" because it "privileges literature, reading, and authorship over screen, viewing, and mass production."[88] Because "texts develop from a network of sources that have no single author," Geraghty celebrates what she calls a "plurality of meanings," which depend in part on the "textual skills and the contextual positioning of the reader"[89]; in other words, much of the success of Foote's screenplay depends on the connection that readers and viewers make individually with the text.

Furthermore, Geraghty argues that scholars should analyze the film or television adaptation itself—separate and apart from its original source—taking into account the transformative impact of "genre, editing, and acting"[90] or, as she later suggests, "space and landscapes."[91] For example, Peck's portrayal of Atticus Finch is his own. He creates a character that readers might or might not have imagined as they immersed themselves in Lee's novel. The fact that Lee often said she appreciated Peck's talent and that he reminded her of her father is, in some ways, irrelevant. An actor's performance may be distinct from what the author imagined and may be either better or worse than the character depicted in the original source.

Also, as the authors of *The Pedagogy of Adaptation* suggest, if a film and the novel on which it is based are "indistinguishable,"[92] then viewers have lost the opportunity to interact with two texts, which, although they are intimately connected, are by definition free-standing and culturally and historically distinct. Reinforcing this viewpoint, Suzanne Diamond writes:

Various contemporary psychological and epistemological findings establish that our notions of the world we inhabit—indeed, our most basic ideas about who we *are*—come to us by way of the story lines our

---

[87]Christine Geraghty, *Now a Major Motion Picture: Film Adaptations of Literature and Drama* (Lanham, Md.: Rowman & Littlefield, 2008) 1-2.

[88]Ibid., 2.

[89]Ibid.

[90]Ibid., 5.

[91]Ibid., 7.

[92]Dennis Cutchins, Laurence Raw, and James M. Welsh, eds., "Introduction," *The Pedagogy of Adaptation* (Lanham, Md.: Scarecrow Press, 2010) xii.

cultures make possible and the work we do with these story lines. We are, in other words, constant and inveterate adapters.[93]

Consequently, Diamond disagrees with critics who want to diminish the importance of fidelity because the original text is a good place to begin a conversation about the multiple adaptations readers and viewers might discover for themselves: "And the serial nature of the adaptation process produces far more complex discourses, rather than simply stating that 'the book was better,' even if that's where the discussion begins,"[94] she said. Specifically, she argues that discussing "how a given adaptation sustains or departs from *any* remembered 'source text'" is itself a fruitful exercise that can lead to a conversation about "who we collectively *are*, how we recall, and what we continue to find important."[95] Analysis of the original and adapted texts makes possible what Diamond calls "social memory work,"[96] which she explains as deriving from a study of culture, history, politics, psychology, and the "function of remembering within all of these."[97]

Unfortunately, one can argue that Foote diminished Lee's novel when he drastically reduced the parts that Mrs. Henry Lafayette Dubose and Charles Baker Harris play. In the screenplay, Jem does not visit Mrs. Dubose, who cures herself of an addiction to painkillers, wanting to be free of them even though she has been diagnosed with terminal cancer. In the novel, foreshadowing his own loss in the Tom Robinson case, Atticus tells his son what Mrs. Dubose represents:

> I wanted you to see something about her—I wanted you to see what real courage is, instead of getting the idea that courage is a man with a gun in his hand. It's when you know you're licked before you begin but you begin anyway and you see it through no matter what...She was the bravest person I ever knew.[98]

---

[93]Suzanne Diamond, "Whose Life *Is* It, Anyway?: Adaptation, Collective Memory, and (Auto)Biographical Processes," *Redefining Adaptation Studies*, ed. Dennis Cutchins, Laurence Raw, and James M. Welsh (Lanham, Md.: Scarecrow Press, 2010) 96.

[94]Ibid., 101.

[95]Ibid., 105.

[96]Ibid., 98.

[97]Ibid.

[98]Lee, *To Kill a Mockingbird*, 128.

Similarly, in the screenplay, Dill, who is based on Lee's lifelong friend Truman Capote, no longer functions as a social conscience in the community, nor does he interact with Adolphus Raymond, who is (thankfully) not what he appears to be. In Lee's novel, Dill provides extensive social commentary and is a deeply sympathetic figure, especially during his encounter with Raymond; in the film, however, he is ancillary to most of the central action. In the novel, Dill's compassion for the black community is profound and based, perhaps, on his own isolation and sense of rejection. He tells Scout that he left home because his mother "just wasn't interested in me,"[99] and when she asks him why Boo Radley never fled the town, Dill replies, "Maybe he doesn't have anywhere to run off to."[100]

It is Dill's identification with the plight of blacks in Maycomb that constitutes the greatest loss in the transition from novel to film. Brokenhearted about the jury's cowardice and the prosecutor's racism during Tom Robinson's trial, Dill "started crying and couldn't stop," and others in the courthouse began to notice him. Jem asks Scout to take him outside. In a tribute to the child's perspective in the novel, Lee lets Scout try to figure out why her friend is distressed ("I guessed he hadn't fully recovered from running away," she thinks, followed closely by another speculation, "Heat got you, I expect—"[101]). When Dill explains how devastated he is by a black man being called "boy," Scout replies, "Well, Dill, after all he's just a Negro," and Dill says, "I don't care one speck. It ain't right, somehow it ain't right to do 'em that way. Hasn't anybody got any business talkin' like that—it just makes me sick."[102] Raymond, who eavesdrops on the children, compliments Dill, even as Scout thinks, "I had a feeling that I shouldn't be here listening to this sinful man who had mixed children and didn't care who knew it."[103] Here, Scout is the voice of the status quo, the spokesperson for a town mired in historical prejudice. It is Dill who refuses to be bound by what is, who dedicates himself—at his own peril—to love. Nodding to Dill, Raymond says to the children, "Things haven't caught up with that one's instinct yet. Let him get a little older and he won't get sick and cry…Cry about the simple hell people give other people—without even thinking. Cry about the hell

---

[99]Ibid., 162.
[100]Ibid., 164.
[101]Ibid., 226.
[102]Ibid., 227.
[103]Ibid., 229.

white people give colored folks, without even stopping to think that they're people, too."[104]

In short, Dill is the child who leads them, the voice Scout hears, the voice that affects her, the voice as yet uncorrupted by the world in which he lives. Because Dill's role in the screenplay is minor, it falls to Jem and Scout to provide his perspective. Foote's decision is understandable—he cannot include all characters or all scenes from the novel—but eliminating the dialogue between Dill and Adolphus Raymond is a terrible loss. Its inclusion in a study of Truman Capote is, of course, imperative. Even as a child, Capote knew he was different, a fact that freed him to identify with and to support other outsiders—something he did all his life.

Childhood in Novel and Film

Mary McDonagh Murphy argues that Foote's screenplay became "what many consider to be one of the greatest screen adaptations of all time."[105] One reason may be that Foote's screenplay remains true to the culture, history, politics, and psychology of *To Kill a Mockingbird* and relies on memory to provide narrative cohesion. Foote also is faithful to the themes Lee develops, especially what Pakula calls in *Fearful Symmetry* the "mysterious" and "secret world of childhood."

Pakula especially praised the beginning of the film, where a marble hits another marble and the music begins. That moment, Pakula said in the documentary about the film, is "magical." In fact, childhood and its mysteries and challenges are at the heart of the novel and the screenplay. In his foreword to *Scout, Atticus & Boo: A Celebration of Fifty Years of* To Kill a Mockingbird, Wally Lamb compares Lee's novel to Mark Twain's *The Adventures of Huckleberry Finn* and J. D. Salinger's *The Catcher in the Rye*: "All three novels, each a product of its era, give voice to outsider American kids trying to negotiate an adult world full of hypocrites."[106]

In addition to its other themes, *To Kill a Mockingbird* addresses social expectations in a small town, where residents delight in dissecting their neighbors. Yet even this theme is tied inextricably to childhood. As Mark Childress writes, even little children such as Scout and Dill are not safe from the scrutiny and criticism of their elders: "The two of them, they were both

---

[104]Ibid.

[105]Murphy, "Part I: Scout, Atticus, and Boo," 31.

[106]Wally Lamb, "Foreword: A Mockingbird Mosaic," in *Scout, Atticus & Boo: A Celebration of Fifty Years of* To Kill a Mockingbird (New York: HarperCollins, 2010) x.

odd birds in their town,"[107] Childress writes, both reinforcing Wally Lamb's reference to "outsider American kids" and highlighting the cruelty of gossip and character assassination. The novel focuses on the criticism that members of the community heap upon the heads of Atticus Finch, Boo Radley, Adolphus Raymond, and others; the pressure Aunt Alexandra puts on Scout to meet the expectations of southern womanhood; and even the anger Jem turns on his sister. The film, too, portrays the proper ways of doing things in the Deep South and the price paid by those who flaunt the expectations of others.

Because film is a visual medium, Foote modified the first-person point of view of the novel *To Kill a Mockingbird*. To say that he abandoned it, as Crowther appears to suggest, is simply not accurate; however, there is no doubt that Scout Finch no longer controls what the reader, or in the case of the film, the viewer, sees and understands. In the screenplay and film, Jem Finch, who is older and, because of his gender, inherits more than his father's pocket watch, often becomes the focal point of the film in a patriarchal community. In one scene, he refuses his father's request that he go home; in another, he asks if he can accompany his father, is told "no," and announces that he's going with him anyway.

Much redeemed at the end of the novel, Aunt Alexandra disappears entirely from the screenplay, perhaps because Foote believed Scout's struggle to adapt to southern womanhood could be addressed adequately by particular vignettes (wearing a dress on the first day of school, fighting Walter Cunningham and Cecil Jacobs, happily accepting the promise of her mother's jewelry, being berated by her brother for behaving more and more "like a girl," etc.). Jem criticizes his sister at least twice in the novel, saying, "I swear, Scout, sometimes you act so much like a girl it's mortifyin'"[108] and "I declare to the Lord you're getting' more like a girl every day!"[109] but it is Aunt Alexandra who wants to mold Scout into a southern belle. In the screenplay, Jem says, "Then go home if you're scared. I swear, Scout, you act more like a girl all the time."[110] In the screenplay, Aunt Alexandra is absent, and it is Calpurnia who loves and guides Scout.

---

[107]Mark Childress, interview, in *Scout, Atticus & Boo: A Celebration of Fifty Years of To Kill a Mockingbird* (New York: HarperCollins, 2010) 80.

[108]Lee, *To Kill a Mockingbird*, 42.

[109]Ibid., 58.

[110]Foote, "To Kill a Mockingbird," *Three Screenplays by Horton Foote* (New York: Grove Press, 1989) 24.

In spite of Foote's editorial changes, the film preserves a decidedly childlike perspective—from the credits that scroll across the screen during the first few moments to Scout's voice-over at the end of the film: "I was to think of these days many times; of Jem, and Dill, and Boo Radley, and Tom Robinson...and Atticus. He would be in Jem's room all night. And he would be there when Jem waked up in the morning."[111] Lee Smith states that the novel is "dead-on about childhood" and adds that "it evokes childhood so beautifully."[112] Foote does not wander far from the novel as he creates a little girl in overalls, a boy who walks like an Egyptian, and a visitor from Meridian, Mississippi, who tries to hide his sadness by inventing a father.

Elmer Bernstein's score, too, reinforces a child's view of the world, as he suggests in *Fearful Symmetry*. The single notes—that imitate the way a child might play a piano—and the cardboard box filled with toys and treasures converge. The viewer hears a ticking watch and the humming of a child. Objects such as crayons, marbles, and a whistle contribute to a viewer's nostalgia for the familiar things of childhood. Allan Gurganus underscores the importance of the opening sequence when he suggests that the "toys and images of the precious things saved" work to let viewers know they're part of a "child's vision."[113]

Nonetheless, Crowther mourns the ways in which the child's perspective is diluted in the screenplay. He suggests that when the viewer is dropped "serenely in the comfort of a grubby Southern town" and the audience encounters a "thoroughly beguiling tomboy" and her father—"clearly the kindest man in town"—the film is nothing short of "bewitching."[114] Crowther appreciates the relationship between the children and their father, writing that it alone is "worth all the footage of the film."[115] The primary issue Crowther has with the film appears in the first paragraph of his review, where he suggests that Foote does not maintain the child's point of view, although he does not clarify how Foote might have done so. He writes:

---

[111]Ibid., 80.

[112]Lee Smith, interview, in *Scout, Atticus & Boo: A Celebration of Fifty Years of* To Kill a Mockingbird (New York: HarperCollins, 2010) 178.

[113]Allan Gurganus, interview, in *Scout, Atticus & Boo: A Celebration of Fifty Years of* To Kill a Mockingbird (New York: HarperCollins, 2010) 97.

[114]Crowther, "To Kill a Mockingbird."

[115]Ibid.

There is so much feeling for children in the film that has been made from Harper Lees [sic] best-selling novel, "To Kill a Mockingbird"...so much delightful observation of their spirit, energy and charm as depicted by two superb discoveries, Mary Badham and Phillip Alford—that it comes as a bit of a letdown at the end to realize that, for all the picture's feeling for children, it doesn't tell us very much of how they feel.[116]

Rather than debating Crowther's perspective again, it might be helpful to suggest a representative scene in which the film undercuts Crowther's claim that the viewer cannot surmise what Jem, Scout, and Dill are thinking. For example, Jem is devastated by the verdict in the Tom Robinson trial, and his agony—not conveyed in a soliloquy, of course—is nonetheless made clear as he sits in the rocking chair on the porch. Although his father tells him he cannot protect him from the horrors of the world around him and although Calpurnia gazes at him compassionately, Jem is alone, revealing by his expression and his posture exactly what he feels. Wrestling with demons too terrifying for a child his age, he sits silently and in disbelief.

Although the film amplifies the role that Jem plays (he babysits for his sister, he accompanies his father, he finds Boo's gifts in the tree, etc.), he is a formidable figure in the novel as well; in fact, as he moves into adolescence, Lee is careful to highlight Jem's moodiness, desire for privacy, and other aspects of his relationship with Scout. Because the novel spans three years and the film compresses the children's experiences into one year, any perceived amplification of Jem's role in the film can in part be explained by the altered timeline and the demands of adapting a full-length novel. Nonetheless, Crowther is correct about the dilution of the child's perspective in the film, although to some extent Jem's voice simply replaces Scout's.

Other changes between the novel and the screenplay occur as well, and a few affect the development of the child's viewpoint in the film, although some of them are incidental to it. Stephanie Crawford becomes Dill's aunt in the film, and Scout fights Cecil Jacobs instead of Francis Hancock. Scout and Jem are not shown inside the school. Jem doesn't read to Mrs. Dubose, nor does he learn why she is Atticus Finch's definition of courage. Maudie Atkinson's house does not burn. The children do not attend Calpurnia's church. None of these editorial decisions diminishes the themes Foote develops, although it is impossible to suggest that they are superfluous in the novel: to a greater or lesser extent, each event serves to enrich the reader's

---

[116]Ibid.

understanding of the plot and makes characters more complex. One of the significant differences between the novel and the film is Foote's insertion of a conversation between Jem and Scout about their mother. The moment when the siblings discuss their memory of her is even more poignant because their father overhears them as he sits on the porch swing:

Scout: How old was I when Mama died?
Jem: Two.
Scout: And how old were you?
Jem: Six.
Scout: Old as I am now?
Jem: Uh huh.
Scout: Was Mama pretty?
Jem: Uh huh.
Scout: Was Mama nice?
Jem: Uh huh.
Scout: Did you love her?
Jem: Yes.
Scout: Did I love her?
Jem: Yes.[117]

Lessons in Social Justice

However, although Scout is, as Crowther notes, "beguiling,"[118] her innocence is shattered by events in her community, and she struggles to maintain hope in a world that is coming apart. She encounters haunted houses, rabid dogs, stories about witches, and, most terrifyingly, a stalker (and erstwhile murderer) in the woods. Although readers and viewers understand that the mockingbirds at the heart of the novel and the screenplay represent the children, there are other wounded people, including Mayella Ewell, Atticus Finch, Arthur (Boo) Radley, and Tom Robinson. Atticus tells the children that "it's a sin to kill a mockingbird,"[119] and Miss Maudie explains why: "Mockingbirds don't do one thing but make music for us to enjoy."[120]

Mayella is hardly a sympathetic figure; however, as Atticus Finch states in the film, he has "nothing but pity" for her, although he says promptly,

---

[117]Foote, "To Kill a Mockingbird," 16-17.
[118]Crowther, "To Kill a Mockingbird."
[119]Lee, *To Kill a Mockingbird*, 103.
[120]Ibid.

"My pity does not extend so far as to her putting a man's life at stake, which she has done in an effort to get rid of her own guilt."[121] Interestingly, in the novel, Scout is the first person to express concern for Mayella: "As Tom Robinson gave his testimony, it came to me that Mayella Ewell must have been the loneliest person in the world...She was as sad, I thought, as what Jem called a mixed child...Tom Robinson was probably the only person who was ever decent to her."[122]

Other mockingbirds exist as well. Atticus frequently is the object of derision and ridicule, criticized in the novel even by his sister. During Atticus's vigil outside the locked jail, Lee and Foote describe his fear (Scout sees a "flash of plain fear"[123] on her father's face, and in the screenplay she notices the "look of fear on his face—"[124]). Of course, this description undercuts Atticus's role as an attorney who never loses his composure. Because of his fragility when confronted by the mob and his desire to protect his children, Atticus is a person with whom the reader and the viewer can identify. Boo Radley is the town's shadowy recluse who is also heroic. Importantly, he remains always a child. When he asks Scout to walk him home at the end of the novel, Lee writes, "He almost whispered it, in the voice of a child afraid of the dark."[125] Throughout the novel, Lee emphasizes Boo's isolation by comparing him to the Radley house itself: "The old house was the same, droopy and sick, but as we stared down the street we thought we saw an inside shutter move. Flick. A tiny, almost invisible movement, and the house was still."[126] Finally, although he pays with his life, Tom Robinson is guilty only of caring about a poverty-stricken, uneducated white woman who lives with her tormentor because she has nowhere else to go.

To shoot Tom Robinson, to exclude Boo Radley, to ignore Mayella Ewell, and to force Atticus Finch—as Miss Maudie Atkinson says—to do what others refuse to do is, in effect, to kill a mockingbird. "I simply want to tell you that there are some men in this world who were born to do our unpleasant jobs for us," Miss Maudie tells the children. "Your father's one of

[121]Foote, "To Kill a Mockingbird," 66.
[122]Lee, *To Kill a Mockingbird*, 219.
[123]Ibid., 173.
[124]Foote, "To Kill a Mockingbird," 50.
[125]Lee, *To Kill a Mockingbird*, 320.
[126]Ibid., 16.

them."[127] Later, she adds, "We're so rarely called on to be Christians, but when we are, we've got men like Atticus to go for us."[128]

In spite of its portrayal of a loving father and his children, *To Kill a Mockingbird* is far from a celebration of childhood. Robert E. Lee (Bob) Ewell spits on Scout's father and tries to murder her and Jem in the dark woods. Boo Radley is trapped in a ramshackle house. A jury of twelve white men finds someone guilty of a crime he could not possibly have committed. Mayella Ewell is lost in ignorance and poverty, motherless, and the sole support for her siblings. Calpurnia—who tells the children she has no birthday, which evokes no surprise on their parts— cannot interact freely with the whites in Maycomb. (Symbolically, Lee gives Calpurnia no last name.) The Great Depression has made agrarian life even more difficult for the Cunninghams and others like them than it had been before.

In fact, as Claudia Durst Johnson notes, the novel introduces the reader to Scout and Jem, who "encounter the strange, sometimes evil reality outside the slow, Edenic existence of their own house."[129] Rooted in what Johnson calls the "persistent past," Maycomb, for all its neighborliness and system of manners, "has been shaped irrevocably by a plantation system, the Civil War, and a cotton-based economy."[130] In a novel in which the "chief defining symbols"[131] are children and mockingbirds, Johnson mourns the treatment of Boo Radley and every black resident, all of whom are relegated to the edges of a dangerous and segregated community.

The novel *To Kill a Mockingbird* outgrew its initial title, *Atticus*. Although Atticus Finch features prominently in the lives of his children and defends Tom Robinson in one of the most famous courtroom dramas in America, the novel is more expansive than any one character. Telling the story through a child's eyes creates a level of identification and empathy that the book might not otherwise possess. The innocence of tire swings and tree houses dissipates, replaced by attempted murder, an unfounded charge of rape, an outcast imprisoned in his own house, the widespread effects of ignorance and poverty, and a little boy who lies about having a father who is a train conductor and a pilot because he is afraid and—except for his visits to

---

[127]Ibid., 246-47.

[128]Ibid., 247.

[129]Claudia Durst Johnson, *To Kill a Mockingbird: Threatening Boundaries* (New York: Twayne 1994) 32.

[130]Ibid., 35.

[131]Ibid., 38.

Maycomb—alone. At the beginning of the screenplay, Scout is six years old; Jem, ten. When Foote introduces them and their friend Dill, he does not patronize them; in fact, Foote's respect for the wisdom of children is apparent even in some of the director's notes. For example, when Dill first appears, Foote describes him as having a "solemn, owlish face, a knowledge and imagination too old for his years."[132]

By the end of the screenplay, the children are only a year older, but Jem and Scout have taken their "longest journey together,"[133] a phrase that denotes far more than their harrowing confrontation with Bob Ewell. They have learned that their father is "civilized in his heart,"[134] and they want to follow his example. It is perhaps Dill who best embodies the conflicting forces in the hearts of the children. In a lavish description of her friend Capote, Lee juxtaposes the magical qualities Dill embodies and reintroduces Boo as a reminder that all is not well in Maycomb:

> Dill was off again. Beautiful things floated around in his dreamy head. He could read two books to my one, but he preferred the magic of his own inventions. He could add and subtract faster than lightning, but he preferred his own twilight world, a world where babies slept, waiting to be gathered like morning lilies. He was slowly talking himself to sleep and taking me with him, but in the quietness of his foggy island there rose the faded image of a gray house with sad brown doors.[135]

It is Dill who—with Atticus—provides the moral center for the novel. When Scout asks him why he thinks Boo Radley has never left the town, he suggests that (like himself) Boo may have nowhere else to go.[136] Obviously, Dill identifies with a mockingbird, which never hurts anyone and simply wants to be safe. He also does what Atticus tells Scout she must do— imagine what it is like to be someone else—something Dill instinctively understands because of who he is and the deprivation he has suffered:

> "First of all," he said, "if you can learn a simple trick, Scout, you'll get along a lot better with all kinds of folks. You never really understand a person until you consider things from his point of view—"

---

[132]Foote, "To Kill a Mockingbird," 9.
[133]Lee, *To Kill a Mockingbird*, 292; Foote, "To Kill a Mockingbird," 72.
[134]Lee, *To Kill a Mockingbird*, 112.
[135]Ibid., 164.
[136]Ibid.

"Sir?"

"—until you climb into his skin and walk around in it."[137]

The novel *To Kill a Mockingbird* and the screenplay and film that followed it highlight issues of social justice and portray a time and place that are perhaps not so different from our own. It is with respect and wonder that Atticus remembers the three children who saved him from the mob at the jail: "So it took an eight-year-old child to bring 'em to their senses, didn't it? ...Hmp, maybe we need a police force of children,"[138] he said. And when Jem asks his father how the jury could have made the decision they made, Atticus Finch again invokes the wisdom of the children: "I don't know, but they did it. They've done it before and they did it tonight and they'll do it again and when they do it—seems that only children weep."[139] These words allude to literature that celebrates the wisdom of children as yet untainted by discriminatory social constructs. They also invoke the Old Testament, where "a child shall lead them."

---

[137]Ibid., 33.
[138]Ibid., 180.
[139]Ibid., 244.

Chapter 7

In Cold Blood in Documentary and Film

The diversity of opinions about Truman Capote and *In Cold Blood* is nothing compared to the wildly different critiques of three films and two documentaries about the Clutter murders and their aftermath. *In Cold Blood* (1967), *Murder:* In Cold Blood (1997), *Capote* (2005), *Infamous* (2006), and *Hey, Boo: Harper Lee and* To Kill a Mockingbird (2010) testify to continuing interest in Capote, the murders, the trial and execution of Richard Eugene Hickock and Perry Edward Smith, and controversies related to Capote's artistic decline, definitions of nonfiction, journalistic practice, and the treatment of sources. The 2016 publication of *The Swans of Fifth Avenue*— Melanie Benjamin's literary exposé about Capote and his friendship with Babe Paley and the other "swans"—further suggests that Capote remains a sensation in American literature and popular culture.

In a study dedicated to some of the voices omitted from *In Cold Blood*, a review of documentaries and films is imperative because each one of them represents the collective voice of actors, directors, producers, screenwriters, and others. Also relevant is a discussion of why—given *In Cold Blood*'s obvious appeal to a new generation—the allegorical tale of good and evil, rural innocence and urban corruption, and God-fearing people confronted by sociopathy endures. In addition, sensationalism helps to explain the tenacious hold the nonfiction novel has on an international audience. Rather than exploring contexts first, this chapter moves chronologically through five seminal film and documentary texts, referring to film reviews, historical analysis, and thematic overviews as appropriate.

In Cold Blood *(1967)*

A film adapted directly from Truman Capote's nonfiction novel appeared shortly after the unprecedented success of the book itself. It would be difficult to imagine a film that reflects more effectively the randomness of violence and the underlying brutality of life than Richard Brooks's *In Cold Blood*, filmed in black and white and employing literary techniques and representations of rural Kansas residents. Capote no doubt made Brooks's task easier by employing crosscuts and highlighting visual effects, which are both important to film. Nonetheless, although the film did not win best picture at the Academy Awards, it lives on as one of the best examples of faithful adaptation. Nominated for best director, best adapted screenplay, best cinematography, and best original music score, *In Cold Blood* was overshadowed by *Bonnie and Clyde*, *The Graduate*, *Guess Who's Coming to Dinner*, *Doctor Doolittle*, and *In the Heat of the Night*, which won best picture that year.

Capote concurred with Brooks's preference for unknown actors, who at that time included Robert Blake (Perry Smith), John Forsythe (Alvin A. Dewey), Paul Stewart (Bill Jensen), and Scott Wilson (Richard Hickock). According to multiple sources, at least two Kansas residents played themselves in the film, and University of Kansas drama majors played Kenyon and Nancy Clutter. Brooks filmed *In Cold Blood* in Holcomb and Garden City, Kansas; at the H. W. Clutter River Valley Farm; and in the actual farmhouse. Invented scenes tie directly to central themes in the nonfiction novel. For example, Hickock discusses pheasant hunting: "Them birds don't know it, but this is their last day on earth." This symbolic reference to the Clutters is echoed in Capote's choice of a section heading, "The Last to See Them Alive." Crosscuts establish connections with events depicted in the novel, as viewers see Smith at the bus station, Hickock on the road, and Herbert, Kenyon, and Nancy Clutter rising and making plans for the day. As the Clutters engage in their everyday activities, two killers are driving 400 miles across Kansas and will slide into Holcomb around midnight. The film is as disturbing as the nonfiction novel: "I promise you, honey, we'll blast hair all over them walls," Hickock tells Smith in the film.

The unexpected collision of forces reflects Capote's concerns about fate and the cruelty that people exhibit toward one another. Entering an unlocked door and carrying a twelve-gauge shotgun and nylon cord, Hickock and Smith murder four people for a pair of binoculars, a transistor radio, and forty dollars. During their inexplicable violence against strangers, the killers ensure their return to prison and their executions at midnight on April 14, 1965. Investigators find few clues. The crime defies logic. The night changes forever the way rural Kansas residents feel about one another and about the safety they once took for granted. In the film, Bill Jensen, a reporter and stand-in for Capote, talks quietly with Alvin A. Dewey, a detective with the Kansas Bureau of Investigation, after the murders: "Don't people around here lock doors?" Jensen asks. Dewey responds, "They will tonight." Further reinforcing the sentiment is a waitress at a local restaurant: "If this can happen to a decent, God-fearing family, who's safe anymore?" she asks.

There are differences between the nonfiction novel and Brooks's film. For example, instead of Hickock, Smith is the one who talks to Nancy in her room. Unlike the facts depicted in one of the other films in this chapter, Smith shoots the entire family, as Capote suggests, but instead of shooting Bonnie Clutter last, he shoots Nancy after her mother dies. Rather than confessing to Capote in a jail cell, Smith confesses to the murders while talking to Dewey in his car. Finally, although it is clear that the nonfiction novel *In Cold Blood* is Capote's argument against capital punishment, the film reinforces the theme through a conversation between Dewey and Jensen. Of the crime, Dewey says, "Well, maybe this will help to stop it." Jensen responds, "Never has."

One of the most powerful similarities with the novel is Brooks's casting of Blake as Perry Smith. Not only did Capote say that when he looked at Blake he thought he was seeing Smith, but Blake, too, saw aspects of himself in Smith: "I think how different Perry's life might have been if whatever talent he may have had for painting and music had been channeled like mine—and how easily I could have turned out the way he did."[1] Also, according to Tison Pugh, Brooks imitates Capote's description of the bond between Hickock and Smith, which some readers and critics perceive to be sexual: "Similar to Capote's restrained portrayal of homosocial desires percolating between the two men," Pugh writes, "Brooks's depiction of Smith and Hickock's friendship balances between homosociality and homoeroticism."[2]

Brooks was drawn to literary classics, making him even more appropriate as the director and author of the screenplay for *In Cold Blood*. Brooks also adapted Tennessee Williams's *Cat on a Hot Tin Roof* (1958) and *Sweet Bird of Youth* (1962), Fyodor Dostoevsky's *The Brothers Karamazov* (1958), Sinclair Lewis's *Elmer Gantry* (1960), and Joseph Conrad's *Lord Jim* (1965). His cinematic techniques earned him both accolades and criticism. For example, as Pugh documents, crosscutting reflects one of Capote's own literary devices, something some critics found effective and others said was useless:

Hickock hears a train whistle in the distance, which soon leads to a shot of a train pulling into Holcomb, Kansas, as the camera then cuts to a series of pastoral shots of the Clutters' home, contrasting the quiet peace of their daily lives with the busy pulse of cars, buses, and trains

---

[1] Tison Pugh, *Truman Capote: A Literary Life at the Movies* (Athens: University of Georgia Press, 2014), 113.
[2] Ibid., 124.

that are bringing the killers to them. This crosscutting of story lines builds until Smith and Hickock meet their prey, creating a sense of foreboding and ineluctable doom in both the book and the film.[3]

Praise and criticism also followed Brooks's decision to transition from place to place by linking images. Pugh writes:

> The construction of *In Cold Blood*, in contrast, registers Brooks's masterful control of his narrative, if at the expense of its realism. The film is edited together with many narrative links uniting the characters and their story lines, such as when Nancy is speaking on the telephone, which cuts to Smith likewise talking on a phone, which cuts to Hickock registering at a hotel with Smith's name, or when Smith throws a cigarette out of their car into a river, which segues to a scene of the investigators dredging a river for the murder weapon.[4]

In an article that explores film techniques in *In Cold Blood*, John Patterson emphasizes memorable moments: "No one who has ever seen it forgets the beginning of Richard Brooks's 1967 adaptation of Truman Capote's 'non-fiction novel' *In Cold Blood*: a Greyhound bus howls out of an ink-black prairie night, Kansas City its destination, on a screaming trumpet note from Quincy Jones's score."[5] Patterson writes:

> All of *In Cold Blood's* virtues are encapsulated in that opening: the black-and-white camerawork of cinematographer Conrad Hall; the music of Jones; and the performance of Robert Blake. Hall's work draws on news-footage aesthetics, achieving a true-crime tabloid griminess…Everything great about *In Cold Blood* comes from his intelligent corralling of the talents above, and his commitment to realism and accuracy, which went as far as his insistence that the murders be filmed in the town, the house, indeed, the very rooms in which they really happened.[6]

---

[3]Ibid., 114.
[4]Ibid., 116.
[5]John Patterson, "*In Cold Blood*: Why Isn't the Movie of Capote's Bestseller a Masterpiece?" *The Guardian*, 7 September 2015, web (accessed 13 August 2018).
[6]Ibid.

Pugh supports the techniques that drive the plot in both the nonfiction novel and the film: "Although one can snipe at Brooks's polished editing and restrained filming of the violence as antithetical to a realist ethos, he succeeds in conveying the ineluctable doom that captures the Clutters in its midst, with a verisimilitude that renders the full horror of their meaningless suffering."[7] In his lengthy critique of *In Cold Blood*, Pugh also argues that the film is realistic, suggesting that Brooks's dedication to authenticity leads to a film that has the feel of a documentary. Bosley Crowther calls the film *In Cold Blood* a "quasidocumentary," referring to the "frequent flashbacks and fragmentations of continuity," the "arrogance of the marauders," and "their wild, smashing outburst of vengeance," which he suggests appears to be "inevitable."[8] "The final scene of the hanging," Crowther writes, "which is realistically done, is like some medieval rite of retribution. It leaves one helplessly, hopelessly chilled."[9] The fact that the scene is filmed at the Kansas State Penitentiary adds more evidence to his claim of Brooks's eye toward documentary.

Pugh describes Brooks's directorial priority: "By putting his characters in the actual settings of their real-life counterparts, Brooks imbued his film with a reality both mundane and unbearable. Indeed, Brooks attempted to re-create every scene as authentically as possible, even trying to acquire the gallows upon which Smith and Hickock were executed."[10] Certainly, the film imitates the cutbacks of the novel. In "Rereading: Truman Capote's *In Cold Blood*," Rupert Thomson contributes an extensive and worthwhile explanation for the technique:

> As late as 1962, Capote was still sticking to his original script—in public, at least. "My book isn't a crime story," he told *Newsweek*. "It's the story of a town." By then, however, he knew the two murderers were central to the story he wanted to tell, that they would give it texture, urgency and shape. He was writing the book in brief, self-contained sections, and as he began to fit them together he found himself exploiting classic crime-genre techniques in order to create resonance and heighten suspense. This is particularly apparent early on, in the tense,

---

[7]Pugh, *Truman Capote: A Literary Life at the Movies*, 117.
[8]Bosley Crowther, "*In Cold Blood*," *The New York Times*, 15 December 1967, web (accessed 13 August 2018).
[9]Ibid.
[10]Pugh, *Truman Capote: A Literary Life at the Movies*, 115.

cinematic inter-cutting between the killers and their victims: as Herb, the rural patriarch, consumes his usual breakfast of an apple and a glass of milk, "unaware that it would be his last", and his daughter Nancy lays out her velveteen dress for church, "the dress in which she was to be buried", the two ex-cons are racing across the wheat plains of the Midwest in their black Chevrolet sedan, Hickock high on Orange Blossoms, Smith crunching handfuls of aspirin for his grotesquely injured legs. Fortunately for Capote, the murderers were not locals, as had originally been supposed. On the contrary, Smith and Hickock symbolised the feckless, degenerate underbelly of the country, the absolute antithesis of Holcomb's God-fearing and law-abiding citizens. Capote's brilliantly atmospheric, sordidly glittery account of the "long ride", as the wanted men drifted from Kansas City to Acapulco to Miami in the weeks leading up to their arrest, supplied the perfect foil to his spare, tight-lipped depiction of a community in shock. The murders represented a sudden, horrifying collision of two wildly divergent Americas. If, as he claimed, Capote had his heart set on making a "big work", then this was more than he could ever have hoped for.[11]

One of the reasons that the film *In Cold Blood* succeeds is that it "leaves the impression of documentary authenticity," said Donald Pizer in "Documentary Narrative as Art": "One way in which Capote gains this effect is by his extensive use of special kinds of 'official records'—letters, diaries, written statements, and even an article in a learned journal—records which he identifies and quotes verbatim."[12] This technique—the heart and soul of journalism itself—contributes to a reader's sense that the novel was well researched and that the film is believable. In the nonfiction novel, "The author appears to be an impartial chronicler of conversation,"[13] Pizer states, and the gruesome murders tell us a great deal about the perpetrators, especially Perry:

We learn of Perry's alcoholic mother and authoritarian father, of his miserable boyhood in homes and asylums, and of his thwarted artistic ambitions and his impossible child-like dreams. Perry has lived a love-

---

[11]Rupert Thomson, "Rereading: Truman Capote's *In Cold Blood*," *The Guardian*, 5 August 2011, web (accessed 13 August 2018).

[12]Donald Pizer, "Documentary Narrative as Art: William Manchester and Truman Capote," *Journal of Modern Literature* 2/1 (September 1971): 111.

[13]Ibid., 112.

less, frustrated life, and he has finally come to center his distrust and hatred on his family and particularly on his father.[14]

In addition to attempting to explain Smith's animosity toward Herbert Clutter, Pizer also addresses why Smith turned his rage on both Clutter and Hickock: "Dick's hesitancy and cowardice at the crucial moment was one more betrayal,"[15] Pizer speculates. He writes, "Mr. Clutter, a rich, imposing, and self-possessed man, was yet another figure of authority...Perry's hate of a 'world' that had mistreated and misunderstood him could cause him to commit an 'instinctive' murder, a murder which appears to be in cold blood because it is superficially emotionless."[16] In what was his ultimate support for Brooks's work, Capote said, "Reflected reality is the essence of reality, the truer truth."[17]

Casting, too, is effective and supports the author's own hopes for the adaptation of his novel. For example, as mentioned earlier, when Capote first sees Robert Blake, he believes he is the reincarnation of Perry Smith: "The first time I saw him I thought a ghost had sauntered in out of the sun-shine...I couldn't accept the idea that this was someone pretending to be Perry, he was Perry—and the sensation I felt was like a free fall down an elevator shaft."[18] In his review of Capote's "Ghosts in Sunlight," Hilton Als describes the time Capote spent on the set of the film *In Cold Blood*:

At one point Capote relates how the actors impersonating the real-life protagonists in his famous "non-fiction novel" unsettled him, rattled him, for there they were, alive and interpreting the thoughts and feel-ings of men he had known long before, dead men he could not shake. Capote describes this experience as being akin to watching "ghosts in sunlight"—a lovely metaphor about memory and the real converging to make the world something else, and the artist someone else, too. Standing on that film set, the Capote who had written *In Cold Blood*

---

[14]Ibid., 115.

[15]Ibid., 116.

[16]Ibid.

[17]Truman Capote, "Ghosts in Sunlight: The Filming of *In Cold Blood*," *Truman Capote: A Capote Reader* (New York: Penguin, 2002) 623.

[18]Ibid.

was a relative ghost to the film being made; he was a specter standing in the sunlight of his former self.[19]

In "Ghosts in Sunlight: The Filming of *In Cold Blood*," Capote expresses his own accomplishment this way: "All art is composed of selected detail, either imaginary or, as in *In Cold Blood*, a distillation of reality."[20]

Transitioning from Brooks's *In Cold Blood* to a documentary in the American Justice series is simple, especially since the first documentary in this chapter so closely resembles the 1967 film in its no-frills approach, its stark treatment of the crime, and its focus on actual Kansas residents. No imaginary characters appear in a documentary—no Bill Jensen steps in to clarify themes and make connections between the film and the novel—and emotional editors and law enforcement officials discuss the day of the murders and the months that follow. Unlike the audience for Brooks's film, documentary viewers meet actual people relating great sorrow. In *Murder:* In Cold Blood, tough law enforcement officials weep openly—the Clutters are their friends, their neighbors. In *Murder:* In Cold Blood, the audience is forced repeatedly to look at crime photos, not flashes of light in a dark basement and in the upstairs bedrooms. It is difficult to look, and, for those hoping to understand the crime without Capote's narrative overlay, it is also difficult to look away. Smith is a black-and-white photograph in the documentary, not a sympathetic figure whose crimes may have resulted from a tortured childhood and poor life choices. The documentary portrays Smith as he was: a murderer who, without apparent motive, extinguishes the lives of four people, flees to Mexico, and returns to Kansas without either understanding or regretting what he has done.

Murder: In Cold Blood *(1997)*

The Kurtis Productions documentary *Murder: In Cold Blood* features interviews with Kansas residents, editors, and local government officials. Shot on location, it is as antiseptic and devoid of artistic intent as *Capote* and *Infamous* are scripted and staged. After entering a town of 270 residents, viewers step onto an 800-acre farm in southwest Kansas, 200 miles from Wichita.

---

[19]Hilton Als, "Ghosts in Sunlight," *The New York Review of Books*, 10 July 2014, web (accessed 13 August 2018).

[20]Capote, "Ghosts in Sunlight: The Filming of *In Cold Blood*," 623.

Reactions of sources—many of whom are now deceased—range from calm to anguished. Mitch Geisler, Garden City police chief, speaks in monosyllables: "Here are my friends who are dead," he says to the camera and, later, "This has happened to our friends and our neighbors," and, as he struggles to explain to the production team the toll the crimes took on Holcomb and Garden City: "You kept your doors locked because maybe it's your next-door neighbor. Maybe it's the guy down the street." Equally effective is Bill Brown, editor of the *Garden City Telegram*, and KBI agent Harold R. Nye, whose eyes fill with tears when he discusses the crimes and their aftershock. Readers of the nonfiction novel may forget that law enforcement officials who knew the Clutter family are among those who went to Mexico to retrieve the binoculars and radio that Hickock and Smith pawned, supported the $1,000 reward given by the *Hutchinson News* for information leading to any arrest, found murder weapons at the Hickock farm, and arrested Hickock and Smith for parole violations and larceny in order to continue building the murder case against them. Among the most interesting of the sources is Duane West, Finney County prosecutor, whose anger against Hickock and Smith is palpable: "I was abused by my daddy. My momma didn't kiss me goodnight...Nonsense. Garbage...It makes me want to throw up." Interestingly, Beecher Avants of the Las Vegas Police Department disagrees with Capote, saying that he thought Smith was "psychopathic" and that Hickock was more approachable and "less cocky" than Smith.

Deliberately and dispassionately, the narrator provides a timeline: the murders occur November 15, 1959; law enforcement officials find Hickock's car December 30, 1959; Hickock and Smith appear at the courthouse January 6, 1960; and the trial begins March 23, 1960 (Floyd Wells, who lied to Hickock about having seen a safe in the Clutter home, claims the $1,000 reward and testifies). The jury deliberates for forty minutes. When Hickock is hanged April 14, 1965, it takes him twenty-two minutes to die. It takes Smith seventeen minutes. The documentary states that Smith did not apologize and that he refused to walk up the steps to the gallows and was carried there. According to the documentary, Capote saw Hickock executed but left before Smith died.

Murder: In Cold Blood provides a vantage point all its own. Only in Bill Kurtis's narrative is there any context or artistry, as he calls *In Cold Blood* a "true crime masterpiece" and a "modern American horror story." The documentary opens with Kurtis's voice describing a "storybook existence" in Kansas, "where the serenity of the fields was broken each year by the comforting roar of the wheat combines." After the murders have occurred, Kurtis reads, "Everybody was a suspect. The gossip ran wild in coffee shop cliques along Main Street. So did the paranoia." It is Kurtis who tells us that the killers "slid into Holcomb" at midnight and Kurtis who divulges that the hired man found the bodies, which differs from events in *Capote* and *Infamous*. In true documentary style, we hear Hickock tell police during his recorded interview: "Smith was bent over Clutter. That's when I seen that he had cut his throat. I jumped down there to see how bad he was cut. I didn't know whether he killed him or what, but he cut the hell out of him." The clinical, reportorial voice of the documentary does not appeal to everyone, of course, but it is in some ways a respite from the fictional reenactment, a moment to remember the actual events and the people to whom the events occurred.

Capote *(2005)*

Most critics consider *Capote* to be better than the films *In Cold Blood* and *Infamous*, although audiences may disagree. Reasons include the talents of the late Philip Seymour Hoffman as Truman Capote and Catherine Keener as Harper Lee (Hoffman won an Academy Award for best performance by an actor in a leading role); the serious tone of the film; its willingness to delve into Capote's character; and the chemistry between Hoffman and Clifton Collins Jr., who plays Perry Smith. The purpose of this chapter is not to provide aesthetic judgment but to argue that all three films attest to a lingering interest in the Clutter murders, which, given the number of murders in the United States, is itself a phenomenon. According to Pugh, director Bennett Miller opens the film "by holding shots of wheat fields and farm settings for several seconds longer than viewers might expect, asking his audience to ponder the majesty and desolation of country life, then contrasts these scenes by introducing Capote at a riotous party."[21]

Drawn from Gerald Clarke's celebrated biography of Truman Capote and filmed predominantly in Winnipeg, Canada, the film *Capote* was nominated for five Academy Awards, including best picture, best performance by an actress in a supporting role (Catherine Keener), best achievement in directing (Bennett Miller), and best writing, adapted screenplay (Dan Futterman). Two premier film critics that celebrate *Capote* are the late Roger Ebert and A. O. Scott of *The New York Times*. Ebert introduces his review by fo-

---

[21]Pugh, *Truman Capote: A Literary Life at the Movies*, 228.

cusing on Capote, who, he says, is "consumed by a story that would make him rich and famous, and destroy him" and who praises the film because it "looks with merciless perception at Capote's moral disintegration."[22] It is primarily Hoffman's performance that captivates Ebert: "Philip Seymour Hoffman's precise, uncanny performance as Capote doesn't imitate the author so much as channel him, as a man whose peculiarities mask great intelligence and deep wounds."[23]

For his part, Scott describes Capote as someone who "pursued literary glory and flirted with moral ruin," someone who struck a "Faustian bargain." Although it is difficult to know whether or not this is a compliment to the film, Scott writes, "Prefiguring the talk show and tabloid self-parody he would later become, this Capote drinks, gossips, teases and whines, but mostly he works, with methodical intensity and ruthless discipline."[24] He also commends Keener: "Through her wary, witty performance, she becomes the bridge that connects Capote with the audience; we take our cues from her as we try to figure out when he should be indulged and when he should be censured."[25] Most important for this study, Scott focuses on Perry Smith—"whose story Capote believes will be the key to the book and whose sensitive, sociopathic temperament is the dark mirror-image of his own"— and refers to the reportorial challenges for a writer beguiled by one of his sources: "Still, in dramatizing this process—in showing how Smith was seduced, betrayed and immortalized by the writer's attention—'Capote' unflinchingly faces the moral abyss at the heart of the journalistic enterprise."[26] In conclusion, the reference to a doppelgänger acknowledges the casting of Capote and Smith and evokes themes in chapter four, and Scott's reference to the journalistic enterprise lies at the heart of the discussions of literary journalism in chapter two. Additionally, Scott's mention of *Capote* as allegory reinforces references throughout *Untold Stories, Unheard Voices*. Scott writes:

In setting out for Kansas, Capote believed himself to be tracing the violent intersection of "two Americas": the conservative, stable world of

---

[22]Roger Ebert, "*Capote*," 20 October 2005, web (accessed 13 August 2018).
[23]Ibid.
[24]A. O. Scott, "Big-Name Novelist, Small-Town Murders," *The New York Times*, 27 September 2005, web (accessed 13 August 2018).
[25]Ibid.
[26]Ibid.

the Clutters and the lawless underworld represented by their killers. That may be the theme of "In Cold Blood," but the collision portrayed in "Capote"—the cultural friction that gives it a frisson of contemporary relevance—is a rather different one, between everyday American life and death and the equally American machinery that turns it into news, spectacle and sometimes art.[27]

Other critics are not as complimentary. Dan Callahan writes that the film has an "axe to grind against its subject, the quite horrible but quite gifted writer Truman Capote," adding that *Capote* is a "brisk, well-made, tonally assured film, and it's engrossing, but it never grows into anything more than a prolonged and detailed character assassination."[28] Although Callahan's assessment does not signify consensus, it provides evidence that critiques of *Capote* exist along a wide continuum.

Capote is strikingly introspective, even in its depiction of New York and of Capote as he charms his way into every room he enters there. "The very emptiness of 'Kansas,' figured in the film's opening of wind blown wheat, eventually becomes the emptiness from which Capote will suffer,"[29] writes Philip Heldrich. With the exception of a few glimpses into colorful, crowded parties in New York and a scene in which a porter is paid to compliment Capote, the film is somber, dominated by gray skies, wheat fields, and the memory of an empty, silent farmhouse. True to the novel on which it is based, *Capote* introduces the celebrity author as he travels to Kansas to conduct research for *The New Yorker* about how the Clutter killings are "affecting the town." Capote looks into the caskets of the Clutters, startled to see their heads covered by swaths of bandages. "It's the book I was always meant to write," Capote says about *In Cold Blood*, adding that he is "blazing a different path by inventing an entirely new kind of writing—the nonfiction novel." William Shawn, too, is in character, telling his friend and client, "This book is going to change everything. It'll change how people see you as a writer. It'll change how people write." Perhaps the most famous line in the films *In Cold Blood*, *Capote*, and *Infamous* is Capote's statement to Harper Lee in *Capote*. Although it does not appear in the nonfiction novel, it

---

[27]Ibid.

[28]Dan Callahan, "*Capote*," *Slant Magazine*, 2 September 2005, web (accessed 13 August 2018).

[29]Philip Heldrich, "*Capote* and *Infamous*," *Kansas in the Movies* website, Center for Kansas Studies (n.d.), web (accessed 13 August 2018).

should: "It's as if Perry and I started life in the same house. One day he stood up and walked out the back door while I walked out the front. With some different choices, he's the man I might have become," Capote tells her.

Ultimately, as noted earlier, *Capote* was nominated for five Academy Awards. Its nominations for best picture and best director point to the talents of Bennett Miller. In "Capote's Co-Conspirators," Patrick Radden Keefe pens a tribute to Miller's commitment and talent:

> Bennett Miller's film "Capote" portrays its title character as a consummate seducer: before Capote can repurpose the narrative tricks of the novel to beguile the unsuspecting reader, he must first get the story, by persuading ornery, suspicious Kansans to open up to him through a kind of velvet sorcery. Miller delivers a particularly grim vision of Capote: he seduces Perry Smith and then betrays him, lying about the title of the book (which would reveal that he was less sympathetic with the killers than he might have seemed), and refusing to help the men find a new lawyer for their appeals (because only when they were finally executed would Capote have his ending).[30]

In production at the same time that *Capote* was being filmed, *Infamous* suffers from being released second and from gaining fewer critical accolades. It was not nominated for an Academy Award. Nonetheless, audiences and critics celebrated the film, in part because it included fine performances by Toby Jones as Capote and Sandra Bullock as Lee and demonstrated why Capote was the life of every party he attended. His charm, his wit, and his ability to listen to his friends are obvious in *Infamous*, especially in scenes with his "swans," as he joins them for lunch and participates in a new dance craze, the twist.

Infamous *(2006)*

The serious tone of *Capote* reoccurs in *Infamous*, but it is less sustained. Devastated by the loss of a fellow farmer and his family, one Kansas resident tells Capote and Lee in the film, "What scares me is that—well, sometimes, out of nowhere—a bad wind comes up…and despite the weight that's holding you to the ground, when that wind comes, it picks you up light as a leaf and takes you where it wants. We're in control until we're not." This state-

---

[30]Patrick Radden Keefe, "Capote's Co-Conspirators," *The New Yorker*, 22 March 2013, web (accessed 13 August 2018).

ment is less representative of *Infamous* than it might be of *Capote*, but both films address naturalism and an inhospitable world. The Clutters were not in control on the night they died. Capote is not in control from the moment he meets Perry Smith. Shocking events occur without warning, and people are in control until they're not. In spite of the more analytical second half of the film and what Kenneth Turan calls a "vivid performance"[31] by Daniel Craig as Perry Smith, *Infamous* was for numerous critics less memorable than the film that preceded it.

Several reviewers are critical of Toby Jones's performance as Truman Capote, although they are in the minority. Turan writes:

> Part of the problem is the casting of elfin British actor Toby Jones as Capote. The actor looks like the writer to a remarkable extent. But the resemblance seems to have encouraged Jones to fall back into a kind of weird impersonation that verges on caricature. It also makes a hash of Capote's legendary ability to charm one and all.[32]

This perspective does not dominate the reviews; in fact, Jones won numerous awards for his portrayal of Capote, and audiences enjoyed his comic gifts. Callahan calls *Infamous* "risky, emotionally raw, maybe not entirely successful, but always searching and intuitive."[33] He adds:

> The previous *Capote* was a solemn, limited chamber piece and one-man show for Philip Seymour Hoffman, who won an Oscar for his work. It's an accomplished performance, but when set beside what Jones does in *Infamous*, it fades in comparison...Jones captures things about Capote that Hoffman could never touch, such as his lightness, his wild humor, and, most importantly, his vulnerability.[34]

Kristin M. Jones adds her own tribute to *Infamous*, also praising Toby Jones:

> Although *Infamous* covers the same terrain as *Capote*, it is a very different film—less freighted with moody gravity but with its own way of

---

[31]Kenneth Turan, "'Infamous' Fails Where 'Capote' Succeeded," NPR, 13 October 2006, web (accessed 13 August 2018).

[32]Ibid.

[33]Dan Callahan, "*Infamous*," *Slant Magazine*, 2 October 2006, web (accessed 13 August 2018).

[34]Ibid.

conveying how the aftermath of the Clutter murders helped trigger Capote's eventual decline into despair and addiction. Comic moments are also plentiful. Played with uncanny verisimilitude by English actor Toby Jones, this Capote is as winsome as he is self-absorbed, strewing sparkling witticisms wherever he goes, his choirboy bangs and eager mannerisms underlining why many pronounced him "adorable."[35]

Director and screenwriter Douglas McGrath and the actors featured in *Infamous* are alternately celebrated and vilified. Like Richard Brooks, director of *In Cold Blood*, McGrath was a logical choice to oversee the adaptation of a book-length work. McGrath collaborated with Woody Allen on *Bullets Over Broadway* (1994), directed Gwyneth Paltrow in the film adaptation of Jane Austen's *Emma* (1996), and directed the adaptation of Charles Dickens's *Nicholas Nickleby* (2002). Peter Travers suggests that McGrath "pushes too hard on the gay angle"[36] in *Infamous*, but both he and Alexandra Calamari praise Sandra Bullock in what he calls a "beautifully nuanced portrait of Capote's confidante"[37] and Calamari terms a "true standout performance."[38] In the end, however, the laughter fades in both *Capote* and *Infamous*, as Capote finds himself "bereft of many treasured imitation friends,"[39] as Jones reminds us.

As they did with *Capote*, Roger Ebert and A. O. Scott weigh in, decidedly mixed in their reviews. Scott lauds the film for its tone: "In general, 'Infamous' is warmer and more tender, if also a bit thinner and showier, than 'Capote,' which focused on the deep ethical questions raised by the writing of 'In Cold Blood' and emphasized the writer's cold, manipulative narcissism."[40] Ebert focuses on the first scene, where Capote joins his friend Babe Paley (Sigourney Weaver) in a club and the two are mesmerized by a rendition of "What Is This Thing Called Love?" sung by Gwyneth Paltrow. "Is this an artist connecting with her material on a personal level, or is it all part

---

[35]Kristin M. Jones, "Review: *Infamous*," *Film Comment*, September/October 2006, web (accessed 13 August 2018).

[36]Peter Travers, "*Infamous*," *Rolling Stone*, 5 October 2006, web (accessed 13 August 2018).

[37]Ibid.

[38]Alexandra Calamari, "*Infamous*," *Cinemablend*, n.d., web (accessed 13 August 2018).

[39]Jones, "Review: *Infamous*."

[40]A. O. Scott, "Truman Capote's Journey on 'In Cold Blood,' Again," *The New York Times*, 13 October 2006, web (accessed 13 August 2018).

of the performance?" Ebert asks. "This question reverberates throughout the rest of the movie."[41] Ebert also appreciates what he calls the complex "extent of the seduction" between Capote and Smith and the film's exploration of "who seduced whom."[42] In summary, Ebert writes, "'Infamous' never finds its proper tone, which should have been set by the peacock performances of [Toby Jones as Capote and Juliet Stevenson as Diana Vreeland]—flaming creatures who are comically flamboyant, self-possessed and just enough over the top to be dazzling."[43]

Based on George Plimpton's biography of Capote, *Infamous* includes a few fictional interview excerpts. For example, an editor speaks directly to the audience, saying, "I want to explore how a crime like this affects a town where everyone trusts each other…Who among us did this horrible thing?" Although Capote did not abandon his desire to create a portrait of a community in crisis, he shifted his gaze to the killers. Both Capote and Lee were familiar with small-town America, although Lee understood that Capote's interest in Holcomb differed from hers, explaining that Capote covered his pain with "grand tales." Much of her own interest in the murders and the trial derived from the fact that both her father Amasa C. Lee and her sister Alice Finch Lee were attorneys. For her, an interest in a rural community and a nationally significant crime meant that Capote's invitation was nothing less than "deep calling to deep."[44]

Infamous subtly refers to *In Cold Blood*, which strengthens its appeal to readers familiar with the nonfiction novel and with the life of Capote himself. For example, Capote tells Alvin A. Dewey (Jeff Daniels) that he is not a reporter ("I'm a writer") and, true to the nonfiction novel, states clearly that he is "trying to create a new kind of reportage…I treated the people with the emotional and psychological detail of a novel." Again talking with Dewey, Capote suggests that the real story is "how this terrible crime has eaten away at the foundation of trust that makes up your community." Of course, the psychological study of a village that Capote planned largely evaporates after he meets Perry Smith, something Dewey appears to forgive even after he arrests Smith and tries to dissuade Capote from befriending the killers. In *Infamous*, Smith kills Herbert and Kenyon Clutter but not Bonnie and Nan-

---

[41]Roger Ebert, "*Infamous*," 12 October 2006, web (accessed 13 August 2018).
[42]Ibid.
[43]Ibid.
[44]"Truman Capote and Harper Lee: Immortalizing Each Other in Fiction," The Library of America, 1 October 2010, web (accessed 13 August 2018).

cy Clutter. Although it is difficult to make sense of this alteration in the plot without hearing McGrath's own explanation, it may be an attempt to make Smith appear less diabolical by making it clear that he was only one of two killers and that neither Hickock nor Smith committed a premeditated act.

As in *Capote*, Lee again criticizes Capote in *Infamous*, perhaps with less damage to their relationship but with no less passion. Her central concern is not Capote's desire to employ fictional techniques (description, dialogue, and narration) in writing *In Cold Blood* but his cavalier use of facts, including facts central to her interviews of Kansas residents. In *Infamous*, Lee employs Bonnie Clutter as an example of Capote's general disinterest in details: "You obviously plan to turn Bonnie Clutter into some faux poetic recluse when what it sounds like is that she was just thrown off by her menopause." The most intense conversation between them follows:

> Capote: Yes, of course it will all be true, but...
> Lee: But what? Either it is, or it isn't.
> Capote: You're not understanding. I'm, I'm going to bring fictional techniques to a nonfiction story.
> Lee: What fictional techniques? The ones where you make stuff up?...
> Capote: What is your stupid fucking point?
> Lee: That you shouldn't be doing what you're doing. The truth is enough.

Ralph F. Voss said the two argue about the definition of fiction and calls it a "possible fault line" between Capote and Lee, "a line of potentially seismic sensitivity in their longtime friendship."[45]

In 2010, along came a documentary that deals primarily with Harper Lee's *To Kill a Mockingbird* but that intersperses references to Truman Capote, who appears in the 1962 film adaptation of her novel as Charles Baker (Dill) Harris. The documentary belongs in the list of films and documentaries derived from *In Cold Blood* because it addresses Lee's lifetime commitment to her childhood friend and to her willingness to accompany him to Kansas.

---

[45]Ralph F. Voss, *Truman Capote and the Legacy of* In Cold Blood (Tuscaloosa: University of Alabama Press, 2011) 179.

Hey, Boo: Harper Lee *and* To Kill a Mockingbird *(2010)*

The novel *To Kill a Mockingbird* covers several years of the Great Depression (1932–1935), an American nightmare that lasted from 1929 to 1939. (The film compresses the action into one year.) At the beginning of the novel, protagonist Scout Finch is six years old; at the end, nine. Harper Lee, who modeled Scout after herself—even giving Scout her own mother's last name, "Finch"—is featured as Idabel Thompkins in Capote's *Other Voices, Other Rooms* (1948) and again as Ann (Jumbo) Finchburg in *The Thanksgiving Visitor* (1967). In the former, Idabel states emphatically, "I never think like I'm a girl; you've got to remember that, or we can't never be friends"[46]; in the latter, Capote describes Jumbo as "a sawed-off but solid tomboy with an all-hell-let-loose wrestling technique."[47]

In *Hey, Boo*, Mark Childress, author of *Crazy in Alabama*, describes Capote and Lee as "odd birds in their town," the nondescript Monroeville, Alabama. In a 1966 television interview included in *Hey, Boo*, Capote calls Lee a "great, great friend of mine." Cynics will suggest that he was tapping into her fame; others more sympathetic to him will recognize a moment when Capote is most secure, most genuinely himself, and most compassionate. He did not amass the number of friends he had—in Alabama, Kansas, New York, and elsewhere—by being entirely self-absorbed. In fact, as we learn in the documentary, on August 8, 1949, Capote wrote a letter to Michael Brown asking him to look after someone the director of the documentary calls his "shy friend from Alabama" who was traveling to New York City. Gestures such as this one attest to Capote's affection for Lee and offset some of the criticism he faces for having been self-absorbed. For example, in an interview Harper Lee's sister says that Truman Capote became "very jealous" because "Nelle Harper" received a Pulitzer—"and he did not." Logically enough, Alice Lee said Capote's anger increased when he began to rely on alcohol and drugs: "It was not Nelle Harper dropping him," she said. "It was Truman going away from her."[48]

These three films and two documentaries make clear that Truman Capote remains central to the American literary consciousness, a chameleon that both charmed and alienated the people who came into his universe.

---

[46]Truman Capote, *Other Voices, Other Rooms*, in *Three by Truman Capote* (New York: Random House, 1985) 79.

[47]Truman Capote, *The Thanksgiving Visitor* (New York: Random House, 1967) 11.

[48] *Hey Boo: Harper Lee and* To Kill a Mockingbird, dir. Mary McDonaugh Murphy, Mary Murphy and Company, 2011.

Dewey remained his friend until he died, although, as discussed in chapter three, Capote appropriated cases that Dewey hoped to use in his own book. According to Alice Lee, her sister did not abandon Capote; instead, he drifted away from her. In the end, Capote lost most of his New York celebrity friends as well, betraying even Babe Paley by disclosing their secrets. Nonetheless, what Capote lacked in his social circle he made up for in his literary one. For all of its controversy, *In Cold Blood* is a landmark achievement that points to Capote's ability to understand themes of universal significance. In an alchemy of allegory and sensationalism, the nonfiction novel remains a classic.

Allegory and Sensationalism in Documentary and Film

Defending Truman Capote is not the point of this study. In no way does his desire for fame excuse him from violating journalistic principles or ignoring essential facts that underpin a larger truth. However, his instincts were razor sharp, and his ability to create allegory helped him enlarge his audience and deal with universal themes. When Crowther asks, "And what does this single explosion of violence indicate as to society's pitiable vulnerability to the kooks that are loose in the land?"[49] he inadvertently underscores Capote's gift for discovering a horrific crime, caring about an ordinary family, and spinning a news event into art. Not all crimes resonate. Not all murders make it to the front pages or reside there for more than a day.

The murder of the Clutter family is unusual but not unprecedented before or after it occurred. What elevated the murders, the investigation, the trial, and the executions into the popular sphere was Capote's skill in making the crime emblematic, metaphorical, representative. Geography played a large part in his portrayal of the Clutter family, as did the people affected by random violence. Holcomb and Garden City, Kansas, are in the center of the nation and are "proud of their neighborliness and of a life free from the sins of the city,"[50] as Pizer suggests. In "Rereading: Truman Capote's *In Cold Blood*," Thomson writes, "His intention was to produce a tightly controlled forensic piece that examined the effects of a savage, senseless killing on an obscure community, and what interested him at the outset was the climate of wariness and suspicion, the insomnia, the loss of faith, the dread."[51]

---

[49]Crowther, "*In Cold Blood*."
[50]Pizer, "Documentary Narrative as Art," 117.
[51]Thomson, "Rereading."

In the allegory of good versus evil, Dewey, too, becomes larger than life. Keefe describes him as "heroic and comfortingly archetypal."[52] Dewey represents the law; he is handsome, modest, relentless. Keefe defends Capote's intentions in "Capote's Co-Conspirators," suggesting that readers appreciate a character's heroic instincts and appreciate a sense of order. Although Duane West and other KBI agents argue that Dewey received too much positive press—especially when he was wrong, as he was when he suggested that the killers were probably local—he is the person Capote trusted to solve the crime, to maintain a personal sense of ethics, and to be merciful:

> Even in the most scrupulously factual (and fact-checked) piece of narrative journalism, the writer uses some details and discards others, focuses on some characters and ignores others altogether, withholds information, and then metes it out as it suits him. If Dewey feels, at times, like a hero in a movie, that's because Capote rendered him that way, with a degree of careful embroidery. So while "In Cold Blood" breaches the signal prohibition of nonfiction writing, it does so in service of a narrative agenda—to arrange chaotic reality into a story that is orderly and emotionally engaging and suspenseful—that more responsible journalists would surely recognize.[53]

Although allegory surfaces throughout this study, it also is important to insert sensationalism into the conversation, although it is too often demeaned in journalism and other literary forms. With *In Cold Blood*, sensationalism bears revisiting because it helps to account for the enduring popularity of the nonfiction novel. Certainly, conflict and violence always have been a part of American media coverage. In *Sensationalism: Murder, Mayhem, Mudslinging, Scandals, and Disasters in 19th-Century Reporting*, editors David B. Sachsman and David W. Bulla collect twenty-one essays that reinforce the appeal of sensationalism in cable news, literature, magazines, newspapers, and film. With *In Cold Blood*, Truman Capote steps into a river that flows from a time long before he existed. In their detailed introduction, Sachsman and Bulla write:

> Sensationalism is a key to the story of how newspapers changed throughout the century to appeal to an increasingly literate workforce

---

[52]Keefe, "Capote's Co-Conspirators."
[53]Ibid.

that included wave after wave of new immigrants. Political scandal-mongering continued throughout the century and continues to the current day, and the crime coverage that was the bread and butter of the penny press rose to new heights in the era of yellow journalism and is now the essential feature of "if it bleeds, it leads" culture of news reporting.[54]

Sensationalism, write the editors, "can be defined in terms of topics, tone, and degree": "Sensational reporting sometimes titillates and sometimes offends the reader—sometimes it does both."[55] The rollicking exploration of crimes, disasters, gore, the grotesque, hoaxes, and stunts asks readers to consider their own preconceptions about sensationalism and its prevalence in contemporary film, literature, and other media forms and recommends that scholars continue to explore why reports about bludgeoning, stabbing, whipping, and war endure.

At least as pertinent to an exploration of the sensationalism in *In Cold Blood*, Meg Greenfield defends readers and viewers who find *In Cold Blood* riveting and suggests that our interest in similar literary texts began long ago. In "In Defense of Sensationalism: The Media and the O.J. Simpson Case," Greenfield writes:

[Much] of what constitutes the frowned-upon preoccupation of readers and viewers—the startling crimes and trials, the passions that wreck lives and destroy families and other institutions—goes to ancient, even primal human concerns. It engages supremely serious questions of good and evil, guilt and responsibility and all the many permutations of these in our lives. Don't be so snobbish about the interest people show in this stuff or so dismissive of its significance. After all, according to Genesis, when the good Lord put us on this earth just about the first two things that happened were a sex scandal and a murder. Great minds ever after have turned to these subjects, meditated on them, explored them. Shakespeare's fascination was consuming. There is a reason, and it is

---

[54]David B. Sachsman and David W. Bulla, "Introduction," *Sensationalism: Murder, Mayhem, Mudslinging, Scandals, and Disasters in 19th-Century Reporting*, ed. David B. Sachsman and David W. Bulla (New Brunswick, N.J.: Transaction Publishers, 2013) xxxii.

[55]Ibid., xxi.

not simply some base or squalid instinct, that draws people to these tales.[56]

In the finale to her essay, Greenfield gives consumers of media permission to stop reading or watching an informative piece about graft in city government if an interesting robbery is taking place: in a reference to the O.J. Simpson trial that followed the 1994 murders of Nicole Brown Simpson and Ronald Goldman, she writes, "If they are discussing unfunded federal mandates for state social programs on TV, you shouldn't feel guilty about switching over to the trial for a look."[57]

Sensationalism is part of the southern gothic tradition familiar both to Capote and Lee, whose novel *To Kill a Mockingbird* makes good use of haunted houses, shadowy figures, and violence. The childhood friends also were drawn to film, and Lee enjoyed significant success with the Academy Award-winning film that was drawn from her first novel. Throughout his life, Truman Capote danced between literature and film, using both artistic forms to reimagine himself into a person who could survive in the social circles he craved. He appeared in at least two films, Neil Simon's *Murder by Death* (1976) and Woody Allen's *Annie Hall* (1977). In the latter, Alvy (Max) Singer (Woody Allen) and Annie Hall (Diane Keaton) are watching people in the park, when Alvy says, "Oh, there's the winner of the Truman Capote Look-Alike Contest." In fact, the person he observes actually *is* Truman Capote himself, although he is not listed in the credits.

Sensationalism is not the final component of films addressed in this chapter. In "The Headless Hawk" (1946), Capote compares a darkened, safe movie theater to religion, elevating his appreciation for film by suggesting that it can reach the heights of allegorical, ideological, and individual truth:

> The movies. Again. In the last month he'd seen so many films, snatches
> of Hollywood dialogue rumbled in his dreams...But Vincent was sensi-
> tive enough to see why; there had been in his own life a certain time of
> limbo when he'd gone to movies every day, often sitting through several
> repeats of the same film; it was in its way like religion, for there, watch-

---

[56]Meg Greenfield, "In Defense of Sensationalism: The Media and the O.J. Simpson Case," *Newsweek*, 26 September 1994: 72.
[57]Ibid.

ing the shifting patterns of black and white, he knew a release of conscience similar to the kind a man must find confessing to his father.[58]

According to Pugh, "In this metaphor of film as religion, the cinema erases
not merely transgressions but consciousness, allowing the penitent to find
freedom from the ravages of his mind."[59] Here, it is clear that Capote shifts
from making cameo appearances to describing the catharsis and containment
possible when he immerses himself into the experience of film.

Capote used the term "nonfiction novel" to describe *In Cold Blood*, and
according to Pugh, "as he increasingly becomes a character from the nonfiction novel that was his life, the various cinematic and stage adaptations featuring him suggest that he has metamorphosed into an avatar of adaptation,
iconically symbolizing the transition from life to page, and from page to
screen."[60] Pugh adds:

> With *In Cold Blood*, his account of the slaughter of Herb, Bonnie, Nan-
> cy, and Kenyon Clutter at the hands of Perry Smith and Dick Hickock,
> Capote credited himself with inventing the nonfiction novel, one that
> couples the linearity of a journalistic account with fiction's depth of
> character, structure, and style. As Capote envisioned, *In Cold Blood*
> would break down the borders between journalism and fiction through
> its unflinching realism. In comparing the two genres, he posited that
> journalism suffers in comparison to fiction because of its inherent line-
> arity: "Journalism, you see, always moves along on a horizontal plane,
> telling a story, while fiction—good fiction—moves vertically, taking
> you deeper and deeper into character and events." In another interview,
> Capote admitted the paradox of the term *nonfiction novel* and confessed
> that he employed it to generate publicity—"About that nonfiction-
> novel business, I wish I'd never said it. People didn't understand. But
> one has to do something."[61]

On another occasion Capote described film's aesthetic influences on *In Cold
Blood*: "I wanted to produce a journalistic novel, something on a large scale

---

[58]Truman Capote, "The Headless Hawk," *Truman Capote: A Capote Reader* (New
York: Penguin, 2002) 55-56.
[59]Pugh, *Truman Capote: A Literary Life at the Movies*, 9.
[60]Ibid., 16.
[61]Ibid., 109.

that would have the credibility of fact, the immediacy of film, the depth and freedom of prose, and the precision of poetry."[62]

While academics, critics, and readers parry and thrust, literary journalist and professor Madeleine Blais stands firm in her support for Capote—both what he attempted and what he achieved:

> Capote's attempt to graft the techniques of imaginative literature onto a non-fiction story was more brazen, more unremitting, and on a larger scale. He came out of the gate firing away, claiming to have invented a new form: the non-fiction novel. Everything about it was innovative: his use of cinematic devices, the way he enters a scene as late as possible and gets out of it as early as possible, the cross-cutting, and especially the agonizing slow motion when he finally gets around to describing the crime itself. He was so successful in raising the bar that today we take his innovations for granted, losing sight of the revolutionary nature of immersing readers in the way people really talk, in a headlong rush, full of loops and asides, without a bunch of stilted "according to's" or other cumbersome, momentum-breaking devices.[63]

In her praise, Blais makes central Capote's use of cinematic techniques in *In Cold Blood* and his ability to fuse two mediums. It is no wonder that the 1967 film *In Cold Blood* does not take a back seat to either *Capote* or *Infamous*. All three alter reality even as Richard Brooks's film achieves a documentary quality; together, however, the three films and two documentaries amplify and sustain Capote's piece of extended nonfiction and allow for multiple and mutually enriching points of view.

---

[62]Truman Capote, "Preface to *Music for Chameleons,*" *Truman Capote: A Capote Reader* (New York: Penguin, 2002) 719.

[63]Madeleine Blais, "Truman Capote's 'In Cold Blood' Still the Standard," *Chicago Tribune*, 25 December 2005, web (accessed 13 August 2018).

Chapter 8

River Valley Farm and Beyond

From one perspective, *In Cold Blood* is the story of a house and the people who lived there. In 1948, Herbert and Bonnie Clutter completed a brick home on prime Kansas farmland. With five bedrooms, three bathrooms, 3,600 square feet of finished space, and an unfinished basement, the house on the outskirts of Holcomb was a source of pride: "The handsome white house, standing on an ample lawn of groomed Bermuda grass, impressed Holcomb; it was a place people pointed out,"[1] writes Truman Capote. Chinese elms, which can grow as high as fifty to eighty feet, shaded a long driveway. These elegant elms produce small leaves that turn to red, purple, or yellow in late fall, their thin branches supporting broad, round heads of foliage. The hardy, resilient trees often are used to line avenues and boulevards and to adorn spacious yards. With enough water and care, Chinese elms can live to be 100 years old.

In their forties at the time of their deaths, Herbert and Bonnie Clutter had three daughters and a son. One of the oldest daughters, Eveanna Clutter Jarchow, was married, and the other, Beverly Clutter, was about to be. The two youngest lived at home and were involved in their school, Garden City church, and 4-H, a youth empowerment program that stands for "head, heart, hands, and health": "I pledge my Head to clearer thinking, my Heart to greater loyalty, my Hands to larger service, and my Health to better living, for my club, my community, my country, and my world." World War II was over, although the Vietnam War loomed. Country, rock and roll, rhythm and blues, and swing dominated the airwaves. Rural life offered some Americans a sense of community and security, and Holcomb residents treasured a sense of shared history. The Clutters and their neighbors planned their lives, did what they could to protect their finances and health, expected more for their children than they had achieved, and worked hard in a nation that advertised—both then and now—the advantages of a middle-class life. Their house was a tribute to their industry, yes, but, more important, it represented their hope in what was yet to come.

---

[1]Truman Capote, *In Cold Blood: A True Account of Multiple Murder and Its Consequences* (New York: Random House, 1965) 9.

Into this world entered William Floyd Wells of Columbus, Kansas, who had worked for Herbert Clutter when he was nineteen and had then drifted into a life of crime. At the time of the murders, Wells, then thirty-one, was serving time at the Kansas State Penitentiary for burglary, and he developed a penchant for the spotlight and a predisposition to lie. In his social circle was his cellmate Richard Eugene Hickock, who took to heart tales of wealthy farmers and safes full of money. During the trial that would follow, Wells claimed a reward, made a deal with prosecutors, and testified: "I told Hickock about working for Clutter and that Clutter was wealthy. I told him the Clutters once told me he spent more than $10,000 in one week, that Clutter was generous and frequently gave his employees bonuses."[2] In *In Cold Blood*, Capote describes Wells's affection for the family whose death warrants he signed. Wells compliments Clutter for helping him when he needed a few dollars, for paying him fairly, and for providing bonuses. He also describes how attached he was to the children, Nancy and Kenyon.[3]

After he testified in the trial of Richard Eugene Hickock and Perry Edward Smith and was released, Wells continued to commit crimes and was imprisoned again, this time at the Mississippi State Penitentiary, a prison for men that is also known as Parchman Farm. The penitentiary now houses approximately 5,000 inmates—a few on Death Row—and its gas chamber has been replaced with an electric chair. It is best known for having "housed" Freedom Riders that came to Mississippi to help register African-American voters during the Civil Rights movement. Years later, on April 5, 1970, in the *Delta Democrat-Times* appeared the headline "Parchman Escapee Killed, 2 Wounded." A few readers may have noticed a short news story on page three below the fold:

PARCHMAN (UPI)—A desperate flight for freedom by three inmates at the Mississippi State Penitentiary ended in death for one and the recapture of the other two Friday on the grounds of a sprawling Delta plantation.

The three made their break on a stolen tractor but were caught on foot within hours before they could make it off the W.D. Patterson plantation grounds about two miles north of the Parchman prison.

---

[2]"Witness Claims Two Took Turns Killing Family: FBI Agent Reveals What He Says Smith Told to Officials," *Lawrence Journal-World*, 24 March 1960, web (accessed 1 August 2018).

[3]Capote, *In Cold Blood*, 160.

Parchman Supt. Tom Cook said 42-year-old inmate William Floyd Wells was gunned down by prison guards and highway patrolmen when he offered resistance. Wells was dead on arrival at a clinic in the nearby community of Shelby.

The other two inmates [both twenty-three years old] were recaptured in the same wooded area of the plantation where Wells was shot.[4]

In addition to the Clutters, Hickock, Smith, and Wells, *In Cold Blood* introduces readers to attitudes about hard work and thriftiness, religion, rural life, and a system of manners that may or may not be familiar to them. *In Cold Blood* also introduces readers to compelling themes, including cruelty, lost innocence, and random violence. In the nonfiction novel, Kansas becomes an insular and evocative world—with its Wheat Lands and Windsor hotels, the First Methodist Church, the Finney County Courthouse, and the home of Alvin A. and Marie Dewey. From Capote's first few words—"The village of Holcomb stands on the high wheat plains of western Kansas"[5]—to the last—"the big sky, the whisper of wind voices in the wind-bent wheat"[6]—readers enter a universe both alien and familiar, both real and allegorical. The author, too, was deeply affected by his time in Kansas, a journey he said he would not repeat if he had known what lay in wait. His most descriptive account of his experience occurred in a conversation with biographer George Plimpton:

> I'm still very much haunted by the whole thing. I have finished the book, but in a sense I *haven't* finished it: it keeps churning around in my head. It particularizes itself now and then, but not in the sense that it brings about a total conclusion. It's like the echo of E.M. Forster's Malabar Caves, the echo that's meaningless and yet it's there: one keeps hearing it all the time.[7]

"Voices in the Wind-Bent Wheat"

The final line of *In Cold Blood* is haunting and wistful. As Alvin Dewey walks away from a (fictional) chance encounter with a "pretty girl in a hur-

---

[4]"Parchman Escapee Killed, 2 Wounded," *Delta Democrat-Times*, 5 April 1970, 3.
[5]Capote, *In Cold Blood*, 3.
[6]Ibid., 343.
[7]George Plimpton, "The Story Behind a Nonfiction Novel," *Truman Capote: Conversations*, ed. M. Thomas Inge (Jackson: University Press of Mississippi, 1987) 68.

ry,"[8] he imagines that Nancy Clutter would be a lot like Susan Kidwell, the young woman he meets in the cemetery, if she had lived. "Then, starting home, he walked toward the trees, and under them, leaving behind him the big sky, the whisper of wind voices in the wind-bent wheat,"[9] Capote writes. Reading *In Cold Blood* would be an even richer experience if it were possible to include the voices of Susan Kidwell and all the other Kansans affected by the murder of the Clutter family. Capote and the filmmakers included in chapter seven tapped into some resources and dismissed others, depending both on the willingness of sources to share their stories and the thematic intent of particular documentaries and films and *In Cold Blood* itself. In the final chapter of this study, several unheard stories are introduced. In addition to the news story about William Floyd Wells that preceded this section, they include two autobiographical essays, one by Donald Cullivan, who knew Perry Smith in the Army and renewed their friendship during Smith's murder trial, and the other by Diana Selsor Edwards, a niece of Herbert and Bonnie Clutter. A newspaper article about Ralph McClung, who served on the actual jury in 1960 and the jury in the film *In Cold Blood* in 1967, follows the essays. Robert (Bob) Rupp, Nancy Clutter's boyfriend, and Donna Mader, owner of what always will be the "Clutter house," gave occasional interviews summarized here. Obviously, all of these contributions are representative—not comprehensive—and much more research needs to occur before historians, literary critics, and readers understand fully the events of November 15, 1959. The value of ongoing oral histories cannot be exaggerated.

Although residents of Holcomb and Garden City, Kansas, differ in their opinions about visitors who come in search of information about *In Cold Blood* and about the time that Capote and Nelle Harper Lee spent in their state, there are those who have welcomed the opportunity to discuss the murders, the trial, the publication of the book, the aftermath of the crimes, and the impact the events had on their community and their families. Included in the numerous articles and news stories about *In Cold Blood* are residents who say they have never read the nonfiction novel (some say they also have not seen *In Cold Blood*, *Capote*, and/or *Infamous*, even though the films highlight local venues and people familiar to them). Reasons they avoid these texts vary, but the phenomenon itself is cause for dismay. Nonetheless, people from all over the world make pilgrimages to Holcomb and

---

[8]Capote, *In Cold Blood*, 343.
[9]Ibid.

Garden City, Kansas, and the Internet explodes with articles, blogs, letters, and questions about Capote, the nonfiction novel, the region, and the time period.

Kansas residents who became part of the international conversation about *In Cold Blood* continue to interest readers. They include Roy Church of the Kansas Bureau of Investigation and adviser to the 1967 film *In Cold Blood*, who died in 1971; Alvin A. Dewey of the KBI and friend to both Truman Capote and Harper Lee, who died in 1987; Marie Louise Bellocq Dewey, also a friend to Capote and Lee, who died in 2002; Clifford R. Hope Jr., attorney for the Herbert and Bonnie Clutter estate and for Capote, who died in 2010; and Dolores (Dodie) Hope, columnist, editor, and reporter for the *Garden City Telegram*, who died in 2014. The Deweys and the Hopes liked Capote and respected *In Cold Blood*. Before he died, Clifford Hope told a reporter with *The Guardian*, "Many people thought he should have written about the Clutter family, rather than the murderers," and Dolores Hope added, "There will always be people who think it's none of anybody's business to come out here and write about their affairs. You will never change their opinions."[10]

Others who continue to interest readers, of course, are Harper Lee, who died in 2016 and was buried in Hillcrest Cemetery in Monroeville, Alabama, and Capote himself, who died in 1984. Some of Capote's cremated remains are at the Westwood Memorial Park in Los Angeles; according to other unconfirmed sources, ashes also were given to his friend Joanne Carson, wife of television talk show host Johnny Carson, and still others were scattered with those of his long-time partner Jack Dunphy off the coast of Long Island, New York, near where Capote and Dunphy had shared a home.

Perry Edward Smith and Richard Eugene Hickock are buried—side by side—in the Mount Muncie Cemetery in Lansing, Kansas. Walter David Hickock, Dick's younger brother, published *In the Shadow of My Brother's Cold Blood* (2010) about the murders and their effect on him and his family. In an interview in 2005, Walter Hickock disclosed that he once considered his brother his hero. Suzanna Adam writes:

> Walter's life was not untouched by the actions of the older brother he called the "hero" of his youth. While Dick faced a series of judges,

---

[10]Ed Pilkington, "In Cold Blood, Half a Century On," *The Guardian*, 15 November 2009, web (accessed 14 August 2018).

Walter's struggle to understand the harsh truth of his brother's crime helped derail three marriages and contributed to his breaking ties with his children. While Capote grew famous, Walter received hate mail, and potential employers denied him jobs....[11]

Walter Hickock believes his brother began to change after an automobile accident in 1950 that "almost killed him," he said. Dick Hickock began writing bad checks and gambling in order to pay hospital bills and other debts. In 1958, he went to prison after stealing a rifle. Their mother Eunice Hickock blamed herself. Quoted in Walter Hickock's book, she said, "Maybe I did do something wrong. Only I don't know what it could have been. I get headaches trying to remember. We're plain people, just country people, getting along the same as everybody else." She and others in the family drove two hours to Lansing State Penitentiary often to visit Dick Hickock; in fact, she and Walter Hickock made a final trip the day before the execution: "We didn't go to the hanging," Walter Hickcock said. "Dick said he'd just as soon we didn't go for it. That would've been hard. But we were there the day it took place, of course."[12] Walter David Hickock died in 2008, two years before the book appeared.

Readers wonder, too, about others in the nonfiction novel. Several of the people featured in *In Cold Blood* are buried in Valley View Cemetery in Garden City (some are listed in the previous paragraph and some here). They include Herbert William Clutter; Bonnie Mae Fox Clutter; Nancy Mae Clutter; Kenyon Neal Clutter; Alvin A. Dewey; Marie Louise Bellocq Dewey; Arthur Milo Fleming, defense attorney for Smith; Clifford R. Hope Jr., whose Garden City law firm managed correspondence and visitation between Capote and officials at the Kansas State Penitentiary; and Wilma Kidwell, mother of Susan Kidwell Armstrong and a friend of Bonnie Clutter's, who died in 1996. Alfred Paul Stoecklein, whom Capote describes as the "sole resident employee"[13] at River Valley Farm, died in 1998, and his wife Geraldine Ann Meier Stoecklein in 2006. Like Hickock and Smith, many readers of *In Cold Blood* wonder how the Stoeckleins could have slept through the gunshots in a house only 100 yards away from the Clutter house.

---

[11]Suzanna Adam, "Left Behind: Man Lives Painful Life in Shadow of Brother's Crime," *Lawrence Journal-World*, 4 April 2005, web (accessed 14 August 2018).

[12]Ibid.

[13]Capote, *In Cold Blood*, 12.

Several figures in *In Cold Blood* are alive and sometimes provide interviews. According to some accounts, Susan Kidwell Armstrong is one of the people who found Nancy Clutter's body November 15, 1959 (the two planned to attend church services that morning). Nancy Ewalt Culbreath, who also is said to have entered the house on that heartbreaking morning, lives in Colorado. Beverly Jean Clutter English and her husband Vere Edward English live part of the year in Arizona and the rest in Kansas. Beverly married Vere three days after the funeral for four members of her family. Eveanna Marie Clutter Mosier lost her first husband, Donald Jarchow, in 1970, and in 1980 married William E. (Bill) Mosier, who died in 2007. She now lives in Arizona. Although Beverly English and Eveanna Mosier stopped giving interviews soon after the murders, they assembled several notebooks of information about their parents for their own children and grandchildren.[14] Duane West, former Finney County attorney and Garden City mayor, led the prosecution against Hickock and Smith and does not like to discuss the murders or the trial, although he occasionally agrees to do so. At the time of the publication of this study, he still resides in Kansas.

One of the central figures in *In Cold Blood* is Robert (Bob) Rupp. Rupp is married, has four children, and lives approximately 800 yards from where his high school girlfriend Nancy Clutter once resided. Occasionally agreeing to interviews, Rupp is one of the Holcomb residents who says he has not read the nonfiction novel. In 2009, Rupp talked with Ed Pilkington, a reporter for *The Guardian*, and again expressed his respect for the Clutter family, especially Herbert Clutter: "He was a big influence in my life—when you know somebody like that it tends to kind of inspire you. He could see above what most people could see, and visualise how things should be,"[15] Rupp said. Pilkington writes that Hickock and Smith were everything Herbert Clutter was not, calling them "impetuous, profane, rootless, lost."[16] Nancy Clutter and Rupp were sixteen years old when the murders occurred, and—with the exception of the killers—he was the last person to see her alive. "She was just a beautiful, outgoing person who had many, many friends," Rupp said. "She was just a stand-out individual."[17] According to the article,

---

[14]Patrick Smith, "Sisters, Family: Surviving Clutter Daughters Hope to Preserve their Parents' Legacy," *Lawrence Journal-World*, 4 April 2005 web (accessed 14 August 2018).

[15]Pilkington, "In Cold Blood, Half a Century On."

[16]Ibid.

[17]Ibid.

Rupp and Nancy Clutter had planned to go to a midnight movie Saturday night, but her father had suggested that they go Friday instead. "Had they kept their original plans," speculates reporter Melissa Lee, "Nancy probably wouldn't have been in the sprawling Clutter farmhouse when two recently released felons drove up the lane and eased through the unlocked doors in search of a rumored safe containing Herb Clutter's fortune."[18] Rupp watched television with Nancy and Kenyon Clutter until 10 p.m., when he left. "He remembers standing on the porch of the brick, two-story Clutter farmhouse with Nancy," writes Melissa Lee. The two hoped to meet the following day to spend the afternoon "cruising Garden City."[19]

Rupp learned about the murders from his father and Clarence Ewalt, and Melissa Lee writes that both men were crying when they talked with Rupp. Rupp remembers thinking, "No. No. This can't happen. You read about this stuff. It doesn't happen here. Not in Holcomb."[20] Rupp and his brother drove to the Clutter property, but there were too many emergency vehicles blocking access. He called Nancy Clutter's friend Susan Kidwell, knowing she would confirm the news if it were true. When he called, her mother answered, crying. Rupp knew the information was true. Rupp was a suspect, and although he told Lee he understands why, the suspicion he faced forced him to leave his high school, which made him ineligible to participate in track or play basketball. Melissa Lee writes, "What he doesn't understand is why, even after he passed the lie-detector test, police went to Holcomb High School the next day and cleaned out his locker—even took his tennis shoes. He doesn't understand why people around town started giving him strange looks. Why even some of his best friends turned on him."[21] At the end of the interview, Rupp discussed the impact of the tragedy on his life, saying that the murderers "took everything from us": "You didn't want to hurt anybody. You weren't 17, 18-year-old kids anymore. You were, but you weren't. Life just turned to the serious. The reality of what the world is really like set in."[22] To this day, either Rupp or his wife Coleen takes flowers to Nancy Clutter's grave every year.[23]

---

[18]Melissa Lee, "High School Sweetheart Recalls the Day His Life Changed Forever," *Lawrence Journal-World*, 3 April 2005, web (accessed 14 August 2018).
[19]Ibid.
[20]Ibid.
[21]Ibid.
[22]Ibid.
[23]Ibid.

Rupp was unimpressed with Capote—"He wasn't the kind of person I wanted to spend time with—he was very, very strange"[24]—and although Capote interviewed him for *In Cold Blood*, the two did not get to know one another. Although he is one of those who has never read the nonfiction novel, Rupp told Pilkington that he thinks Capote was unfair to the Clutters because the book emphasizes their deaths instead of their lives: "I don't think he did the Clutter family justice, is all."[25]

Diana Selsor Edwards, too, thinks the nonfiction novel spends less time celebrating the lives of the Clutter family than it does on the personal histories of Richard Hickock and Perry Smith. To help to address the vacuum of information, she published an essay, included here in its entirety. Edwards is the niece of Herbert and Bonnie Clutter, cousin to Eveanna, Beverly, Nancy, and Kenyon Clutter. She and Nancy were "crib mates,"[26] as she says, and the Clutter farm was a refuge from a difficult home life. Elaine Clutter Selsor of Palatka, Florida, is Diana Selsor Edwards's mother, whose name appears in a list of those whom authorities notified after the murders were discovered.[27] Elaine Clutter Selsor was the youngest of five siblings (Lucille, Clarence, Arthur, Herbert, and Elaine), closest in age to Herbert Clutter. Now a cultural anthropologist and a therapist in Silver City, New Mexico, Diana Edwards is in private practice and also lectures on adoption, grief, and loss. Her article, "The Rest of the Story," is part of a longer memoir and first appeared in November 2009 in *Desert Exposure*. Her essay follows.

"The Rest of the Story"

"It is time we had a family reunion long enough to really get acquainted again. This is our invitation to *each* of you to be one family in our home for two days minimum and longer if possible. Activities will include gabbing, games of all kinds, hunting, horse back riding, after dinner naps, looking at family pictures of films, eating, watching TV football games."

This was our 1959 Clutter Family Reunion invitation from Uncle Herbert, Aunt Bonnie and children. We had not had a Thanksgiving

---

[24]Pilkington, "In Cold Blood, Half a Century On."
[25]Ibid.
[26]Diana Selsor Edwards, "The Rest of the Story," *Desert Exposure*, November 2009, web (accessed 14 August 2018).
[27]Capote, *In Cold Blood*, 71.

reunion since Grandma Clutter died in 1953. I was 16 and needed that secure nest of extended family. But the family reunion that November proved very different than planned.

As *Time* magazine reported in its Nov. 30, 1959, issue: "The showplace farm of Herbert Clutter, set in the peaceful, prosperous, picturebook country west of Garden City, Kansas (pop. 11,000), seemed the nation's least likely setting for cold-blooded, methodical murder. And the Clutter family seemed the nation's least likely victims. Herb Clutter, 48, a well-heeled wheat-grower, was just about the most prominent man in the region. He was chairman of the Kansas Conference of Farm Organizations and Cooperatives, a former member of the federal Farm Credit Board, a civic leader who headed the building committee that got Garden City's new Methodist Church translated from hope into brick. His wife Bonnie was active in the Methodist Women's Society of Christian Service. The Clutters' well-behaved, teen-age children, Kenyon and Nancy, were popular, straight-A students at the local high school. Both were scheduled to receive 4-H awards at last week's Finney County 4-H Achievement Banquet. They never collected their prizes."

I found the *Time* magazine article and the unanswered invitation—along with other family letters, newspapers and magazines about the murders—in a battered suitcase in the attic, after my mother died in 1998.

Uncle Herbert and Aunt Bonnie were touchstones of security for me. Where my parents were unpredictable and often absent, Herbert and Bonnie were predictable and present. My mother, Elaine, was beautiful and talented. She played the piano by ear, and fantasized about playing professionally someday. But she met my father before she finished high school, and by age 20 was burdened with three children. Herbert was the brother who always looked out for her and provided a home and security for our family when we needed him.

My father was also good-looking and talented, another dreamer and unrealized artist. When they first married, he painted Idaho mountain scenes from his brief stint in the Civilian Conservation Corps, selling the oil paintings to supplement his earnings as a rural milkman.

Uncle Herbert earned a college education and became a respected farmer and agricultural expert. He was a caring husband to Bonnie and a fond father to Eveanna, Beverly, Nancy and Kenyon. He and Bonnie designed and built a beautiful and modern home, where they'd lived since Nancy and I were six.

Nancy and I were crib mates, born a month apart. Since we needed to feel superior to someone, we tried to ignore Kenyon—a year younger—just as Beverly and Eveanna ignored us.

When I was nine, my family moved to Florida, against my mother's wishes. My father loved deep-sea fishing and hated Kansas winters. A "rolling stone," as relatives called him, he bought an airplane, joined the Flying Farmers, and flew to Mexico on fishing trips. Everyone else raised wheat and cattle and stayed home.

Our second Christmas in Florida, in 1953, Herbert's, as we called their family, drove down to visit. Our new cinderblock house near Brooksville was finished and we had room for visitors. They had never been to the South. We took them to see flamingoes and alligators and a man who could milk rattlesnakes. I was eager to show Nancy the town library where I had a library card and planned to read every book, systematically.

Other summers and holidays in the 1950s, we drove to Kansas and made the rounds of family. Frequently, I got to stay at Herbert's on my own.

The summer of 1959, we were growing up. Eveanna had already graduated from college and married a veterinarian; they lived in Illinois with their new baby. Beverly was completing her college nursing program and planning her wedding. That summer, Nancy and I spied on Beverly and her fiancé, Vere, kissing; we were nosy girls and wanted to know everything about growing up.

For a 4-H project that year, Nancy had redecorated the basement rec room, creating a space for her, Kenyon and their friends to hang out, play music and dance. On the new couch she'd selected, we still giggled and whispered secrets. Nancy and I also plotted how to get Uncle Herbert to let her drive me the two hours to Grandpa Clutter's in Larned. At 16 and licensed for all of five months, we were eager to try out our independence. When we got up our courage to ask, he said no. I liked knowing that he cared and wanted us to be safe, but we both recognized the freedom I had that Nancy did not.

That summer, Kenyon was engaging and impossible to ignore. He was smart, funny and ordinarily soft-spoken. He liked working with his hands and usually had some carpentry or other project going. For the first time, I was curious about what he thought and what he wanted to do when he grew up.

He and I played intense games of ping-pong. We made up excuses to chase each other around the table and up and down the stairs, laughing and teasing. He had become tall and very good-looking. I was reluctant to return to Palatka, Florida, where we now lived.

The night they were killed, I was at a weekend beach party with girlfriends.

When I came home Sunday afternoon to an empty house, my parents were still out fishing. They had gone to St. Augustine, where my father kept his boat. My sister, Janet, was in Sarasota at the Ringling School of Art; my brother, Gary, was in the Army in Korea. A neighbor boy brought over a handwritten note the police had given them to deliver because we weren't home: "Four members of the Clutter family killed in Holcomb, Kansas." There was a local number to call.

I was brought to my knees. *This can't be possible.* I had no voice to make a phone call. It might have been an hour; it might have been 30 minutes. I was outside of time. When I could, I telephoned my boyfriend John for help. He came over and made the call. It was true. The bodies of Uncle Herbert, Aunt Bonnie, Nancy and Kenyon had been found that morning when Nancy's friends arrived to go to church with them. When no one answered, they opened the unlocked door to check.

I had no way to contact my parents and let them know. Nor did I want to be the one to tell my mother. When I was young, she cried a lot, and was taken several times for electric-shock treatment at the Menninger Clinic in Topeka. Would this trigger another breakdown? Would the "nerve pills" she carried in her purse be enough?

John stayed while we waited for my parents. I don't remember what my mother did when I told her, only that she sent home the neighbor woman who brought coffee. "We don't drink coffee."

We packed my father's blue-and-silver Impala and, early Monday morning, started the journey home.

By then, the family tragedy had become a national event. In each city where we stopped for gas, the newspapers headlined the "savage" murders: the Jacksonville *Florida Times-Union*, "Farm Family of 4 Murdered in Home; *The Montgomery Advertiser*, "Bound, Gagged Bodies of 4 in Family Found." In Kansas, *The Hutchinson News'* headlines spanned the front page, with photographs not only of the family when alive, but of officials bringing out the bodies. Teddy, the family dog, sat by the door.

I was embarrassed that my father would point to the newspaper photos and say proudly to the filling-station clerk, "That's my wife's brother."

The funeral was Wednesday, Nov. 18. The First Methodist Church in Garden City, Kansas, overflowed with people, standing in the aisles and outside. We were escorted through the front side doors. At best, it would have been difficult for me to walk; I was shaky and ungrounded. But I was also wearing my new brown suit and first pair of high heels— bought for the Homecoming football game. If I stumbled, my mother would be ashamed.

We sat in the front pews, too close to the four closed, cold metallic caskets. My mother cried softly and intermittently, clutching a white handkerchief embroidered by Grandma Clutter. Herbert's surviving daughters, my cousins Beverly and Eveanna, were supported on either side by the men who loved them. Vigilant policemen sat and stood among us, as did plainsclothes detectives from the Kansas Bureau of Investigation.

Although the minister, Rev. Leonard Cowan, knew the family well, his task was difficult. How could God have allowed this to happen? "The good purposes of God have been thwarted by sin and evil from the beginning of historical record," Cowan preached. He likened Jesus on the cross to Herbert and Bonnie, Kenyon and Nancy at the hands of their killers. He assured us that the family's unquestioning faith sustained them in their time of extremity. His words made no impression on me.

Afterwards, the great line of cars that had followed the hearses to the cemetery slowly returned to town. My aunts and uncles and other cousins came to the potluck dinner at the church. People ate, talked with one another, traded stories and memories; some even laughed. I knew few townspeople and was glad to be invisible. When someone did speak to me, I tried to find something "normal" to say, though I wasn't sure what normal might be. Beverly and Eveanna seemed at ease, visiting with friends and family they had known from birth. Herbert's family was rooted in community; we were not.

My sense of unreality deepened as my Kansas aunts, practical as always, decided we should go to Herbert's house, clean and get things Beverly would need to set up housekeeping when she got married.

I will never forget being in that house, at that time. The home that had always meant life, love and security was now a house of death.

In Nancy's room, my mother looked through her closet and drawers. *I don't think we should be doing this.* Nancy would not want her aunts looking through her things. I sat in a chair against the wall and gripped the seat. *I know we should not be here.* At any moment I was afraid I'd start screaming. Stuck to the wall above Nancy's bed was a fragment of flesh and dried blood, overlooked by whoever did the first cleaning, and now overlooked by my mother. She was focused, like a detective looking for clues. In triumph, she found Nancy's watch in a shoe in the closet—proof to her that the killers were strangers, burglars.

Was it a robbery? Apparently all that was missing was $40 and a transistor radio from Kenyon's room. Nancy's $2 for Sunday school remained in a church envelope on her bedside table as her attacker tied and gagged her. The rumored wealth that Uncle Herbert supposedly kept in a safe did not exist; his tortured death yielded nothing. Aunt Bonnie was a housewife, rich only in family and community.

The intruders did gain something: the power of life and death. And they wielded it with savage carelessness.

Three days after the funeral, Beverly and Vere were married. The wedding had been planned for Christmas, but the family was already gathered and Beverly had no place to come home to on school vacation.

The church seemed different this time, decorated for a celebration, though again filled with family friends and relatives. Beverly came down the aisle on the arm of her mother's brother, radiant in her long white gown. Waiting at the altar was Vere, handsome and strong. When they exchanged vows, love shone on their faces and brought light into the shadows. It was a fairy-tale wedding in the middle of a nightmare.

We drove back to Florida and I returned to school, shy and in turmoil. It felt wrong to take part in Homecoming—I was part of the "royalty"—as though nothing had happened. I asked my English teacher. She said I shouldn't disappoint others or myself by missing this honor. And so, a week after the funeral, I wore my ice-blue taffeta formal gown, sat on the back of a convertible and rode down Lemon Street in the parade, waving to onlookers as though I were still a real person. By that time, nothing felt real or right. No one spoke with me about what happened—not at school, not at home.

Twenty-five years after the deaths, I began to face the past, hoping that doing so would help me heal from that trauma and other losses. For the first time, I read Truman Capote's *In Cold Blood.* I was angry and disappointed. The Clutters became cardboard figures, hardly more than a backdrop for Capote's sympathetic depiction of the killers. I felt powerless to correct his version of the truth. In the face of Capote's fame, I would have been as invisible as I was in Kansas in 1959.

Nonetheless, for me, Uncle Herbert and Aunt Bonnie, Kenyon and Nancy continue to live, both in memory and in the strengths they engendered in us.[28]

The funeral that Edwards attended is described in *In Cold Blood*, as are references to and information about the wedding of Beverly Clutter and Vere English that followed soon after the burial in order to avoid inconveniencing the numerous friends and relatives who had traveled to Holcomb for the funeral of her parents. "Beverly was engaged to a young biology student, of whom her father very much approved; invitations to the wedding, scheduled for Christmas Week, were already printed,"[29] Capote writes. Later, he refers to the devastating reality that a funeral preceded a wedding: "Indeed, the better part of those on the Clutters' Thanksgiving guest list were either telephoned or telegraphed, and the majority set forth at once for what was to be a family reunion not around a groaning board but at the graveside of a mass burial."[30] Capote cites the headline "Clutter-English Vows Given in Saturday Ceremony" and adds, "Miss Clutter had worn white, and the wedding, a full-scale affair...had been 'solemnized at the First Methodist Church'—the church in which, three days earlier, the bride had formally mourned her parents, her brother, and her younger sister."[31] Capote quotes from the *Garden City Telegram*: "Vere and Beverly had planned to be married at Christmastime. The invitations were printed and her father had reserved the church for that date. Due to the unexpected tragedy and because of the many relatives being here from distant places, the young couple decided to have their wedding Saturday."[32]

On the other side of the continuum is another person willing to talk about his connection to the crime, Donald Cullivan of Reading, Massachusetts, a friend of Perry Smith's who served with him in the Army. Capote

---

[28]Edwards, "The Rest of the Story." The author continues to write about her family and her experiences in Kansas. Edwards and *Desert Exposure* maintain full copyrights, and the article appears here courtesy of the magazine.

[29]Capote, *In Cold Blood*, 7.

[30]Ibid., 71.

[31]Ibid., 106-107.

[32]Ibid., 107.

mentions Cullivan several times in *In Cold Blood*, especially with respect to Smith's isolation and self-hatred. For example, Smith tells Capote he is "like somebody covered with sores. Somebody only a big nut would have anything to do with."[33] Into the void came a letter from Cullivan, which Capote quotes in its entirety.[34] References also include Cullivan's attendance at the trial.[35] One descriptive section is particularly important here:

> Many observers of the trial scene were baffled by the visitor from Boston, Donald Cullivan. They could not quite understand why this staid young Catholic, a successful engineer who had taken his degree at Harvard, a husband and the father of three children, should choose to befriend an uneducated, homicidal half-breed whom he knew but slightly and had not seen for nine years....[36]

Cullivan has never made excuses for his former friend's horrendous acts, but after Smith's arrest, Cullivan reached out to him because of their military service. "There was this fellow who just got back from Korea. He and I had bunks together. It was Perry Smith. He was a really likable guy, smiling, happy all the time,"[37] said Cullivan in a 2015 article titled "Fifty Years Later, *In Cold Blood* Still Fresh for Oak Bluffs Man." While looking through *Time* magazine, Cullivan saw a story about the Clutter murders and the arrest of Hickock and Smith in Las Vegas, Nevada, December 30, 1959. "I wrote him a letter. My letter is verbatim in Capote's book. It was kind of a preachy letter. I was going to save his soul. It was meant to be an act of Christian charity,"[38] he said.

Cullivan is an important figure in the nonfiction novel because although he did not know Smith well, he was motivated by his faith and his compassion for a fellow soldier to be a character witness for Smith. In the article, Cullivan said, "It was all on my nickel. Here I am a junior engineer, with two children and a third on the way, not making a hell of a lot of money. I felt it was a Christian obligation. We didn't tell anybody in the family,

---

[33]Ibid., 260.

[34]Ibid., 260-61.

[35]Ibid., 280, 288-92, 296.

[36]Ibid., 288.

[37]Steve Myrick, "Fifty Years Later, *In Cold Blood* Still Fresh for Oak Bluffs Man," *Vineyard Gazette*, 24 September 2015, web (accessed 14 August 2018).

[38]Ibid.

or any friends."[39] He later maintained correspondence with Smith while Smith waited on Death Row at the Kansas State Penitentiary. Additionally, Cullivan knew and liked Truman Capote and met both Harper Lee and photographer Richard Avedon through the popular author. Cullivan's compassion for others is obvious when he says, "Where would I be, if I had a drunken mother who was a prostitute, and an overbearing father who was a tyrant, two [siblings] that committed suicide? Where would I be?"[40]

Researchers who study inmate case files at the Kansas Historical Society discover troubling documents. One of the notes in Smith's file reads, "Time Smith arrived in Warehouse—12:55. Time Trap Sprung: 1:02. Time Pronounced Dead: 1:19" (Perry Edward Smith Inmate Case File No. 438). Just as startling is a handwritten letter to Smith from Cullivan dated April 11, 1965. The letter did not arrive before Smith was executed April 14, 1965. It reads:

Dear Perry:

Your letter mentioned a new date set for April 14—if so, this letter will be too late. It seems, however, that I've rather come to depend upon indefinite postponements. I guess it's this reluctance to face up to the fact that one day your appeals will all have been denied which has prompted me to write you anyway.

Life has been so terribly good to me—and I have been so manifestly undeserving of such goodness—that I sometimes feel that I'm storing up a great pile of debts which I shall be called upon, some dreary future day, to make payment.

I suppose you can discuss, theoretically, the pros and cons of execution vs. life (as it affects the prisoner himself, I mean) but I expect the gift of life is precious (and while hope exists) that very few actually prefer to die. I know the choice is not a very pleasant one.

I'm starting to finish up my work here as we'll be returning to the States the first week of May. I'm going to teach a special one month water supply course in June at the University of North Carolina and we'll be going to Dacca, Pakistan, in early September. I've been traveling quite a bit lately, as usual. Last week I was in Rio again and, for the first time, São Paolo. The latter city has a population of over 5 million and is really impressive.

---

[39]Ibid.
[40]Ibid.

I appreciate your last letter very much. I too have enjoyed your friendship and I hope I hear from you again.

Sincerely,

Don Cullivan (Perry Edward Smith Inmate Case File No. 384)

The phrases "too late" and "last letter" are reminders that human beings do not control time, a theme central to *In Cold Blood*. In the nonfiction novel, Capote meticulously describes details in the lives of the Clutters, Nancy Ewalt, Susan Kidwell, Bobby Rupp, and others. In "The Last to See Them Alive," Capote alludes to the Bible verse "Take ye heed, watch and pray: for ye know not when the time is."[41] Biblical scholars often refer to the verse from Mark 13:33 as a warning to Christians to be alert to instructions from God or even to anticipate the second coming of Christ. Capote, on the other hand, injects this particular verse, which he sees on a bookmark in Bonnie Clutter's room, as a way to heighten one of his central themes: no matter how diligent they are, human beings cannot predict what will occur. On April 20, 1965, Warden S. H. Crouse wrote to Cullivan, "Your letter of April 11, 1965, addressed to Perry Edward Smith arrived too late. The execution was carried out, as scheduled, early on the morning of April 14, 1965" (Perry Edward Smith Inmate Case File No. 383).

Cullivan was a union carpenter for two years between high school and his freshman year at Northeastern University. Delaying his college graduation were the three years he spent in the Army as a heavy equipment operator. In 1956 Cullivan graduated from Northeastern with a degree in civil engineering, and in 1957, Cullivan earned a master's degree in environmental engineering from Harvard. Beginning what he describes in a September 2, 2016, e-mail message as a "long and interesting professional career as an international engineer," Cullivan worked in Bangladesh, Brazil, and Thailand for seven years. In total, Cullivan worked in almost 100 countries, including Russia. When he was seventy-nine years old, he completed his last assignment, this time in Tajikistan. In addition to his other interests, Cullivan was a pilot for fifteen years. Cullivan and his wife Lorraine have five children and lived on Martha's Vineyard for almost thirty years before moving to Winchester, Massachusetts.

The following essay, "Truman Capote and Perry Smith," addresses Cullivan's connection to Avedon, Capote, Lee, and Smith. It is included

---

[41]Capote, *In Cold Blood*, 30.

here in its entirety, altered only for stylistic consistency. Cullivan offered his friendship to Smith during what he described in a September 3, 2016, e-mail message as the "lowest point" in the condemned man's life. Having taken copious notes—and numerous photographs—throughout his life, Cullivan is working on a memoir.

"Truman Capote and Perry Smith"

"Twisted legs, twisted mind" is what Perry Smith wrote on the back of the picture taken of his badly damaged legs, following the crash of his motorcycle in early 1952. When we were fellow soldiers at Ft. Lewis, Washington, Perry had borrowed my leather jacket before I went home on leave for Christmas of 1951. He was wearing it when he slid on a sandy patch and all but killed himself. After the crash, he walked with a limp and was in nearly constant pain. This led to his lifetime habit of chewing several aspirins at a time.

Perry Smith served in the Korean War. I was an enlisted man in the Army, trained as a heavy equipment operator, stationed in Ft. Lewis. In the fall of 1951, Perry had been assigned to our outfit to spend his remaining time before discharge. Like me, he was a tractor-trailer driver and operator of heavy equipment, such as bulldozers, road graders and cranes. We had adjacent bunks and often worked together. On one occasion, we were each driving a large tractor-trailer truck carrying bulldozers to a distant site, on a very cold day. These trucks were spartan units with no heaters, and it was very cold crossing the Cascade Mountains. Before this trip, Perry showed me that he had used metal cutters to open a hole to allow the engine heat to pass into his cabin. I, in my freezing truck, worried he might be charged with destruction of Army property. He, in his warm one, never had a care. He was an excellent driver and equipment operator, always with a smile, and good company. We didn't socialize much away from the Army base. I may have been among a very small number of soldiers who did not drink until several years later, so I tended to remain on base and read.

Even though he left school after the third grade, he had an extensive vocabulary and extraordinarily good penmanship. He also wrote poetry and was a talented artist. He came from a family as broken as is possible to imagine. His father, John (Tex) Smith, of Irish ancestry, was a tough old bird, a non-drinker, who ended up kicking the teenage Perry out of "Trapper's Den Lodge," the proposed motel they were building in Juneau, Alaska. One freezing winter night they had a knockdown fight, after which he threw Perry and his clothing out the door, and locked it behind him. (Tex committed suicide when he was 92.) Perry's mother, Florence (Flo) Buckskin, was an Indian with a serious drinking problem. She was also a prostitute. Separated from her husband and family, she was living in San Francisco where she died an early death from an alcohol overdose. Perry was 13. After her death, her four children were placed in an orphanage. Perry said they were badly mistreated there.

Perry had a brother and two sisters. His brother and one sister committed suicide. His other sister was married and had children. Living a normal life, she distanced herself from the family madness. Perry joined the Merchant Marine when he was sixteen. Because Perry was only 5 feet 6 inches tall, one wonders how he survived on ships at sea for long periods with crews of grizzled seamen in their thirties and forties. He was only twenty years old when he joined the Army later.

I learned later that during his four years in the Army, much of it in Korea, he spent extensive time in the stockade for carousing and fighting. I knew little of his life after he left the Army, from about age twenty-five to thirty-one, at the time of the murders of the Clutter family members. He drifted a lot, engaged in small-scale theft, and had an arrest record. He dreamed of finding buried treasure and appeared to have no plans for his life. It was during this period that he met Dick Hickock, when both were in jail in the Kansas State Penitentiary in 1959. It was there that they heard from a fellow prisoner about a "rich farmer" in Garden City.

I finished my three years in the Army in early 1954. I returned to college and earned degrees in engineering. In 1960 I was married with two children and working in Boston as a consulting engineer on water supply projects. One Sunday afternoon at my house in the suburbs, I was reading the January 18, 1960, issue of *Time* magazine. It included a very brief account of the capture of two men charged with the murder of four members of the Herbert Clutter family in western Kansas on November 15, 1959. The article included small pictures of the alleged murderers. With shock, I recognized one of them—my Army buddy, Perry Smith. The other man was Dick Hickock, from Olathe, Kansas. After the initial rush from this news, I could not stop thinking of the tragedy and of Perry. That afternoon I wrote him a letter. He later replied, "Dear Don, Hell yes, I remember Don Cullivan." Shortly after that, I received a letter from his court-appointed lawyer, Arthur Fleming, asking me to come to Garden City, Kansas, as a "character" witness. No funds were available for my expenses. I was a junior engineer with two children and a third on the way, so money was tight in our family. Nevertheless, I felt an obligation to go to Kansas, so I paid for my flight and all my expenses in Garden City. I also had to use vacation time for the week I would be gone.

I first met Truman Capote at the trial of the murderers of the Clutter family in western Kansas in March 1960. Truman's *In Cold Blood* has become that rare phenomenon, a book written about fifty years ago that is still being taught in college courses today and is mentioned over and over again in newspapers and magazines. Some of these articles point out alleged factual errors in Truman's book, mostly on minor matters. In our exchanges, Truman asked if he could use my own name in his book. I said yes. He also said that, as the writer, he could not appear in the book, but he needed to convey the essence of his involvement in some manner. He asked if it was possible for him to use me as his surrogate in some such cases. Again, I said yes. However, he never did so, as the references about me in the book were all related to my activities. In fact, many of these were experiences Truman and I shared.

The trial began on Tuesday, March 22, 1960. I flew from Boston to Wichita on Wednesday the 23rd, where I boarded a bus for Garden City that left well after midnight. I slept most of that five-and-one-half-hour bus ride on the 24th and arrived in Garden City just before 7 a.m. Mr. Fleming, Perry's lawyer, met my bus and took me to the quirky Windsor Hotel. A few hours later, he drove me to the courthouse and whispered to the bailiff, who took me inside the railings to a folding chair, directly beside Perry, where we were able to whisper to each other during the trial. Today, one can only wonder at the lack of security and at how casual things were at that time and under those circumstances. The prosecuting attorneys, aided materially by written confessions from the two defendants, had an airtight case, which they stretched out for four days. At the next break that morning of Thursday the 24th, a small man with a distinctive manner of speech introduced himself to me with these words "My name is Truman Capote. I'm a reporter for *The New Yorker* magazine, and I wondered what you are doing at the trial?" After describing my connection to Perry, I asked, "Didn't you write *The Muses Are Heard*?" He beamed, and the two of us hit it off from that time on. The next day, on the walk leading to the courthouse, I was just behind two local farmers in overalls. We were just a few yards behind Truman, who was wearing a wide-brimmed hat and a colorful cape. He had a jaunty, prancing walk. Truman was not one to hide his gay-ness. One of the farmers turned to his friend and said, "Now, don' he look jess like a banty rooster?" I had to admit that he did.

The trial recessed for the weekend on the afternoon of Friday the 25th. I had come to know Perry's jailers, Deputy Sheriff Wendle Meier and his wife Josie. They had an apartment on the right side of the third floor that also contained a single jail cell for women prisoners. Josie was responsible for feeding any prisoners jailed there. The rest of the floor housed cells for any male prisoners. Dick Hickock was out in the main jail room, while Perry was in the single "woman's" cell. They separated the two to prevent them from coordinating their statements. The Meiers invited me to come by and talk to Perry that evening, where Wendell locked me in the cell with Perry.

I talked with Perry from 8:30 to 10:30 p.m. on Friday, March 25. He had a hard time getting started. Perry asked me, "How about a cup of water?" He handed me a cup with a broken handle and we both went over to the faucet and filled our cups with lukewarm water. We returned to his cot and sat, side by side, just inches apart, on the edge and hunched forward, heads close so we could speak in confidence. He then started talking, and continued for almost two hours, with just an occasional question from me. This is what I wrote the next day, of what Perry said to me that evening:

He started talking about the night of the Clutter murders. He said he didn't like the setup from the time they got there. It was too open, and there was another house nearby. The story essentially was what Perry had written in an unsigned statement. Al Dewey, the Kansas Bureau of Investigation officer, had just testified at the trial about this statement. Dick went in the house first because he knew the layout. Perry said they were badly prepared. For example, he said they should have worn sneakers instead of boots, because the sound from the boots as they walked on the wood floors sounded deafening to him. They went upstairs and heard the Clutters in the bathroom. He said the family probably heard them but were too scared to come out. They looked for things to steal upstairs, but in order to make a complete search, they decided to tie up the family. First, they took Mrs. Clutter (Bonnie) to her bedroom and tied her there. Perry then took Mr. Clutter (Herb) down to the cellar, and later the boy (Kenyon). I asked Perry why they separated them so widely. He said they were afraid that one of them might crawl over and untie another. When Perry returned, Dick was talking to the girl (Nancy). Perry never mentioned their names. He referred to them only as "the boy," "the girl," "Mr. C," and "Mrs. C." They then withdrew from her hearing, and Dick told Perry he was going to rape her. Perry got very angry at that, also as reported in Al Dewey's testimony, and told Dick that he wasn't going to touch her.

Perry said there was no thought of violence at that time. He said they tied up the family so they could carry out a detailed search, but they never manhandled them. After a long and unsuccessful search—no safe, and less than $50 in cash—they held a whispered conversation down in the basement. Perry says he was calm but very angry at Dick because things had turned out so badly. He said that Dick had been boasting about how he was going to rob and kill the Clutters. Perry said he knew a lot of the guys up at Lansing (the state prison) had heard Dick say that he was going to splatter hair all over the walls. Perry said this because of his anger at how things had turned out, a result, Perry believed, of Dick's inefficiency and Dick's boasting. Perry now started to taunt Dick. Perry said, "Well, what are we going to do now?" Dick: "I don't know. What do you think we should do?" Perry: "Do you have any qualms? You know what will happen if they identify us. It won't be a short stretch. It'll be ten or fifteen years." Dick: "Yeah, I know." Perry says he was trying to get Dick to say, "Yeah, let's kill them." Then, Perry said, he planned to talk him out of it, but Dick didn't say anything, and Perry said he kept getting angrier. Perry then said he decided to go over to Mr. Clutter and pretend to kill him, just to see what Dick would do. Perry kneeled down with difficulty because of the pain in his legs, knife in hand. Then, he said, right up to that point, he still had no violent intentions.

He said it all then started boiling up in him—the fiasco of the results, the frustrations, and his anger at Dick. At that point, he said, he acted on all these things by striking out at Mr. Clutter, as though he were the embodiment of all Perry's torments. He stuck the knife in Mr. Clutter's throat. Dick looked on in silence as Perry rose. Sounds came from Mr. Clutter's throat. Perry told Dick, "He's suffering. We can't leave him that way." He then gave the knife to Dick and told him, "Come on now. You've got to do your part." Then Dick knelt down and repeated what Perry had done. Perry said he thought Dick just put the knife in the same wound. At any rate, the sounds continued. They then talked about shooting him. Perry said he believes Dick would have done it without question, but Perry took the shotgun, held it next to Mr. Clutter's head, and fired. He said there was a bright blue flash from the muzzle, and by this light, he saw the skull split apart. Perry said the noise was deafening, and he couldn't imagine how the family in the neighboring home didn't hear it.

After that, they ran out of the room, but Dick remembered to pick up the expended shell casings. Perry says he remembers thinking that now they all had to go—the penalty for four is no worse than for one. He said he was in such a state that he just ran from room to room—Dick right there holding the flashlight, with no other lights on in the house—and shot the other three. After he had shot Mrs. Clutter, they headed down the stairs, Dick in front. Perry said that he came awfully close to shooting Dick then. Perry said that Dick had so filled Perry's mind with the idea of leaving no witnesses, he thought Dick had to go, too. In response to my question, Perry said that he got along just fine with Dick all the time they were together afterwards. At one point, while describing the killings as we were together in the cell, he laughed. Then he caught himself and said he knew that was a hell of a thing to be laughing about, but that he never had any feelings of compassion for his victims or remorse for what he had done. He told me he tried to feel sorry for them, but he just didn't.

I met Truman and his two friends the next day, Saturday, March 26, at the office of a local photographer, Jack Curtis, who had taken quite a few photos of Perry and Dick, and of the Clutter house and farm buildings. Truman, Nelle Harper Lee and Richard Avedon were talking about the legal aspects of the trial. Nelle talked so knowledgeably about legal matters that I asked her if she was a lawyer. (I later learned that she had legal training. George Plimpton's book on *Capote* [1997] said she completed law school but never practiced and that she was the daughter of a lawyer.) She replied, "Ah'm a rhattah." I started to ask her again before I realized that in her part of Alabama, a "rhattah" was a "writer." I suspect she was laying on the accent a bit for the "not-with-it" proper Bostonian. It was at this meeting that I learned that Nelle had just written *To Kill a Mockingbird*. The book is largely autobiographical, and she and Truman were both from Monroeville, Alabama...Richard Avedon, who I later learned was a famous fashion photographer, had worked with Truman in a coffee-table-style book, *Observations*, published in 1959. Avedon had expected to provide pictures related to the Clutter family murders. While he took quite a few pictures, the only ones Truman used were the pairs of eyes of Perry and Dick that are in the frontispiece. Truman told me later that Avedon was quite upset about this limited use of his photos.

Later that Saturday morning I met with Perry in his cell from about 10 a.m. to 1 p.m. As I walked up to the entrance of the courthouse on my way to see Perry, I saw a piece of paper flutter down from Perry's third-floor cell. It fell in the freshly watered garden up against the building. It was a note from Perry asking me to get him a bottle of Fitches Shampoo and a jar of Wildroot Cream Oil. These were popular products for men's hair care at that time. Perry's hair was always heavily slicked. Up in his cell, Perry told me he was feeding a small bird that came to his barred window, overlooking the front of the courthouse. He said he loved to watch quietly as the bird ate. He said that when the bird flew off, he pictured himself as the bird, with the capacity to slip through the bars and fly away to freedom.

Truman invited me to drop by the Warren Hotel that afternoon for a chat. The Warren Hotel was quite upscale from the "old frontier" style of the Windsor Hotel where I was staying. Truman had a two-bedroom suite there. The Warren no longer exists, but the ancient Hotel Windsor was completely remodeled some fifty years later. Truman was alone and bare-chested when I arrived. Truman was thirty-five years old at that time and he was at the top of his game, both physically and mentally. It was a chilly March day, and while the room heat was cranked up, the toplessness seemed a bit much. He was bare-chested in another way, in that his chest was completely without hair. It seemed a bit strange, but our talk was innocent of anything untoward, and I never asked him why he was shirtless. Just possibly this was something simple and rational, like the room being too hot, and he felt more comfortable without a shirt. Maybe!

He offered me caviar and vodka, which he had set out. He had a small refrigerator. The caviar was in a small silver bowl, and the vodka was iced. It was a lovely presentation. Unfortunately, I have no notes of that meeting. I'm sure it was mostly about the trial and its progress. That was also the time I told him the details of my Friday night meeting with Perry, and Perry's description of the night the Clutters were murdered.

I was awakened by a phone call at about 11 later that Saturday evening, from a man with a deep and "old" voice. He identified himself as Mr. W.L. Gooding, of Modoc, Kansas, about thirty-five miles north of Garden City. He said he was a farmer, and that, as I was a friend of Perry Smith, he told me he had information that could help Perry. He wanted me to come out to his home and see him now. He suggested that I ask Dick Hickock's father for a ride. I told him I didn't know Mr. Hickock and had no intention of going anywhere at that time. I did agree to meet him at my hotel at 3 p.m. the following day.

I went to the 9 a.m. Mass at St. Dominic church that Sunday morning of March 26. Following Mass, I took a long walk around the town, returned to the hotel, and then went over to the Meiers' at 11:30 a.m. in time for "dinner." "Am I early?" I asked. Wendle, in slacks and T-shirt, drawled, "Little bit," but he invited me up. I talked to the Meiers for about twenty minutes, and Wendle asked me if I wanted to see Perry. Naturally, I did, but I didn't want to ask because I realized the delicacy of Wendle's position. Officially, as undersheriff, he had rules to follow and was answerable to Sheriff Earl Robinson for any breach of those rules. As human beings, he and Josie were warm and loving people, and clearly had taken a liking to Perry the person, as opposed to Perry the prisoner and accused murderer.

When I went into Perry's cell, it was just noon. It was fairly warm and sunny, as it was most of the time I spent in Kansas, and the cell was in the condition it was always in—clean and orderly. Perry mopped the floor several times a day. The blanket on his bed was stretched tightly enough to bounce a nickel, a test Army sergeants used to check how well our bunks had been made. His books were neatly lined up on the wide sill of the only window, and his prized possessions—his collection of maps, letters, poems and clipped-out magazine articles—were laid out on top of the little wooden table in one corner. Perry had on his dungarees with several folds on the cuffs to adjust to the shortness of his legs, a clean white T-shirt, white socks, and shiny black shoes with tops that snapped down. We talked for about two hours—nothing much on crime or about the trial—when Wendle came in and asked if I'd rather eat with Perry in his cell, and, of course, I answered yes. It was now 3 p.m., and I realized I had made an appointment to see a local farmer who asked last night to meet with me. I left the courthouse and returned about an hour later.

When I got to my hotel, there were two messages. One was from Truman, who asked me to give him a call. He was confirming our plans to get together at his hotel later that evening. The other was a verbal message from the hotel clerk who told me that the woman behind me had been asking for me. This small, elderly woman said she was Mrs. Gooding, the wife of the man who called me the night before. At this point, Mr. Gooding came into the lobby. Like his wife, he was about in his seventies. He reminded me of a ponderous John Foster Dulles. We then went up to my room to talk. Mr. Gooding commended me for my actions in trying to help Perry. He said he knew that I was a "Cat-a-lic," and added that he knew a few who weren't bad fellows. He said he was a farmer and that he was convinced that Perry and Dick had not acted alone but had been paid to kill Herb Clutter. It was all, he said, a conspiracy by some unknown enemies who wanted to destroy the grain producer's cooperative, and of course, Herb was a ranking official in that organization.

They seemed such a nice old couple, but his reasoning was so illogical and based on such misinformation and wild flights of imagination that it was painful to listen to him. He gave me copies of letters he had written to the editors of the Garden City and Hutchinson newspapers that they had refused to print. I promised to bring this "startling new information" to the attention of the proper authorities, and I tried to get rid of them as it was now 4 p.m. They didn't want me to leave with them since "someone might be watching." After they went into the hotel's creepingly slow elevator on the second floor, I ran down the stairs and was on my way back to the Meiers' before the Goodings were halfway down to the lobby.

My haste was not entirely necessary, for Josie was still preparing the meal—a feast, as it turned out. I remained out in the kitchen, which was adjacent to Perry's cell but with a windowless wall between them. The door to Perry's cell faced a blank wall in the short hallway to the Meiers' home from the rest of the third floor. The cell door had a small barred window. I talked with the Meiers for a while. Josie's kitchen was clean and attractive, and the apartment was warm and moist from her work. There were red and yellow print curtains on the window, a bright, shiny canister set on the counter, and just-used utensils piled in the sink. It was about 4:30 p.m., and dinner was ready. Wendle opened the cell door and asked Perry to clear off the top of the table. The table wasn't much more than two feet square, and slightly rectangular. Wendle then gave Perry a tablecloth for it. This had to be one of Josie's best, as it was made of heavy material and looked rather new or rarely used. It was in a bright print pattern and had crisp folds. The door was left open while Wendle and I brought in the dishes Josie handed us. Perry stood at the back of the cell by the window, watching this unusual scene. His near-perpetual grin was broader than usual, and I felt myself wondering what his thoughts might be. I also thought that this might be the best day of the rest of his life.

On the table were tall graceful goblets, each full to the brim with milk. There was a tremendous platter of roast wild goose laden with rich, brown slices of breast meat, and both drumsticks. Separate plates were brought in containing steaming mashed potatoes, seasoned stuffing, and gravy. Green string beans and king-sized individual jellied salads followed. The last to come was a dish of hot biscuits, only seconds out of the oven, and wrapped in napkins. The heat of the biscuits was contained by the folds of a large cloth napkin, which overlapped on four corners. For dessert, Josie had freshly baked a cherry pie.

The entire setting—goblets, plates, platters and bowls, salt and pepper shakers, butter tray, silverware—obviously represented the very best table that Josie could set. And, what a table it was! It fairly groaned with the weight of all the food she had prepared. We sat down to eat. I asked Perry's permission to say grace before eating, and he willingly agreed. "Oh sure," he said. It was the simple, non-flowery grace typically used by Catholics.

The food was delicious—one of the finest meals I ever had. It was also the first goose I had ever eaten. Perry mentioned that the two meals a day (standard practice in Kansas prisons) he received at Garden City were so much better than anything he had ever eaten at any jail that there was just no comparison. Later I mentioned that there was food enough for half a dozen people. Perry snickered and said he had gained over ten pounds and still had so much left over that he sometimes flushed it down the toilet so that Josie wouldn't be offended that he didn't eat all she had given him.

Perry talked a while about how he and Dick used to eat on the road in their many travels. Walk into a grocery store, stuff something under their shirts (usually Dick, "he had a mania for it"), go back to the car and just wolf it down as they drove. "We used to eat like a couple of animals," he said. We finished the meal and Perry carefully washed and wiped all the dishes, spurning my offer of assistance. I handed all of them out to Josie and then we sat down to talk. I removed my shoes and sat cross-legged on the bed while Perry sat on the small wooden desk chair, shifting frequently in attempts to find a position more favorable to relieve the pain from his aching knees and hips (though never a word of complaint). It was during this meeting that he told me, once again, and for the last time, about the order of events at the Clutter home. It was dark when Wendle appeared and suggested that our visit end. Perry said he was tired and would go right to bed. Normally lights were turned out at 10, but when he wanted to get to sleep earlier, he would take the broom by the handle and press the bristles around the single light bulb that was mounted on the ceiling, some nine feet above the floor. Then, by exerting sufficient pressure on the broom and twisting it, he was able to succeed in unscrewing it enough to break the contact. I said goodnight to Perry, then the Meiers. I thanked them for the evening, and Wendle walked me down to the front door of the courthouse, which he unlocked to let me out. Looking at my watch as I walked down the exterior courthouse steps, I saw that it was just 9 o'clock.

After I left the courthouse, I walked over to meet Truman at his hotel, as agreed earlier. I was about two hours late for this meeting. Truman had invited me to meet at the restaurant at his hotel, the Warren. Truman was with his friends, Nelle Harper Lee and Richard Avedon, both of whom I had met the day before. They had finished dinner some time before and now were having a second round of drinks. We were seated at a table in the restaurant. When I showed up, Truman, who knew that I was meeting with Perry, said: "I pictured you as stone cold dead, stretched out on the floor of the cell." I remember turning down an invitation for a drink as I was fasting from liquor during Lent. Nelle, as everyone called her, was sitting beside me...Avedon had very little to say that evening, or the day before. At the end of the year, I received a New Year's greeting from Jack Curtis, the photographer in whose room we met the day before, in his office at the *Garden City Telegram*. He wrote that he hadn't yet read *Mockingbird*, but was looking forward to reading a book written by the lady who created a tomato-based drink she called the "Bloody Clutter."

The trial, which had started on Tuesday March 22, resumed on Monday the 28th, with the defense making its weak and futile arguments. I lasted only a few minutes on the witness stand that morning, as the prosecutor, Logan Green, interrupted my few opening comments, shouting, "Objection! Irrelevant and immaterial." This was quickly sustained by Judge Roland Tate, and I stood down. The defense rested that same day. The trial ended the next day, Tuesday the 29th at 11:30 a.m., the day I had to leave. It took the jury only forty minutes to reach a unanimous verdict of guilty, on all counts. Perry and Dick were sentenced to death by hanging, the practice in Kansas at that time.

My bus to Wichita was scheduled to leave at 6:45 p.m. I finally was able to see Perry a little after 6. As I entered the Meiers' apartment, with his cell just to my right, Perry had a big grin, and said, referring to prosecutor Logan Green's comment at the trial, "No chicken-livered jurors, they!" He added, "Guess I'll have to start my neck-stretching exercises." Then, for about the first time since I had known him, the grin vanished completely and he dropped his eyes. The silence was awkward and heavy, but neither of us had much confidence in our ability to talk without our voices breaking. Perry and I finally managed a bit of small talk before the sheriff said our time was up. Just before I left, we grasped each other's hands through the small barred window on the door, and we both wept. It was the last time I saw him. I left the courthouse and just barely caught the bus back to Wichita for my flight home to Boston.

I was back in my home in Reading, Massachusetts, just north of Boston. Perry and I exchanged a half dozen letters before and after the trial, but shortly after he was transferred to the state prison in Lansing, Kansas, a new warden returned my letter to Perry, informing me that I was no longer on the list of persons allowed to write to Perry. This lasted for much of 1961 and 1962. However, Truman remained on the list and he kept me reasonably informed of Perry's status during this period. At one point, Perry went on a hunger strike and had to be force fed for quite some time. Shortly after this, Truman moved to the Costa Brava in Spain. His letters to me were largely requests for copies of certain things I had written to Perry, permission to quote from them and passing along news he thought would be of interest to me. He returned to the U.S. in June 1960, with stationery indicating his address as 70 Willow Street in Brooklyn.

By July, Truman was back in Spain. There is a gap in letters to or from Perry for almost a year, but in a letter dated November 1, 1961, Truman was writing from a condominium he said he had purchased in Verbier, Switzerland. In that letter, he said he was "still working on the book, which is now slightly more than half done." This letter had a long list of requests for information from me. He also said he was returning to Kansas to do a bit more research and to talk to Perry's sister in San Francisco. In that same letter, he wrote, "Nelle asked me the other day if I'd heard from you. I suppose you know her book won the Pulitzer Prize? Anyway, we both send you every greeting. Truman." In a letter to Truman dated December 4, 1962, I mentioned that our family was going to Brazil early in 1963 on a water project for the U.S. Agency for International Development (USAID). He replied on the 11th, telling me that he visited there ten years ago and had been to Rio, Bahia and Recife. I was to be stationed in Recife in the Northeast. In another interesting note he wrote, "I can't tell you much about Nelle's new book. It's a novel, and quite short. But she is *so* sensitive." He also said that his book was "perhaps 80 percent finished."

Now living and working in Recife, Brazil, I was still not on the list of those allowed to communicate with Perry. But in March 1963, the ban was finally lifted by a new warden. I was very busy with my work in Brazil and spent a lot of time traveling, as my territory of responsibility for conducting studies of water supply conditions and needs included the entire Northeast, an area about the size of France. It bothers me now that I wrote Perry only a half dozen times, while he wrote me some seventeen letters. My letters were largely descriptions of what I was doing and places where I worked, all of which fascinated Perry, ever the one for travel to foreign lands and adventures he pictured for himself.

I was nearing completion of my two-year assignment in Northeast Brazil, working on water projects funded by USAID. Shortly before returning to the U.S. in May 1965, I read a brief article in the *Brazil Herald* that Perry Smith and Dick Hickock had been hanged in Kansas on April 14, 1965. In the last letter I received from Perry, he mentioned this as the next date set for his execution, after he had survived several earlier "appointments." While this ending was expected, the reality of the news still came as a shock.

On our return from Brazil, we took our four children to the World's Fair being held in New York City in the summer of 1965. We stayed with my wife Lorraine's sister who lived with her husband on Long Island. While there, I received a call from Truman, asking that we join him that evening for dinner and talks. At his suggestion, we met at the 21 Club, a famous Manhattan restaurant at 21 West 52nd Street. Truman talked Lorraine into having roast pheasant under glass, while he had a "21 Hamburger."

After dinner, we took a cab to El Morocco, a very "in" nightclub at that time, and another favorite of Truman's. Lorraine started to follow a waiter to a distant table when Truman took her arm and said, "My dear, *those* tables are for the nobodies. Tonight we are *somebodies!*" At that point, a waiter appeared with a postage stamp-sized table over his head and placed it on a corner of—and *inside*—the tiny dance floor.

Another waiter followed with three small chairs. It's amazing what fame can achieve. We had another drink or two at El Morocco, and then Truman took us to "Trudy Heller's," a popular disco at 418 Avenue of the Americas, on the southeast corner at Ninth Street. This was in Greenwich Village, and it was another favorite of Truman's. Lorraine danced with him several times there, and she told me later that he was a very smooth dancer. At the end of the evening, at our last watering hole, whose name I can't recall, and with quite a few drinks behind us, the three of us were sitting close together at a tiny table. Truman described his witnessing Perry's execution. He hunched his shoulders and stared down at the table. Then he looked up and said, "What wasted lives—murders, alcoholics, suicides, and an execution." With tears flowing, he looked right at me and said, in words burned in my soul, "*I loved that boy!*"

That's not a moment I'm likely ever to forget. We ended up at a mansion in Brooklyn at 70 Willow Street in the early morning hours. He apologized for all the sheets covering the furniture and explained that the house was closed up, as he was "not at home," having moved to the Hamptons for the summer. This house in Brooklyn was the subject of one of his essays, "A House on the Heights." I later learned the house was not his, but he had access to a small room in it. He had clearly commandeered the luxury living room of the absent owner for the night. Afterward, Lorraine and I drove slowly and carefully back to Long Island. It was a night full of lasting memories. It was also the last time I saw Truman.

In his next to last letter to me dated January 10, 1965, Perry wrote, "Herb Caen of the *San Francisco Chronicle* reports that Capote was seen in one of our favorite restaurants, La Bourgogne, carefully guarding a big package containing the proofs of his new book, *In Cold Blood*." Perry added no comments on the title. He had written Truman years earlier, saying he heard that the name of the book Truman was writing was *In Cold Blood*. Truman denied it at that time, but Perry was not surprised at reading the name of the book in Caen's article. Herb Caen's daily column of local goings-on and insider gossip, social and political happenings appeared in the *San Francisco Chronicle* for almost sixty years into the 1990s.

The last letter I received from Perry was dated March 21, 1965, about three weeks before his execution. His handwriting had deteriorated from the days of our early correspondence. He said he had not been feeling well. Here are a few items from that letter:

Well, one of these times you're going to write and there won't be any more response from your old (I feel it too!) Army buddy. We've gotten another date set for April 14th, and we had one a couple of weeks ago—February 18th, and your letter (was) dated February 22nd, so I was fortunate to be in a condition to read it, and to be writing now.

He mentioned the picture I had sent him of my son Paul when he was about five years old, that he promised to use as the basis for one of his paintings. He apologized about not completing it and hoped the delay would be temporary until he was once again given permission to do artwork.

In his final paragraph, he said, "Well, I haven't been well at all and am still suffering from ailments almost a year old since my clavicle and cervical vertebrae areas are swollen, tender and painful, and I feel very debilitated. Best wishes and regards—Always, Perry."

Perry was right. The last letter I wrote to him came after he was executed, and it was returned to me.

I received a letter dated April 27, 1965, from Chaplain Jim Post. He wrote, "The letter is being written to you as one of the last wishes of Perry Smith before he met his Creator on the gallows at Kansas State Penitentiary, April 14th, at 1:20 a.m."

Truman was a witness at the executions. Near the end of his book, he reported what he saw and heard. Dick Hickock was hanged first at 12:41 a.m. Perry followed and, according to Truman, these are Perry's last words before he was hanged: "I think it's a helluva thing to take a life in this manner. I don't believe in capital punishment, morally or legally. Maybe I had something to contribute, something—" His assurance faltered; shyness blurred his voice, lowered it to a just audible level. Then, after he recovered, in a barely audible voice he added, "It would be meaningless to apologize for what I did. Even inappropriate. But I do. I apologize" *(In Cold Blood* 340).

Truman wrote in his book that they put a hood on him, opened the trap, and it was followed by "the thud-snap that announces a rope-broken neck." The time was 1:19 a.m., April 14, 1965.[42]

---

[42]Donald Cullivan, "Truman Capote and Perry Smith." The author continues to write about his experiences with Truman Capote, Harper Lee, and Perry Smith. He has updated the version of "Truman Capote and Perry Smith" published here and maintains full copyrights. The essay appears here courtesy of Donald Cullivan.

Although Cullivan figures prominently in the second half of *In Cold Blood*, a voice missing entirely from the nonfiction novel belongs to Ralph McClung, who served on the jury during the 1960 trial of Richard Hickock and Perry Smith and whose role was reprised in the 1967 Richard Brooks film *In Cold Blood*. McClung was born May 16, 1927, in Elkhart, Kansas, and he and his wife Ann reared six children in Garden City, Kansas. When McClung died November 2, 2011, the following news story appeared in the Longmont, Colorado, newspaper. Reporter Scott Rochat of the *Longmont Times-Call* writes:

LONGMONT—Ralph McClung was a family man. A pharmacist. And, for a short time, a part of one of the last capital-punishment cases in Kansas.

McClung, who died Nov. 2, was juror on the Clutter murder case, the 1959 killings immortalized in Truman Capote's book "In Cold Blood." In March 1960, Dick Hickock and Perry Smith were convicted of killing Herb and Bonnie Clutter and two of their children during a bungled robbery in the Clutters' Holcomb, Kan., home.

Hickock and Smith were sentenced to death and executed in 1965. In later interviews, McClung said he never regretted the result.

"Cancers in society have to be eliminated," he told the Lawrence Journal-World in a 2004 interview. "They were always losers. What do you do with someone like that?"

McClung's funeral was Monday in Longmont. He was 84.

Born in Elkhart, Kan., McClung trained as a pharmacist in Dodge City, where he met and married his wife. The couple lived in nearby Garden City—just a few miles from Holcomb—from around 1955 until 1972, when they moved with their family to Colorado, where he had been hired by the King Soopers chain.

His son Tom McClung of Colorado Springs, who was 3 years old at the time of the trial, remembered his dad as a loving man who often worked 12-hour days and bred independence in his children from an early age.

"From the moment we were born, when he was feeding us, he'd put our hands on the bottle and clasp his hand around ours," Tom McClung remembered. "He was saying 'Kid, you're going to hold your own bottle sooner than you think.'"

Ralph McClung's role on the jury would be a brief one. The case took one week to try in court, after which the jury deliberated for 40 minutes before reaching its guilty verdict.

Curiously, McClung would get to come back for a second go-around of sorts. He and several other jurors were picked to play themselves in the film version of "In Cold Blood," released in 1967 and starring Robert Blake, Scott Wilson and John Forsythe (all of whom McClung got autographs from).

"It was actually losing him money," Tom McClung said with a chuckle. "He had to leave his pharmacy in town to go film the movie trial. But it was so much fun, he thought it was worth it."

He also remembered a 2005 University of Nebraska coffee-table book that compared another juror on the trial, the one who had had mixed feelings for years after the case concluded, with his father's more resolute stance toward Hickock and Smith.

"He was kind; he was a family man," Tom McClung said. "But they were bad men."[43]

In Cold Blood means many things to many people. To a few, it remains the story of a house and the people who inhabited it and the ones who drive past it and remember. The Clutters were its first residents, followed by Robert (Bob) Byrd, who rarely stayed in the house and offered it to the movie crew that used it to film *In Cold Blood* in 1967. Byrd committed suicide elsewhere, and the house again went on the market. Leonard Mader, who had worked the property, talked with his wife Donna, and the two of them decided it would provide the space they needed for a growing family. In 1990, they purchased what always would be known as the "Clutter house."

In April 2005, Donna Mader talked with Crystal K. Wiebe of the *Lawrence Journal-World*. Like some other Holcomb and Garden City residents, she has not read *In Cold Blood*. The first five paragraphs of the news story are well worth inclusion:

Space is one of the things Donna Mader likes best about her house.

So much, in fact, that when she moved there in 1990, she hardly knew how to fill it all. Having been cramped with six children into a

---

[43]Scott Rochat, "Longmont Resident Ralph McClung Served on 'In Cold Blood' Jury." *Longmont Times-Call*, 8 November 2011, web (accessed 14 August 2018).

smaller place on the main highway for years, Donna simply didn't have enough stuff.

Possessions have a tendency to accumulate, though, and over time, Donna and her husband Leonard, a retired farmer with a broad face, have managed to settle in....

Along with the extra closets and bedrooms in this house came something else, a lingering history. The Maders own the house on Holcomb's southwestern edge, at the end of a long drive lined with dying Chinese elm trees, but the place will always be synonymous with another name: Clutter. The story of a family killed there 45 years ago draws strangers to the doorstep, driveway and telephone, constantly reminding the Maders that their home will never be only theirs.

The couple looks at the Clutter legacy with ambivalence. Although they resent their ever-violated privacy, they speak glowingly of the interesting people they've met because of it. In one instant, they talk of turning the house into a bed and breakfast; in another, they look forward to the prospect of selling it on eBay.

Respectful of the structure's original inhabitants, the Maders have maintained many of the house's original features and décor. Bench seats in the breakfast nook in the kitchen retain their original blue vinyl covering. Wood paneling on the dining room walls and the carpet the last owners laid over the oak floors have been removed. But the frame-and-brick house is hardly a shrine to an old tragedy. It's a warm setting for lives that go on, a place for a sprightly, graying farmer's wife to hold evening card parties and holiday noodle-making sessions with her grandchildren.[44]

Donna Mader is especially proud of what appears to be a "piece of wood...between two drawers" in the kitchen: "Too low to be a cutting board, it's a step for little girls who are too short to reach the highest cabinet," she tells Wiebe. Mader remembers the day of the murders, when she saw a hearse drive back and forth from the Clutter house. According to Wiebe, "Paranoia gripped Holcomb as word of the murders spread," and Donna Mader told her that "no one could sleep." Leonard Mader nailed their windows shut.[45]

---

[44]Crystal K. Wiebe, "In the End, Just a Home: A House with a History of Murder Finds New Life," *Lawrence Journal-World*, 6 April 2005, web (accessed 1 August 2018).
[45]Ibid.

In October 2006, Sue Wieland, daughter of Leonard and Donna Mader, offered the house for sale at auction. The asking price for the house and the seven-acre lot was $275,000. The description of the home reflects the respect the real estate company had for its legacy and the homage the realtors paid to Herbert Clutter, who designed the house:

> The Clutter home was built in 1948 on a tract of land known as the "River Valley Farm" west of Holcomb, Kansas. The home was designed with many custom features popular at the time. Original hardwood floors are throughout the main and second floor of this brick two-story home. The living room features a wood-burning fireplace and the formal dining room has a built-in china hutch. The sunny breakfast nook with dining bench boasts the original fabric. Block glass and ceramic tiles create a unique main floor bathroom.
>
> This beautiful home designed by Herb Clutter with family in mind offers 5 bedrooms, three baths, a large utility room, spacious kitchen and unfinished basement with a second fireplace. The utility room and basement provided ample space for the children to work on 4-H projects and school activities....[46]

The national historic home did not receive a high enough bid, and an article in the *Hutchinson News* suggests there were only two offers. "The house is just bigger than they need," Wieland said of her parents. "They're just wanting to scale down."[47] Wieland does not discount the appeal of the house for visitors to Holcomb, and the article suggests there are between five and twenty-five per weekend: "There are always cars, somebody coming down the lane. They just stop, look at the house, maybe take a picture, then they just leave."[48] Sadly, Leonard Mader died in 2007. Donna Mader also lost her sons, Wesley and Bryan Mader, in 2005 and 2014, respectively. All are buried in Valley View Cemetery in Holcomb, Kansas.

The stories of Robert (Bob) Rupp, Diana Selsor Edwards, Donald Cullivan, Ralph McClung, and Donna Mader are not postscripts; they are part of the fabric of a collective story about people devastated by an

---

[46]"The 'In Cold Blood' Murder House Is for Sale" (n.d.), web http://www2.ljworld.com/news/2005/apr/06/in_the_end/ (accessed 1 August 2018).

[47]"Few Bids Trickle in for Clutter Home Auction," *Garden City Telegram*, 20 September 2006, web (accessed 1 August 2018).

[48]Ibid.

unthinkable crime. They also are representative of other stories of other victims, oral histories that must be made public in order for readers of *In Cold Blood* to understand fully the breadth and reach of all crimes and other tragedies that change lives forever. Even for those such as Bob Rupp, Diane Selsor Edwards, and Donna Mader—who knew the Clutters and believe that Capote did not do them justice in his nonfiction novel—it remains important to acknowledge that Capote himself was a victim of the murders, finding himself lost and unmoored after his six-year pilgrimage toward what he hoped would be his first Pulitzer Prize. Instead, he was devastated by the murders and their aftermath, broken by a complicated relationship with a murderer and his eventual execution. Perhaps the end of Charles McGrath's essay expresses for all of them (and critics and readers as well) the emotions that remain after experiencing tragedy or reading about it in *In Cold Blood*, a particularly dark tale of unremitting loss, of "blooms beginning to fade":

> Capote loved tropical shadow and the spooky half light, just as he loved Venetian mists, rooming houses, cemetery statuary. From his descriptions, it's sometimes hard to tell one place from another—Capote's Brooklyn is practically indistinguishable from New Orleans—and that's because all his landscapes aspire in a way to the remembered South of his childhood. Even when he describes the present, many of the pieces feel nostalgic, and there hangs over almost all of them a scent of over-ripeness, of blooms beginning to fade.[49]

One of the aspects of nonfiction that draws readers is that the stories are real, the people are real, and the events take place in actual time and actual geographical locations. The problem, of course, is that no one—not even public figures such as Alvin Dewey—can foresee what will happen to them or to their communities. Neither the author who records their lives nor the people who want to meet and know more about them are blameless. A nonfiction novel as riveting as *In Cold Blood* promises that the people who fill its pages will forever be part of an event that may or may not define them. In fact, perhaps implicit in the publication of *In Cold Blood* and similar works is that communities such as Holcomb and Garden City, Kansas, are forever compromised.

---

[49]Charles McGrath, "Shades of Capote," *The New York Times*, 2 December 2007, web (accessed 14 August 2018).

Conclusion

In spite of the controversies that swirl around it, Truman Capote's *In Cold Blood* is a masterpiece of creative nonfiction. This study suggests ways to embrace the classic nonfiction novel more fully, including examining contexts that illuminate it and becoming more familiar with the voices that Capote could not or did not incorporate into his tale of crime and punishment. *Untold Stories, Unheard Voices* explores the enduring popularity of the nonfiction novel and its place in American literary journalism. It compares *In Cold Blood* to other Capote murder mysteries, specifically *Handcarved Coffins* and "Then It All Came Down." It connects *In Cold Blood* to motifs, symbols, and themes—including the doppelgänger and sensationalism—that make Capote's tale more accessible.

Untold Stories, Unheard Voices also introduces perspectives omitted from *In Cold Blood*, in particular editor, publisher, and reporter Starling Mack Nations; Pulitzer Prize-winning author Nelle Harper Lee; the directors, producers, and screenwriters responsible for three films and two documentaries that feature Truman Capote and *In Cold Blood*; and the residents of Kansas and beyond who endured the crime, its aftermath, and the ongoing intrusion into their lives. Ultimately, any study of *In Cold Blood* must begin and end with a tribute to the lives of Herbert, Bonnie, Nancy, and Kenyon Clutter. In the novel, when Kansan Josephine Meier begins to get to know Perry Smith—who is "very shy" and responds to her offer of a meal by saying, "One thing I really like is Spanish rice"—she tells her husband that "he wasn't the worst young man I ever saw."[1] Frustrated by her affection for Smith, Wendle Meier tells his wife he wishes she had helped investigators discover the bodies. She then tells Capote about her encounter with Smith and about her husband's response: "He said they'd cut out your heart and never bat an eye. There was no denying it—not with four people dead. And I lay awake wondering if either one was bothered by it—the thought of those four graves."[2]

This study of contexts and voices is not meant to be exhaustive; instead, it anticipates future critical work that will address the nonfiction novel's

---

[1] Truman Capote, *In Cold Blood: A True Account of a Multiple Murder and Its Consequences* (New York: Random House, 1965) 253.
[2] Ibid., 254.

place in adaptation studies, in regional literature, in gay and lesbian fiction and nonfiction, and in other intellectual frameworks. Authors of the American South have not been explored fully, and the treatment of issues related to the lesbian, gay, bisexual, and transgender community below the Mason-Dixon line remains a rich area of inquiry. For example, while this book was in production, a call for papers for a collection titled *Queering the Deep South: Research on Queer Studies and LGBTQ Lives in the U.S. Southeast* appeared, further reinforcing the importance of ongoing scholarship in LGBTQ studies, sociology, women's studies, and other equally interdisciplinary and important fields.

No one but Truman Capote could have written *In Cold Blood*, a book that is so much about himself that he could have inserted the words "I" and "me" throughout the narrative—a practice common to many literary journalists. In "Preface to *Music for Chameleons*," Capote writes:

> From a technical point, the greatest difficulty I'd had in writing *In Cold Blood* was leaving myself completely out of it. Ordinarily, the reporter has to use himself as a character, an eyewitness observer, in order to retain credibility. But I felt that it was essential to the seemingly detached tone of that book that the author should be absent. Actually, in all my reportage, I had tried to keep myself as invisible as possible.[3]

Perhaps Capote feared he would violate an increasingly obsolete definition of "objectivity" by intruding into the text when, in fact, literary journalism—a subset of creative nonfiction—encourages an authentic voice and all-but-full disclosure. In spite of his reticence to use first-person point of view, Capote is hardly absent; his opinions about capital punishment, religious institutions, the Clutter family, the criminal justice system, the Midwest, and other topics are obvious. Capote's presence in the events as they unfolded makes it clear that he, like Perry Smith, is an outsider. Hilton Als writes:

> As an artist, Truman Capote treated truth as a metaphor he could hide behind, the better to expose himself in a world not exactly congenial to a Southern-born queen with a high voice who once said to a disapproving truck driver: "What are you looking at? I wouldn't kiss you for a dollar." In so doing, he gave his readers, queer and not queer, license to

---

[3]Truman Capote, "Preface to *Music for Chameleons*," *Truman Capote: A Capote Reader* (New York: Penguin, 2002) 722.

imagine his real self in a real situation—in Kansas, researching *In Cold Blood*.[4]

Like William Faulkner, Carson McCullers, Flannery O'Connor, Eudora Welty, Tennessee Williams, and other unreconstructed southern writers, Capote found himself both at home in and abandoned by his region of origin. Like Kansas, Alabama had been a refuge and not a refuge at all; the rural American South was both familiar and unwelcoming, inviting and hostile. New York provided Capote with a wide—albeit fickle—social circle, but, like Dixie, it would ultimately not be a place on which he could rely. Summarizing the work of various scholars across several disciplines, Tison Pugh writes that Capote relied broadly upon southern literary history and specifically on gothic narratives:

> Also, he relied heavily on southern gothic tropes—mysterious events and family secrets, the legacy of the Civil War in the decadent South, grotesque characters in nightmare worlds—in *Other Voices, Other Rooms* and other works. Robert Lee sees the gothic "as somehow always integral to Southern writing," and its influence on Capote's southern fictions is apparent in his decaying landscapes and grotesque characters. Moreover, Capote's use of southern gothic elements builds upon his treatment of homosexuality, showcasing the complementarity of these interweaving themes. Louis Gross observes that the gothic, with its emphasis on repression and secrecy, serves as an apt genre for addressing homosexual themes: "the entire Southern Gothic movement of Tennessee Williams, Truman Capote, Carson McCullers, and William Inge is shaped by those qualities culturally associated with gays, and therefore defined as unhealthy. No other genre so welcomes culturally defined 'sickness' and horror as the Gothic." Southern gothicism imbues several of Capote's fictions with a foreboding atmosphere in which repressed desires circulate uneasily; it is difficult to envision how these stories would have survived if transplanted to other geographies.[5]

Pugh discusses both the film and the nonfiction novel *In Cold Blood* at length, although he argues in his overview that the themes and tropes com-

---

[4]Hilton Als, "The Shadows in Truman Capote's Early Stories," *The New Yorker*, 13 October 2015, web (accessed 16 August 2018).
[5]Tison Pugh, *Truman Capote: A Literary Life at the Movies* (Athens: University of Georgia Press, 2014) 6-7.

mon to literature of the American South are less discernible in *In Cold Blood* than they are in other Capote works: "*In Cold Blood*, Capote's masterwork detailing the aftermath of a multiple murder in Kansas, straddles the border between gothic horror and nonfiction reporting, yet Capote does not employ in it many of the standard tropes of southern gothicism, as he did in *Other Voices, Other Rooms*."[6]

Capote is the voice of the ostracized and the marginalized—but not entirely in a moral sense. Rather than arguing that human beings should be more inclusive and empathetic, Capote simply sets out to learn about a Midwestern community that is as foreign to him as Bourbon Street might be to a Southern Baptist from rural Iowa. Capote did not want or need to belong to particular groups—churches, families, political parties, or literary enclaves; therefore, the nonfiction novel reflects not only a moral sensibility, as important as that is, but also a desire to embrace the unfamiliar and to encourage readers to do the same.

In spite of the fact that *In Cold Blood* can only be set in Kansas—both because the crime occurred there and because the region represents a certain gestalt—Capote asks the reader to join him on his pilgrimage to the heartland but does not clarify much for the critic or reader interested in the centrality of place, especially as it is privileged in southern fiction. Small-town life and heteronormative cultural attitudes are not so much analyzed as presented. In spite of his references to Kansas as a foreign landscape, Capote actually is not far from Monroeville, Alabama, with its dirt streets and horses standing listlessly by. Capote knows Herbert Clutter and others like him— although they may speak with different accents—and Capote also understands how faith and social conservatism define the family, its work ethic, its values. Nancy Clutter goes to bed on the last night of her life with an envelope on her bedside stand. It contains two dollars for the church offering plate the next morning. Kenyon Clutter is guided not only by the Methodist services he attends each Sunday but by the pledge of allegiance to the 4-H Club. Accompanied by Harper Lee, Capote found himself in a profoundly unfamiliar place—but one that he well recognized.

Asked about his place in the community of artists in the Deep South, Capote tells Lawrence Grobel, "Flannery O'Connor had a certain genius."[7] Later, he expands his response to include other southern writers: "I've never

---

[6] Ibid., 7.

[7] Lawrence Grobel, *Conversations with Capote* (New York: New American Library, 1985) 36.

been aware of direct literary influence, though several critics have informed me that my early works owe a debt to Faulkner and Welty and McCullers. Possibly. I'm a great admirer of all three; and Katherine Anne Porter, too."[8] In another interview with Grobel, however, Capote disavows any creative connection with Faulkner, considered by many to be the best novelist of the twentieth century:

> Well *he* was completely reckless. I'm not a great admirer of Faulkner. He never had the slightest influence on me at all. I like three or four short stories of his…and I like one novel of his very much, called *Light in August*. But for the most part, he's a highly confusing, uncontrolled writer. He doesn't fit into my category of the kind of writer I really respect. I knew Faulkner very well. He was a great friend of mine. Well, as much as you could be a friend of his, unless you were a fourteen-year-old nymphet. Then you could be a great friend![9]

Chapter six makes clear that Harper Lee was far more kind to the American South than was Capote, and although she lived periodically in New York, she resided in the family home in Monroeville, Alabama, with her sister Alice Finch Lee until shortly before she moved to an assisted living facility late in her life. In an interview with Roy Newquist, Harper Lee's gentility and affection for the Deep South is obvious, as is her admiration for her childhood friend Truman Capote:

> But it will take quite a while to take the small town out of the South— we're simply a region of storytellers. We were told stories from the time we were born. We were expected to hold our own in conversation. We certainly don't have literary conversations, we have conversations about our neighbors. Some of it's straight fact, some of it's a bit embroidered, but all of it's part of being tellers of tales.[10]

About her own role in the emergence of novels, poetry, and short stories in the land of her birth, Harper Lee tells Newquist:

> As you know, the South is still made up of thousands of tiny towns. There is a very definite social pattern in these towns that fascinates me.

---

[8]Ibid., 130.
[9]Ibid., 131.
[10]Roy Newquist, *Counterpoint* (New York: Rand McNally, 1964) 408.

I think it is a rich social pattern. I would simply like to put down all I know about this because I believe that there is something universal in this little world, something decent to be said for it, and something to lament in its passing.

In other words all I want to be is the Jane Austen of south Alabama.[11]

Critical Assessment of In Cold Blood

On November 16, 1959, Capote read a *New York Times* article about the murder of a Kansas family, and soon after, he traveled to Kansas with Harper Lee. *In Cold Blood* was published first as a four-part series in *The New Yorker* beginning September 25, 1965, and in book form by Random House in January 1966, although the nonfiction novel bears a 1965 copyright date. (The Library of Congress lists 1966 as the publication date.) Since then, *In Cold Blood* has been published in more than thirty languages and has been at the heart of much debate.

However, it is not the timeline or even the book's critical reputation that interests readers the most. The stylistic masterpiece continues to be popular because, although readers know how the mystery ends, they are mesmerized by the unraveling of the crime and by its impact on a rural population that even today is defined in part by the horrific and random events of November 15, 1959. One fact is too often minimized: Capote, too, was deeply affected by the experience and the resulting narrative. In fact, it was a story he said he could not escape. In an interview with Grobel, Capote said:

> I didn't choose that subject because of any great interest in it. It was because I wanted to write what I called a nonfiction novel—a book that would read exactly like a novel except that every word of it would be absolutely true...I settled on this obscure crime in this remote part of Kansas because, I felt, if I followed this from beginning to end it would provide me with the material to really accomplish what was a technical feat. It was a literary experiment where I was choosing a subject not because of a great attraction to the subject, because that was not true, but because it suited my purposes literarily speaking...I became so totally involved in it personally that it just took over and consumed my life. All the trials, the appeals, the endless research I had to do—something like eight thousand pages of pure research—and my involvement with the

---

[11]Ibid., 412.

two boys who had committed the crime. Everything. It was a matter of living with something day in and day out...I spent six *years* on *In Cold Blood* and not only knew the people I was writing about, I've known them better than I've known *anybody*.[12]

In several interviews, Capote said that if he had known the emotional price he would pay for completing *In Cold Blood*, he would not have begun the project. "Well, I certainly wouldn't do it again," he told Grobel. "If I knew or had known when I started it what was going to be involved, I never would have started it, regardless of what the end result would have been."[13] Even more descriptively, Capote said, "No one will ever know what *In Cold Blood* took out of me. It scraped me down to the marrow of my bones. It nearly killed me. I think, in a way, it *did* kill me."[14] The most descriptive recounting of his experience occurs in a conversation with one of his biographers:

I'm still very much haunted by the whole thing. I have finished the book, but in a sense I *haven't* finished it: it keeps churning around in my head. It particularizes itself now and then, but not in the sense that it brings about a total conclusion. It's like the echo of E.M. Forster's Malabar Caves, the echo that's meaningless and yet it's there: one keeps hearing it all the time.[15]

Capote's contemporaries could be both laudatory or damning in their assessment of his work. Most interesting is Harper Lee's praise for Capote, who rarely returned the favor. One reason for his reticence may have been jealousy, as Alice Finch Lee proposes in chapter six. Whatever the reason for Capote's lack of generosity, Harper Lee said Capote was "the greatest craftsman we have going" and said she looked forward to the publication of *In Cold Blood*: "There's probably no better writer in this country today than Truman Capote. He is growing all the time. The next thing coming from Capote is not a novel—it's a long piece of reportage, and I think it is going

---

[12]Grobel, *Conversations*, 112-13.

[13]Ibid., 117.

[14]Thomas Fahy, *Understanding Truman Capote* (Columbia: University of South Carolina Press, 2014) 8; Gerald Clarke, *Capote: A Biography* (New York: Simon and Schuster, 1988) 398.

[15]George Plimpton, "The Story Behind a Nonfiction Novel," *Truman Capote: Conversations*, ed. M. Thomas Inge (Jackson: University Press of Mississippi, 1987) 68.

to make him bust loose as a novelist. He's going to have even deeper dimension to his work."[16] Gore Vidal and others criticized Capote's fiction but seemed to rethink their positions when *In Cold Blood* appeared. Having called Capote "ruthlessly unoriginal," Vidal later offered a half-compliment: "Then he turned to reportage, the natural realm of those without creative imagination, and began to do interesting work. In other words, he'd found his own voice, and that is what writing is all about."[17]

Current criticism of Capote's canon varies, but Madeleine Blais, a journalism professor at the University of Massachusetts, is unflinching in her praise for *In Cold Blood*. In "Truman Capote's 'In Cold Blood' Still the Standard," Blais describes the novel as "revolutionary" and the "high-water mark, the North Star and the gold standard against which its many imitators in the genre of narrative nonfiction are measured."[18] She adds:

> Capote's attempt to graft the techniques of imaginative literature onto a non-fiction story was more brazen, more unremitting, and on a larger scale. He came out of the gate firing away, claiming to have invented a new form: the non-fiction novel. Everything about it was innovative: his use of cinematic devices, the way he enters a scene as late as possible and gets out of it as early as possible, the cross-cutting, and especially the agonizing slow motion when he finally gets around to describing the crime itself. He was so successful in raising the bar that today we take his innovations for granted, losing sight of the revolutionary nature of immersing readers in the way people really talk, in a headlong rush, full of loops and asides, without a bunch of stilted "according to's" or other cumbersome, momentum-breaking devices.[19]

Although *In Cold Blood* deserves the attacks on its attention to facts and its invented scenes, in "Shades of Capote," Charles McGrath adroitly addresses these well-worn issues. He responds to a statement in Capote's "Self-Portrait" about the author's tendency to exaggerate in order to make an event "come alive." The full statement from Capote, which comes in response to a question about Capote's being a "truthful person," reads, "As a writer—yes, I think so. Privately—well, that is a matter of opinion; some of my friends

---

[16]Newquist, *Counterpoint*, 409.
[17]Grobel, *Conversations*, 130.
[18]Madeleine Blais, "Truman Capote's 'In Cold Blood' Still the Standard," *Chicago Tribune*, 25 December 2005, web (accessed 16 August 2018).
[19]Ibid.

think that when relating an event or piece of news, I am inclined to alter and overelaborate. Myself, I just call it making something 'come alive.' In other words, a form of art. Art and truth are not necessarily compatible bedfellows."[20] McGrath responds to Capote's deflection and self-defense by addressing his habit of misleading readers and prevaricating, something he suggests may best be called "lying":

> You could also call it lying, and in an earlier piece, in which he apologizes for telling tales about his life in New York to an old woman named Selma, who used to cook for his aunts in Alabama, he says as much: "But mostly they were lies I told; it wasn't my fault, I couldn't remember, because it was as though I'd been to one of those supernatural castles visited by characters in legends: once away, you do not remember, all that is left is the ghostly echo of haunting wonder."[21]

People who are angry about the mischaracterization of a friend or family member will not find solace in McGrath's circuitous and inadequate speculation about Capote's divergences from the truth. People who challenge Capote's claim that everything in *In Cold Blood* is accurate will not be persuaded either. In correspondence with Wayne Flynt, even Harper Lee voiced—albeit with humor and affection—her opinion of Capote and his relationship with truth: "I do laugh, though, because so much of Truman's own manipulative talent is being used on him—coming back to haunt him, as it were. I can hear him complaining, 'Can they tell the TRUTH about it?' No more than he could."[22]

Nonetheless, what remains is a mystery writ large, one that will no doubt continue to captivate readers, draw visitors to Holcomb and Garden City, and inspire critics and others who prefer nonfiction to fiction, even when the genre can best be described as fiction based on fact. Evidence of the continuing allure of *In Cold Blood* lies in the proliferation of related autobiographical essays, biographies, histories, memoirs, and other nonfiction tomes. Furthermore, professors, reporters, and high school teachers invested in journalism as art and as practice teach their students that although Capote

---

[20]Truman Capote, "Self-Portrait," *Truman Capote: A Capote Reader* (New York: Penguin, 2002), 633.

[21]Charles McGrath, "Shades of Capote," *The New York Times*, 2 December 2007, web (accessed 16 August 2018).

[22]Wayne Flynt, *Mockingbird Songs: My Friendship with Harper Lee* (New York: HarperCollins, 2017) 55.

was not trained as a journalist and failed to uphold the ethics of journalism, he contributed one of the classics of literary journalism. Evidence of the endurance and preeminence of *In Cold Blood* lies, too, in the number of people who engage on social media, sharing stories about their time in Kansas and asking questions about the people whose names appear in *In Cold Blood*. In short, the more critical studies and oral histories that emerge, the more historians, journalists, and the public at large will understand the impact of the last book Capote completed—and the emotional price he paid. In 2012, biographer Gerald Clarke reaffirmed that Capote's "self-destruction" began in Kansas with Perry Smith's execution. In short, publishing *In Cold Blood* required that Perry Smith and Richard Hickock die: "He wrote that he wanted them to die—that started the decline,"[23] Clarke said.

For Truman Capote himself, his rise to fame was splendid; his finale, a terrible and prolonged unraveling, both for him and for the nation that watched. It is his friends and acquaintances—not literary critics—who should have the last word, and Sam Kashner's 2012 article in *Vanity Fair* provided them with that opportunity: Caroline Lee Radziwill, sister of Jacqueline Kennedy Onassis, said, "It was pitiful. Heartbreaking, because there was nothing you could do. He really wanted to kill himself. It was a slow and painful suicide."[24] Long-time partner Jack Dunphy said Capote looked "tired, very tired": "It's as if he's at a long party and wants to say good-bye—but he can't."[25] Gossip columnist Mary Elizabeth (Liz) Smith expands her own grief into a comment on New York literary society itself: "I still miss him. New York doesn't seem to have epic characters like Truman Capote anymore. There are no major writers today that matter in the way that he mattered."[26]

Although no one will ever know exactly what led to Capote's creative demise, there is little doubt that his identification with Perry Smith was a catalyst. In "Capote's Swan Dive," Kashner writes that "it would have been easy for Truman to look into Perry Smith's black eyes and think he was looking at his darker twin."[27] In the end, most of us cannot separate a Kansas murder tale from Truman Capote's rise and fall—nor should we. *In Cold*

---

[23]Sam Kashner, "Capote's Swan Dive," *Vanity Fair* (December 2012): 213.
[24]Ibid.
[25]Ibid.
[26]Ibid., 214.
[27]Ibid., 213.

Blood remains a searing narrative, perhaps more autobiographical than the author, who fancied himself a detached journalist, intended.

Works Cited

Adam, Suzanna. "Left Behind: Man Lives Painful Life in Shadow of Brother's Crime." *Lawrence Journal-World* (4 April 2005). Web. <http://www2.ljworld.com/news/2005/apr/04/left_behind_man/>.

The Age of Innocence. Dir. Martin Scorsese. Columbia Pictures, 1993. Film.

All the President's Men. Dir. Alan J. Pakula. Wildwood Enterprises, 1976. Film.

Als, Hilton. "Ghosts in Sunlight." *The New York Review of Books* (10 July 2014). Web. <http://www.nybooks.com/articles/2014/07/10/ghosts-in-sunlight/>.

———. "The Shadows in Truman Capote's Early Stories." *The New Yorker* (13 October 2015). Web. <http://www.newyorker.com/books/page-turner/the-shadows-in-truman-capotes-early-stories>.

Alter, Alexandra. "Harper Lee, Author of 'To Kill a Mockingbird,' Is to Publish a Second Novel." *The New York Times* (3 February 2015). Web. <http://nyti.ms.1DBoqlA>.

Anderson, John. "Scorsese Rules This 'Island.'" *Wall Street Journal* (19 February 2010). Web. <http://online.wsj.com/article>.

The Aviator. Dir. Martin Scorsese. Warner Bros., 2004. Film.

Axelrod, Daniel. "In Cold Fact, In Cold Blood: Exposing Errors, Finding Fabrication and Unearthing Capote's Unethical Behavior." *The Newsletter of the International Association of Literary Journalism Studies* (Winter 2014): 18-20, 22-23, 25-31. Print.

Badham, Mary. Interview. *Scout, Atticus & Boo: A Celebration of Fifty Years of* To Kill a Mockingbird. By Mary Murphy. New York: HarperCollins, 2010. 45-50. Print.

Bardach, A.L. "Jailhouse Interview: Bobby Beausoleil." *Oui Magazine* (November 1981). Web. <http://www.bardachreports.com/articles/oa_19811100.htm>.

Berendt, John. *Midnight in the Garden of Good and Evil*. New York: Vintage, 1994. Print.

Betrayal. Dir. David Jones. 20th Century Fox, 1983. Film.

Betrayed. Dir. Konstantinos Gavras. United Artists, 1988. Film.

Black Widow. Dir. Bob Rafelson. 20th Century Fox, 1987. Film.

Blais, Madeleine. "Truman Capote's 'In Cold Blood' Still the Standard." *Chicago Tribune* (25 December 2005). Web. <http://articles.chicagotribune.com/2005-12-25/entertainment/0512240030_1_dick-hickock-clutter-family-truman-capote>.

Boatwright, Alice Lee (Boaty). Interview. *Scout, Atticus & Boo: A Celebration of Fifty Years of* To Kill a Mockingbird. By Mary Murphy. New York: HarperCollins, 2010. 51-56. Print.

Brokaw, Tom. Interview. *Scout, Atticus & Boo: A Celebration of Fifty Years of* To Kill a Mockingbird. By Mary Murphy. New York: HarperCollins, 2010. 61-65. Print.

Brontë, Charlotte. *Jane Eyre*. New York: Penguin, 2006. Print.

Brontë, Emily. *Wuthering Heights*. New York: Penguin, 2002. Print.

Bugliosi, Vincent. *Helter Skelter: The True Story of the Manson Murders*. New York: W.W. Norton, 2001. Print.

Bunyan, Paul. *Pilgrim's Progress*. New York: Penguin, 2009. Print.

Burr, Ty. "'The Two Faces of January': Holding a Mirror to Mr. Ripley." *Boston Globe* (9 October 2014). Web. <https://www.bostonglobe.com/arts/movies/2014/10/09/movie-review- the-two-faces-january>.

Calamari, Alexandra. *"Infamous." Cinemablend* n.d. Web. <http://www.cinemablend.com/reviews/infamous-1863.html>.

Calhoun, John. "The True Story Behind 'True Story.'" *Biography* (16 April 2015). Web. <http://www.biography.com/news/true-story-movie-michael-finkel-christian-longo>.

Callahan, Dan. *"Capote." Slant Magazine* (2 September 2005). Web. <https://www.slantmagazine.com/film/review/capote>.

——. *"Infamous." Slant Magazine* (2 October 2006). Web. <https://www.slantmagazine.com/film/review/infamous>.

Camus, Albert. *The Stranger*. Trans. Matthew Ward. New York: Vintage, 1989. Print.

Capote. Dir. Bennett Miller. Sony Classics, 2005. Film.

Capote, Truman. *In Cold Blood: A True Account of a Multiple Murder and Its Consequences*. New York: Random House, 1965. Print.

——. "The Duke in His Domain." *Truman Capote: A Capote Reader*. New York: Penguin, 2002. 517-44. Print.

——. "Ghosts in Sunlight: The Filming of *In Cold Blood*." *Truman Capote: A Capote Reader*. New York: Penguin, 2002. 621-27. Print.

——. *Handcarved Coffins. Truman Capote: A Capote Reader*. New York: Penguin, 2002. 463-514. Print.

——. "The Headless Hawk." *Truman Capote: A Capote Reader*. New York: Penguin, 2002. 44-62. Print.

——. *Music for Chameleons*. New York: Random House, 1980. Print.

——. *Other Voices, Other Rooms. Three by Truman Capote*. New York: Random House, 1985. 11-130. Print.

——. "Preface to *The Dogs Bark*." *Truman Capote: A Capote Reader*. New York: Penguin, 2002. 642-44. Print.

——. "Preface to *Music for Chameleons*." *Truman Capote: A Capote Reader*. New York: Penguin, 2002. 717-722. Print.

——. "Self-Portrait." *Truman Capote: A Capote Reader*. New York: Penguin, 2002. 632-41. Print.

——. *The Thanksgiving Visitor*. New York: Random House, 1967. Print.

——. "Then It All Came Down." *Truman Capote: A Capote Reader*. New York: Penguin, 2002. 455-62. Print.

——. *Truman Capote: A Capote Reader*. New York: Penguin, 2002. Print.

Chapman, Wes. "Human and Divine Design: An Annotation of Robert Frost's 'Design.'"*American Poetry* (8 March 2006). Web. <http://titan.iwu.edu/~wchapman/americanpoetryweb>.

Childress, Mark. Interview. *Scout, Atticus & Boo: A Celebration of Fifty Years of* To Kill a Mockingbird. By Mary Murphy. New York: HarperCollins, 2010. 76-84. Print.

Cieply, Michael. "Telling a True-Life Story, Following a 'True-Film' Style." *The New York Times* (17 April 2013). Web. <http://www.nytimes.com/2013/04/18/business/media/true-story-is-based-on-the-conning-of-a-shamed-journalist.html>.

Clark, Jonathan Russell. "In Search of the Real Truman Capote." *The Atlantic* (10 September 2015). Web. <http://www.theatlantic.com/entertainment/archive/2015/09/in-search-of-the-real-truman-capote/403978/>.

Clarke, Gerald. *Capote: A Biography.* New York: Simon and Schuster, 1988. Print.

Clarke, Gerald, ed. *Too Brief a Treat: The Letters of Truman Capote.* New York: Random House, 2004. Print.

Cohen, Patricia. "'To Kill a Mockingbird' Author Repudiates Journalist's Memoir About Her." *The New York Times* (27 April 2011). Web. <http://artsbeat.blogs.nytimes.com/2011/04/27/to-kill-a-mockingbird-author-repudiates-journalists-memoir-about-her>.

Connery, Thomas B. "Discovering a Literary Form." *A Sourcebook of American Literary Journalism: Representative Writers in an Emerging Genre.* Ed. Thomas B. Connery. New York: Greenwood Press, 1992. 3-37. Print.

———. "Preface." *A Sourcebook of American Literary Journalism: Representative Writers in an Emerging Genre.* Ed. Thomas B. Connery. New York: Greenwood Press, 1992. xi-xv. Print.

Cox, David. *"Shutter Island's* Ending Explained." *The Guardian* (29 July 2010). Web. <https://www.theguardian.com/film/filmblog/2010/jul/29/shutter-island-ending>.

Crane, Stephen. *Maggie: A Girl of the Streets and Other Tales of New York.* New York: Penguin, 2000.

Criminal Law. Dir. Martin Campbell. Hemdale, 1989. Film.

Crouse, S.H. Letter to Donald Cullivan. Perry Edward Smith Inmate Case File #383. Kansas Historical Society (20 April 1965). Web. <http://www.kansasmemory.org/item/208964/page/340>.

Crowther, Bosley. *"In Cold Blood." The New York Times* (15 December 1967). Web. <http://www.nytimes.com/movie/review>.

———. "'To Kill a Mockingbird': One Adult Omission in a Fine Film." *The New York Times* (15 February 1963). Web. <http://www.nytimes.com/movie/review?res=9D06EED143CEF3BBC4D52DFB4668388679EDE>.

Cullivan, Donald. Letter to Perry Smith. Perry Edward Smith Inmate Case File #384. Kansas Historical Society (11 April 1965). Web. <http://www.kansasmemory.org/item/208964/page/341>.

———. "Truman Capote and Perry Smith" (25 June 2016). Unpublished.

Cutchins, Dennis, Laurence Raw, and James M. Welsh, eds. "Introduction." *The Pedagogy of Adaptation.* Lanham, Md.: Scarecrow Press, 2010. xi-xix. Print.

———. *Redefining Adaptation Studies.* Lanham, Md.: Scarecrow Press, 2010. Print.

Dangerous Liaisons. Dir. Stephen Frears. Warner Bros., 1988. Film.

Davidson, Sara. "Introduction." *Cowboy: A Novel.* New York: HarperCollins, 1999. ix-xi. Print.

———. "The Gray Zone." *Book* (July/August 1999): 49-50. Print.

———. *Leap!: What Will We Do with the Rest of Our Lives?* New York: Random House, 2007. Print.

———. Lecture. "Literary Journalism: What Are the Rules?" School of Journalism and Mass Communication. University of Colorado. Boulder, Colo. (22 November 2002).

———. *Loose Change: Three Women of the Sixties.* Berkeley: University of California Press, 1977. Print.

"Deaths of Ensign Man, Wife Were Dual Murder?" *Salina Journal* (2 July 1974): 1.

Defoe, Daniel. *The Storm.* New York: Penguin, 2005. Print.

DeFore, John. "Hoffman Gives Soul to the Role of Capote." *Austin American-Statesman* (28 October 2005): 1E+. Print.

The Departed. Dir. Martin Scorsese. Warner Bros., 2006. Film.

Dewey, Alvin A. "The Clutter Case: 25 Years Later KBI Agent Recounts Holcomb Tragedy." *Garden City Telegram* (10 November 1984): 1A+. Print.

Diamond, Suzanne. "Whose Life *Is* It, Anyway?: Adaptation, Collective Memory, and (Auto)Biographical Processes." *Redefining Adaptation Studies.* Ed. Dennis Cutchins, Laurence Raw, and James M. Welsh. Lanham, Md.: Scarecrow Press, 2010. 95-110. Print.

Dickens, Charles. *Bleak House.* New York: Penguin, 2003. Print.

———. *Great Expectations.* New York: Longman, 2004. Print.

———. *Oliver Twist.* New York: Penguin, 2002. Print.

Didion, Joan. "Some Dreamers of the Golden Dream." *Slouching Towards Bethlehem. We Tell Ourselves Stories in Order to Live: Collected Nonfiction.* London: Knopf, 2006. 13-29. Print.

———. *The White Album. We Tell Ourselves Stories in Order to Live: Collected Nonfiction.* London: Knopf, 2006. 179-342. Print.

To Die in Jerusalem. Dir. Hilla Medalia. HBO Documentary Films, 2007. Film.

Dillard, Clayton. "The Two Faces of January." *Slant Magazine* (20 September 2014). Web. <http://www.slantmagazine.com/film/review/the-two-faces-of-january>.

The Door in the Floor. Dir. Tod Williams. Focus Features, 2004. Film.

Dreiser, Theodore. *An American Tragedy.* New York: Signet, 2010. Print.

———. *Sister Carrie.* New York: Penguin, 1994.

Du Marnier, Daphne. *Rebecca.* New York: Avon, 2002.

Ebert, Roger. *"Capote"* (20 October. 2005). Web. <http://www.rogerebert.com/reviews/capote-2005>.

———. *"In Cold Blood"* (6 February 1968). Web. <http://www.rogerebert.com/reviews/in-cold-blood-1968>.

———. *"Infamous"* (12 October 2006). Web. <http://www.rogerebert.com/reviews/infamous-2006>.

———. *"Shutter Island." Chicago Sun Times.* (17 February 2010). Web. <http://rogerebert.suntimes.com/apps/pbcs.dlll/article?AID>.

"Editor's Note." *The New York Times* (21 February 2002). Web. <http:www.nytimes.com/2002/02/21/nyregion/editors-note-731463.html>.

Edwards, Diana Selsor. "The Rest of the Story." *Desert Exposure* (November 2009). Web. <http://www.desertexposure.com/200911/prt_200911_in_cold_blood.php>.

Elias, Justine. "After Midnight." *US* (December 1997): 89-97, 113.

Epps, Garrett. "The True Story Behind *True Story.*" *The Atlantic* (24 April 2015). Web. <http://www.theatlantic.com/national/archive/2015/04/the-real-story-behind-true-story/391376/>.

Fahy, Thomas. *Understanding Truman Capote.* Columbia: University of South Carolina Press, 2014. Print.

Fatal Attraction. Dir. Adrian Lyne. Paramount, 1987. Film.

Faulkner, William. *Light in August.* New York: Modern Library, 2002. Print.

———. Presentation. University of Virginia. 21 February 1958. Web. <http://faulkner.lib.virginia.edu/display/wfaudio21>.

———. Speech. Washington and Lee University. 15 May 1958. Web. <http://faulkner.lib.virginia.edu/display/wfaudio31>.

Fearful Symmetry: The Making of To Kill a Mockingbird. Dir. Charles Kiselyak. Universal, 1998. Film.

"Few Bids Trickle in for Clutter Home Auction." *Garden City Telegram* (20 September 2006). Web. <http://www.hauntedcolorado.net/In-Cold-Blood-House.html>.

Fiedler, Leslie A. "The Fate of the Novel." *Kenyon Review* 10.31 (1948): 519-27. Print.

Finkel, Michael. "Is Youssouf Malé a Slave?" *The New York Times Magazine* (18 November 2001. Web. <http://www.nytimes.com/2001/11/18/magazine/is-youssouf-male-a-slave.html>.

———. *True Story.* New York: Harper Perennial, 2005. Print.

Flanders, Judith. *The Invention of Murder: How the Victorians Revelled in Death and Detection and Created Modern Crime.* New York: St. Martin's, 2011. Print.

Fletcher, Angus. *Allegory: The Theory of a Symbolic Mode.* Ithaca: Cornell University Press, 1964. Print.

Flynt, Wayne. *Mockingbird Songs: My Friendship with Harper Lee.* New York: HarperCollins, 2017.

Foote, Horton. "Foreword." *Three Screenplays by Horton Foote.* New York: Grove Press, 1989. xi-xvii. Print.

———. "To Kill a Mockingbird." *Three Screenplays by Horton Foote.* New York: Grove Press, 1989. 1-80. Print.

Fretts, Bruce. "A Writer Watches His Life Unspool on Film." *The New York Times* (14 April 2015). Web. <http://artsbeat.blogs.nytimes.com/2015/04/14/a-writer-watches-his-life-unspool-on-film/>.

Frost, Robert. "Design." *The Poetry of Robert Frost: The Collected Poems.* Ed. Edward Connery Lathem. New York: Henry Holt, 1969. 302. Print.

Gangs of New York. Dir. Martin Scorsese. Intermedia Films, 2002. Film.

"Garden City Couple Recount Friendship with Truman Capote, Harper Lee." *Lawrence Journal-World* (15 April 2011). Web. <http://www2.ljworld.com/news/2011/apr/15/couple-recount-friendship-capote-lee/>.

Gates, David. "Literature's Lost Boy: The Self-Destruction of an American Writer." *Newsweek* (30 May 1988): 62-63. Print.

Geraghty, Christine. *Now a Major Motion Picture: Film Adaptations of Literature and Drama.* Lanham, Md.: Rowman & Littlefield, 2008. Print.

Gillman, Peter. "The Truth about Truman Capote." *The Sunday Times* (17 February 2013). Web.

<http://www.peterleni.com/Capote%20Sunday%20Times%20Feb%2017%202013.
pdf>.

Gillman, Peter and Leni. "Hoax: Secrets That Truman Capote Took to the Grave."
Longform Reprints (June 1992). Web. <http://reprints.longform.org/hoax-truman-capote-secret>.

Going, William T. "Truman Capote: Harper Lee's Fictional Portrait of the Artist as an
Alabama Child." *Alabama Review* 42.2 (1989): 136-49. Print.

Greenfield, Meg. "In Defense of Sensationalism: The Media and the O.J. Simpson
Case." *Newsweek* (26 September 1994): 72. Print.

Grobel, Lawrence. *Conversations with Capote.* New York: New American Library, 1985.
Print.

Gurganus, Allan. Interview. *Scout, Atticus & Boo: A Celebration of Fifty Years of* To Kill a
Mockingbird. By Mary Murphy. New York: HarperCollins, 2010. 95-103. Print.

Hammer, Joshua. "How Two Lives Met in Death." *Newsweek* (15 April 2002): 18-25.
Print.

Harris, Paul. "Mockingbird Author Steps Out of Shadows." *The Observer* (4 February
2006). Web. <http://www.guardian.co.uk/world/2006/feb/05/books.usa>.

Harris, Robert. "Elements of the Gothic Novel." *VirtualSalt* (22 Nov. 2011). Web.
<http://www.virtualsalt.com/gothic.htm>.

Hartsock, John C. *A History of American Literary Journalism: The Emergence of a Modern
Narrative Form.* Amherst: University of Massachusetts Press, 2000. Print.

Hawthorne, Nathaniel. *The Scarlet Letter.* New York: New American Library, 1959.
Print.

Hayes, David, and Sarah Weinman. "The Worthy Elephant: On Truman Capote's *In
Cold Blood.*" *Hazlitt* (27 January 2016). Web. <http://hazlitt.net/feature/worthy-elephant-truman-capotes-cold-blood>.

Heldrich, Philip. *"Capote* and *Infamous."* "Kansas in the Movies." Center for Kansas
Studies (n.d.). Web.
<http://www.washburn.edu/references/cks/mapping/movies/capoteinfamous/>.

Hellman, John. *Fables of Fact: The New Journalism as New Fiction.* Champaign: Illinois
University Press, 1981. Print.

Henderson, Odie. "The Two Faces of January" (26 September 2014). Web.
<http://www.rogerebert.com/reviews/the-two-faces-of-january-2014>.

Hersey, John. *Hiroshima.* New York: Vintage, 1989. Print.

Hey, Boo: Harper Lee and To Kill a Mockingbird. Dir. Mary McDonaugh Murphy. Mary
Murphy & Company, 2011. Film.

Highsmith, Patricia. *The Boy Who Followed Ripley.* New York: W.W. Norton, 2008.
Print.

———. *Ripley Under Ground.* New York: W.W. Norton, 2008. Print.

———. *Ripley Under Water.* New York: W.W. Norton, 2008. Print.

———. *Ripley's Game.* New York: W.W. Norton, 2008. Print.

———. *The Talented Mr. Ripley.* New York: W.W. Norton, 2008. Print.

———. *The Two Faces of January.* New York: Grove, 1964. Print.

Hotel New Hampshire. Dir. Tony Richardson. Orion, 1984. Film.

In Cold Blood. Dir. Richard Brooks. Columbia Pictures, 1967. Film.

"The 'In Cold Blood' Murder House Is for Sale" (n.d.). Web. http://www2.ljworld.com/
news/2005/apr/06/in_the_end/.

Infamous. Dir. Douglas McGrath. Arclight, 2006. Film.

Inge, M. Thomas, ed. *Truman Capote: Conversations.* Jackson: University Press of Mississippi, 1987. Print.

Irving, John. *Hotel New Hampshire.* New York: Ballantine, 1995. Print.

———. *A Widow for One Year.* New York: Ballantine, 1999. Print.

Jagged Edge. Dir. Richard Marquand. Columbia, 1985. Film.

Johnson, Claudia Durst. *To Kill a Mockingbird: Threatening Boundaries.* New York:
Twayne, 1994. Print.

Jones, Kristin M. "Review: *Infamous." Filmcomment.* (September/October 2006). Web.
<http://www.filmcomment.com/article/infamous-review>.

Kafka, Franz. *The Trial.* New York: Penguin, 2000. Print.

"Kansas Trails: Dedicated to Free Genealogy" (n.d.). Web.
<http://genealogytrails.com/kan/gray/anton.html>.

Kashner, Sam. "Capote's Swan Dive." *Vanity Fair* (December 2012): 200-207, 210-14.

Keeble, Richard. "Introduction: On Journalism, Creativity, and the Imagination." *The
Journalistic Imagination: Literary Journalists from Defoe to Capote and Carter.* Ed.
Richard Keeble and Sharon Wheeler. New York: Routledge, 2007. 1-13. Print.

Keefe, Patrick Radden. "Capote's Co-Conspirators." *The New Yorker* (22 March 2013).
Web. <http://www.newyorker.com/online/blogs/books/2013/03/capote-co-
conspirators-in-cold-blood.html>.

King, Stephen. *Secret Window, Secret Garden. Four Past Midnight.* New York: Penguin,
1990. 247-399. Print.

Kolker, Robert. "The Great Pretender?" *New York Magazine* (9 March 2013). Web.
<http://nymag.com/nymetro/news/media/features/5740/>.

Kroll, Jack. "Truman Capote: 1924-1984." *Newsweek* (3 September 1984): 69. Print.

Kudun. Dir. Martin Scorsese. Touchstone, 1997. Film.

Kuna, Franz. "The Janus-Faced Novel: Conrad, Musil, Kafka, Mann." *Modernism: A
Guide to European Literature (1890-1930).* Ed. Malcolm Bradbury and James
McFarlane. New York: Penguin, 1991. Print.

Lamb, Charles. *Essays of Elia.* Paris: Baudry's European Library, 1835. Print.

Lamb, Wally. "Foreword: A Mockingbird Mosaic." *Scout, Atticus & Boo: A Celebration of
Fifty Years of* To Kill a Mockingbird. By Mary Murphy. New York: HarperCollins,
2010. ix-xiv. Print.

Lawrence of Arabia. Dir. David Lean. Horizon Pictures, 1962. Film.

Lee, Alice Finch. Interview. *Scout, Atticus & Boo: A Celebration of Fifty Years of* To Kill a
Mockingbird. By Mary Murphy. New York: HarperCollins, 2010. 119-29. Print.

Lee, Harper. *To Kill a Mockingbird.* New York: HarperCollins, 1999. Print.

Lee, Melissa. "High School Sweetheart Recalls the Day His Life Changed Forever."
Lawrence Journal-World (3 April 2005). Web.
<http://www2.ljworld.com/news/2005/apr/03/high_school_sweetheart/>.

Lehane, Dennis. *Gone, Baby, Gone.* New York: HarperCollins, 1998. Print.

———. *Mystic River.* New York: HarperCollins, 2001. Print.

———. *Shutter Island.* New York: HarperTorch, 2003. Print.

Lehmann-Haupt, Christopher. "Books of *The Times*." *The New York Times* (5 August 1980). Web. <https://www.nytimes.com/books/97/12/28/home/capote-music.html>.

Lule, Jack. "Myth and Terror on the Editorial Page: *The New York Times* Responds to September 11, 2001." *Journalism and Mass Communication Quarterly* 79.2 (Summer 2002): 275-93. Print.

Malcolm, Janet. *The Journalist and the Murderer*. New York: Alfred A. Knopf, 1990. Print.

Masquerade. Dir. Bob Swaim. MGM, 1988. Film.

McCarthy, Cormac. *No Country for Old Men*. New York: Vintage, 2006. Print.

McElwaine, Sandra. "'To Kill a Mockingbird' Makes Its Mark, 50 Years After the Film's Release." *The Daily Beast* (31 January 2012). Web. <http://www.thedailybeast.com/articles/2012/01/31/to-kill-a-mockingbird-makes-its-mark-50-years-after-the-film-s-release.html>.

McGrath, Charles. "Shades of Capote." *The New York Times* 2 December 2007. Web. <http://www.nytimes.com/2007/12/02/books/review/McGrath-t.html>.

Mclean, Norman. *A River Runs Through It*. Chicago: University of Chicago Press, 2001. Print.

Melville, Herman. *The Confidence-Man: His Masquerade*. New York: New American Library, 1954. Print.

Michener, James A. "Foreword." *Conversations with Capote*. By Lawrence Grobel. New York: New American Library, 1985. 1-12. Print.

Milbank, Alison. "Gothic Fiction Tells Us the Truth About Our Divided Nature." *The Guardian* (27 November 2011). Web. <http://www.guardian.co.uk/commentisfree/2011/Nov/27/gothic-fiction-divided-selves>.

Minzesheimer, Bob. "'Kansas' Imagines Truman Capote-Harper Lee Rift." *USA Today* (18 December 2007). Web. <http://usatoday30.usatoday.com/life/books/reviews/2007-12-17-powers-capote_N.htm>.

"Monroeville: Truman Capote and Harper Lee." *The Southern Literary Trail* (n.d.). Web. <http://www.southernliterarytrail.org/monroeville.html>.

Montesano, Anthony P. "The Film That Never Was." *Movies on My Mind* (18 March 2006). Web. <http://moviesonmymind.blogspot.com/2006/03/film-that-never-was.html>.

The Morning After. Dir. Sidney Lumet. Lorimar, 1986. Film.

Mr. Brooks. Dir. Bruce A. Evans. Element Films, 2007. Film.

Murder: In Cold Blood. Kurtis Productions, 1997. Film.

"Murder of Kansas Couple in 1974 Remains a Mystery." *Lawrence Journal-World* (29 April 1992): 2C.

Murphy, Mary McDonagh. "Part 1: Scout, Atticus, and Boo. *Scout, Atticus & Boo: A Celebration of Fifty Years of* To Kill a Mockingbird." New York: HarperCollins, 2010. 1-42. Print.

———, ed. *Scout, Atticus & Boo: A Celebration of Fifty Years of* To Kill a Mockingbird. By Mary Murphy. New York: HarperCollins, 2010. Print.

"Music for Chameleons." Kirkus Reviews (10 October 2011). Web. <https://www.kirkusreviews.com/book-reviews/truman-capote/music-for-chameleons/>.

Myrick, Steve. "Fifty Years Later, *In Cold Blood* Still Fresh for Oak Bluffs Man." *Vineyard Gazette* (24 September 2015). Web. <https://vineyardgazette.com/news/2015/09/24/fifty-years-later-cold-blood-still-fresh-oak-bluffs-man>.

"Mysteries Hold Year After Anton Murders," *Garden City Telegram* (30 June 1975): 3.

Nabokov, Vladimir. "The Strange Case of Dr. Jekyll and Mr. Hyde." *The Strange Case of Dr. Jekyll and Mr. Hyde.* By Robert Louis Stevenson. New York: New American Library, 1987. 7-34. Print.

Nations, Mack. "America's Worst Crime in 20 Years." *Male* 11.12 (December 1961): 30-31, 76-83. Print.

Newquist, Roy. *Counterpoint.* New York: Rand McNally, 1964. Print.

No Way Out. Dir. Roger Donaldson. Orion, 1987. Film.

Norden, Eric. *"Playboy* Interview: Truman Capote." Ed. M. Thomas Inge. *Truman Capote: Conversations.* Jackson: University Press of Mississippi, 1987. 110-63. Print.

Nuttall, Nick. "Cold-Blooded Journalism: Truman Capote and the Nonfiction Novel." *The Journalistic Imagination: Literary Journalists from Defoe to Capote and Carter.* Ed. Richard Keeble and Sharon Wheeler. New York: Routledge, 2007. 130-44. Print.

O'Connor, Flannery. "The Fiction Writer and His Country." *Mystery and Manners.* New York: Farrar, 1969. 25-35. Print.

———. "A Good Man Is Hard to Find." *A Good Man Is Hard to Find and Other Stories.* New York: Harcourt Brace, 1976. 1-22. Print.

"Officers Question Man in Ensign Murder Cases." *Salina Journal* (11 July 1974): 21.

Orlean, Susan. *The Orchid Thief: A True Story of Beauty and Obsession.* New York: Ballantine Books, 2000. Print.

Orwell, George. "Shooting an Elephant." *Facing Unpleasant Facts: Narrative Essays.* New York: Harcourt, 2008. 29-37. Print.

"Parchman Escapee Killed, 2 Wounded" *Delta Democrat-Times* (5 April 1970): 3.

Patterson, John. *"In Cold Blood:* Why Isn't the Movie of Capote's Bestseller a Masterpiece?" *The Guardian* (7 September 2015). Web. <https://www.theguardian.com/film/2015/sep/07/in-cold-blood-a-near-masterpiece>.

Pauly, John J. "Damon Runyon." *A Sourcebook of American Literary Journalism: Representative Writers in an Emerging Genre.* Ed. Thomas B. Connery. New York: Greenwood, 1992. 169-77. Print.

———. "The Politics of the New Journalism." *Literary Journalism in the Twentieth Century.* Ed. Norman Sims. New York: Oxford University Press, 1990. 110-29. Print.

Peschock, T. Madison. "A Well-Hidden Secret: Harper Lee's Contributions to Truman Capote's *In Cold Blood."* Diss. Indiana University of Pennsylvania, 2012. Print.

Pilkington, Ed. "In Cold Blood, Half a Century On." *The Guardian* (15 November 2009). Web. <https://www.theguardian.com/books/2009/nov/16/truman-capote-in-cold-blood>.

Pizer, Donald. "Documentary Narrative as Art: William Manchester and Truman Capote." *Journal of Modern Literature* 2.1 (September 1971): 105-18. Print.

Plimpton, George. "Capote's Long Ride." *The New Yorker* (13 October 1997): 62, 64-71. Print.

———. "The Story Behind a Nonfiction Novel." *Truman Capote: Conversations.* Ed. M. Thomas Inge. Jackson: University Press of Mississippi, 1987. 47-68. Print.

———. *Truman Capote: In Which Various Friends, Enemies, Acquaintances and Detractors Recall His Turbulent Career.* New York: Anchor, 1998. Print.

Poe, Edgar Allan. "The Cask of Amontillado." New York: Doubleday, 1966. 191-96. Print.

———. "The Fall of the House of Usher." New York: Doubleday, 1966. 177-91. Print.

———. "The Pit and the Pendulum." New York: Doubleday, 1966. 196-207. Print.

Powers, Kim. *Capote in Kansas: A Ghost Story.* New York: Carroll and Graf, 2007. Print.

Pugh, Tison. *Truman Capote: A Literary Life at the Movies.* Athens: University of Georgia Press, 2014. Print.

Raging Bull. Dir. Martin Scorsese. United Artists, 1980.

Rainone, Anthony. "Island of No Return." *January Magazine.* Web. <http://januarymagazine.com/crfiction/shutterisland.html>.

Reed, Kenneth T. *Truman Capote.* Boston: Twayne, 1981. Print.

"Reward Offered in Anton Murders." *Garden City Telegram* (17 February 1975): 3.

Ringle, Ken. "Just Savannah Good Time." *Washington Post* (24 February 1994): C1. Print.

Rochat, Scott. "Longmont Resident Ralph McClung Served on 'In Cold Blood' Jury." *Longmont Times-Call* (8 November 2011). Web. <http://www.timescall.com>.

Rosenblatt, Roger. "Dreaming the News." *Time* (14 April 1997): 102. Print.

———. "Journalism and the Larger Truth." *State of the Art.* Ed. David Shimkin and others. New York: St. Martin's Press, 1992. 132-34. Print.

———. "The Killer in the Next Tent: The Surreal Horror of the Rwanda Refugees." *The New York Times Magazine* (5 June 1994): cover, 39-42, 44-47. Print.

———. "Once Upon a Time." *Online NewsHour with Jim Lehrer* (24 December 1999). Web. <http://www.pbs.org/newshour/essays/2000>.

Rudnick, Paul. "Midnight Snack at Tiffany's: Answered Prayers." *Los Angeles Times* (27 September 1987). Web. <http://articles.latimes.com/1987-09-27/books/bk-10366_1_capote-prayers-answered>.

Sachsman, David B., and David W. Bulla, ed. "Introduction." *Sensationalism: Murder, Mayhem, Mudslinging, Scandals, and Disasters in 19th-Century Reporting.* New Brunswick, N.J.: Transaction Publishers, 2013. xvii-xxxiv. Print.

Salinger, J.D. *Catcher in the Rye.* New York: Penguin, 2010. Print.

Schultz, William Todd. *Tiny Terror: Why Truman Capote (Almost) Wrote* Answered Prayers. New York: Oxford University Press, 2011. Print.

Scott, A.O. "Big-Name Novelist, Small-Town Murders." *The New York Times* (27 September 2005). Web. <http://www.nytimes.com/2005/09/27/movies/bigname-novelist-smalltown-murders.html>.

———. "'True Story' Stars Jonah Hill and James Franco." *The New York Times* (16 April 2015). Web. <http://www.nytimes.com/2015/04/17/movies/review-true-story-stars-jonah-hill-and-james-franco.html>.

———. "Truman Capote's Journey on 'In Cold Blood,' Again." *The New York Times* (13 October 2006). Web. <http://www.nytimes.com/2006/10/13/movies/13infa.html>.

Secret Window. Dir. David Koepp. Columbia Pictures, 2004. Film.

Secret Window: From Book to Film. Dir. Laurent Bouzereau, 2004. Film.

Shafer, Jack. "The Return of Michael Finkel." *Slate Magazine* (27 July 2007). Web. <http://www.slate.com/articles/news_and_politics/press_box/2007/07/the_return_of_michael_finkel.html>.

Shakespeare, William. "Sonnet 59." *The Riverside Shakespeare.* Vol. 2. Boston: Houghton Mifflin, 1974. 1760. Print.

Shelley, Mary Wollstonecraft. *Frankenstein: Or, The Modern Prometheus.* New York: Penguin, 2003. Print.

Sherrod, Kerryn. "To Kill a Mockingbird." Turner Classic Movies. Web. <http://www.tcm.com/this-month/article/35384%7C0/To-Kill-a-Mockingbird.html>.

Shields, Charles J. *Mockingbird: A Portrait of Harper Lee.* New York: Henry Holt, 2006. Print.

Shutter Island. Dir. Martin Scorsese. Paramount, 2010. Film.

Siegle, Robert. "Capote's *Handcarved Coffins* and the Nonfiction Novel." *Contemporary Literature* 25.4 (Winter 1984): 437-451. Print.

"Sifting for Clues: KBI agents sift ashes of Richard Anton home near Ensign." *Salina Journal* (3 July 1974): 13.

Sims, Norman, ed. "Preface." *Literary Journalism in the Twentieth Century.* New York: Oxford University Press, 1990. v-x. Print.

———. "The Literary Journalists." *The Literary Journalists: The New Art of Personal Reportage.* New York: Ballantine Books, 1984. 3-25. Print.

Smith, Lee. Interview. *Scout, Atticus & Boo: A Celebration of Fifty Years of* To Kill a Mockingbird. By Mary Murphy. New York: HarperCollins, 2010. 176-80. Print.

Smith, Patrick. "Sisters, Family: Surviving Clutter Daughters Hope to Preserve their Parents' Legacy." *Lawrence Journal-World* (4 April 2005). Web. <http://www2.ljworld.com/news/2005/apr/04/sisters_family_surviving/>.

Sondheim, Stephen. "Not While I'm Around." *Sweeney Todd.* <https://www.stlyrics.com/lyrics/sweeneytodd/notwhileimaround.htm>.

Sophie's Choice. Dir. Alan J. Pakula. Universal Pictures, 1982. Film.

Stevens, Wallace. "The Idea of Order at Key West." *The Norton Anthology of Modern Poetry.* Ed. Richard Ellmann and Robert O'Clair. 2nd ed. New York: W.W. Norton, 1988. 291-92. Print.

Stevenson, Robert Louis. "A Gossip on Romance." *Memories and Portraits. The Works of Robert Louis Stevenson.* Vol. 6. New York: Greenock Press, 1906. 119-31.

———. *The Strange Case of Dr. Jekyll and Mr. Hyde.* New York: New American Library, 1987. Print.

The Still of the Night. Dir. Robert Benton. United Artists, 1982. Print.

Stoker, Bram. *Dracula.* New York: Penguin, 2003. Print.

Streitfeld, David. "Capote's 'Coffins.'" *The Washington Post* (19 July 1992). Web. <https://www.washingtonpost.com/archive/entertainment/books/1992/07/19/capotes-coffins/7020e401-3adc-47da-a622-5b2ee6ff4018/>.

Swift, Graham. *Waterland.* New York: Vintage, 1983. Print.

The Talented Mr. Ripley. Dir. Anthony Minghella. Mirage Enterprises, 1999. Film.

Thomson, Rupert. "Rereading: Truman Capote's *In Cold Blood.*" *The Guardian* (5 August 2011). Web. <http://www.theguardian.com/books/2011/aug/05/truman-capote-rupert-thomson-rereading>.

Tompkins, Phillip K. "In Cold Fact." *Esquire* 65.6 (June 1966): 125, 127, 166-68, 170-71. Print.

Toobin, Jeffrey. "American Gothic: What Rushes into the Newsless Void?" *The New Yorker* 73.21 (28 July 1997): 4-5. Print.

Toppman, Lawrence. "'*Shutter* Yields Shudders—and Ideas." *The Charlotte Observer* (18 February 2010). Web. <http://events.charlotteobserver.com/reviews/show/151425-review-shutter-island>.

Travers, Peter. "*Infamous.*" *Rolling Stone* (5 October 2006). Web. <http://www.rollingstone.com/movies/reviews/infamous-20061005>.

True Story. Dir. Rupert Goold. Plan B Entertainment, 2015. Film.

"Truman Capote and Harper Lee: Immortalizing Each Other in Fiction." Library of Congress (1 October 2010). Web. <http://blog.loa.org/2010/10/truman-capote-and-harper-lee.html>.

Turan, Kenneth. "'Infamous' Fails Where 'Capote' Succeeded." NPR (13 October 2006). <http://www.npr.org/templates/story/story.php?stststoryid=6259809>.

Twain, Mark. *The Adventures of Huckleberry Finn.* New York: Penguin, 2002. Film.

The Two Faces of January. Dir. Hossein Amini. StudioCanal, 2014. Film.

Underwood, Doug. *Chronicling Trauma: Journalists and Writers on Violence and Loss.* Urbana: University of Illinois Press, 2011. Print.

Unger Funeral Chapel. "Barbara E. Beausoleil." Web. <http://www.ungerfuneralchapel.com>.

Vertigo. Dir. Alfred Hitchcock. Paramount Pictures, 1958. Film.

Villon, Francois. "Ballade Des Pendus." Trans. A.S. Kline. 2004. <http://www.poetryintranslation.com/PITBR/French/Villon.htm>.

Voss, Ralph F. *Truman Capote and the Legacy of In Cold Blood.* Tuscaloosa: University of Alabama Press, 2011. Print.

Watson, Courtney. "Other Rooms: Safe Havens and Sacred Spaces in the Works of Truman Capote." *Studies in American Culture* 37.1 (October 2014): 101-16. Print.

"Wealthy Farmer, 3 of Family Slain." *The New York Times* (16 November 1959). Web. <https://www.nytimes.com/books/97/12/28/home/capote-headline.html>.

Webb, Joseph M. "Historical Perspective on the New Journalism." *Journalism History* 1.2 (1974): 38-42, 60. Print.

Weber, Ronald. *The Literature of Fact: Literary Nonfiction in American Writing.* Athens: Ohio University Press, 1980. Print.

"What Happened to Other Characters in Capote's Book?" *Lawrence Journal-World* (3 April 2005). Web. <http://www2.ljworld.com/news/2005/apr/03/what_happened_to/>.

Whitby, Gary L. "Truman Capote." *A Sourcebook of American Literary Journalism: Representative Writers in an Emerging Genre.* Ed. Thomas B. Connery. New York: Greenwood, 1992. 239-48. Print.

Wiebe, Crystal K. "In the End, Just a Home: A House with a History of Murder Finds New Life." *Lawrence Journal-World* (6 April 2005). Web. <http://www2.ljworld.com/news/2005/apr/06/in_the_end/>.

Wiegand, David. "After Getting Fired by the *New York Times* for Lying in Print, a Reporter Stumbled on the Story of His Life." *SFGate* (11 June 2005). Web. <http://www.sfgate.com/entertainment/article/After-getting-fired-by-the-New-York-Times-for-2451380.php>.

Wilde, Oscar. *The Picture of Dorian Gray.* New York: Modern Library, 1992. Print.

Williams, William Carlos. "Asphodel, That Greeny Flower." *Asphodel, That Greeny Flower and Other Love Poems.* New York: New Directions, 1994. 9-42. Print.

Winfrey, Oprah. Interview. *Scout, Atticus & Boo: A Celebration of Fifty Years of* To Kill a Mockingbird. By Mary Murphy. New York: HarperCollins, 2010. 199-204. Print.

"Witness Claims Two Took Turns Killing Family: KBI Agent Reveals What He Says Smith Told to Officials." *Lawrence Journal-World* (24 March 1960). Web. <http://www2.ljworld.com/news/1960/mar/24/witness_claims_two/.>

Wolcott, James. "The Truman Show." *Vanity Fair* (December 1997): 124, 126, 128, 130, 132, 134, 136. Print.

Wolfe, Tom. *The New Journalism.* New York: Harper & Row, 1973. Print.

Wolfe, Tom, and Bonnie Angelo. "Master of His Universe." *Time* 133.7 (13 February 1989): 90-93. Print.

Young, Andrew. Interview. *Scout, Atticus & Boo: A Celebration of Fifty Years of* To Kill a Mockingbird. By Mary Murphy. New York: HarperCollins, 2010. 205-209. Print.

Index

Author's Note

Recipient of the 2014 Boulder Faculty Assembly Excellence in Research and Creative Work Award and the 2013 Edward R. Murrow Teaching Award, Jan Whitt is a professor of literature and media at the University of Colorado at Boulder.

Whitt has published numerous journal articles on American literature, literary journalism, media studies, popular culture, and women's issues. Her books include *Allegory and the Modern Southern Novel, Burning Crosses and Activist Journalism: Hazel Brannon Smith and the Mississippi Civil Rights Movement, Dangerous Dreams: Essays on American Film and Television, Rain on a Strange Roof: A Southern Literary Memoir, The Redemption of Narrative: Terry Tempest Williams and Her Vision of the West, Reflections in a Critical Eye: Essays on Carson McCullers, Settling the Borderland: Other Voices in Literary Journalism,* and *Women in American Journalism: A New History.* She is working on a book for Mercer University Press and two for Lexington Books, a division of Rowman & Littlefield.

Whitt received a B.A. in English and journalism and an M.A. in English from Baylor University. She completed her Ph.D. in English at the University of Denver.